Writing a Romance Novel For Dummies®

Cheat Sheet

Reader Expectations

Writing a romance is a creative process and far from formulaic. But romance readers pick up each and every novel with certain expectations firmly in place. To write a winning romance, you have to meet these expectations each and every time:

- ✔ A sympathetic heroine
- ✔ A strong, irresistible hero
- ✔ Emotional tension
- ✔ An interesting, believable plot
- ✔ A happy ending

D0774927

Getting Ready to Write

Before you sit down to start writing your romance, make sure you have the following list covered. Accomplishing these tasks will make the writing process easier and more productive.

- ✔ **Choose a space that can become your home office:** Although an entire room would be great, you can turn any unoccupied corner into dedicated writing space.
- ✔ **Reconcile your family to the project:** Finding time to write can be difficult. Involving your family and getting them on your side from the start makes life easier for everyone.
- ✔ **Collect your supplies:** Grab everything from a computer to a coffee mug, ahead of time.
- ✔ **Surround yourself with relevant research:** Collect research materials before you start writing so that the information is at your fingertips—instead of at the end of a 20-minute drive to the library or bookstore.
- ✔ **Make a schedule:** Block out regular writing time and stick to your schedule, unless you have a real emergency.

Putting It All Together

Keep these tips in mind throughout the writing process:

- ✔ An outline is just a guide, so write one. Yes, really.
- ✔ Let your characters—your hero and heroine—drive the plot.
- ✔ Leave your readers wanting more. Start and stop every chapter (and every scene) so that your reader simply must keep reading.
- ✔ Master the techniques of effective pacing.
- ✔ Build both the emotions and the action to a climax, and follow it with a satisfying resolution.

For Dummies: Bestselling Book Series for Beginners

Writing a Romance Novel For Dummies®

Cheat Sheet

Practicalities Make Perfect

Romance writing and publishing is a business — a business filled with professionals. If you want agents, editors, and everyone else to take you and your work seriously, you have to walk the walk. When you submit a manuscript you want it looking polished and professional. Keep these details in mind:

- ✔ **Accuracy counts:** Check and double-check your research.
- ✔ **Know the rules:** Grammar and punctuation are important. You can break them, but do so with a purpose and only for effect.
- ✔ **Simple is usually better:** Don't go thesaurus-crazy.
- ✔ **Proofread:** Don't just use your computer's spellcheck.
- ✔ **Formatting matters:** Get your margins right and make your font and spacing readable.
- ✔ **Count accurately:** Come up with an accurate word count.

Targeting the Right Publisher and Editor

You can significantly increase your chances of getting published by knowing who's who in the market (publishers and editors) and the types of romance they're publishing.

- ✔ **Check bookstores:** Make use of both the brick-and-mortar and online varieties to see who's publishing books similar to yours. Bookstore employees may also be able to offer insight in the direction publishers are going in the near future.
- ✔ **Read writers' magazines and market guides:** Check these sources to see who's looking for books like yours.
- ✔ **Network:** Keep your ears and eyes open at writers' conferences and talk to everyone you can.
- ✔ **Make full use of the Internet:** Publishers' own sites give you accurate sources, and online writers' bulletin boards, e-mail lists, and related sites have all kinds of useful information — but watch out for unsubstantiated rumors.
- ✔ **Read in-book dedications:** Authors often mention their editors' names.

Stages from the Sale to the Bound Book

The fun isn't over after you've written and submitted your manuscript. Here's a brief outline of the path your book will take on its way to store shelves:

1. Contract negotiation
2. Revisions
3. Deflag and copy edit
4. Galley and author alterations
5. Dedication and acknowledgments
6. Cover — art, copy, and quotes
7. Personal PR

For Dummies: Bestselling Book Series for Beginners

Writing a Romance Novel
FOR DUMMIES®

by Leslie J. Wainger

Foreword by Linda Howard

Wiley Publishing, Inc.

Writing a Romance Novel For Dummies®

Published by
Wiley Publishing, Inc.
111 River St.
Hoboken, NJ 07030-5774
www.wiley.com

For general information on our other products and services or to obtain technical support, please contact our Customer Care Department within the U.S. at 800-762-2974, outside the U.S. at 317-572-3993, or fax 317-572-4002.

Wiley also publishes its books in a variety of electronic formats. Some content that appears in print may not be available in electronic books.

Library of Congress Control Number: 2004103028

ISBN: 978-0-7645-2554-4

10 9 8 7 6 5 4

1O/SQ/QU/QU/IN

WILEY

About the Author

Leslie Wainger has been editing romances and general women's fiction for twenty-five years. She started as the editorial assistant for Silhouette Books and is now an executive editor for Harlequin/Silhouette, where she handles the editorial direction and acquisitions for several romance series. She also edits both series and mainstream novels and works with a roster of authors that includes multiple *New York Times* and *USA TODAY* bestsellers. In the course of her career, she's traveled extensively to speak at conferences, and she's done both local and national PR in print, on radio, and on TV, including National Public Radio, the *Wall Street Journal,* and Fox News. She's written articles, been featured in industry guides and how-to books, and currently has a *Letters to the Editor* bulletin board in the Community/Learning To Write section of the eHarlequin.com Web site.

When she can get away, she enjoys extended travel vacations; recent destinations have included Australia (where she ate a grub on her first visit and held a baby wombat on her second), New Zealand (where she wisely refrained from swimming in a lake of acid), Peru (where she ate a local delicacy called *cuy,* aka guinea pig, and — more enjoyably — visited Macchu Pichu), Bolivia (where she tasted alpaca), and Spain (where she fell in love with Gaudi's architecture). Next trip? With any luck, somewhere where she can see monkeys in the wild.

That she's an admitted bookaholic goes without saying, but she's also an all-too-avid collector of CDs and DVDs, with a bent toward popular films (especially romance in any form) and TV series she's known and loved. Additional collections include tacky salt and pepper shakers and (of course) monkeys.

She's also been a fangrrrrl her entire life, and that shows no signs of stopping. Davy Jones was the first great love of her life (and she still insists they would have been perfect for each other, if only he could have waited for her to get from twelve to twenty-two). Current obsessions include everything related to "The Lord of the Rings" (especially Viggo Mortensen, with a note to include the fact that she's been a fan since "Ruby Cairo"), "Farscape" (if you want to see an amazing romance, check out Ben "John Crichton" Browder and Claudia "Aeryn Sun" Black), and James "Spike" Marsters, formerly of "Buffy the Vampire Slayer" and "Angel."

Additional useless trivia: She has three cats and the commute from hell.

Dedication

To all my authors, past and present: Thank you for making me look good.

Author's Acknowledgments

As the dedication says, I have to thank all the authors I've worked with. Every single one of them has made me a better editor, and many of them have also become some of my best friends. Special thanks to Linda Howard for the intro and Patricia Gardner Evans for the tech read. For additional technical help, special thanks also to Nancy Yost, who had the (bad?) luck to be scheduled to have lunch with me right when I needed a piece of info and came through in spades, and to Joan L., who answered a library question for me and gets collies in return.

I also want to acknowledge the support I received from everyone at Harlequin/Silhouette/MIRA. Thank you to Donna and Isabel for allowing this to happen, KO for not only jumping on the bandwagon but revving the engine, and especially to Tara, who gave me a push in the "write" direction. And I can't forget Grayling's Leslee Borger, for all the additional engine revving.

Family and friends are the backbone of everyone's life. Mom, Dad, Judi, Polly and your attendant crews . . . thank you. Thanks also to all the friends — real-life and on-line — who've supported, pushed, commiserated, laughed, cried, and promised to buy (and even requested autographs). If I start naming names, I'll either go on for pages or leave out someone crucial, so basically, if you think you should be included . . . trust me, you are. (But special mention has to be made of Melissa, at whose baby shower this book — or at least my participation in it — was also born, Kimm, AZ, Mario, Cheryl, Shelly, Linda K. and Mr. B., all of whom went above and beyond at various points.)

Finally, kudos to my Wiley crew: Tracy Boggier, Joyce Pepple, Holly Gastineau-Grimes, Mike Baker, Michelle Dzurny, Laura Miller, Lesa Grant, and April Fazio.

Publisher's Acknowledgments

We're proud of this book; please send us your comments through our Dummies online registration form located at www.dummies.com/register/.

Some of the people who helped bring this book to market include the following:

Acquisitions, Editorial, and Media Development

Project Editor: Mike Baker

Acquisitions Editor: Tracy Boggier

Copy Editors: Michelle Dzurny, Laura K. Miller

Assistant Editor: Holly Gastineau-Grimes

Technical Reviewer: Patricia Gardner Evans

Editorial Manager: Jennifer Ehrlich

Editorial Assistants: Courtney Allen, Elizabeth Rea

Cartoons: Rich Tennant, www.the5thwave.com

Composition Services

Project Coordinator: Adrienne L. Martinez

Layout and Graphics: Andrea Dahl, Joyce Haughey, Heather Ryan, Jacque Schneider, Melanee Wolven

Proofreaders: David Faust, Aptara

Indexer: Aptara

Publishing and Editorial for Consumer Dummies

> **Diane Graves Steele,** Vice President and Publisher, Consumer Dummies
>
> **Joyce Pepple,** Acquisitions Director, Consumer Dummies
>
> **Kristin A. Cocks,** Product Development Director, Consumer Dummies
>
> **Michael Spring,** Vice President and Publisher, Travel
>
> **Brice Gosnell,** Associate Publisher, Travel
>
> **Kelly Regan,** Editorial Director, Travel

Publishing for Technology Dummies

> **Andy Cummings,** Vice President and Publisher, Dummies Technology/General User

Composition Services

> **Gerry Fahey,** Vice President of Production Services
>
> **Debbie Stailey,** Director of Composition Services

Contents at a Glance

Table of Contents

Foreword

I admit it: When I wrote my first romance book, I didn't know what I was doing. Of course, I was only nine years old and didn't know what I was doing most of the time. What I did know was that I loved writing, and I took great joy in creating these rambling, clichéd stories that swooped in and out of different characters' points of view as the plot galloped from one country to another — all without a single chapter break. I *knew* what chapters were; I just didn't care. All that mattered was telling the story.

My love of writing never faded. I eventually learned to break the tale into chapters (just as I learned the rules of grammar), although I still hate all that wasted white space on a page. Margins are for sissies. Do you know how many words you can get on one sheet of paper when you make your handwriting really, really tiny so you can actually get two lines of prose inside one ruled line of notebook paper, and write from one side of the paper to the other? A lot. And I wrote on both sides of the paper. I think one sheet held close to 1,500 words. Ah, the good old days. Now stories have to be typed and double-spaced on only one side of the paper; not only is a lot of white space wasted, but the challenge of seeing how small I can write and having the words still legible is gone.

But fast-forward a couple of decades, roughly. I was still writing. I had never stopped, and writing was the great private joy of my life. I wrote westerns; I wrote science fiction; I wrote fantasy; and I wrote thrillers — but they all had one thread in common: They all had romances in them. I *connected* to romances, but I wrote everything by the seat of my pants. I hadn't researched or studied anything and had no idea of any do's or don'ts — I just had the stories. Finally, one morning I woke up and decided to see whether I was good enough to be published. Then I did some research. I found out how to prepare a manuscript (margins were required) and how to submit it. Everything else, I did the usual way: by the seat of my pants.

I wrote a book and sent it to Leslie Wainger, my dear friend and editor of over 20 years now, who bought it. That's how she became my dear friend and editor. I was a newbie in the business; she was fairly new herself. What I knew about writing would have rattled around in a peanut shell, but I loved what I did know. Leslie loves books, and she taught me the publishing lingo, how a manuscript gets into book form, and all the other details that become part of a writer's life. Her editing — good heavens, how I needed editing — taught me more about the *structure* of writing than anything else I'd learned since learning the English language.

Little did I know that my chosen genre, romance, was the toughest one to write. It can't be, you say; so many romance books are out there — it can't be difficult. Oh, yeah? Try it. Romance readers are probably the most prolific readers on the face of the earth, and they don't read just romance. They read everything. As a group, they're frighteningly knowledgeable. They know their genre, they know what they expect, and they like being surprised. How do you give them what they expect and surprise them at the same time? Sheer dumb luck, and a lot of hard work.

Romance is the best discipline for writers. It forces you to learn how to make your characterization so strong that the characters not only live on in the readers' minds, but the readers also have a personal connection to the books. A romance writer has to learn pacing, how to tell a coherent, cohesive, and engrossing story in 80,000 words or less, depending on the category line. It's a tough challenge. Any tips are appreciated.

There weren't any tips when I started writing, back in the dark ages B.C. (Before Computers). No one had analyzed the hearts and parts of numerous romance books and broken them down for me to study so I could polish my craft, tighten my plot, and otherwise get a head start.

I feel cheated. Why wasn't this book written 25 years ago????

But it's written now, by an expert in the romance publishing field, for you to enjoy and learn from. Have fun!

I still feel cheated.

— Linda Howard

Introduction

· ·

Romance is far and away the best-selling genre in all of fiction. The specific numbers are constantly changing, but on average, 50 percent of all mass market paperbacks sold are romances. Add to that the growing sales of trade-paperback and (especially) hardcover romances, and the picture is even more impressive. Just take a look at the bestseller lists: They're filled with romance novels.

Romance is a something-for-everyone genre. Looking for a quick read to keep in your purse and pull out whenever you have a few minutes free? A 55,000-word category romance may give you just what you want. Want a complex story that can keep you turning pages for days as you relax on the beach or the porch of a mountain cabin? Try a 150,000-word mainstream. Whether you like history, the here-and-now, or even the future, whether you're looking for comedy, suspense, something spooky, or an inspirational read, the romance genre has something for you.

Because romance is so popular with readers, it's also popular with would-be writers — many of whom started out as readers and then suddenly decided that they had a story to tell, too. If you're one of these aspiring writers, this book is for you, because there's always room for one more.

A lot of outsiders have a very clear — and clearly wrong! — image of the typical romance writer. They picture her as someone dressed all in pink (boa included) who taps computer keys with the long, red nails of one hand while picking up bon-bons with the other — unless she's writing in the tub, artfully camouflaged by bubbles and probably shorting out a computer per day.

The real truth, as insiders know, is that romance writing is hard work, but it's also extremely rewarding work, allowing successful authors to express their creativity and earn money for it, all the while making thousands — sometimes even millions — of readers happy. Not a bad job if you can get it, and if you've read this far, I'm betting it's a job you want. So welcome to the *inside* of the romance business. It's time to start your new career.

About This Book

I've been in the romance biz for 25 years (okay, 24½, as of this writing). I started as an editorial assistant and worked my way up to my current position of executive editor. In that time, I've seen the romance industry grow and cycle through all kinds of changes. Gothic romances, one of the staples of my teenage years, were only a memory until recently. Regency romances, as epitomized by

Georgette Heyer (whose books I also devoured as a teen), have hung on as possibly the hardiest subgenre of romance novels. Sometimes historical romances have been on top, sometimes contemporary romances. Right now, romantic suspense novels seem to be *the* way to break into the big-time, but romantic comedy novels are climbing fast, and inspirational romances are showing strength outside religious bookstores.

Some things, though, never change. Readers are always looking for *a good story.* I've heard that phrase more times than I can count, and when I probe a little deeper, it always comes down to the same things. Readers are looking for strong, compelling characters, a story that makes them feel things right along with those characters, and a happy ending that lets them experience the thrill of falling in love all over again with each book.

As a writer, your job is simple: Give the readers what they're looking for. But the practicalities of that mission are complex. You not only need to know the basics of writing any novel, you also need to know — and master — the specifics of writing a romance. You need to put emotion on the page, and that can be a bit like catching lightning in a bottle.

In this book, I distill everything that I've learned as a romance editor into a step-by-step, topic-based guide to help aspiring romance authors take an idea and grow it into a published novel. I'm not big on rules and regulations when it comes to writing a romance novel, because I think too many do's and don'ts make a writer self-conscious and stifle her creativity. And writing a romance novel is all about finding creative ways to make the reader happy. Instead of dictating to you or using the dreaded F-word, *formula,* I'm going to do for you what I've done for writers throughout my career: I'm going to give you the tools you need to write well, and to understand what a reader needs and how to give it to her. Then I'm going to turn you loose to tell the story of *your* heart so you can touch *your reader's.*

Foolish Assumptions

Every author — whether she's writing a romance novel or *Writing a Romance Novel For Dummies* — has to make assumptions about her audience. And I've made a few, at least one of which I suspect is true of you:

- ✔ You're interested in making a serious effort at writing a romance novel and getting it published.
- ✔ You're sitting down to write your first book, and you're looking for advice on everything from creating a proposal to writing the manuscript to finding the perfect agent or publisher.
- ✔ You have a stack of unpublished manuscripts under your bed that has yet to grace an editor's desk.

✔ You've met with some success in the romance-publishing world, but, like most authors, you're always looking for tips, tricks, or advice to help you improve your craft.

If any of these descriptions sound familiar, you've come to the right place. You can find something here to help you improve your writing skills and guide you to success in your career.

How This Book Is Organized

I've organized *Writing a Romance Novel For Dummies* into six parts, each one designed to help you with a separate stage of the writing process.

Part I: Welcome to the World of Romance Writing

This part provides rock-solid advice for how to set up your career, in both creative and practical terms. Begin here if you're looking for an overview of the topics I cover in the book, as well as an in-depth look at the romance marketplace. As a writer, you're a *creative professional,* and you have to develop both halves of that description. As you begin (or go on) writing, you need to have a sense of your strengths and goals, and that means knowing what's out there and where your book can fit in.

This part also focuses on the practicalities of being a writer: how to set up a home office; how to handle the sometimes difficult, even touchy, problem of claiming time as your own so that you can write; and how to take full advantage of all the available resources for writers in general and romance writers in particular. Everything in this part is about getting ready to write, so after you start writing, you can exercise your creativity as uninterruptedly as possible.

Part II: Laying the Foundation: The Building Blocks of a Great Romance

In this part, I talk about the crucial elements you need to have thought out before you begin actually telling your story, starting with your characters (after all, everything depends on them and their relationship). I also talk about coming up with ideas, something many would-be writers worry about, and turning an idea into a full, complex story, complete with conflict and emotional tension. A lot of writers often overlook or under-use setting as a component of a good romance, but I give it plenty of attention here. Finally, I demystify outline writing and show you how to view an outline as a useful tool, rather than something to be afraid of.

Part III: Putting Pen to Paper

This third part focuses on the heart of the writing process — taking everything that you've come up with and turning it into an actual story. I concentrate quite a bit on the idea of voice — yours, as the teller of the story, and your characters' — as the reader's way into the book. When you combine voice with pacing, another topic I concentrate on in this part, you really have the key components of the writing process. If Part II answered "what," Part III tackles "how."

Because the topic is romance, you need to know how to handle one more crucial component — love scenes. Done right, they can completely cement your reader's identification with the characters and their story.

Part IV: Putting It All Together: Mechanics Count, Too

After you've done all the creative work and gotten your first draft down on paper, you need to go back and work on structure to make sure that you're telling your story as effectively as possible. You need to take care of the things that you (quite rightly) may not have paid much attention to as you wrote in the first burst of creativity.

This part talks about how to make the most of all the book's transition points — the opening scene and the way that you start and stop each chapter, even each scene — because the movement between scenes and chapters can build your reader's interest and keep her going.

After you've completed the first draft, you also know what facts you still need to check and what additional research you need to do. So, although some of the advice in this section will also prove helpful to you in your pre-writing prep work, you especially need it after you're done with the main part of the writing process, because that's when you get your last chance to get everything right before you try to impress an editor.

And you still need to take a few more important last steps to help maximize your chances of selling. Some steps are more mechanical than creative, but they're no less important. You need to make sure that you're not messing around with the rules of grammar (unless you're doing it to make a point about a character, for instance), proof and reproof your spelling, and then, finally, format your manuscript professionally.

Part V: Submitting Your Manuscript — and Making the Sale!

You've done it! You've finished the book, done your rewrites, and now you're ready to submit. Or are you? After you have the book ready to go, you need to send it to the right place. In this part, I give you advice on targeting the right publisher — even a specific editor — for your book, looking for an agent, submitting your manuscript (including how to write a query letter and synopsis), and dealing with rejection and revision, which are almost inevitable parts of the process for any writer.

After that, I get into the good stuff: getting the call from an editor to say she wants to buy your book, negotiating a contract, and then dealing with everything that happens as your romance novel goes from manuscript to actual book.

Part VI: The Part of Tens

Every *For Dummies* title contains The Part of Tens. And who am I to break with tradition? These chapters are packed with ten-point lists meant to help you with specific situations you may face. I help you meet such challenges as beating writer's block, avoiding beginners' mistakes, deciphering rejection, and coming up with a winning title.

Icons Used in This Book

I've scattered some icons throughout the book for easy reference. Here's a sneak preview along with their descriptions, so that you know what to keep your eyes peeled for in the rest of the book.

This icon clues you in to a bit of romance-writing wisdom, some advice that you may want to consider using. This icon signals something that's definitely worth checking out — and putting to use.

Text by this icon gives you advice on things to avoid to keep your romance writing on the right track.

You can find this icon next to important bits of information that (what a surprise) I don't want you to forget. The accompanying advice can really help you in your quest to write the perfect romance — and create the perfect romance-writing career. If you skim through the text, stop and check these points out.

This fine piece of art accompanies text that, while interesting, is a bit more technical in nature. If you want to skip over this info, you're romance-writing potential will not suffer.

Where to Go from Here

If you're familiar with the *For Dummies* books, you already know a bit about how they're set up. If not, let me clarify the *For Dummies* experience a little. You can read this book in two ways. The first way is to go cover to cover. I present the topics in the order that a writer's likely to deal with them, starting with understanding the market and finishing with the stages a manuscript goes through on the way to becoming a bound book. So, you can read it in one front-to-back gulp as an overview to help you get started, or you can read it in order but in pieces, tackling the relevant chapters as you reach that stage in your own writing process.

The other way to read this book is piecemeal and out of order, investigating only the subjects you need, as you need them. If you've been a romance reader all your life, you may never need to read Chapter 2, but you may find the chapters on plotting and pacing (Chapters 5 and 10, in case you're interested) key. You may want to read some chapters in their entirety, and then skim others only to glean the answer to a specific question or concern. Check out the table of contents and index if you want to track down something specific.

Bottom line? The only right way to read this book is the way that works best for you. But in the end, wherever you start in *this* book, I hope your ultimate destination is the shelves of your local bookstore — as the published author of your *own* book.

Part I
Welcome to the World of Romance Writing

The 5th Wave   By Rich Tennant

THE HOME REPAIR ROMANCE NOVEL

© RICHTENNANT

READING
GUS SVABODA
FROM HIS NOVEL
"THE WHISPERING
DRAIN PIPE"

"Rebecca shuddered with anticipation as she and Drake approached the broken flush valve. Drake smiled, and gently reached for his 3/8" wrench and plumbers tape..."

In this part . . .

After you've made the all-important decision to become a romance writer, you have to start thinking like the professional you hope to be. In this part, I give you an overview of what it takes to write, and sell, your romance novel. Then I delve into detail about the multifaceted romance market and help you figure out where you fit in. Finally, I show you how you can organize your life and your surroundings so that after you start writing, you're free to create without unnecessary interruption.

Chapter 1

Romance Writing at a Glance

*T*he world of romance writing and publishing is exciting. Being part of a business that's all about making people happy is wonderful: The writers get to tell their stories, and the readers get to read them. At the end of the day, it's great going home knowing that because of my efforts, a lot of people are going to smile. But romance publishing can also be complex — even daunting — especially when you're approaching it for the first time. So, I've taken up the challenge of demystifying this world for you. Whether this book marks your first foray into writing romance novels or you've been hard at work honing your skills for years, I'm glad you're here. As you read, you'll find lots to interest you and, most of all, help you write a winning romance novel.

In this chapter, I provide you with a snapshot of the romance-writing process and the romance industry as a whole. By extension, the information I present also provides you with a sneak peak at the subjects I cover elsewhere between these yellow and black covers. I start by talking about the market, defining romance novels in general, and then talk briefly about some of the different types of romances you find on the shelves.

I then move on to the heart and soul of the matter at hand: the elements that every romance novel needs to be a success. Without sympathetic characters, an interesting plot, compelling emotional conflict and, of course, a happy ending, you don't have a romance novel (much less one that's going to leave readers eager to find your next book the minute it comes out).

I finish up by taking you for a quick behind-the-scenes tour of the business end of publishing romance novels, because no matter how good your book is, you'll never get anywhere as a writer if you can't master the submission process. And knowing what's expected of you *after* you make a sale, as your novel goes from manuscript to store shelves, never hurts, either.

Tuning in to the Market

Many aspiring writers sit down to tell a story without a clear idea about what kind of story they're writing, whether (and where) a market exists for it, or what they'll do with the manuscripts when they're done writing. Now, I won't tell you that an unplanned approach to writing never works, because a lot of books get published every year, and some of them undoubtedly follow that path.

But if you want to write popular fiction in general and romance novels in particular, you can cut down the time you spend on both writing and submitting, as well as increase your odds of success, by researching the marketplace and paying attention to what readers and editors are looking for.

What makes a romance a romance?

A large portion of the fiction books that you find on store shelves — from mysteries, to science fiction, to horror, and pretty much everything else — have romantic elements in them. But they're not romances. If you want to define your book as a romance novel, you need to keep certain things in mind.

At its heart, a *romance* distinguishes itself from other forms of fiction because the romantic relationship is the focus of everything that happens — it's the driving force behind the story, the one thread that makes the entire tapestry fall apart if it's removed.

Romance readers are knowledgeable. They're very aware of the elements in a book that make them happy and the elements that make them *un*happy. Romance readers have very specific expectations for every book that they pick up. They want to identify with the heroine and love the hero. They want to root for the relationship to overcome the seemingly insurmountable obstacles in its path, and at the end of the day, they want an interesting plot that delivers a happy ending. When you meet these expectations and focus on the central romantic relationship, your book becomes a romance novel. (See Chapter 2 for more details on meeting readers' expectations.)

Contrary to popular belief (a belief you've probably run up against, if you've been a romance reader for a while), romance novels do *not* follow a prescribed formula. You just have the reader's basic expectations, which means that, as a writer, you have a lot of freedom in what you write and how you satisfy those expectations.

Subdividing romances for fun and profit

Approximately 50 percent of all mass market paperbacks sold are romance novels, making romance the single most popular genre. But not all romances are the same. Within romance publishing in general, all kinds of distinctions exist. Each type of romance comes with its own set of reader expectations that you must meet. In Chapter 2, I go into great detail about the different types of romances. But every writer needs to know the two big distinctions:

- **Contemporary versus historical romances:** The first big decision you need to make — one that affects every page of your novel from first to last — is whether to set your book in the past or the present.

  - **Historical romance:** Your readers expect your research — into clothes, everyday life, occupations, social structure, language, and everything else — to be accurate and your characters to behave in ways that are appropriate to their world and its society. (I devote Chapter 13 to research specifics.) Certain story lines and plot twists work perfectly in a historical context, while others are completely out of place — and it's your responsibility to know which is which.

  - **Contemporary romance:** These novels are set in your reader's own time, so they're often subject to even closer and more knowledge-able scrutiny. Slang that's even slightly out-of-date or characters who feel like they're from the 1950s (when women were expected to cook, clean, and do just what the man said), will turn a reader off faster than you can type "Chapter 1."

- **Category versus mainstream romances:** This concept is based on the ways that books are packaged and marketed to the reader.

  - **Category romance:** Also known as *series romances,* these novels are published on a monthly schedule in groups, which usually consist of four or six novels. The groups are referred to as *lines* or *series,* and all the books in a given series are similar in certain basic ways such as length, editorial focus, and cover design. Series books appear together on store shelves and are marketed to readers as part of a series rather than as individual titles. Most series are contemporary romances, but that's always subject to change.

  - **Mainstream romance:** These novels are also known as *single titles,* which is an accurate description of how they're perceived and sold. Each book stands alone and fits its own individual vision, though that vision often identifies the book as belonging to a sub-genre like romantic suspense, western, or Regency. A single title has unique packaging and is placed on the bookracks separately, usually in alphabetical order by the author's last name. Single titles almost always have larger page counts — sometimes substantially so — than series books, which allow them to have more complex plotting and a bigger cast of characters.

Beyond the basic distinctions I list above, the romance genre is also divided into all kinds of more specific *subgenres*. Subgenres can include romantic suspense, inspirational, western, romantic comedy, and the others I detail in Chapter 2, where I also help you figure out where you — and your novel — fit into this spectrum.

Practicing Your Craft

After you know the marketplace and what kind of romance you want to write, you have to take care of a few everyday matters before you start hitting the keyboard. Writing's a creative profession, and after you and your muse get in "the zone," the last thing you want is to be yanked back to reality because your printer needs ink, your kids are fighting over the remote, or you have a question about grammar or British history and have no idea where to go for the answer. Here are a few suggestions (I include many more in Chapter 3):

- Set up a workspace for yourself, even if it's only a corner of your bedroom or family room.
- Get your family invested in your writing so that they're happy to pitch in so you can succeed.

Only after you have the mundane under control can you sit down, face that blank screen and blinking cursor, and start telling your story.

No one can make you a storyteller or magically inject you with talent, but if you have the drive and creativity to be a writer, you *can* hone your craft so you make every book as strong as it can possibly be. Writing has many practical aspects, and the bulk of this book focuses on helping you master them. Here's a quick look at just a few of the topics I tackle.

Everything starts with characterization

Without compelling characters to win over the reader, a romance novel simply won't succeed. The heroine, in particular, is key, because she becomes the reader's alter ego. Your heroine needs to be strong, smart, and attractive, but also vulnerable and emotionally accessible. She needs to be an interesting and admirable woman who your reader enjoys sharing time with. Your hero needs to be just that: heroic. But that doesn't mean he has no flaws. He definitely needs to be vulnerable, otherwise he won't have a place for the heroine in his life or his heart. Your hero has to be a man that your heroine — and your reader — can fall in love with. (Chapter 4 covers creating characters, making it one of the most important chapters in this book.)

Both your hero and heroine should be fully realized human beings, with complete and complex inner lives. They need to have more going on than just sexual attraction — although, as I discuss in Chapter 11, sexual attraction and emotionally involving love scenes are important, too. Every character also needs an individual voice. Chapter 9 sets you on the right path to creating unique ways of speaking — ways that are also distinct from your *own* voice — for all your characters, especially the star couple.

It's all about emotional tension

Emotional tension is the driving force of every romance. Your hero and heroine are more than just pretty faces. Make their relationship the driving force of your novel, because your reader's main reason for picking up a romance novel is to experience the roller-coaster thrills of falling in love.

To keep that roller coaster going, you need to create emotional tension between your hero and heroine, something that comes from who they are that can believably keep them apart for the course of the book. Maybe your wealthy hero has a hard time believing that the heroine's not just like all the other gold diggers. Maybe the heroine thinks no man can be trusted to stay for the long haul because her father left her mother, and her own relationships have never lasted longer than six months. In every book, the emotional tension is unique to that heroine and hero, grows out of who they are, and is enhanced by their situation.

I explain how to use emotional tension to propel your plot and create momentum in the hero and heroine's relationship in Chapter 5. Compelling emotional tension gets your reader involved even more deeply in your characters, and the more deeply involved your reader feels, the more quickly she'll turn the pages to see what happens next. Best-selling novels aren't referred to as page-turners for nothing.

Plotting, pacing, and point of view

Once you have your characters and their conflict down, your job is to plot out, and then tell, their story. Think of your novel as the context in which the hero and heroine can work out their issues. But plotting is more than just figuring out what happens in the story. You need to structure events in a way that keeps your reader's interest. You need an *external conflict* — something that gives your hero and heroine something to argue about and deal with when they can't talk about the emotional conflict that's *really* bugging them.

In Chapter 5, I give you tips on how to use conflict to build the reader's involvement as the action escalates. In Chapter 10, I focus on pacing, especially achieving the all-important balance between showing and telling: knowing when to let your characters show the readers what they're doing and thinking, and when using narrative is the most effective tool for getting the reader from Point A to Point B.

When you're telling your story, guard against letting *your* voice call a lot of attention to itself, which can overshadow the characters, their voices, and their points of view. I provide strategies for finding your own voice and using it for greatest effect in Chapter 8.

Finding the right spot to begin your book and knowing how to start and stop every chapter and every scene for maximum effect are crucial aspects of structuring your plot. As you work on these mechanics, creating cliffhangers, and knowing how to resolve them, is likely to become one of your most effective strategies. For more information on beginnings and endings, not to mention on how to leave your reader dangling (but in a good way), go to Chapter 12.

Submitting Your Manuscript

Submitting your manuscript, and then waiting to hear its fate is generally considered a lot more nerve-wracking than the writing process. Although you can't control the process after your manuscript's out of your hands, you *can* take steps beforehand to weight the odds in your favor.

Choosing the perfect publisher

You can give your book its best shot at being published by targeting the most appropriate publisher and, when possible, a specific editor whose taste runs to books like yours. You can't ensure a sale, but finding an appropriate publisher helps you on two fronts:

- ✔ Doing so obviously increases your chances of success.
- ✔ If your manuscript is going to sell anyway, you can save yourself — and your book — a lot of time.

Once again, you need to research the market. This time, you look past what's out there to see who's publishing it. I provide tips on how to compare what you're writing to what each house is publishing, how to figure out what a particular editor likes to see, and other helpful strategies in Chapter 15.

Do you need an agent?

Authors are always asking, "Do I need an agent?" which is frequently followed by: "How do I get an agent?" You may need (or at least want) an agent for two main reasons:

- ✔ **Your publisher of choice requires one.** Most mainstream publishers don't accept *unsolicited manuscripts* — manuscripts that are unagented and haven't been specifically requested (perhaps as the result of an author/editor appointment at a conference).
- ✔ **You want someone else to handle the business details.** Finding an agent for this reason is based on preference rather than necessity. Agents perform a whole host of services for their clients, and many authors especially rely on agents during contract and advance negotiations.

I discuss getting an agent in more detail in Chapter 15. I also give you tips for finding an agent because that can sometimes be — or at least feel — as difficult as finding a publisher.

Putting together a selling submission

Every publisher has its own rules about submissions, what they look at, and what they buy. Those rules often vary based on whether a project's agented and whether an author's brand-new or has been published elsewhere, even if in a different genre. Whatever you submit, you want it to be as perfect as possible to increase your chances of making a sale.

You can submit your manuscript in three types of formats: complete manuscript, partial manuscript, and query letter. A complete manuscript is self-explanatory, but the latter two require some explanation. Query letters and partial manuscripts both involve a synopsis of your manuscript (I discuss them in greater detail in Chapter 15). In a query letter, your synopsis has to be brief, and it's all an editor sees of your novel. The good news is you don't need to convince her to buy your book based on your query; you only need to convince her that she wants to see more of it. And in the scheme of things, it's easier to get an editor to invest her own time, rather than the company's money. A partial manuscript consists of a longer synopsis and chapters — usually three chapters, always starting with the *first* chapter. This manuscript gives an editor a fuller look at what you're capable of.

In most cases, an editor likes to see a complete manuscript before going to contract with a brand-new author. Getting a request for a complete manuscript, based on your query letter or partial manuscript, is no guarantee that you're going to make a sale, but you're that much closer.

Submitting a *complete,* as it's called, also means that you have to make sure every possible detail of your manuscript is perfect. For tips on formatting and advice on grammar and spelling — two aspects of writing and manuscript preparation that every author thinks she has under control (and which many authors are wrong about) — check out Chapter 14. My biggest suggestion on that score? Use or ignore spell-check — whatever makes you happy — but *always* proofread by eye.

Somewhere along the way, you're almost certainly going to deal with rejection, because very few authors sell the first books they write — but possibly rejection leavened by a request for revision. Dealing with rejection can be the hardest time in a writer's career, but forewarned is forearmed. In Chapter 16, I talk about the different kinds of rejection letters — and how to revise and resubmit your manuscript, because getting a request for a revised manuscript is the next best thing to making a sale.

You sold your book — now what?

It's finally happened. An editor made an offer on your book, and you're about to become a published author. But before that can happen, you still need to negotiate a contract. Every publisher has its own boilerplate contract, but you're likely to run up against certain common terms and clauses, no matter what publisher you're dealing with. I help you close the deal in Chapter 17.

You and your editor-to-be both want the same thing: to see your book published and sold to as many readers as possible. Don't be afraid to ask her questions so that you understand what you're agreeing to and are happy with your deal. To help you achieve the goal of signing your name on the dotted line, I give you strategies for win-win negotiating and questions you need to make sure you get answers to.

Last, but far from least, understanding what happens to your book after you've sold it is helpful, because your role's far from over. Your editor and publisher will expect input from you as your book passes through the various stages from manuscript to bound book. Chapter 18 covers what comes next.

My ultimate advice for you? If your book is rejected, don't lose heart. You're a storyteller, so start telling the next story, and then the one after that. Work on your craft, get all the input you can and factor it in. And *keep writing and keep trying.* And if the best happens — as I hope it will — and you get published? My advice isn't very different. Don't sit on your laurels. Go back and do it all again, because editors aren't looking to buy single manuscripts — we're looking to build authors, book after book to greater success.

Chapter 2

Romancing the Marketplace: Identifying Your Options

In This Chapter

▶ Knowing your audience

▶ Looking at the different romance subgenres

▶ Figuring out which kind of romance you should write

*T*he single most important decision you can make, after you've decided to be a romance writer in the first place, is what kind of romance to write. Despite what skeptics, non-romance readers and plain old killjoys believe, romances are *not* all the same.

Romance accounts for about 50 percent of all mass market paperback fiction sales, and the genre has made strong inroads into the hardcover and trade paperback markets in the last few years. A close look makes it clear that all romances aren't the same. Not only do their settings range from the past to the present and even into the future, the books themselves range in length from around 50,000 words to 150,000 words or more. They can be highly sexy, or sweet and tender; suspenseful, humorous, or glitzy; highly realistic, populated by vampires, ghosts, and werewolves, or filled with barely dreamed of technology.

But all romance novels share one thing in common — they're all built around the romance between one man and one woman who find their way past all obstacles in order to live happily ever after together.

In order to choose what to write, you need to know what kinds of romances publishers are releasing, who's reading them and why, and where your own interests and strengths lie. In this chapter, I introduce you to the average romance reader and the vast array of choices you and she both have, and I give you tips for figuring out where you can best fit in.

Knowing Your Reader

Romances are popular fiction, with the emphasis on *popular.* That means the entire romance industry is driven not by capital-L Literary concerns but by a desire to make as many readers as possible as happy as possible. It's a market-driven genre.

I'm not saying that creativity and talent aren't important, because they definitely are — very important. With literally thousands of romance novels being published every year, it's incredibly difficult to stand out — to give the readers what they want while still maintaining a unique voice and approach.

Your creativity and talent come from within. You're born with the talent and desire to tell stories. But you can acquire craft and the ability to write what readers want to read. That part of the equation starts with knowing your market, which boils down to knowing the reader and what she wants.

Meeting the romance reader

Writing is a solitary profession, especially when you're unpublished and don't have an editor to talk things over with. Published authors have an editor, but even they don't really have a boss. Instead, you, like all writers, have thousands of bosses — all the readers you're hoping will one day be your readers. No two romance readers are exactly alike, but as a group, they have a lot in common.

Not surprisingly, the vast majority of romance readers, like the vast majority of romance writers, are women. The youngest readers are somewhere in their teens, and the oldest are in their 80s and 90s. But the bulk of readers range in age from their 20s into their 60s (with baby boomers making up the largest group, just as they do in the general population). A few more characteristics:

- Most romance readers have at least some college education (and plenty of them are doctors, lawyers, and other highly educated professionals).
- Most readers work outside the home part or full time, and their median income is slightly above the national average.
- Most readers are or have been married, and many of them have children.
- For most readers, reading provides their key source of entertainment, and when they do sit down in front of the television, they're more likely to watch the news than soap operas.

Romance readers are strong, smart women who know what they want and, in terms of fiction, expect you to give it to them.

And now, a word from the men in our audience

Yes, some men read romance novels, too. Not a lot, in the grand scheme of things, but some definitely do. Most of them fall into one of two categories:

✔ **Men without women:** Men on oil rigs, in prison, and in other places where women are uncommon to nonexistent like to read romances. Personally, I think it's really nice

that when you get right down to it, their fantasy relationships are the same as women's.

✔ **Men who are a captive audience:** However they get there, you can find a lot of romances in hospitals and senior residences, so the men there read them, right along with the women.

Meeting the romance reader's expectations

Many people — way too many (okay, one would be too many, in my book) — think of romances as formula books. As far as I'm concerned, a formula is something scientific. Toothpaste, laundry detergent, and nail polish all have formulas, but romance novels come in too many styles and sizes to be based on something as limiting as a formula.

Romance novels are built around reader expectations. Every romance reader picks up a book — contemporary or historical, mainstream or category, Regency, romantic suspense, or inspirational — with certain expectations firmly in place, and the author has to satisfy those expectations with *every* book. The five basic expectations that every romance reader shares and that you, as an author, implicitly promise to fulfill are simple and leave you a lot of room for creativity:

✔ **A sympathetic heroine:** The heroine is the key to every romance. The reader's sense of identification with the heroine draws the reader into the book and keeps her reading. Your heroine needs to be sympathetic — strong without being hard, vulnerable without being weak, intelligent, ethical, interesting, capable (but not perfect), beautiful (but not unreal) — in short, a surrogate for your reader as she wants to see herself. (See Chapter 4 for more information on both heroines and heroes.)

✔ **A strong, irresistible hero:** Both your heroine and your reader need to fall in love with the hero. He has to be strong without being overbearing (or borderline abusive), yet vulnerable enough to need the heroine; as intelligent, ethical, and capable as she is; fascinating; and, of course, good-looking (and good in bed, even if the reader never sees his skills).

✔ **Emotional tension:** The heart of every romance is the emotional conflict that keeps the hero and heroine from being together, even though they both want to be. You need to create a source of tension that's complex, interesting, and believable, and that grows intrinsically from the characters you create; then allow the characters to deal with their issues as the book unfolds (check out Chapter 5 to find out more about plotting, including creating conflict and tension).

✔ **A believable plot:** Though your plot is the context for the characters' all-important emotional journey, not the point of the story itself, it still needs to be believable, logical, and interesting, so that your reader stays immersed in the world you've created.

✔ **A happily-ever-after ending:** Every romance novel ends with the hero and heroine together. They commit to a future as a couple, with marriage generally somewhere in the offing (if they're not already married or engaged). In a romance novel, happiness is part of the promise.

Fulfill these five expectations, and you're well on your way to writing a successful, and publishable, romance novel. Of course, your reader may have secondary expectations stemming from the type of romance you're writing — expectations for an inspirational and a Gothic romance, for example, will be quite different — and you have to keep them in mind, too. (For more on the different types of romance, see the "Getting to Know Your Genre" section later in this chapter and the "Secondary expectations" sidebar in this chapter.)

Starting from Square One: Reading

There's no substitute for reading. That fact holds true no matter what you want to write. Whether you look at reading as a way to learn the so-called rules, figure out where the publishing industry has set the bar, or scope out the competition, you need to know something about your chosen genre and the elite company of published authors you're hoping to join.

Many authors don't like to read in their genre while working on a book, afraid of being subconsciously influenced in their own writing. That decision is understandable, and you may feel the same way while you're writing. But you should read extensively before you start writing and when you're in between manuscripts. You're not writing in a vacuum, and romance is *popular* fiction, which means you need to use every tool you can to figure out what can make you popular, too. The more you read, the more you know what works.

Drawing up a reading list

When you start reading within the romance genre as an aspiring writer (rather than as a normal reader simply looking for enjoyment), read broadly, across a number of different time periods and subgenres, quite possibly also moving between mainstream and series romances. Take this broad approach, even if you've been reading romances for years, because you need to become objective about the market and your best chance for fitting into it (see the section "Choosing Your Path" later in this chapter).

After you've read broadly and decided what you may want to write, narrow your focus and concentrate your reading on the type of book you're thinking of writing — contemporary or historical, series or mainstream, or a particular subgenre (see "Getting to Know Your Genre" later in the chapter).

You can also keep an eye on the bestseller lists to see what's selling and then focus on reading the books that draw in the most readers. You may find this approach especially helpful if you have a limited amount of time for reading. Here are some of the most well-respected bestseller lists:

- *The New York Times*
- *USA TODAY*
- *Publishers Weekly*
- *Waldenbooks*

Or go to the Romance Writers of America (RWA) Web site to see a number of bestseller results all gathered in one place. RWA is the biggest organization of published and aspiring romance writers, and you can find their Web site at www.rwanational.com.

Reading like a writer

As an aspiring author, don't just read for pleasure. Instead, read like a critic, like an analyst. As you read, look at every aspect of the novel, all the things that this book talks about: Characterization, plotting, writing, pacing . . . everything you can think of counts. Constantly ask questions:

- Where did the author get it right, and where did she go wrong?
- What can you do better? (What do you already know how to do well?)
- What did the author do better than you can? (What do you still need to figure out how to do?)

When you read a book you like, think about what made it work for you. When you read a book you don't like, think about what didn't work: Recognizing and avoiding mistakes before you make them can save you a lot of time and disappointment. Also, think about why a book you didn't like got published. Something in it spoke to an editor, so try to spot that element. You can often learn more from the books that you consider creative failures, or at best only semi-successful, than from the ones that are letter perfect. Even after you've published a book — or 20 — you'll find that you can still learn from reading other authors, just as you hope that someday aspiring writers will be able to learn from you.

You can easily look at a book you don't like and think, "If *that* got published, I can throw together *anything* and still find a publisher." Don't count on it. No editor sets out to publish a weak book, but sometimes a book just never pulls together the way the editor hoped, or practical needs — time constraints, the need to publish a certain number of books, and so on — mean putting out a book that isn't as strong as the house had hoped. Or you may dislike a book that other people like a lot, because everyone's tastes are unique. If you set your goals low, you're going to write a book that isn't anyone's first choice.

You owe it to yourself to write the best book you can every time you sit down and type "Chapter 1." Aiming to do your best work improves your chances of getting published and gives you your best avenue to winning the readers' hearts — and getting them to spend their money on you.

Getting to Know Your Genre

You need to know the different types of romance novels so that you can define what you're writing and discuss your work like a professional when you talk to other writers and, eventually, when you submit your book to an editor or an agent. Plus, readers have differing expectations for every general romance type and specific subgenre.

In many cases, there's nothing mutually exclusive about the distinctions within the genre and between the subgenres I discuss in this section. A book can be a mainstream historical romantic suspense, for instance, or a mainstream contemporary paranormal romantic comedy. You can mix and match to your heart's content. Just make sure to choose elements that work together, target a house that can publish your book, and keep things simple (not trying to do too many things at once). And never forget that, whatever the trappings, you're writing a romance, so your focus needs to stay on your hero and heroine and their developing relationship.

Historical versus contemporary

You need to make several important big-picture distinctions and a lot of smaller ones that may help you. First, you have to decide whether to write a historical or a contemporary romance. And to make this decision, you need to know what each consists of. The basic distinction is obvious, and I feel a little silly pointing it out. Historical romances are set in the past, and contemporary romances are set in the present. But the differences don't end there.

Contemporary romances account for the bulk of sales, in large part because most series romance lines are contemporary, but historical romances (including the Regency subgenre) are also extremely popular.

Paging through history

Technically, any book set between the Stone Age and today is a *historical* book because it's set in the past. But readers and publishers define a historical romance more narrowly than the preceding description.

You can find exceptions, but the earliest era that shows up regularly in historical romances is the Medieval period (knights and chivalry are quite popular). At the other end, publishers used to set the late 1800s as the cutoff point for historical romances, but you could still find books set as late as the San Francisco earthquake of 1906 or the days of Pancho Villa (who was active from around 1910 to 1920). Now that we're in the 21st century, the cutoff date may continue to shift, with individual editors deciding, based on individual books, what they feel comfortable with.

That definition leaves a big chunk of the recent past in limbo, including both World Wars, the '50s, and the '60s. These time periods are too recent to be considered historical but too far in the past to be considered contemporary. (Check out the "Mainstream versus category" section later in this chapter for more about this limbo period.)

Also, most historical romances are set in one of two places: the United States, especially the West (it's the cowboy mystique, though Native Americans are quite popular, too), or Europe, especially England. Plenty of exceptions exist (just off the top of my head, I can recall books set in ancient Rome, Asia, Egypt, and South America), but offbeat settings can make for a harder sell. I'm not saying that you shouldn't choose a different setting if you have a great story you're dying to tell. You just need to know that you may have a tougher time when you're ready to submit your manuscript.

Living in the present

Contemporary romances are pretty much what they sound like: books that feel as if they're taking place at the same time that the reader is reading the book. I like to say they're happening in the *eternal present.*

In the "Mainstream versus category" section later in this chapter, I talk about the distinction between mainstream and series romance and explain that the definition of *contemporary* varies a bit between the two. In contemporary series romance, the books *must* take place in the eternal present. You can't do a prologue set in 1999 and then headline Chapter 1 "Three Years Later." (If you need to make the timeline clear, headline the prologue "Three Years Ago" and Chapter 1 "Today.")

In mainstream romance, you have a bit more flexibility. You can go back a few years or specify a specific year and still consider the book contemporary. As with the cutoff date in historical romances, nothing's hard and fast in contemporary romances. One editor may let you go back to the '70s, another only to the '90s.

If you choose the eternal present, you need to keep certain things in mind as you write so that you don't date your book:

- ✔ **Never mention the year in which the book's taking place.** This tip sounds like common sense, but you can easily forget and mention the hero's brand-new 200-whatever Porsche.

- ✔ **Don't talk about current events.** Don't talk about the current presidential election or refer to specific big events you read about in the papers or see on the news. If you need that kind of dramatic background, make something up. Invent a president and his challenger, make up a global conflict, name your own hurricane . . . whatever you have to do to avoid tying your story to a time that'll be long gone when your book comes out.

- ✔ **Be careful about pop-culture references.** Today's hit is tomorrow's trivia question. So when it comes to pop culture references — music, movies, television, best-selling books, and even computer games — you're better off having your characters rent a DVD (videos are already passé) of a classic like *Casablanca* or *M*A*S*H,* or listening to a standard like Billie Holiday rather than something that's current (and will probably be forgotten by the time the book comes out). Or, just as good, mention that they rent a *just-released hit* or tune the radio to *a station playing all the latest hits,* which lets you avoid mentioning any specifics.

- ✔ **Don't try too hard to sound too cool.** Slang changes overnight. Avoid using slang as much as possible, and when you do use it, try not to be too cutting edge. Use expressions that have been around for a while and are still in use, like "cool," "radical," and "bad" (meaning good, of course).

✔ **Set trends instead of following them.** This tip holds especially true when you're talking about fashions. Luckily, the fashion magazines or the latest teen-angst nighttime soaps probably don't dictate to your heroine, but those influences may be important for secondary characters, especially younger ones. So don't get too specific about what people are wearing if you want their clothes to be cutting edge. The same holds true for whatever else your characters share with the in-crowd. Talk in general terms, or create a fashion statement or a trend of your own. That way, you can never be behind the times.

Mainstream versus category

The second big distinction publishers, readers and, of course, writers make is between mainstream (single title) romances and category (series) romances. The main differences involve length and the way the books themselves are marketed to the reader.

Making the most of mainstream

Mainstream romances are the genre's "anything goes" books. You still need to satisfy the basic tenets of any romance and give the reader what she wants, but you have a lot of freedom in how you do that. Mainstream romances can be contemporary or historical, and they can belong to any subgenre: western, futuristic, inspirational, romantic suspense, or anything else. Most mainstream novels are 100,000 words or longer, but you don't really have a limit, upper or lower — other than what an editor and a publishing house think that they can market.

Publishers also refer to mainstream romances as *single titles* because of the way they market them — singly. In contrast to *category romances* (see the next section, "Keeping track of category" for more info), which publishers market in related groups, called *series,* single titles stand on their own. Publishers sell each one into stores individually, and then, in most cases, stores put them on shelves alphabetically by the author's last name, so readers generally need to know who they're looking for in order to find your book.

You have a lot of freedom when you write a single title. Your creative instincts have plenty of room to play, and every born storyteller finds that freedom exciting. You don't have any restrictions (other than those restrictions based on subgenre, if you're working in one) on

✔ The kind of story you can tell

✔ The language you and your characters can use

✔ Your characters' behavior in the bedroom (or anywhere else that appeals to them)

And you can incorporate gritty realism, way-out fantasy, or anything in between that you want. You have the freedom, and the room, to create more fully realized subplots and a larger cast of characters, and to use additional points of view to tell your story. (See Chapter 9 for details on using different points of view in your novel.)

A mainstream editor can feel free to publish books set in that limbo period between where historical romances leave off and contemporary romances pick up, and books from that period definitely get published. (See the "Historical versus contemporary" section earlier.) It *is* a tough sell, though, in part because you don't have an easy way to define the book in terms of a larger grouping, so it's harder for editors, marketers, PR people, and sales reps to talk about the novel. You shouldn't look at this limbo period as impossible for you to work with, but it *is* more difficult.

The bestseller lists almost exclusively contain mainstream books, and most of the well-known names in the business got so well known by writing single titles (though most of them didn't become stars with their first books). Very few romance novels get made into big Hollywood films or even made-for-TV movies, but most of the ones that do are mainstream romances. Those six- and seven-figure advances you read about? They go to mainstream writers, too.

The rewards of writing single titles can be huge, but it's a tough market to crack. Far more authors aspire to sell a mainstream than there's room for in the market, and actually getting published is no guarantee of the kind of success and fame most authors dream of. For every giant advance and matching print run, a dozen or more mainstream authors get advances that don't pay the mortgage for more than a few months. Most authors' books don't get the advertising and PR push to support the big print runs that turn a novel into a bestseller, so luck, as much as talent, often makes a star.

But don't let the challenges turn you away, because I firmly believe that a good book can always find a home. Going in, though, you need to have a clear idea of what you're up against, because the road to your first sale is likely to be long and paved with rejection letters. If you're aware of the challenges, you're less likely to get depressed if things are hard, and you'll be pleasantly — even ecstatically — surprised if things go unexpectedly easily.

Keeping track of category

Category romances, often called *series romances,* sit at the other end of the spectrum from single-title romances. Series romances are published, as their name implies, in a series. Each series, or *line* (and there are many), puts out the same number of titles (usually four or six) every month.

All the books in any given series have the same number of pages and the same approximate word count (as of this writing, different series range from 50,000 to 100,000 words), which is necessary so they'll fit the prescribed page count. Each series has a consistent look — with a particular art style, graphic design, and the series name featured almost as a brand — so that readers look not (or not only) for particular authors but for particular series, because they know that each series can be counted on to provide a particular reading experience.

Each line has a *strongly defined* editorial personality, shared by all the books in the series. Some series are so sexy that they're just short of erotica, and others feature a low level of sensuality but with sexual tension so thick you can cut it with a knife. Some series feature a wide range of plot types, while others are defined by subgenre (see the "Subgenres and niche markets" section later in this chapter).

Most category romance series are contemporary romances, but historical romances are represented, too, and more could enter the category marketplace at any time.

Publishers have so well defined the different series' personalities that they have *tip sheets* to describe the specifics of each series, including its editorial focus, level of sensuality, and length requirements. Tip sheets frequently also include specific editors' names and information on how to prepare and submit a manuscript. When a publisher offers tip sheets, they're available by mail (send a self-addressed, stamped envelope) directly from the publisher, online, and at conferences.

The category approach, with its use of tip sheets to guide aspiring authors, is completely different from mainstream, where you're left to your own devices to decide what you write and where to submit it. Category romance requires creativity of a different sort than mainstream does, because you have definite and clearly defined requirements and expectations, and you need to be creative and establish your unique style and abilities within those boundaries.

Writing for series has both upsides and downsides, just as writing mainstream does. Category-only writers can never earn the huge advances that some mainstream writers receive, and they rarely star on the national bestseller lists or become household names. On the other hand, most mainstream authors can publish only one book per year, either because of the time it takes to write a long novel or because most single-title publishers find that a one-book-a-year schedule works for them. But publishers encourage series authors to write multiple titles per year. Plus, series authors can often contribute to several different series. So the advances may be smaller, but several per year, plus royalties, can add up.

Another huge plus to writing for series romance is that it provides a great point of entry into the business, for a number of reasons:

- ✔ **Large need for books:** Most romance readers don't just read, they read voraciously. Every month, publishers put out over 70 original titles in series romance.

- ✔ **Migration from series to mainstream:** Many mainstream authors, including some of the biggest and most successful, got their starts in series. As authors move on to mainstream romances, they either stop writing series books altogether or cut down on the number of series titles they produce, making room for new stars in the category world. This migration is constant, so publishers constantly need new authors.

Subgenres and niche markets

The biggest distinctions in the romance genre are the ones I describe earlier: historical versus contemporary romances, and mainstream versus series romances. But romance also has all sorts of subgenres. *Subgenre* refers to books intended to appeal to a specific niche within romance as a whole. Some subgenres can be historical or contemporary, while others (those tied to a specific era) can only be historical. Some are subject-based, while others are defined by their approach to storytelling, and most can be mainstream or category romances. You can even combine several subgenres if that's what makes your story work. Some subgenres are widely popular, and others appeal to a smaller but devoted group of readers. Not every book fits into one of these subgenres; plenty of romances are just contemporaries or historicals, and the writer gets to decide the specifics. But every editor and experienced author knows the subgenres, so you need to know them, too.

You may be tempted to aim for the themes with the broadest possible appeal, but niche markets can be profitable, too. What a niche market lacks in numbers of readers may be made up for by the devotion of those readers it does have, who buy virtually everything in their area of interest. You can make a name for yourself more easily in a niche market, too. It's the old big-fish-small-pond situation.

Keep an eye on what subgenres are currently popular, but remember that things change. Just like in Hollywood, you only need one big success to change the face of the industry. An unexpected bestseller puts every publisher on alert to the marketing possibilities, and suddenly every editor is looking for good books to appeal to the same readers who drove "That Book" onto the bestseller lists.

Ultimately, you should make your decision about what type of romance to write based on a combination of factors, your knowledge of the market's possibilities and its relative popularity being one of them. (See the section "Choosing Your Path" later in this chapter for the factors you may want to consider when choosing what type of romance to write.)

Futuristic: Looking ahead

A *futuristic romance* isn't true science fiction, because you emphasize the characters and their relationship, just as you would in every other romance. No strange, monstrous aliens need apply, and futuristic romances are usually set here on Earth — just Earth in the future. You set the book in the future for a reason, though, whether because technology plays a part (maybe someone's developing computer technology to bring world governments to their knees), or because it's set in a post-apocalyptic world. You may even set it in space or on another planet, but both of those settings can make for a tougher sell.

Whatever futuristic trappings you put on your story, though, those trappings aren't the point of the book. You should still structure your story like any romance. The setting should help drive the plot and create an atmosphere, but it's never the story.

Gothic: Simply sinister

I remember when *Gothic* romances, whether historical or contemporary, were the rage. Every one of these books had a similar cover: A woman, at night, running away (often along a cliff-edge path, with one scraggly tree leaning ominously into the abyss) from a menacing castle or a huge, turreted Victorian house. And a light was always shining from a single window. Rumor — never substantiated, as far as I know, but intriguingly believable — says that one publisher left out the light in the window on one cover, and sales tanked.

In the Gothics' heyday, the basic plotline involved an innocent heroine who found herself living in the sinister hero's equally sinister house, falling in love with him — sometimes even already married to him — while wondering whether he was actually out to kill her, because clearly someone was, judging by the "accidents" and outright attempts on her life that kept on happening. Gothic romances faded almost out of existence more than 20 years ago, but they've never quite died. These days, the covers don't give away the subgenre as they once did, and the heroines are less innocent and have more backbone, but the heroes are still dark and sinister, even scary. The defining characteristics remain the spooky (but rarely paranormal) setting and the sense of encroaching menace, which is tied to the hero, though ultimately someone else turns out to be the real threat. The romance world has room for a good Gothic every now and then, though they're often disguised as so-called psychological thrillers, which may contain romance but aren't necessarily romances themselves.

Inspirational: Relying on faith

Inspirational romances are non-denominational Christian romances, and they feature faith and faith-based issues as an important element of every plot, in addition to the developing relationship. Whether the characters' lives are simply shaped by their religious beliefs, which feature in all their actions and decisions, or one character has lost faith and finds it again, or anything in between, this faith-based thread is what makes an inspirational an inspirational.

The books aren't sermons, however. Like every romance, they feature strong, sympathetic characters who must overcome their own emotional issues on the way to happily ever after. They don't feature sex or even a level of sensuality that would be out of place in a '50s TV show. You don't just close the bedroom door and keep the reader from peering inside. Your characters — especially unmarried couples — don't go into the bedroom at all. Traditional one-man/one-woman values generally drive romances, but inspirational romances are far more traditional than any other books in the genre.

Inspirational romance is a growing niche market with a devoted (no pun intended) readership. For many years, inspirational romances were almost all historical romances, but in recent years, contemporary romances have entered the mix in increasing numbers. You can find inspirational single titles and series, and romantic suspense is popular. This subgenre is expanding, both in terms of the kinds of books it includes, and in number of readers, all the time.

Paranormal: Hauntingly good

Paranormal romance, with its mystical, even mythical, elements, isn't for everyone, because it can require a particularly strenuous willing suspension of disbelief, especially in its more extreme forms. A lot of readers don't find it too

---

Romance by invitation only

What about anthologies and continuities? *Anthologies* usually consist of three novellas (occasionally more) on a similar theme, frequently holiday-based. Sometimes the novellas are editorially connected, but most of the time only the common theme ties them together. *Continuities* are series of linked books, usually 12, with an umbrella story that runs from the first to the last alongside each individual romance. Continuities are bible-driven, with all the authors working from an editorial blueprint.

Storywise, anthologies and continuities are quite different, but they share one key element in common: They're contracted by invitation only. As an aspiring writer, don't waste your time attempting to write for either of these formats. Concentrate on becoming a successful multi-published romance novelist, which provides your best chance of being invited to participate in one of these exciting projects.

much of a stretch to accept a haunted house, a heroine with ESP, or maybe even a reincarnation story, with the hero and heroine fated to complete a romance set into motion a century ago, and paranormal romances like those tend to have the broadest appeal. Time travel, sometimes considered a sub-genre of its own, can sometimes even sneak in and get published as a historical or a contemporary romance, depending on when the bulk of the book takes place. But a hero who's a vampire or a heroine who's a werewolf . . . those plot lines can be harder for some readers to accept, making them harder for a writer to place. The more extreme paranormals are usually — though not exclusively — published as mainstream, rather than series, books.

With something as extreme as paranormal romance, you really need to buy into the fantasy yourself. Even if you treat the subject humorously, instead of with drama or a sense of menace, you don't want to be tongue-in-cheek, implying that it's all really rather silly. That destroys the mood and prevents the reader from identifying with your characters and their romance, because it's as good as telling her that she's a fool if she does.

Regency: Crowning success

Regency romances are a subgenre of historical romance that is set in a spe-cific time period. A traditional Regency romance is different enough from most historical romances that it's given its own category and discussed sepa-rately. The actual Regency period was quite short (1811–1820) and got its name from the fact that George, Prince of Wales (later to be King George IV), was appointed Regent due to his father's increasing insanity. Prinny, as he was called, lived a lavish lifestyle that the titled class aspired to share. He ascended to the throne in 1820, marking the literal end of the period. In romances, the late Georgette Heyer popularized the period, and her name is still synonymous with the Regency romance. Her books, more than any histo-ries, continue to inform the subgenre.

Two things distinguish a traditional Regency romance:

- ✔ **Length:** Most historical romances are at least 100,000 words long (Harlequin Historicals, with a minimum length of 90,000 words, are an exception), but the traditional Regency is shorter, around 65,000 words.

- ✔ **Tone:** The traditional Regency is also generally lighter in tone, often almost a comedy of manners, and both the author and the characters pay a great deal of attention to the ins and outs of society and the social whirl. Though Regencies were once very low-key in terms of sensuality, a lot more variety exists these days, and some can be quite sensuous.

In more recent years, Regencies have expanded, so publishers have put out full-length (in historical-romance terms) Regencies, many of them darker sto-ries that explore the underside of the society of the time and allow their char-acters to face heavier issues.

Houses publish these longer Regencies much like any historical romance, but traditional Regencies remain a niche market that very few publishers are active in. The players change with relative frequency, so if you're interested in writing a traditional Regency, you need to research the market for yourself to see what houses are currently publishing them.

Romantic comedy: Looking for laughs

Romantic comedy isn't only a box-office draw, it's also a growing presence in romance fiction. Real-life romance makes people happy — lovers have fun in each other's company. *Romantic comedies* capture that sense of fun while simultaneously throwing up emotional roadblocks between the lovers.

Although humor can have a place in pretty much any book, a romantic comedy is humorous throughout and at every level: characters, plot, and writing style. In my experience, romantic comedies are always contemporary, with a hip, flip tone, and usually feature characters on the younger end of the spectrum — 20s rather than 40s — who are frequently unattached and child-free. The books are upbeat, with a sense of fun throughout, and they're not the place to explore emotional trauma or experiment with social realism.

If you write romantic comedy, avoid slapstick and physical comedy. Let the humor come from the characters themselves, from their reactions to situations, rather than from bizarre setups that would throw anyone for a loop.

Romantic suspense: Thrills and chills

This subgenre is one of the most popular, as of this writing. It's also one of the fastest growing. As its name implies, *romantic suspense* is a mix of romance with suspense and mystery, so you propel the reader through the story not only by her desire to see the romance reach a happy conclusion but by her need to make sure everyone lives, and the danger, whatever form it takes, is averted.

One of the challenges of writing successful romantic suspense is that you need to write a strong, complete, and compelling romance *and* a strong, complex, and believably threatening suspense plot. Too often, writers feel that they can slack off on one or the other, so either the emotional conflict gets settled too soon, leaving the hero and heroine as romantic allies for the rest of the book as they work together to solve the mystery, or the suspense angle is too simplistic and the solution transparent. One failing I see constantly is that either the hero or heroine is a suspect in whatever's going on, and there's only one other possible villain. Because the reader knows (despite her willing suspension of disbelief) that the hero or heroine will turn out to be innocent, there ends up being no mystery at all, and any feeling of suspense is severely compromised, if not totally lost.

Secondary expectations

Depending on what kind of romance you're writing, your reader may have secondary expectations you need to keep in mind (in addition to the big five I outline in the "Meeting the romance reader's expectations" section in this chapter). This list is far from comprehensive, but here are some things you may want to think about:

✔ **Historical accuracy:** Every historical romance needs to stay true to its period while still satisfying a modern reader's desire for characters she can identify with and writing that doesn't sound stiff to her ear.

✔ **An appropriate level of sensuality:** Mainstream romances don't dictate a sensuality level, but many category romance series do, and so do inspirationals. So it's up to you to live up, or down, to what's expected.

✔ **A convincing mystery/level of suspense:** Romantic suspense readers aren't easily fooled. They're good at picking up on clues and spotting red herrings. It's your responsibility to plot out the suspense side of your book believably, to put your characters in real jeopardy, and to make any mystery sufficiently mysterious to keep the reader guessing.

True romantic suspense novels shouldn't be confused with suspense novels that include an element of romance, which don't need to satisfy a romance reader's expectations (see the "Meeting the romance reader's expectations" section earlier in this chapter) in dealing with the relationship. Both of these kinds of novel have one thing in common, though — both men and women like to read them. Romantic suspense is the genre most likely to attract a crossover readership, and that's partly why many of the romances you see on national bestseller lists are romantic suspense.

Western: Riding the range

Western romances have been popular forever and continue to sell well. *Westerns* are set in the American (and sometimes Canadian) West. They can be either contemporary or historical romances. The key is that they're decidedly non-urban in tone and usually in setting. Dallas, Denver, and Santa Fe are all western cities, true, but books set in them often have just as much, if not more, in common with books set in New York, Chicago, and Los Angeles as with those books set on a ranch or during a cattle drive.

The real draw of the western lies in the hero — usually a cowboy, a rancher, or a Native American. He's a quintessential American type: rugged, strong, usually solitary, and very definitely not a touchy-feely sensitive, new-age guy. He lives in a rugged land that tests men's courage, and he passes the test every time. He can tame a wild horse, rope a runaway steer, and sleep as comfortably on a mountainside as in his own bed. In Chapter 4, I talk about

Alpha heroes, and this guy is Alpha to the max. You may sometimes find the western hero in a boardroom, but it's usually not by choice, and he's probably still wearing his broken-in boots, hoping to get out of the office and back on horseback long before the end of the business day.

Westerns are less appealing to overseas publishers, where readers see the fantasy these books depict as quintessentially American and not as appealing as some of the other subgenres. Because North America is the single biggest romance-buying market in the world, you can still make plenty of money if you write a successful western, even if your overseas rights never sell.

Related women's fiction markets

A number of non-romance genres, often grouped together as women's fiction, are closely related to romance and sometimes referred to in the press and by readers as romances. All these genres contain elements of romance, even though they're different in terms of structure and focus. Because you're likely to run into them as you navigate the publishing maze, I want to quickly cover these related genres.

Chick lit

Chick lit focuses on young (mostly twenty-something) heroines navigating the perils of single life. These books are very heroine-focused, and the author often tells the story in first-person point of view, which differs from the usual third-person approach of romance novels (see Chapter 8 for more on voice). Key themes include men and how to deal with them, but the heroine's entire life and its travails (often humorous) form the backbone of the plot, and a happily-ever-after ending isn't required and is often pointedly avoided. Most chick lit novels are published in trade paperback.

Mom-lit has emerged as a spinoff genre of chick lit. It deals with slightly older characters who are at a different place in life — married (or divorced) with children. Again, the book focuses on the heroine's whole life, with romantic relationships playing only one small part in the whole.

Erotica

Many romances are sexy, even extremely sexy, but they're still romances, with a focus on the characters' emotions and their ultimate union in every sense. *Erotica* focuses on sexual relationships rather than emotional ones, and the plot makes no pretense that the relationship will be a lasting one. Erotic novels are about sexual thrills, not emotional highs. And although they do have actual characters and plots (something pure — a very strange term, under the circumstances — pornography lacks), the real point of these books is to explore the characters' sexuality in great detail, at great length (yes, including *that* length), and often in ways (kinks and multiple partners, separately and simultaneously) that even highly sensuous romances don't.

Family sagas and multi-generational novels

Family sagas and multi-generational novels are the mini-series of the publishing world, painted on a broad canvas and covering the lives and loves of several generations of the same family, though in slightly different ways.

- ✔ **Family sagas:** These novels cover many years, so the first generation that the reader meets will get old, maybe even be long dead, by the time the most recent generation takes center page.
- ✔ **Multi-generational:** The story in these novels covers far less time, but members of several generations feature prominently.

In both types of novels, you usually find strong, and strongly-drawn, romances of the same sort any romance novel features, but those romances are only pieces of a much bigger story. Family relationships, births and deaths, the economic ups and downs of a family, the way a marriage evolves over time . . . these life moments are all of equal importance and help define the broad canvas against which the romances also play out.

Young adult

Young adult, or YA, novels come in all forms, and some of them are romances. Because the characters are in their teens — the same age as the readers, maybe even slightly older — they're almost always dealing with the challenges of first love, along with all the issues that go along with adolescence. This very different focus, a simple function of age, makes YA romances too different from romances aimed at the adult market for me to discuss them in tandem. In addition, even if a book ends with the young couple still together and planning to stay that way, it's unlikely, given their ages, that they really will live happily ever after the way an adult couple can.

Choosing Your Path

After you know everything the romance genre offers a writer and a reader, you need to focus and choose what kind of romances you want to write. Making that choice is important because your success depends on making the right match between your interests, your talents, and the market's needs.

Too often, I hear an aspiring author say that she has several ideas: a historical romance, a sexy series title, and a romantic suspense. It's clear that her creative energies and attention are divided among the three, that she has no idea what to write first or how to move forward. I always tell her to focus, to look at all the ideas objectively, and start with the strongest one — whether it's the premise she likes the best or the one she thinks is the most salable.

Making a choice now also affects future choices. If you sell your manuscript, you'll have a good reason to continue writing more of the same, to develop a readership who's willing to follow you into another subgenre. Even if you don't sell this one, any success (like getting feedback from an editor) may merit sticking with that subgenre so you can follow up on the contacts you've made.

You may have a particular idea that just won't let you go, in which case you need to write it and give it a chance. But often aspiring authors are torn, knowing they want to write romances but not sure exactly what kind. If that sounds like you, you need to ask yourself questions like those I pose in the following sections, and then let the answers combine with practicality to illuminate your path to publication and success.

By comparing what you like, what you're good at, and what the market's up to, you can probably arrive at the answer to "What should I be writing?" without even having to stress. Then let your mind start wandering, see what idea captures your imagination, sit down at the computer, and get started. Your romance-writing career has begun.

What do you like to read?

Sometimes the answer to this question is simple. You're strongly drawn to something very specific — inspirational romantic suspense, for instance. But a lot of writers like many kinds of books. Historical *and* contemporary romances. Series *and* mainstream romances. The first step to choosing what you should be writing is to narrow down your options. Use this list of questions to help you figure out what direction you may want to go:

- ✔ Do you read more of one type of book than another?
- ✔ Who are your favorite authors, and what do they write?
- ✔ Do you like to do research?
- ✔ Does the past fascinate you?
- ✔ Do you enjoy solving puzzles?
- ✔ Do you ever read outside the romance genre for fun? What kinds of books do you read? Mysteries? Science fiction? Nonfiction?
- ✔ What kinds of movies and TV shows are your favorites?

Follow your heart — at least as much as possible — in choosing what kind of romance to write. Romances are all about the heart, so if yours isn't engaged, your reader's won't be, either. And loving what you write helps you write the best book you're capable of, and only your best has a chance to sell.

If you don't like romance novels, can't love your hero and heroine, or only want to write a romance because you know they're popular and you think you can sell a few to make some money before moving on to "real" books, do us both a favor and put this book down now. Don't waste your time on the impossible, because love can't be faked — and that includes the kind of love found between the covers of a romance novel. Choose a genre that *does* appeal to you and start exploring *those* possibilities.

By asking yourself the preceding questions, you may be able to pinpoint a single type of romance that you're meant to be writing, in which case you've taken your first important step on the path to publication. If your interests are so specific, you need to be aware of what the market looks like but not let that be a factor in choosing what to write. But maybe you've just narrowed things down to a few possibilities that appeal to you, in which case, it's time to bring practicality to bear on creativity.

How do you fit into the market?

After you have a sense of what you may want to write, you need to get practical: Look at your own strengths, compare them to the state of the market, and see where the two come together to give you your best shot at publication. It all comes down to asking questions and analyzing the answers.

Knowing your own strengths

Knowing what you're good at is more than just knowing what you like — though knowing what you're interested in is certainly a big part of it. I love to watch equestrian show jumping, but if you put me on a horse and aim me at a 5-foot fence? Just watch me faint dead away.

You may love to read long, complicated romantic suspense novels, but writing something similar that's complex and tightly plotted enough to fill 150,000 words may be more than you feel up to right away. On the other hand, a 75,000-word Harlequin Intrigue may feel much more within your reach. Or maybe you have no facility for plotting suspense at all, in which case, you can always enjoy reading romantic suspense but need to look for something more romance-centric to write.

Based on your answers to the questions in the preceding section about what you like, ask yourself whether what you like and what you can do are the same thing. Take a practical look at the realities of your life, too. Are you working full time and also taking care of children, a husband, and a house? How much time can you realistically expect to steal for yourself so that you can write? If the answer is "not very much," you may want to think about series romance, even one of the shorter series, rather than a lengthy mainstream romance that takes much longer to complete.

The following list of questions can help you narrow down your choices, helping you figure out what kind of romance is the best choice for you because you not only enjoy it, but it also plays to your existing strengths:

- ✔ Have you always been fascinated by history, maybe even one period in particular? Do you sometimes think you were born a hundred years too late and that you'd fit in so much better if the world moved a little slower? Historical romances probably fit you just right.

- ✔ Feel uncomfortable writing love scenes, the more explicit the more uncomfortable? Or do you love to write them, looking on each one as a reward for your hard work writing the rest of the book? Let your own comfort level with sensuality guide you, because writing compelling love scenes is an important part of writing a romance.

- ✔ Do your friends think you're the funniest thing on two feet? Romantic comedy is going to be a natural match for you. Or can you screw up a knock-knock joke? Romantic comedy as an option? Not so much.

- ✔ Is Christianity a key component of your life, or have you forgotten the last time you went to church? You're going to have a hard time going against your natural inclinations, so why not make things easy for yourself and follow them?

Matching yourself with the market

After you have a sense of what you'd be good at, figure out that particular market's strengths and weaknesses. This step can be challenging, because the romance market shifts constantly. No matter how much info you gather, you can never be sure where things will stand even a month or two in the future, much less by the time you get your finished book in front of an editor, which can be a year or more away. But you can try to track and predict trends and collect as much helpful information as possible. And I have a number of rock-solid avenues for you to take when the time comes for your market research.

- ✔ **Writing resources:** In Chapter 3, I talk about writing resources, and many of those resources — writers' organizations, writers' conferences, magazines, and Web sites — are great sources for market information, giving you a timely idea of what's hot and what's not.

- ✔ **Bestseller lists:** Keep an eye on the bestseller lists to see what authors and what kinds of books are represented.

- ✔ **Media:** Read the papers and the pop culture magazines to see what's selling and getting critical acclaim, and who's getting paid the big bucks.

- ✔ **Retailers:** Talk to your local booksellers and get their take on things. They not only know what's selling but what kinds of books publishers are pushing for the future.

- ✔ **Online writers' communities:** No one person is an infallible source of all information — and that includes published authors — but if you get your information from a variety of sources and analyze it carefully, you can put together a reasonable picture of what's going on in publishing.

When you're gathering information, don't just look at what's selling through to the readers, either. Look at what the publishers are up to. Find out who's buying and what they're looking for. The category market is always hungry for new writers, and you may find a perfect fit in one of the many different series. Mainstream houses and editors often have more specific needs, and it never hurts to know whether one editor or a dozen are looking for what you want to write.

Never make your decision about what to write based solely on what's selling the best or the hot new trend. Just as you shouldn't be writing a romance novel at all if you don't love the genre, you shouldn't choose a plot type or a subgenre that you don't enjoy just because you think that's where the money is. You need to write the best book possible if you want to sell, and that requires an emotional and creative commitment on your part.

Chapter 3

Setting Up for Stardom

· ·

In This Chapter

▶ Setting aside the right place and time for writing

▶ Getting the right technology and supplies for writing

▶ Finding resources you can rely on

· ·

*O*n TV and in the movies, romance writers always seem to wear frou-frou negligees, spend about five minutes a day writing, and forego a desk and a computer for the sake of a bubble bath and a notebook. Unfortunately, real life is a little bit different. In real life, you have practicalities to consider, like carving out space and time for writing, as well as figuring out what kinds of supplies you need to keep on hand. Taking care of those practical considerations before you start writing is important, because when you get into your creative zone, you won't want to break your concentration to run out for printer software or sticky notes.

Another important part of getting yourself ready to write is knowing what writing-related resources are available. Organizations, publications, Web sites, and more offer information and instruction for the would-be writer. Some resources are more general, while others are romance-specific.

The exact realities of your situation are going to differ from everybody else's, but your basic needs aren't, and that's where this chapter can help. In this chapter, I talk about all these real-world concerns, so you can get set, forget, and write.

Finding the Perfect Place and Time to Write

Some successful writers (or writers who start out with money to burn) rent out-of-the-home offices that let them get away from all the interruptions of day-to-day life and turn writing into their full-time jobs. Most writers, however — especially just-getting-started writers — aren't so lucky. Chances are that you, like most of your peers, need to find space somewhere in your house to write and to make time for your passion in the midst of holding down a job and/or taking care of a family. Pursuing your writing may not always be easy, but you're starting out with two big advantages:

- ✔ **You're creative:** That means you can find clever, unique solutions to challenges, including finding space and time.

- ✔ **You're good with people:** Romances are all about people and their emotions, and if you can deal with the emotions of fictional people, you can also deal with the real emotions of your family.

Creating at-home office space

If you really want to be a writer, the first thing you need is a place to write. Having a place to write doesn't mean you won't be scribbling notes on a notepad or the back of an envelope while you're on the bus or eating lunch with the kids. (In fact, you may want to keep a small tape recorder in your purse so that you can even capture an idea while you're driving.)

But when you're ready to put all those great notes and ideas together, having a place of your own is important. If you're lucky, you have an extra room in your house that you can make into an office: A closed door can be your best protection against unnecessary interruptions, although if you have small children, this idea may not always be practical.

If you can't take over an entire room, try finding a permanent place where you can reserve a computer desk and maybe a small bookshelf and a bulletin board for your own use. From day one, think of yourself as a professional. Setting up an office, however small, tells the world (and reminds *you*) that you're serious about writing, so everyone else needs to take your writing seriously, too. Here are some solutions for setting up your own office when you don't have an entire room to spare:

- ✔ Can you take over a corner of your bedroom? (Corners are especially good because they have two walls and give the illusion of privacy.) Or maybe a corner of the family room?

- ✔ Do you have a not-too-grubby basement or attic that you can co-opt?

- ✔ Do you use your dining room only for special occasions? If so, you can make it your office, or you can make it the regular site of family meals and use the kitchen table as your desk. Be creative.

What if you literally have no way to make a permanent office or even a corner space for yourself? First and foremost, *don't let that stop you from writing.* Not having your own personal writing space does make sitting down to write harder, because you have to re-establish your boundaries every time (for instance, sharing the couch with the family). But if you're driven to write, you know that the challenge is worth the hassle.

If you don't have a set place for your writing, consider a laptop computer so you can turn any unused corner of the house into your office-of-the-moment. Depending on how good you are at tuning out the outside world, you might even try working at a library, bookstore, or local coffee shop, especially if it has a place to plug in a laptop. Some libraries also offer computers for their patrons to use; just be sure you save your work to a floppy disk so you don't lose it.

Making time to pursue your dream

Setting up a place to write is only half the job. The second — and often much harder — half is finding the time. These days, everyone seems to be on the go from the moment they get up to the moment they go to bed. Every minute is crammed full of something. Mothers of toddlers know all too well that sometimes privacy only comes in the bathroom. In order to take advantage of the place you set up for yourself, you need to make time for your writing.

Reconciling your family to the new you

Women are traditionally the caretakers, the ones who handle the bulk of the child-rearing and homemaking duties, even though most women these days also work outside the home. Standing up for yourself and insisting on some time for what you want — and for something that may not have any immediately obvious benefit, financially or otherwise — is difficult. But if you want to be a writer, you're most likely going to have to stand up and insist. And, because your boss probably won't pop the cork on a celebratory bottle of champagne if you tell her that you can work only five hours a day from now on, your writing time is going to have to come from the rest of your schedule.

Chances are you're married and have kids, in which case, your decision to write is going to affect your husband and children — sometimes in ways that don't make them very happy. Fancy dinners may give way to plainer fare, and your husband and children, depending on their ages, may have to start doing more to help out around the house (cooking, cleaning, and the older kids helping to take care of the younger ones).

If you get serious about your writing, you may not have as much time for helping with homework or driving your children everywhere, and at first that may make you feel bad — like you're letting your family down. At the risk of sounding hard-hearted, get over it. I'm not advocating ignoring your family, because they are — and should be — the most important people in your life. But, like most women, you've probably structured your life so that every spare minute is spent taking care of them and your house. Now they can take some responsibility for themselves. Their reward? A happy wife and mother who's doing something that makes her feel fulfilled and makes her even better than ever to have around.

Factoring in your new priorities

So how can you find time to write and keep your family happy while you do? Here are some tips for balancing your time:

- ✔ **Schedule everything you can.** Most of us move through the day without a hard and fast plan, playing a lot of our tasks by ear. Make yourself a to-do list and set aside specific amounts of time for specific chores. Keep track of your time and keep to your schedule. Streamline your housework (do you really need to vacuum every room every day?) and plan your errands so you don't have to zigzag all over town.

- ✔ **Simplify mealtime.** You can make quick and easy meals, or you can prepare meals ahead of time; a lot of cookbooks are available that can give you hints. Slow-cookers are a great invention and free up time for other things. Not all takeout is bad or bad for you, and nothing is wrong with scheduling a weekly dinner out somewhere inexpensive and fun.

- ✔ **Can you afford help?** If you can, why not hire someone to help, even once a month or every couple of weeks, with the housework? You can hire a teenage girl to do childcare, even for an hour or two once or twice a week. Think of it as an investment in your future — one you can even finance by giving up small luxuries that you can live without, like a magazine subscription, buying so many books (support your local library!), or even cigarettes.

- ✔ **TV or not TV?** Most folks (like me) have favorite TV shows, and I'm not advocating that you give them up. But you may spend plenty of time watching shows you don't really care about just because the TV's on and everyone else is gathered around it. Or the show you like finishes, but inertia keeps you in front of the set and you start flipping channels to find a movie to watch. Cut out the nonessential TV, watch (or rent) even one less movie a week, and you can buy yourself valuable writing time. You may even want to tape your week's shows (writing while they're on) and watch them later all at once, fast-forwarding through the commercials.

- ✔ **Stay up late or get up early.** I've lost track of how many authors have told me that they wrote their first books by getting up an hour or two early and writing when everyone else was still asleep. You can also stay up later than everyone else to get in some writing time. This strategy is especially helpful if you have young children who can't be on their own as much as older ones.

- ✔ **Say no.** You don't always have to be the one to drive to and from lessons, sports, the mall, or the movies. Your kids' friends have parents, too. Work out a fair division of labor — which may demand compromise from your kids as well as other parents — and stick to it. If you're a full-time mom, you're probably used to doing all the driving because the working moms figure that you have nothing better to do. Well, that was never true, but you're writing now, so this assumption is even more off base. Writing is your job, and you're going to have to tell people you need time to do it.

✔ **Make your time with family count.** Quality instead of quantity really does count. When you're with your family, be present in the moment; don't cook dinner and help with homework at the same time. When you take a break to play a game or go prom-dress shopping, get into it wholeheartedly.

✔ **Share the responsibilities.** As I mention earlier in the chapter, your family can probably help out more than they have been. I don't want to sound like a broken record, but the point bears repeating. Older kids can learn to cook and can certainly help clean up, no matter who did the cooking. Your husband can pitch in, too (at least sometimes). You may discover that your husband actually likes having more one-on-one time with the kids. And he can do a driving shift, too. The more involved he is in his kids' lives, the better for all of them.

✔ **Make finishing your book a family goal.** Plan to have a special family outing or take a real vacation after you complete your writing. If you get your family invested in your dream, you can bet they'll be more willing to give you time to accomplish it. You can even break things down incrementally, promising a favorite meal, a special dessert, or a family trip to the movies at the end of every chapter.

Building a Writer's Tool Kit

After you find your office space, you need to furnish it so you can take advantage of the time you carve out for your writing. You don't need me to tell you the basics of getting a desk, chair, and bookshelf. Just get what fits (with emphasis on a comfortable chair, because you'll spend plenty of time in it). The following sections discuss some other items that you need to think about more carefully.

Counting on your computer: Technology is your friend

These days, I don't know a single author who doesn't do the bulk of her writing on a computer. Using a computer makes revising a breeze, compared to the old days of typewriters. If possible, get your own computer to use for your writing and online research. Then you don't have to compete with your family for computer time, and claiming your computer as a tax deduction will be easier (for more on taxing matters, see the "Booking it: Accurate financial records" section later in this chapter).

You may already have a computer at home, and maybe you'll end up using that computer for your writing. But if you're lucky enough to pick out a new system, think about the features that you want most, and don't pay for things that you don't need. When picking out a computer, keep these basics in mind:

✔ **Get the best monitor that your budget can swing.** Why did I start with this tip and not something techie? Because you're going to stare at that monitor for hours at a time, so be kind to your eyes and get the clearest, sharpest, and biggest one you can. You'll be glad you did.

✔ **Bigger really is better.** At least when you're talking about memory and hard-drive size. You're going to be working with — and storing — a lot of information. With prices for these features coming down all the time, you may as well buy as much as you can afford.

✔ **Choose necessary software.** Don't load up your computer with programs you don't need. They just take up space and tempt you to waste time (especially with games) that should be spent writing. The only thing you absolutely have to have is a good word-processing program, although a good suite of office tools that contains spreadsheets and other programs will probably be worth investing in. After that, choose cautiously and think carefully about everything else that you add onto your system.

✔ **Pick a basic printer.** A romance novel manuscript consists entirely of text, so you don't have to worry about printing figures or pictures, so you won't need a color printer. You want sharp black text on white paper to save your eyes and an editor's. And speed counts, because you'll want to be able to print out your manuscript quickly if an editor or agent asks to see it.

Sooner or later, you'll probably need to get your computer repaired. And you won't want to be without it any longer than you have to be, so pick a brand that has a good reliability rating, equally reliable customer service (including by phone) and, if possible, repair service that's available either in your home or locally.

Plugging in: Phones, faxes, and photocopiers

You don't need a lot of actual equipment to set up your office, which is a big help when you're working with limited space, as most writers are.

I know you have a phone, but you may want to get a separate line for your office, because you definitely need to be accessible via phone. Talkative teenagers who tie up the line or children who continue screaming at one another as they answer the phone doesn't necessarily say "I'm a pro" to publishing contacts. Also consider whether a separate phone line (or cable connection) is necessary for Internet access. Much like the teenager who talks on the phone nonstop, a Web-surfing adolescent (or spouse) can render you unreachable. Another argument in favor of a separate line no one else is allowed to answer? You always get your messages (no forgetful teens or toddlers). But, whatever line you use, be sure that you have a reliable way to get messages.

As for faxing, the days of stand-alone fax machines are gone. As long as your computer is hooked up to the Net (and you want to be, so you can do research), you can use fax software and send information directly from your system to any fax number.

Unless you live literally in the middle of nowhere (and maybe not even then), you don't need a photocopier. Copy shops are everywhere. Most of the time, printing out an extra copy is just as easy (but not when you're going over a copy edit, for example, as I discuss in Chapter 18). Plus, you should be saving everything on disk, too.

Sharpening up your office supplies: More than just pencils

You're probably not going to need a lot of supplies, and most of the ones you do need are pretty basic. (You don't want to be scrambling around looking for a pencil when an editor calls.) Here's a list of basic office supplies to get you started:

- **Bulletin board and thumbtacks:** If you have space to hang one, I recommend getting a bulletin board. If not, getting a small one that you can bring out whenever you need it is still a good idea. Bulletin boards can be helpful in all kinds of ways: keeping track of timelines, listing character traits, listing key research facts, and so on.

- **Paper and pads:** Keep plenty of paper on hand for your printer; you also want to keep pads handy for taking notes. Always keep a pad near the phone. You may also want some quality stationery for making letterhead. (Preprinted letterhead is an unnecessary expense now that quality printers are widely available.)

- **Pens, pencils, and erasers:** Computers are great, but sometimes you need to write things down the old-fashioned way. Keep a few red pencils and pens around, too, so you can write notes on the hard copy of your manuscript.

- **Sticky notes and index cards:** Sometimes all you need is a small surface for a small note. These supplies are great because you can put them on your bulletin board, computer monitor, your husband's forehead, or anywhere else.

- **Rubber bands:** Be sure you buy a size that's big enough and strong enough to hold an entire manuscript together. No wimpy rubber bands here. You don't want them to break and leave your manuscript loose in an envelope or, worse, all over an editor's floor. *Always rubber band your manuscript horizontally and vertically.*

- ✔ **Envelopes:** You need different sizes for mailing full and partial manu-scripts, and be sure that they're strong enough to travel without tearing. You also need business-size envelopes for correspondence.

- ✔ **Other stuff:** You also need such basics as tape, a stapler, binder clips, paper clips, and so on.

Keep your supplies organized (and don't let your children raid your desk drawers), so they're always at hand when you need them.

Dusting the shelves: Your home library

In the best of all possible worlds, you'd have the room and money to sur-round yourself with every book you could ever need. In real life, however, you need to limit yourself. But having certain books around will be useful. As a romance writer, your basic home library is likely to include some or all of the following:

- ✔ Grammar reference

- ✔ Dictionary

- ✔ Thesaurus

- ✔ How-to books and guides on writing romance, writing in general, and marketing book-length fiction

- ✔ Research books for topics covered in your romance (see Chapter 13 for more information about research).

Don't overload yourself with writing references. Find a few that work for you and stick with them.

Booking it: Accurate financial records

Most creative writers don't like thinking about money and numbers because they're so, well, *uncreative*. But you have to think about finances, because they're part of having a home office and earning money (which you're plan-ning to do with your writing). You need to think about how writing and its attendant costs affect your tax status, and you probably also want to keep an eye on your expenses. In this section, I give you a few basics so you can get started and thinking in the right direction, but what you really need is expert advice, which you can get from books, a financial planner, an accountant, a tax advisor, or any combination of these options. Tax laws vary from state to state, and your specific situation needs to be examined individually, because getting it wrong can have legal and financial repercussions.

Here are some supplies that can help you keep your finances straight:

- ✔ **Financial ledger:** Get a basic financial ledger — one that lets you keep track of income and expenses — and write everything down, annotating entries to help you remember details.

- ✔ **Folder or file for receipts:** Save all your writing-related receipts. Write notes on the back if you need to, or get an accordion folder with dividers so you can separate different types of expenses.

Err on the side of caution. If you think that something may be relevant to your writing finances, save it or write it down. You can decide later whether or not to write it off on your taxes.

What kinds of expenses may be tax-deductible? This list is far from comprehensive, and different types of expenses are covered for one person and not for another. (See why I told you to get expert advice?) As a start, though, you might keep track of:

- ✔ **Capital expenses:** These expenses are the big goods, like furniture or a computer.

- ✔ **Real estate:** In some cases, you can write off a portion of your mortgage or rent.

- ✔ **Telephone:** You may have a separate line for your business calls or your computer, or just have writing-related calls made on your home phone.

- ✔ **Office supplies:** Paper, printer cartridges, sticky notes, and so on fall into this category. If you pay to have a manuscript photocopied, that cost is another office-related expense.

- ✔ **Books:** Other romance novels, books on writing (like this one), or research books may also be written off on your taxes.

- ✔ **Software/Internet provider:** Did you buy a word-processing program or a dictionary on CD-ROM? Do you use the Internet for research? These items may be deductible expenses.

- ✔ **Entertainment and news:** Depending on what you're writing, you may be able to deduct the cost of some movies, magazines, or newspapers that give you an idea about contemporary society and concerns.

- ✔ **Travel:** You may travel for research or attend conferences that are related to your writing.

Getting comfy: Strategies for making your workplace work for you

Feeling at home and being productive is more than just setting up furniture and sitting down in the comfiest chair you can find in front of your computer. You need to make your workspace *your* workspace. If you're a minimalist and hate even a hint of clutter, this section may not be for you. But for those of you who enjoy personalizing your space, here are some tips for making your workspace a place that brings out all your creative instincts:

- **Picture this.** Whether they're family pictures (so you feel a little less like you're abandoning them when you sit down to write), artistic images that speak to you, or photos of your favorite actor (obviously a good source of inspiration), use available wall space, a spot on your bulletin board, or the extra space on your shelves and desk to put up pictures that please and inspire you.

- **Let your kids contribute.** If you have young kids, make them feel like part of your career by putting up their artwork around your office space. You can even "commission" a new piece every week and make a little ceremony of the hanging process.

- **Don't knock knick-knacks.** Do you have a favorite stuffed animal left over from childhood? Or a collection of, well, anything (for me, it's monkeys) that makes you happy? A

memento that always makes you feel content or, better yet, romantic? Find a place to put one or two of these small things around you so you feel good about being at your desk.

- **It makes scents.** Many people find specific fragrances soothing, and that scents open pathways to calmness and creativity. If you're one of them, you can burn a scented candle or keep a dish of potpourri nearby.

- **Music matters.** Some people can work only in complete quiet, but for many others, music is a must. Whether you prefer wordless classical or jazz, or hard rock and roll, play your favorite. Most computers play CDs, but if yours doesn't, invest in a small shelf system so you can always have your music at hand. You may want to invest in a pair of good headphones, too, so your music doesn't disturb anyone and so you can block out extraneous sounds. *Hint for lovers of quiet:* Good headphones can help keep noise at bay, even if you're not playing any music. They can also serve as a do-not-disturb sign for your family.

Basically, do whatever you want to make your workspace feel homey and relaxing, because you can't be creative or do your best writing when you feel uncomfortable or edgy.

Accessing Resources for the Would-Be Writer

I want to spend a little time talking about writing-related resources. Many sources are available that give you a chance to interact with other writers, both aspiring and published, or find guidance and instruction for your craft. I can't give you a complete list, but I can offer you some places to start and tips for finding more resources.

Joining writers' organizations — romance-related and otherwise

Here are a few organizations that you can check out:

- **Romance Writers of America (RWA),** 16000 Stuebner Airline Rd., Suite 140, Spring, TX 77379; phone 832-717-5200, fax 832-717-5201; Web site www.rwanational.com. The RWA is the main organization in North America for published and unpublished romance writers. The organization publishes a monthly magazine and has an annual conference that features workshops taught by editors, agents, and published authors, as well as other related professionals. The conference also offers opportunities to meet individually with editors and agents. Numerous RWA chapters are located across the United States and Canada, many of which publish monthly newsletters and hold local meetings and conferences.

- **Novelists, Inc.,** P.O. Box 1166, Mission, KS 66222-0166; fax 913-432-3132; e-mail ninc@kc.rr.com, Web site www.ninc.com. This organization is for published authors, although you don't necessarily need to be published in romance fiction. Novelists, Inc., puts out a newsletter and holds an annual conference.

- **National League of American Penwomen,** Pen Arts Building, 1300 17th St. NW, Washington, DC 20036-1973; phone 202-785-1997, fax 202-452-6868; e-mail info@americanpenwomen.org, Web site www.american penwomen.org. The National League of American Penwomen is an organization that fosters women's participation in the arts, specifically letters, art, and music. The organization has several hundred local branches in the U.S. and sponsors writers' workshops and conferences.

Going where the writers are: Conferences and more

Writers' conferences are located all over the U.S. and Canada throughout the year. Some conferences are specifically for romance writers, while others cover multiple genres. The RWA and other writers' organizations sponsor many of these conferences. *Romantic Times Bookclub Magazine* (see the section "Finding magazines for writers") and many universities also sponsor annual conferences. Check the publications listed in the last section of this chapter for upcoming conferences.

Make the most of an appointment with an author or editor. If you can arrange a conference-sponsored one-on-one appointment with an editor, make sure you request your appointment with an editor who handles the type of book you're writing. Go prepared with a project to pitch or specific questions to ask. Don't take up an editor's time just to say "hi" (even if your agent, your mom, or anyone else told you to) or to pitch a project that's already on her fellow editor's desk.

Informal local writers' groups are another option for meeting and interacting with other writers. To see whether there's a group in your area, check local college or library bulletin boards or ask around in likely places, such as colleges, bookstores, and libraries. You can also put up your own notice in the same places, asking for information on existing groups or even volunteering to start your own if enough like-minded people are interested.

Taking advantage of courses and critique groups

Many community colleges and adult-education programs offer writing courses. You may have a tough time finding a class specifically for writing romance novels, but you should have much less trouble finding a class for fiction writers. You may luck out and find one specifically for popular fiction.

Because editors can't be writing teachers and because they can respond only to specific manuscripts, many aspiring writers find a course in learning and practicing the basics of story structure, character development, and so on in a very feedback-heavy environment helpful. Many writers also find having a critique partner or being part of a larger critique group helpful, again because of the hands-on feedback. RWA chapters and writing courses are prime spots for meeting potential critique partners and setting up what is, essentially, your own self-directed writing course. For more information on critique groups and whether or not they're for you, see Chapter 5.

Searching the Web

Nothing seems to shift faster than the online environment. Sites that were old faithfuls suddenly disappear without a trace, while new sites spring up, just waiting to be discovered. So instead of giving you specific writing-related Web sites, I'd like to offer a few tips for finding sites that meet your individual needs:

✓ **Use well-defined, narrow searches:** When using a search engine like www.yahoo.com or www.google.com to search for writing-related sites, try narrowing your search to get the best results. For instance, don't just search for "romance writers"; instead, search for "Silhouette Intimate

Moments authors" or "historical romance writers Medieval." The more keywords you put into your search phrase, the more specific your results will be. And if one word doesn't work, try substituting another. For example, change "writers" to "authors" and see what you get.

✔ **Follow the links:** If your favorite author has a home page, look around it for suggested sites — you can often find useful links. Many authors also provide an e-mail address so you can write to them. I've found that romance writers are incredibly generous, so a politely worded (and brief — don't ask for the moon) request for direction is very likely to receive a response. Some authors even offer writing advice on their sites.

Checking in with publishers

Major publishers have official Web sites, and most sites provide information on submission procedures and, in some cases, editorial guidelines or tip sheets. A direct link for submission guidelines may be supplied, but in many cases the "About Us" or "Contact Us" link can get you to that information. You can find out a lot about companies' needs just by looking around their Web sites and noticing what they're currently publishing. Check out these companies' Web sites for more information:

✔ **Harper Collins' Avon imprint:** www.harpercollins.com/hc/aboutus/imprints/avon.asp

✔ **Dorchester Publishing:** www.dorchesterpub.com

✔ **Kensington Books:** www.kensingtonbooks.com

✔ **MIRA Books:** www.mirabooks.com

✔ **Penguin Books:** us.penguingroup.com

✔ **Ballantine Books:** www.randomhouse.com/BB

✔ **Bantam and Dell imprints:** www.randomhouse.com/bantamdell

✔ **St. Martin's Press:** www.stmartins.com

✔ **Warner Books:** www.twbookmark.com/index.html

One site deserves special mention, and not just because I work for the company: The official Harlequin (and Silhouette) Books site (www.eharlequin.com) features an entire "Learn To Write" section for aspiring writers, along with a section called "Community," that between them offer tip sheets for all the company's series, as well as submission procedures, articles, bulletin boards, and even chat rooms. Published authors and editors (including me) also log on from time to time.

Finding magazines for writers

Membership in RWA gets you a subscription to *The Romance Writers' Report,* a magazine that contains market updates, topic-specific writing tips, interviews with successful writers, editor and agent interviews, and more. But several other magazines that can provide you with practical writing advice are available for you to subscribe to or purchase on the newsstand. A few magazines you may want to check out are

- ✔ *The Writer:* Along with subscription information, this magazine's Web site (www.writermag.com) provides access to articles for registered members (registration is free) and other helpful links.

- ✔ *Writer's Digest Magazine:* The magazine's Web site (www.writers digest.com) provides subscription information, articles, and links to a number of other resources for writers.

- ✔ *Romantic Times Bookclub Magazine:* An additional romance-related magazine to look at is *Romantic Times Bookclub Magazine.* Although the magazine is mainly aimed at romance readers, *Romantic Times Bookclub* also interviews editors and agents, provides tips on new developments in the industry, and has reviews of virtually every romance novel published each month. The Web site is also full of helpful features and links (www.romantictimes.com).

Part II
Laying the Foundation: The Building Blocks of a Great Romance

The 5th Wave   By Rich Tennant

"I think drawing inspiration from your dreams is a valid approach to writing romance novels, but yours seem a bit overburdened with talking cookware, flying monkeys, and sidewalks made out of quicksand."

In this part . . .

*E*very great romance novel has a few essential elements — compelling characters and an interesting and exciting plot. In this part, I tell you how to create irresistible heroes, sympathetic heroines, a setting to showcase their romance, and a plot that's based on compelling emotional conflict and builds to a climax no reader can resist. In addition, I give you tips for writing a outline — something even many experienced writers hate to do — and show you why doing so is important.

Chapter 4

Creating Compelling Main Characters: Alpha Males and Fiery Females

*E*veryone dreams of falling in love, and it's the reason romance novels exist: So readers can experience the vicarious thrill of falling in love as if for the first time with every new book. More than anything — more than a clever plot, an exotic setting, or beautiful prose — what makes that possible are the characters.

In this chapter, I talk about why characterization is so important, and I also offer tips on creating sympathetic heroines and irresistible heroes, so your reader finds herself caught up in your book and eagerly turning pages. Of course, your hero and heroine don't exist in a vacuum, so I provide some tips for handling secondary characters, too, because they make your book's world seem real, and add color and complexity to your novel. Finally, I give you some general tips on characterization to help you create rounded, interesting characters, no matter how large or small their roles.

Depending on Your Characters

Romances are all about emotion, and emotion comes from people. In real life, our family and friends bring emotion into our lives. In a romance novel, your characters, especially your heroine and hero, are responsible for fueling the emotional fire.

Romance, by definition, involves two people. And in a romance novel, those two people are the entire reason for the book's existence. In other genres, a romance can exist in the background or as a secondary element in relation to a mystery, a family drama, a battle against evil aliens from outer space, or any other scenario that the author dreams up. But in a romance novel, the hero and heroine's relationship takes center stage. Their romance isn't just part of the action — it *is* the action. And your readers view every other plot development through this lens. (For that reason, I devote most of this chapter to stand-alone heroine and hero sections.)

The heroine is the reader's alter ego. She's key, the gateway for the reader to get involved in the novel on a personal level. The reader's identification with the heroine keeps the reader involved in your story because everything that happens to the heroine also happens to the reader. And the hero? Not only does the reader vicariously fall in love with him as the book progresses, but she also feels the excitement as he falls in love with her, too.

Your hero and heroine must be interesting enough to capture the reader's imagination, strong enough to move the plot forward, and admirable enough to deserve a happy ending. They don't have to be 100 percent perfect; in fact, as I discuss later in this chapter, perfection is a problem. But your hero and heroine must deserve being called a hero and a heroine. You can define your supporting cast by moral ambiguity, but your hero and heroine need to be genuinely good people, even if they've made mistakes or are on a journey of redemption from something in their past.

A romance requires more than an interesting and appealing couple. For one thing, the characters have to find each other interesting, too. And their interest in each other has to strike several kinds of sparks. They must have romantic sparks — that wonderful, almost indefinable electricity that two people feel for each other — that tell them they have a shot at something wonderful. I talk more about this type of spark in Chapter 11, when I discuss love scenes. A second kind of spark is also crucial — and that spark comes from conflict. I talk in detail about conflict in Chapter 5. But because you need to keep conflict-based sparks in mind when creating your characters, and because all good conflict is character-driven, I also touch on it in this chapter.

The Key to Every Romance Is the Heroine

Most romance readers are women, and naturally, they want to see themselves reflected in their choice of reading. That desire for reflection doesn't mean that every heroine has to be straight from everyday life (even everyday life in, say, the 1800s); however, the heroine does have to feel real and be interesting and emotionally complex enough to keep the reader interested in your story.

Your heroine has to be the most accessible character, because the packaging (the cover art, copy, and often the title) usually focuses on her. And in most cases — unless the author is already one of the reader's favorites — the packaging is crucial to making the sale to the reader.

Your heroine needs to be at the center of the plot. Your story is really *her* story. Fifteen or twenty years ago, her point of view was usually the only one. Nowadays, authors make room for the hero's point of view, and sometimes even secondary characters'. But a romance novel is still the story of the *heroine's* romance — she's the focus, the pivot on which all action turns. In the end, the happy ending is happy because she literally gets her man.

Drawing the reader into your story

Because she's the reader's alter ego — the reader's avenue into the story — your heroine directly controls everything the reader feels, and whether or not she keeps reading. To get your reader involved in the novel, convince her that your heroine's not only someone she would like to know, but is also someone she would like to *be*.

When the reader identifies — whether consciously or subconsciously — with the heroine, she takes on the heroine's thoughts and feelings as her own. As she reads the story, the reader feels everything's happening to *her*, not just a fictional character.

The reader's identification is your secret weapon to make the reader fall in love with the hero. He has to be appealing on his own merits. But suppose you make him a cowboy, and your reader generally goes for suit-and-tie guys? Your heroine's thoughts and feelings — as she falls for the hero — become the reader's thoughts and feelings, too, until suddenly the reader has fallen in love with her first cowboy.

Making your heroine feel real

To foster the reader's identification with the heroine, you need to make your heroine feel real. Making her feel real doesn't necessarily mean depicting her as someone your reader could be or might know. Instead, it means giving her character reference points that readers recognize, which let your readers easily slip into the heroine's role and internalize her thoughts and feelings. In the following sections, I line up five rules for creating believable heroines.

Responding realistically

Make your heroine's emotional responses realistic. She's certainly going to experience things in the course of the book that most women never experience in real life, so your reader can't say, "I remember how I felt when that happened to me." So how do you get the reader to go along for the ride when your heroine's in the protective custody of a handsome detective, or playing incognito sex games with the suave publisher of a men's magazine? Simple. Just make her respond as the reader would. If a woman would be scared or shocked (and also attracted to the hero, of course) in real life, let your heroine feel that way, too. Her realistic response to a seemingly unrealistic situation will make sense to the reader and keep her caught up in your story.

Sowing the seeds of conflict

The sparks of all conflict come from your characters, and the best conflict is emotional. (See Chapter 5 for more on conflict.) Your heroine's the key character, so root the novel's conflict in your heroine's emotions. When the heroine's emotions feel real, her emotional conflict also feels real.

The circumstances may be unrealistic — like my previous example of the incognito sex games with the suave publisher — but her conflict can still be one the reader identifies with. What if your heroine has always been unsure of her ability to attract — and hold — the attention of a man, so she's afraid that when the hero finds out who she really is, he'll lose interest in her? This conflict is emotionally based and is one your reader can empathize with.

Exhibiting identifiable traits

Give your heroine character traits that feel real. She often has a job or lifestyle that your reader will never have. Maybe your heroine is a spy, a federal judge, a minister, or the daughter of a millionaire and her first car was a Mercedes. On the surface, she may seem too far outside the reader's realm of experience for that crucial sense of identification to occur, but a few well-chosen character traits can change that. Maybe she likes to drive too fast or is always playing with her hair. Maybe she has a soft spot for stray dogs or coos at babies in the supermarket.

Something small and human that you briefly mention just once or twice can resonate with the reader and make her realize that, for all their differences, she and the heroine aren't so dissimilar after all. Just don't mention these traits over and over again, because then they seem forced, which will distance your reader instead of drawing her in.

Keeping complexity in mind

Make your heroine a complex and interesting human being. You may think that having a complex and interesting heroine goes without saying, but not all writers realize this necessity. I've seen many heroines who were just plain boring. They had whatever character traits the author decided were necessary for the plot — curious, lonely, and intelligent, for example — but that was it. I didn't feel I was reading about a real person who had quirks, contradictions, and layers worth uncovering.

I think I'm a pretty interesting and complicated woman, and for me to identify with a heroine, she needs to be pretty interesting and complicated, too. And believe me, your readers feel the same way I do. Of course, don't go to such extremes that your heroine feels like a mass of tics, insecurities, and disconnected enthusiasms. She needs to be strong, admirable, and intelligent, and she should definitely feel like herself and no one else.

Overlooking her own great looks

Don't let your heroine realize she's beautiful. This tip may seem like a small point, but especially in our visually driven society, it's actually an important one. Most women are very critical of their own appearances. I look in the mirror and see flaw after flaw, not my good points — even though I know I have them!

Most romance heroines are quite attractive, but if all your heroine does is admire her own beauty, readers aren't able to identify with her. So, instead of working your heroine's description into the story through her point of view, let the reader see her through the hero's eyes. After all, no one can object if *he* finds her beautiful. Giving her a flaw or two doesn't hurt, either. Maybe her hair is a beautiful shade of red but has a tendency to frizz in the humidity, or maybe she needs glasses to read. Little touches like these make her more human and easier for the reader to empathize with.

Introducing imperfection

True heroines are strong but flawed. An imperfect heroine makes a perfect heroine. At first glance, I know that doesn't seem to make any sense, but trust me, it does, and for several reasons:

- **Readers can't identify with a perfect heroine:** No one is perfect. So if you make your heroine perfect, without flaws, fears, or vulnerabilities, your reader won't feel the bond that keeps her inside the heroine's head and turning the pages. By introducing weaknesses and vulnerabilities, you let the reader create that all-important bond with the heroine.

- **Static characters are boring:** Your heroine (and yes, your hero, too) can't remain static over the course of the book. As the plot progresses, you need to make your heroine develop, change, grow, and discover things about herself and her abilities — especially how to love and live with her hero. If your heroine starts out perfect, she has nowhere to go. But if she has insecurities, past failures to put to rest, doubts about herself and her abilities, or an out-and-out bad habit — maybe a quick temper, or impatience that leads to rash, unwise decisions — she has room for progress, and readers will want to see how she masters the challenges of the plot and the romantic relationship.

✔ **Imperfections call for complementary strengths:** Part of what makes a couple right for each other is that they complement each other; they need each other, and bring out the best in each other. The same must be true of your hero and heroine, so the reader believes they belong together.

Your heroine's insecurities and flaws allow room for the hero in her life and in her heart. As an example, perhaps your heroine comes from a broken family, which left her doubting her ability to succeed in a relationship, much less be a successful mother. Pets are the most she can manage, she's decided. So who moves in next door? A single father whose 5-year-old daughter just can't stay away from the heroine's golden retriever. Suddenly she finds herself playing mom at unexpected moments — not to mention having dinner at the hero's house so he can thank her for her help, where she discovers that maybe she does have what it takes to win the love of a good man after all. Without her insecurities, you wouldn't have a story — *or* a romance.

Naming your heroine

I've never heard of an editor turning down a manuscript because she didn't like a character's name, but the names you choose for your characters can subliminally express whether you have an ear for language or a knack for thorough research. Although a rose by any other name might smell as sweet, the idea of buying a dozen skunk cabbages doesn't appeal to most people. Names carry both connotations and information, so as a writer, you want to make your characters' names work for you, not against you. And because your heroine's your key character, her name is also key.

Ultimately, select the name that simply *is* your heroine's name, the name that belongs to her as an individual. Listen to your instincts as an author. At the same time, know the consequences of your decision, so you can make them work for you as you write your romance.

Choosing an accurate name

Taking accuracy into account when naming a character may sound odd, but the idea is important. You want your heroine's name to fit seamlessly into her world. Her name is part of the illusion that makes her feel real.

For instance, if you're writing a Medieval romance, don't name your heroine Tawanna or Tiffany. In any historical romance, choose a name that's appropriate to the period. When you don't choose a historically accurate name, the editor may question the accuracy of *all* your research. And research — especially in a historical novel, where most readers have to be told how people dressed, what they ate, and any other details of their lives — is crucial, so an editor needs to know she can rely on you to get it right.

The accurate-naming rule applies to ethnicity and region, too. If your heroine's Scandinavian, the names Ellie and Rose aren't appropriate first names, and Smith and Weinstein aren't suitable surnames. If your heroine's from New England, she's unlikely to go by Sarah Kate, because that double-name construction is more indicative of the American South.

But watch out for place-based stereotypes, such as Sarah Kate from down South. If your heroine's name sounds like a cliché, your reader may think the heroine herself is a cliché, too. You also want your heroine's name to sound unique so she'll stand out from the other characters in your book, who may need to be defined by their names more than your heroine does.

Connotations count: Pretty is as pretty does

Some names just sound nicer than others, like *rose* versus *skunk cabbage*. Every generation has its own standards of beauty — in clothes, cars, and names. With no offense meant to anyone who has a mother, aunt, or sister named Myra, it's a tough name to pull off for a heroine these days. Younger generations are conditioned to think of Myra as an old-fashioned name, so if you choose it, you're fighting an uphill battle to convince the reader that the name isn't an accurate indication of the heroine's personality. That's not to say you can't choose a name that creates challenges for you, just know what those challenges are so you can overcome them.

Be aware of any connotations the name you choose carries so you can work with them or against them to create your heroine. Choose a name that has no real connotations, so you can create your heroine from scratch, or pick one that communicates *what you want to convey* about your heroine. Is she brash and iconoclastic? Bree (with its echo of "breezy") may work. Quiet and feminine? Perhaps Emma or another name that hints at the past and has a soft sound. A tomboy? Try Meg or Becky — something that has a playful lilt. Or, if you choose a name that has connotations that clearly don't fit your heroine — Emma for a tomboy or Mabel for an adventurous astronaut, for example — be aware of the mismatch so you can work to counter it. You may even have another character comment on her name, so you can bring it out into the open and get it out of the way.

Covering gender

Unisex names are trendy now. (Obviously, when I was named Leslie many years ago, my parents were cutting edge.) But, if you name your heroine Jamie or Sam (short for Samantha), be aware of one challenge in her future: back-cover copy. For a reader, flipping a book over and reading about the perfect romance between Jamie and Jake or Sam and Rafe can be a little jarring. Unisex names are less of a problem in the books themselves, but know that you're creating a challenge on the marketing end.

Is exotic erotic?

The short and oh-so-definitive answer is . . . sometimes. Exotic (meaning different, not necessarily from an exotic locale) names can be beautiful, musical, romantic, and enticing. Romina. Michelline. Shoshanna. But exotic names can also be so strange, attention-getting, and unpronounceable that they stop the reader in her tracks, pulling her out of the story to sound out a name. Shivareena. Caledonia. Briganta. Don't try so hard to choose something different that you work against your own best interests.

Creating Your Hero

Your hero's almost as important as your heroine, because a one-person romance is . . .well, not a romance. Every heroine needs a hero. Your reader needs to empathize with your heroine, but she needs to fall in love with your hero. Don't worry. This prerequisite doesn't mean that you have to create some too-true-to-life (boring!) man your reader may run into in the course of everyday life. This guy isn't called a hero for nothing. Like the heroine, he doesn't have to be perfect; he just has to be perfect for *her,* and that's something altogether different.

Heroes are for loving

The heading sums up what you need to know about your hero. In the rest of this section, I talk about how to make him worthy of your heroine's — and your readers' — love. Think of your hero as a prize, the prize the heroine wins after all the conflict is resolved. (By the way, just so you don't think I'm being sexist: Make your hero realize that the heroine's love is the prize *he* wins.) From the moment he appears, something about him has to affect the heroine in a way no other man ever has — even if she (thinks she) hates him.

Because conflict is the driving force of a romance novel, you can't let your heroine love your hero (or vice versa) right away. But you *do* need to demonstrate immediately that your characters have a connection and an excitement between them that marks him as the hero and tells the reader that these two characters are going to be madly in love by the end of the book.

So how can you show that special something that tells the heroine this guy is different — and special? The possibilities are as limitless as your imagination, but in the following sections, I present a number of sure-fire ways to show that your hero's special.

Selling the sizzle

Make him gorgeous. Sure, this approach has been used literally a million times, but it works. A big part of what makes a fictional romance appealing is something that works in real life: chemistry. And a big part of chemistry is finding your partner physically irresistible.

Maybe he's a millionaire who's just stormed into your heroine's flower shop to accuse her of stealing his frozen sperm so she could get pregnant and force him to hand over a ton of money in child support. She gets furious because, as far as she knows, that was her late husband's sperm. And yet, as angry as she is, she can't help noticing — maybe even to the point of derailing her train of thought — how incredibly good-looking he is. Showing the heroine responding so viscerally to the hero is a big clue that they're meant to be.

Digging deep

Give him moral, intellectual, and emotional strength. Remember the literal meaning of the word *hero*. Your hero has to be more than a male protagonist. He has to embody all the virtues the heroine deserves in a partner.

He needs to be honest and live by a strong moral code that is present in everything he does, even if he's overcoming a difficult past or makes mistakes in the present. He needs to be intelligent; no empty-headed pretty boys need apply for *this* position. And last (but far from least) he needs to be emotionally strong and reliable — and faithful, not necessarily from the beginning (although the reader doesn't want to see him sleeping around, even if the romantic relationship hasn't been solidified yet), but definitely by the end of the book. The reader needs to close the book knowing that these two people can be happy together forever, which means knowing his love for her is strong and true.

Creating conflict from character

Because the best conflict is emotional and is generated directly from your characters, your hero, just like your heroine, needs to have internal issues that drive him and contribute to the tensions separating him from the heroine. Like your heroine, your hero shouldn't be perfect, or he won't be interesting and won't have any room to develop as the book progresses; and it's from his flaws and insecurities that his conflict will come. (For more on the subject of creating emotional conflict, see Chapter 5.)

Making things equal

Show him as the heroine's equal. Whether they're exchanging barbed remarks at a boring dinner party where the hostess seated them next to each other, not realizing they're lawyers on opposite sides of a custody battle, or fighting their way to freedom side by side after being taken hostage by rebel forces during a luxury tour of the Amazon, don't let the heroine dominate or be dominated by the hero. If she's so strong or witty that she makes him look weak or stupid, or if he's superior and demeaning and undercuts her strengths (and by proxy the reader's), then they're not going to make a lasting match, because no one can be happy spending life in a one-down position. But if they're equals, the reader sees their potential as a match because they can go through life enjoying each other's company and meeting challenges together.

Shining but not outshining

Give your hero strengths that differ from but also complement the heroine's. Just as, in real life, good couples need each other, your hero and heroine should also need each other to feel complete. Maybe your couple is taken hostage by South American rebels and meet during an escape attempt. He's the tough guy who fights past the guards, and she's the clever one who talks their way onto a boat so they can escape. They both shine, but neither outshines the other, because they're not competing in the same arenas.

Revealing his softer side

Let the hero's inner soft side be visible to your heroine. Maybe he and your heroine first encounter each other across the bargaining table during a hostile corporate takeover. She's about to lose the family firm to him, which really hurts, because her employees are like family to her and he has a reputation for being ruthless to his staff. Just when the situation is tensest, his young daughter, who's escaped from her nanny, runs in and turns the place upside down. Suddenly the heroine sees the hero's human side as he hugs his daughter, smiles, and forgets all about what's going on around him so he can hear about her first day of kindergarten. The heroine melts, and after that she never quite sees him as the bad guy again, no matter how much she tries.

Laughing it up

Never forget the power of humor. Laughter is sexy. Studies show that couples who laugh together have stronger relationships, so if your hero makes your heroine laugh, it's a good sign for their future. The hero and heroine's meeting may be difficult or awkward: They're playing lovers in a movie, and on the first day of shooting they have a sexy love scene. She's uncomfortable, not just because of the situation but because he's her ex-husband, and all she can remember is how much it hurt when they broke up. He senses her nervousness and decides to put her at ease, so he pratfalls out of bed, and suddenly she's laughing and remembering all the times they laughed together, not to mention wishing their love scene were for real, not just for the cameras. The key is to make sure the humor's character-driven, not slapstick, and that it's appropriate to their ages and situations.

Holding out for a hero: Alphas and others

Not every hero is the same, but certain *types* of heroes exist that writers, editors, and, often, readers recognize. Each type of hero has his own appeal. Of course, you can combine attributes of the various types as you create your own hero, which allows you to craft just the right guy for your heroine *and* make a hero who's memorable to readers.

Any discussion of types of heroes is meant only as a starting point, because your goal is to always make your hero (like your heroine and your secondary characters) feel real. The tension between your couple needs to arise from the people they are, not from a contrived meeting of a stereotypical hero and heroine — so make your hero your own. As a basis for understanding heroes, here's some info on the kinds of men readers are used to falling for.

Just as relationships depicted in romance novels don't mirror real-life relationships, the heroes also aren't like the men that women are looking to get involved with in real life. Romance novels are full of tension and drama, and romance heroes do their part to contribute. A perfect real-life boyfriend has no problem showing his feelings, and an imperfect real-life guy never figures out that he has any. Either way, these real-life boyfriends don't work as the hero of a romance novel. Real-life men and relationships are wonderful and fulfilling, but they lack the drama to power a compelling novel and keep readers turning pages. Be sure to avoid the true boy-next-door hero.

Leading the pack: The Alpha hero

Have you ever heard of the Alpha wolf? He's the leader of the pack. The one all the other wolves defer to. The wolf with all the power, and he takes his position for granted. An Alpha hero is a lot like that wolf, except he wears a suit and tie, or maybe jeans and a leather jacket. Occasionally he even wears the human equivalent of sheep's clothing, but underneath, he's still all Alpha.

- ✔ An Alpha hero takes charge of situations and people the minute he enters the room. To others, particularly the heroine, he generally seems dictatorial, rigid, even a big pain in the butt who needs to be taken down a peg. (Part of the heroine's conflict is almost always butting heads with an Alpha guy to establish her own strength.)

- ✔ An Alpha hero is often a loner, and he usually works in an appropriately Alpha job: corporate CEO, rancher, spy, policeman, fighter pilot. He's unlikely to be a teacher, and when he is, he's probably assuming the role for a reason. (Think Arnold Schwarzenegger in *Kindergarten Cop,* but not played for comedy.) In his job, being tough is an asset; being tough helped him get to the top and stay there.

✔ An Alpha hero can make decisions and implement them in a second, and frequently the welfare of others — sometimes economically, sometimes their lives — depends on him. He's not used to thinking about feelings, his or anyone else's, and often women are eye- and arm-candy, because he doesn't let anyone get close — until he encounters the heroine.

✔ An Alpha hero appeals to the heroine (and the reader) because she gets to him as no woman ever has before. He may have been involved or even married before, but chances are his relationship broke up because of his Alpha inability to let her in. Or maybe the relationship ended because she used him for his position and power (reinforcing his inability to trust a woman) or because she was a more traditional, submissive partner who died and provides a real contrast with the heroine. The heroine, however, is ultimately as strong as the Alpha hero and breaks through his defenses. She makes him feel, and she gives as good as she gets, because she's his equal, which makes the two of them a match.

Twenty-five years ago, every hero was an Alpha, and a wide gap usually existed between him and the heroine in every way — age-wise, financially, and in career and social position. Throughout the book, he kept her in a one-down position, even though she did her best to combat him, and he never let on that she was getting to him. At the very end, he confessed his feelings for her and let her know how much she mattered to him.

These days, Alpha heroes have a lot more range. Some still follow that classic pattern (particularly in historical romances, where that kind of relationship is more accurate for the time period, and in some series romances), but in most cases, the Alpha hero is more complex. For instance, including his point of view lets the reader see what the heroine can't: that he's feeling something for her beyond sexual attraction, and that he's often exaggerating his Alpha tendencies to keep her from knowing how much she means to him.

As I discuss in the "Introducing imperfection" section earlier in the chapter, perfect characters aren't very interesting. An Alpha guy may look perfect, but if he really were perfect, what would he need the heroine for? By giving him flaws and vulnerabilities, you also give the heroine a way into his life and his heart. Maybe he's suddenly presented with a 3-year-old daughter, the result of a long-ago one-night stand, and has no idea how to deal with the upheaval. Maybe he has demanding, disapproving parents, and envies the heroine's boisterous, loving family, and her own open, outgoing nature. Using such elements, you create chinks in his Alpha armor, giving the heroine a way to reach him and the reader a reason to love him.

Opening up (but slowly): The Beta hero

The Beta hero is so-called simply because he provides a contrast to the Alpha hero. The Beta hero is still a true hero, but he's not as tough and unbending as an Alpha hero. A Beta hero interacts more with the heroine instead of just barking out orders, but he's no pushover — strong tension still needs to exist between them. Here are the Beta basics:

✔ A Beta hero can be in pretty much any profession. He can excel at an Alpha-style job, but he can also do jobs that don't come as naturally to an Alpha, such as a teacher, doctor, writer, or scientist.

✔ A Beta hero is more likely to be a family man who has important relationships with his children, parents, or siblings, and he often has close friends, as well. Unlike the loner Alpha, a Beta has a support system, and sometimes the heroine envies *his* good relationships. If a Beta has a relationship in his past, it was quite possibly a good one, where he and his wife were a great couple, and either she died or the relationship ended in a more real-world way, like two nice people who just grew in different directions and divorced.

✔ A Beta hero's emotional issues are likely to be out on the table. Whereas an Alpha hero refuses to acknowledge his issues with the heroine, the Beta hero gets them out in the open piece by piece throughout the book. For example, if he has trouble trusting women, he won't hide that inside but will find ways to let her know he's not sure he can trust her, either — even though his attraction to her is clear. A Beta hero comes with baggage, but he hasn't been as extremely affected by it as an Alpha, even when their issues are the same. A Beta hero's easier for the heroine — and the reader — to understand.

But just because the issues are discussed doesn't mean he and the heroine discuss them calmly and rationally. (Where's the tension in that?) The issues between them are obvious to both of them — and to the reader — even if they seem unlikely to find a way to sort things out.

Breaking the rules: The bad-boy hero

The bad-boy hero is more accurately the reformed bad boy. When he was young, he was the town bad boy, the tough kid who scared the locals with his swagger, his hot car, and his I-don't-give-a-damn approach to the rules. He usually came from the wrong side of the tracks and often wasn't half as bad as the locals thought. And if he *was* bad, he wasn't bad in a big way, although that may not have saved him from taking the rap for anything from theft to rape to murder. Despite everything, he was usually irresistible to the local girls — or one local girl, in particular, who turns out to be the heroine.

The bad boy's transformation from outcast to hero can take various forms. Sometimes he stayed in town all along, possibly overcoming the stigma of his past and winning the locals' respect. Sometimes he lives on the fringes, the victim of whispers and finger-pointing. Sometimes he's just come back to town, possibly looking for revenge after a stint in prison for a crime he didn't commit, or maybe to show everyone he's made something of himself.

The bad boy's appeal lies in the old Beauty-and-the-Beast fantasy. Something's appealing about the edge of danger he carries, and something's seductive about being the one woman to tame him. In the end, he turns out to have all the essential heroic qualities, and his bad-boy persona becomes a thing of the past.

Feeling the pain: The tortured hero

The tortured hero hasn't been literally tortured, although it *is* a possibility, depending on the past you invent for him. Rather, he's emotionally tortured by something in his past, and that something causes him to put up barriers between himself and emotional intimacy.

Perhaps he's a former cop, and his wife and child were killed by a car bomb intended for him. Now he's tortured by guilt and never wants to get close to anyone again, because he can't bear the thought of putting anyone else at risk or of feeling the grief of such loss again. Maybe he had a terrible childhood that left him believing he's simply not capable of love. Maybe he's a vampire in love with a woman and is tormented that his only choices are to watch her wither and die of old age or to turn her into an immortal yet hunted creature like himself.

So what's the appeal of the tortured hero? Psychologists say that women are nurturers; they like to fix people and relationships. So a tortured hero is the ultimate challenge. In reality, this kind of guy is probably damaged goods and a bad bet for a relationship. But in a romance novel, he's a perfect romantic fantasy — a prize worth winning because the heroine alone can heal him.

Living and loving in style: The playboy hero

This type of hero is especially suited to a sexy romp or a battle of the sexes. He's the irresistible guy who has a woman — or two, or three — in every port. He loves women — all women. But settling down with just one isn't on his agenda. A playboy hero may know that he's using his attraction to all women as a form of self-protection, a method of making sure he isn't attracted to just one woman, thereby leaving himself vulnerable. Or he may genuinely think he's happy without strong emotional ties, because he hasn't seen love and marriage work. Maybe he became a playboy in response to a relationship gone wrong, or maybe he's a natural flirt who's just taking the path of least resistance through life and love.

Whatever made him a playboy, one thing is guaranteed: His world is rocked when he meets the heroine. Suddenly all other women lose their appeal — something that radically alters his self-image and makes him very unhappy at first. Almost always, his tension comes from that unhappiness when he realizes that he's been blindsided by love. But by the end of the book, he's very grateful for that emotional accident.

The hero is the prize the heroine wins, and a playboy can be thought of as the ultimate prize. The heroine becomes, in a sense, the world's most successful woman, the one who makes all other women fade to nothing in the eyes of the ultimate connoisseur of the female sex. Talk about the perfect couple!

Looking for love in all the wrong places

Some kinds of heroes are a proven hard sell. I'm not saying it's impossible for you to find success with these heroes, because specific books with "problematic" heroes *have* sold — and very well. As the writer, you need to decide whether or not to let this information influence your decisions:

✔ **Locales:** I don't always understand why readers dislike certain things, but I know that they've made certain dislikes clear. For whatever reason, heroes from certain locales (or whose names indicate a connection with those locales) tend not to be popular. Heroes from Germany, Scandinavia, and the former Soviet Union and its current descendent states have all proven a difficult sell.

✔ **Job descriptions:** Unless you're a superstar author whose books sell on your name alone, back-cover copy is crucial in getting the reader to buy your book. One of the key pieces of information that back-cover copy conveys and that readers respond to is your hero's occupation. For the readers, certain jobs are shorthand for masculine: cowboy, spy, soldier, CEO, and cop. Other occupations indicate just the opposite and can negatively affect sales: playwright, dancer, sculptor, and painter.

✔ **Athletic endeavors:** Sports superstars don't make super heroes. This idea seems to run counter to logic, but it's true. Perhaps sports-star heroes aren't popular with readers because many of the athletes who make headlines do so for less than heroic reasons. Or maybe because readers' real-life husbands are obsessed with sports, readers don't want to hear about a hero who's similarly obsessed. Whatever the reason, readers' associations with sports-star heroes are generally negative.

If you choose a known unpopular element, you need to give your readers plenty of compelling emotional conflict (see Chapter 5) so the back-cover copy (and the book) can focus on what the readers want, not what they don't.

Hello, my name is . . .

Just as the heroine's name is a crucial part of how the reader sees her, the hero's name says a lot about who he is, and it also needs to be chosen carefully. A reader needs to recognize your hero the minute he shows up on the page, and the right name tells her immediately that she's found her man. Listen to your instincts when naming your hero. Always be aware of the name you choose and how to make it work for you.

Strong men need strong names

You're probably not going to call your hero Casper Milquetoast, a name that screams — no, make that mumbles — weeniness. But you still have to be careful and avoid choosing a name that has connotations that work against the character you're creating.

In general, short names sound masculine and strong: Rafe, Gabe, and Jake. They're not fussy sounding, and heroes aren't fussy guys. Of course, longer names can work, too, as long as they sound masculine, like: Rafael, Gabriel, and Jacob. They carry a certain weight and have a certain history to them, and their connotations work to your advantage. Active names, like Chase, sound strong and heroic, and hard sounds — Cord, Kyle, and Rick — also indicate strength and masculinity. Compare those names to Myron or Frances, which are generally considered geeky or weak sounding.

Avoiding childish nicknames

Charlie and Stevie are fine nicknames for little boys, but remember that your hero's a man. He may be a Charles or a Steven, even a Steve, but if you give him a cute, little-boy nickname, the reader's likely to think of him as *her* little boy, and you want her to see him as the man she's falling in love with.

Hitting your mark: Accuracy counts

Being accurate when naming your hero is important. If your book is a historical romance, make his name specific to the time period. Seth and Caleb both have a strong sense of history to them that Pierce and Keshawn lack. If he comes from a particular country or region, give him a name that also comes from that area. Miguel works if he's Hispanic, for instance, or Jean Paul if he's French. Names can even feel job-specific, in a way. For example, you're more likely to find a cowboy named Rafe than a corporate CEO.

Native American heroes are particularly popular in historical and contemporary romances, which has led to an extra challenge: finding a name that indicates the hero's background without sounding phony or clichéd. I've lost count of how many characters named Hawk I've seen, so even if you use Hawk as part of his name, know that you need to work hard to make him stand out as an individual.

Switching order: Last names as first names

In romance novels (and often in real life), men are frequently referred to by their last names. Alex Chance may become Chance, while Keith McCord may become McCord or Mac. For this reason, you may want to give extra thought to your hero's surname.

Keepin' It Real: Secondary Characters

Although the hero and heroine are the key characters in any romance, they don't live in a vacuum. Like all of us, they have family, friends, and co-workers. These supporting characters are called *secondary characters*. Secondary characters range from parents, children, best friends, and bosses to villains and romantic rivals who create a sense of threat, to waitresses or mechanics who may have only a line or two of dialogue or description. Pay plenty of attention to them (even though you may not give them a lot of space), and you maximize your chances of creating a world that feels real.

Secondary characters can be harder to create than your hero and heroine, because you use fewer words and pages to describe them.

Remembering their roles

In most cases, secondary characters exist because they play a specific role in the plot (especially true of villains and romantic rivals). They

- ✔ **Provide a sense of place and reality:** Secondary characters make your hero and heroine's world feel full and real. With names, voices, and behavior, secondary characters give a sense of where and when things are happening, saving you from relying on narrative to get everything across.

- ✔ **Parallel or contrast with the hero and heroine's relationship:** Using secondary characters in this way allows you to shed more light on the main characters' romance. A secondary couple may act as an example of two people who overcame issues similar to those that the hero and heroine face. Or they can serve as a cautionary tale, as an example of what the hero and heroine want to avoid. A secondary character who's open about wanting to find love can also provide a good contrast to a hero or heroine who's determined to avoid emotional entanglements and the risk of ending up unhappy.

- ✔ **Help move the plot forward:** Your hero and heroine shouldn't — and probably can't — do everything for themselves. A villain or romantic rival plays a role no hero or heroine can, but sometimes a secondary character's role is less dramatic or obvious. You may just need someone to get hurt or trapped so your hero or heroine can demonstrate his or her skills; it can be something as mundane as fixing a car or as dramatic as making a critical scientific discovery — whatever your story needs.

✔ **Provide crucial information:** Secondary characters are helpful in providing two types of information:

- **Factual information:** A secondary character may know something the hero and heroine don't, whether it's a clue to solving a mystery, how to break a horse, or how to negotiate a contract.

- **Emotional information:** Secondary characters may also know pieces of emotional information. The hero and heroine can't sit down and discuss their feelings with each other, but they can talk about those feelings (the heroine, especially) with *other* characters. Conversations with friends and family are a good opportunity to let your hero and heroine start to express and understand their feelings about each other.

Don't let your secondary characters take over the story. Remember that the role of a secondary character is to support. Their lives and stories aren't important by themselves; they're important for the ways that they illuminate the central characters and their romance.

Avoiding stereotypes

You have to watch out for stereotypes in all aspects of your novel. But falling into the trap of using types instead of individuals for your secondary characters is *very* easy. Avoid relying on the supportive best friend, the nit-picking boss, the leering villain, or the overprotective older brother.

You can give recognizable characteristics to secondary characters because you don't have the time or space to develop them in as much detail as your hero and heroine; however, they still must resonate as individuals. Be selective in the descriptions you include, so your secondary characters feel real, mixing unique details with broader brushstrokes.

Speaking up

Voices count. You don't want every character in your book, no matter how minor, to have such a quirky way of speaking that your novel sounds like lunchtime at the Tower of Babel. You can use voice to quickly and easily define your most important secondary characters: For instance, older characters probably talk with more formality than a thirty-something or a slang-slinging teen; someone from the South may speak with a relaxed cadence; and a non-native's accent may come across through syntax. Also, don't let your own speech and vocabulary come from every character's mouth, or all your characters will sound the same in such an obvious way that they won't seem real. (For specifics on creating and using your characters' voices, see Chapter 9.)

Naming the baby (and everyone else)

What's in a name? More than you might think. For better or worse, people often draw conclusions based on names, so use that to your advantage when you're creating your secondary characters because you don't have a lot of room to develop them. When someone's heritage — national, regional, or racial — is important, choose a name that conveys it. Keep names consistent with their generations, too.

For example, old-fashioned names usually indicate grandparents or baby boomers' children. Made-up names or brand names used as baby names are indicative of teens and younger children. Names in a historical romance must fit the period. Also, don't use too many similar names, because the reader becomes confused instead of being able to distinguish your characters from each other. For the same reason, don't start too many names with the same letter, and keep a running list to be sure you don't give two (or more!) characters the same last name. Keeping your main characters' names straight is easy, but not confusing all the minor characters' names is more difficult.

Factoring in the future

You may set up a secondary character to be the hero or heroine of a future connected book. In this case, focus on that character just a little more than you normally would and raise an unanswered question or two about him or her. The unanswered questions are a cue to the reader that she can expect to see that character again in a starring role.

Just don't pay too much attention to this character by explaining and focusing on him or her too often in *this* book. If you start telling his or her story, it will compete with your hero and heroine's romance.

Also be very sparing and discriminating when you use secondary characters' points of view (see Chapter 9). As a general rule, including secondary characters' points of view isn't only unnecessary, it's often a problem because it diffuses the focus of the book.

Laying Concrete Strategies for Creating Characters

You need to know your characters inside and out. In the end, you'll know far more about them (especially the secondary characters) than you ever tell your readers. But the fact that you created your characters so completely helps them come across as real people. Here are some strategies for making them real in your own mind so they also feel real to your readers:

- **Find pictures that look like your characters.** Whether you use movie-star photos or pages pulled from catalogues or magazines, find pictures of people who look like your characters and hang them up in your workspace to help you visualize them and keep the details in your mind as you write. Especially find pictures for your hero and heroine, but don't be afraid to add pictures that represent your secondary characters.

- **Know your characters' voices.** You should hear your characters in your head as you write. If their voices are specific actors' or singers' voices, you can listen to them by playing a movie or CD in the background (if you're not distracted by it).

- **Create a character board.** Whether you use index cards on a corkboard, stick-on notes on the wall, or keep a list on your computer, keep a file on every character that tells you everything you need to know about him or her. You need to know every detail of his or her appearance, job, romantic history, family and educational backgrounds, favorite color, music, TV shows, movies, how he or she dresses, and whether he or she likes animals, staying up late, getting up early, or sleeping away the weekend, and so on. Know the nuances of your characters' personalities and lives as well as you know your own or your best friend's.

- **Run role-playing exercises for your characters.** Doing role-playing exercises is useful, especially when you're developing your hero and heroine. You need to know how they respond in all kinds of situations so their actions feel natural and believable when you commit them to the page. Before you start writing, give some thought to role playing. Think up situations your characters may face together and individually; then, based on everything you've decided about them, come up with their logical actions and responses. You can use everyday situations — like getting a flat tire on the way to a job interview — and extreme possibilities — like being carjacked on the way home from the grocery store. Writing your book is easier when you know how your characters react in different situations, because as they face each new plot twist, their responses are second nature to you.

Chapter 5

Crucial Ingredients for Every Plot: Conflict, Climax, and Resolution

• •

In This Chapter

▶ Coming up with ideas

▶ Creating suspense

▶ Crafting believable emotional conflict

▶ Letting conflict drive your plot

▶ Building to climax and reaching resolution

• •

*P*lot isn't just the heart of your story, it literally *is* your story. Your plot provides the context in which your hero and heroine's romance unfolds, but it's more than just the framework for that romantic picture. A plot moves, just as your romance moves. Ultimately, the plot and the romance should be like two completely entangled strands: Neither one can exist or make sense without the other. Plot brings your hero and heroine together, and then their romance moves the plot forward. Their decisions affect what happens, and what happens affects their future decisions. This chain of events doesn't end until happily ever after.

All romance plots consist of a number of key structural components — suspense, conflict, climax, and resolution. Suspense keeps the reader turning the pages and creates her need to know what happens next. Conflict gets your readers as emotionally involved in the story as the characters are and propels your plot forward. And finally, climax and resolution provide the grand finale — everything your plot has been building toward.

In this chapter, I explain how to create each piece of the plot puzzle and the ways in which they work together. Along the way, I unravel the plot and romance connections to help you discover how to seamlessly weave these elements together in your work. Because you can't fill in plot particulars until you have an idea for a story, I begin by providing suggestions on how you can generate ideas for your novel.

You Can't Have a Novel without a Plot

To be more accurate, maybe I should say that you can't have a romance novel (or any piece of popular fiction) without a plot. There are literary novels and examples of experimental fiction that don't have what's conventionally defined as a plot, but we're talking about romance novels, so plots are definitely on the agenda.

Every successful romance novel has a plot. In its simplest form, a *plot* is a series of interconnected events that progress through three stages:

- ✓ A beginning, where the story is set in motion
- ✓ A middle, where the bulk of the action takes place
- ✓ An ending, where everything is resolved, the loose ends are tied up, and a satisfactory conclusion is reached

The beginning of a book is crucial. So crucial, in fact, that I devote an entire chapter (Chapter 12) to the mechanics of creating a great beginning and *how* to start your story. In this chapter, I focus on the *what* of your story — the process of conceptualizing the story you want to tell, starting with the idea.

Where do ideas come from?

I wish I had a simple answer to this question — and so do the many published authors who hear "Where do you get your ideas?" all the time. Many of those authors are so instinctively attuned to the storytelling process that they aren't even conscious of where their ideas come from. For a writer like this, her subconscious does the work for her, so by the time an idea hits her conscious mind, it seems to have sprung full-blown out of nowhere.

You may never have ideas without any conscious effort on your part, but you can teach yourself to find ideas when and where you need them. The real question isn't really "Where do ideas come from?" as much as "How do I recognize an idea?" As I often say at conferences, there's no such thing as an idea store, even though Ideas Express would make our jobs as writers and editors much easier. Instead, the entire world is your idea store. Ideas are literally everywhere. What you need to do is train yourself to recognize them.

Approaching the world from different angles

You can begin your quest for the elusive idea in any number of ways, but in general, I see two perspectives from which you can approach this task:

- ✓ **Emotional:** With this approach, you're examining the world for an idea that will drive the romantic, personal aspects of your story. For example, your starting point may be how a formerly abused woman learns to trust (and love) again, or how a lone-wolf hero finds his defenses penetrated by a bubbly 6-year-old blonde and her warm-hearted mother. Because romance novels are all about emotion, starting from this perspective works well, because you develop the key element first. Think of it as working from the inside out. After you have an idea in place, you can then move beyond the characters' personal concerns to construct the larger, external events around your emotional core.

✔ **Intellectual:** This approach is like working from the outside in. You look for your ideas in larger-scale events (a scientific discovery, a paranormal event, a study on why marriages failed), rather than on the personal level. This approach can be trickier, because your job then is to insert the key ingredient — the romance — into this larger external plot.

How you get your ideas doesn't matter — what matters is simply that you get them. You can even develop your own approach that's unrelated to anything I suggest. The keys are to find a way to recognize ideas and capitalize on them, and to develop the emotional core that will drive your story before you start writing.

Finding ideas around every corner

You probably move so quickly through life, juggling family, friends, work, and everything else, that you don't give yourself time to recognize all the ideas that are begging for your attention. Even so, we see and hear things every day that catch our imaginations. As a storyteller, you just need to take the next step and give yourself permission to notice and explore those promising ideas, with the thought of turning them into the basis for a romance. Ask yourself questions, the most effective of which usually start with "What if?" Questioning yourself is a great way to brainstorm and take your ideas to the next level, turning them into a story, and then populating that story with characters your readers will enjoy knowing.

Ideas are in the newspapers, on the TV news, in a local church bulletin, in gossip you overhear in line at the grocery store, in an article in your favorite magazine, in a story Uncle Ed tells at the family Thanksgiving dinner . . . anywhere and everywhere you find yourself interacting with the world.

Here are some examples of situations you run into every day, some of which are likely to catch your attention emotionally, others intellectually, and all of which give rise to the kinds of what-if situations that form the basis of a romance novel:

✔ **The papers are full of an especially juicy piece of romantic celebrity gossip.** Celebrities are people who've chosen careers that lead to fame. What if someone who has no desire to live in the public eye, who even has good reason (like being in Witness Security) to feel threatened by it, falls in love with someone who's chosen to live the celebrity life, and then is catapulted into that world herself?

✔ **Scientists discover a promising new treatment for childhood leukemia.** What if a scientist is focused on finding a cure for leukemia because his sister died of the disease, but now the big drug interests are threatening to sideline his research in favor of another approach they think is more promising (and potentially profitable)? What if he must convince — by any means necessary — the beautiful but by-the-numbers corporate accountant to loosen the purse strings?

✔ **Archeologists dig up a trove of Viking gold in a field in England.** How did the gold get there? What if a British maiden fell in love with a Viking warrior? Did he steal the gold from his lord and bury it, so he could run away with his true love and start a life with her? Why was he unable to retrieve the gold? What course did their love follow?

Anything you hear or see that interests you may potentially be an idea for your romance novel. Tune in your radar to the world around you, and don't let anything pass by — big or small, a human-interest story or a breaking headline — without turning it over in your mind, looking at it from all angles, and deciding whether there's something there that you can use.

At first, you may have to make an effort to tune in to the world around you. You may have to consciously tell yourself to pay attention and think more deeply about things. But eventually, there's a good chance that tuning yourself in will become a learned behavior. If you're lucky, it can become second nature, letting you go from worrying that you may never have an idea to having so many that you can't find time to write all of them.

Keep an idea file. Whether the file is a manila envelope stuffed with clippings and notes or an entire file drawer full of neatly alphabetized information, save your ideas for future use and look through them periodically to give your subconscious something to work with. An added benefit to saving articles, in particular, is that you already have a starting point for doing research later.

Asking questions develops your characters and plot

No matter how you're initially drawn to your idea, by the time you're ready to work with it, you should be looking at it in emotional terms, thinking of the ways in which your characters (see Chapter 4 for more on creating characters) are going to respond and react, both intellectually and emotionally, because their reactions help drive your story forward. Ultimately, your entire book is based on the answers to the "What if?" questions you've asked yourself.

Frame your questions in emotional terms. Make them complex enough so that answering them takes a while; otherwise, you're not going to have enough story to tell. One of the most important interviewing rules is to never ask questions with yes and no answers, or else you can end up with the shortest, most boring interview on record. Instead, ask leading questions. For example, don't ask, "Mrs. Smith, did winning the lottery change your life?" Instead, ask, "Mrs. Smith, how did winning the lottery change your life?" Apply this strategy to shape the idea that will begin your book. Your initial "What if?" should be open-ended and/or complex enough that the answer spawns an entire scenario, allowing you to develop your characters and propel the plot. Essentially, your characters act out the scenario your "What if?" gives rise to, and that's your story.

Ask questions that require your characters to grow, change, and explore their emotions. Ask questions that push their buttons and their boundaries. Don't ask, "Would falling in love with a movie star change my heroine's life?" Instead, ask, "How would falling in love with a movie star change my heroine's life?" It's in describing the "how" that you find your story. By phrasing your question not in terms of *whether* but in terms of *how,* you ensure that the answer is in the form of a story and you focus the story on character experience and growth, a crucial element to all romances.

Letting your characters drive the plot

Although other types of popular fiction can be — and often are — plot-driven, romances are character-driven. A romance novel is based on emotional conflict, which is part of who your characters are and determines how they respond to each other and how they operate in tandem with the plot you create. By setting up a story that focuses on character growth, you set up a story that, as long as you emotionally challenge your hero and heroine, is automatically based on emotional conflict.

Throughout the course of your book, your characters' actions — which you've made the central focus of the story — are driven by their emotions, because emotion is the key motivating force in a romance novel. Your characters, their decisions, actions, and responses, propel and control the plot, keeping your reader interested — all because you knew how to spot an idea and think about it the right way.

You should be able to describe the setup of your book for anyone who asks. A *setup* is a brief (that's key) explanation of what will drive your story and make it interesting to a reader. The best setups contain everything a writer or an editor needs to know in as few words as possible. I sometimes half-jokingly say that I work with authors who could write me one line on a cocktail napkin and, based on that, I would trust them to write an entire book. I say that because, in just a line or two, the right setup can contain enough information to make the characters and their conflict vivid and complex, which is a signal that the author has the basis for an entire book.

A sample setup, presented as briefly as possible, is: An heiress who (thinks she) doesn't like kids runs away from an arranged marriage and finds herself masquerading as a nanny to the 3-year-old twin sons of a rancher who's sworn off love. In that one sentence, you get a quick-and-dirty sense of who the characters are, where they're likely to butt heads, and even where some of the plot details are likely to come from: different worlds (big bucks versus the ranch life). Try writing your own setup in a line or two and see if you can include the key information that tells an editor you have a story to tell.

Suspense: Every Story Has It

A good idea is a necessary starting point, but you need more than that to have a successful book. You also have to execute it well. Two writers starting with the same potential-filled premise will write two entirely different books. The one who understands suspense will write a page-turner; the one who doesn't will write the cure for insomnia.

In your romance, a reader cares about what's happening because of two reasons: her interest in and identification with your characters (see Chapter 4), and the emotional conflict inherent in your setup. After you've created compelling characters and an emotionally intriguing idea to hook your reader's interest, you can move on to maintaining her interest by creating suspense and using it to your advantage.

When I talk about suspense in storytelling, I'm not talking about the kind of suspense that involves dark alleys, dead bodies, and smoking guns. Those elements *are* one definition of the word, and a very legitimate one. As I discuss in Chapter 2, romantic suspense novels are one of the most successful romantic subgenres. But dark-and-dangerous suspense isn't the only kind. All good storytelling involves suspense in a more general form. In a broad sense, a reader is prey to suspense when she cares about what's going to happen to a particular character or in a particular situation and then has to wait to find out. Her desire to know more is what keeps her turning pages.

A writer who knows how to handle suspense understands that to keep her reader reading, she has to do two things: Make her reader care about what's happening in the story, and create suspense by doling out information — the payoff — in increments, withholding the most important pieces until the end. Every scene not only moves the story and the romance forward, but it also leaves the reader wanting, needing, to know more. Whether the scene ends on a cliffhanger or simply raises a new complication that's followed up on later, the reader is left in suspense, and that leads her to read the next scene, and the next, in hope of getting the answers she wants.

Using romance to create suspense

Working with suspense is a bit like mimicking the rise and fall of the sea. First you rev your reader's interest to a high pitch, then you drop back without completely satisfying her, and then you do it again. You work incrementally, getting a little closer to fulfillment — for your characters and your reader — with every scene, but you always stop short of giving them everything they want.

In a romance novel, the reader's main interest is in the relationship's progress, so your most effective strategy for building suspense is through that relationship. Your reader wants to see the relationship deepen in two areas as the romance develops:

- ✔ **Physical intimacy:** Anything from a kiss to full-on lovemaking
- ✔ **Emotional intimacy:** The final payoff

When you're building suspense, don't develop these two types of intimacies in tandem. They work most effectively when developed independently of each other. In a real-world romance, physical and emotional intimacy tend to develop at a matching pace. As a couple grows closer emotionally, their physical relationship deepens. (Not that a proposal is always a prerequisite for lovemaking, but both people usually sense that the relationship has potential.) This scenario is wonderful in the real world, but it doesn't have enough suspense to support a romance novel.

In a romance novel, the reader doesn't want the course of the relationship to run smoothly; if it does, she gets bored. She wants to worry that your hero and heroine won't end up together — even though she knows they belong together and that the very fact she's reading a romance novel means they will be together in the end. But she pretends she doesn't know, and you let her. That's where suspense comes into play. Whether you use the characters' own emotional issues or a clever plot twist to keep them apart, by depriving them of ultimate romantic satisfaction you're also depriving the reader — and keeping her in suspense as she waits for that happiness. See the "Taking two steps forward and one step back" section later in this chapter for information on just how to do this.

Other ways of creating twists and turns

Even though your reader's main interest and your most effective tool for creating suspense is the central romance, it's not the only tool you have available. You can also use both plot-related twists and your secondary characters to keep readers guessing.

One advantage to both of these *secondary suspense* tools, which form a helpful backup to your primary source of suspense — what will happen with the hero and heroine's relationship? — is that you can pay them off as you go along, giving your reader satisfaction on one level while still withholding the ultimate payoff of the romance.

Critique groups: Pros and cons

Many authors find working with critique partners both helpful and enjoyable. In a *critique group*, members present their works-in-progress to each other for constructive feedback and provide moral support at every stage of the writing process. The decision to join a critique group is an individual one. Writing is a very personal process, and for some, it's a private one; others love to share their work. Either approach can be successful; go with the one that makes you most comfortable and frees your creativity. But make an informed decision. Talk to people who are already in critique groups to get a firsthand opinion about how they work. Here are some additional points to consider:

- ✔ **Are you comfortable sharing your work while it's still in progress?** Each writer works on her own manuscript, but being a member of a critique group means being part of a collaborative process. Do you feel comfortable letting others see what you're working on, and are you open to making changes based on others' opinions?

- ✔ **How well do you handle criticism?** In a critique group, your work is subjected to a variety of close readings and comments. You'll hear some compliments, but you're also likely to hear a lot of criticism. If negative comments, even when phrased constructively, cause you to become defensive or hurt, a critique group may be difficult for

you. Another part of handling criticism is determining which critique-based changes will help your book and which won't.

- ✔ **Do you work and play well with others?** It's a two-way process. You can benefit from others' attention to your work, but you need to cede the spotlight so that every member's work gets equal attention and be able to comment on other manuscripts with a combination of diplomacy and honesty.

- ✔ **Do you have the time?** Groups meet on a regular basis, though the frequency varies, and meetings can be long. Plus, some groups require members to read manuscripts ahead of time, rather than reading and critiquing passages on-site.

- ✔ **Will you be bothered if other members sell their manuscripts before you do?** Everyone in the group is working toward publication, and everyone makes that journey at her own pace. You need to handle others' successes without letting it get you down.

One last thing: Critique partners can help strengthen a manuscript, but they can also weaken it by watering down a book's strengths or creating problems. As an editor, I've seen examples of both. As a writer, you may have difficulty discerning if a suggestion helps or hurts. You must decide whether this is a risk you feel comfortable accepting.

Working your plot

Plot elements can be interesting in their own right. Even though the reader picks up the book for the romance, plot elements work on a subsidiary level, and the desire to see how they turn out is another factor that keeps her reading. Will the serial killer be caught? Where's the deadly formula? How will the custody battle be resolved? If you pose the question intriguingly enough, your reader will definitely want to know the answer.

Plot developments that are also closely tied to the progress of the romance are the strongest source of secondary suspense. For example, is the missing formula hidden — unknown to her — in the heroine's purse? Is the hero actually an undercover operative sent to retrieve it? After she discovers who he really is, her immediate response is likely to be that he's been romancing her not out of genuine interest, but because she has something that he wants. Plot affects emotion, and the relationship is in trouble again. Every plot offers opportunities to affect your characters' emotions, and the more closely you intertwine the plot with the characters' emotional lives (something I discuss later in this chapter, in the "Letting conflict complicate your plot" section), the more frequent and effective those opportunities will be.

The more you make your hero and heroine care about the outcome of any plot-related question, the more your reader will care about it, too.

Using secondary characters

Secondary characters can also provide a secondary source of suspense. Although their fates shouldn't rival the hero and heroine's relationship, their stories can still capture and hold your reader's interest. Secondary characters' plotlines often exist to parallel or illuminate the central romance, which gives them added interest. Will a secondary character have a healthy baby, find his missing son, or recover from her heart surgery? The answers aren't earth-shattering, but they *will* matter to your reader, so use them to your advantage.

Making Sense Matters

Your hero and heroine's emotional conflict, which works to keep them apart even when they want to be together, is the single most important factor in driving your plot and creating your reader's need to finish the book. But your plot still has to make sense, so making the elements in your story move logically is crucial.

Every plot dictates its own internal logic. A romantic suspense plot requires careful fact- and timeline-checking, while a marriage-of-convenience plot has fewer concrete demands but still requires you to move the book along in a believable time frame and not change the rules — for instance, the setup of the marriage — midstream.

Getting so caught up in your characters' emotions that you forget to keep an eye on the outside world can be easy. But without acknowledging how things work in real life, the plot falls apart before it's even begun. Editors keep track of how the book's moving on every level, and if you get the mechanics wrong, they'll notice. Major mistakes in anything from the timeline to the topography pull an editor out of the book, and for this editor, at least, make it likely that the novel will never see the light of day.

I could give you a lot of examples, but the following mistake is obvious enough to make my point. I've seen this mistake a number of times, and it undercuts a book so thoroughly from the beginning that it doesn't matter how well-drawn the hero and heroine's emotions are, because the book will never make sense.

The heroine comes home to find her apartment ransacked. Upset, she runs next door, where the handsome hero (probably just moved in) is waiting to help and offer support. They go back to her place to see what they can figure out and spend the rest of the book solving the mystery and falling in love (in spite of the requisite emotional suspense and conflict, of course). The problem? The hero and heroine don't call the police anywhere along the way, and no official crime scene investigation ever occurs. On top of that problem, in most cases, neither the hero nor the heroine has the skills or expertise to solve the case, which makes the reader skeptical about the plot's plausibility.

The problem isn't that the basic plot setup can't work — the author just has to acknowledge how things happen in the real world first. She can do so in plenty of ways:

- ✔ **Have the characters call the police.** Let the police start an official investigation. If they're not taking it as seriously or being as thorough as the hero and heroine would like, they can still investigate on the side.

- ✔ **Give the heroine a good reason for not contacting the police.** Her ex-husband is a cop and she doesn't want to give him a way back into her life. Her three overprotective older brothers are all cops and will use the break-in as an excuse to pressure her to get married, move back home, and so on. If she's not being physically threatened by what happened (and what's likely to happen next), you can get away with an explanation like this, so long as you acknowledge that calling the police would be the logical response and come up with a reason for her not to.

- ✔ **Give the hero or heroine the expertise to deal with the problem.** In the circumstances I lay out, the hero is likely to be a cop, ex-cop, private investigator, and so on. Either way, the decision to go it alone makes much more sense if one of them has the skills to investigate.

Your characters' actions always need to be believable and believably motivated, both emotionally and in terms of real-world logic.

Emotional Conflict and Tension: The Only Reason to Turn the Page

The conflict, or tension, between your hero and heroine should always drive your plot. Your novel should also have a certain story-related momentum, but the key factor that keeps your reader turning pages is the progress of the romance, which is driven by the conflict between the hero and heroine.

You can use different techniques and combinations of techniques to create conflict between your hero and heroine. However you craft that conflict, though, one point is key: You need to create a source of emotional conflict and tension for your hero and heroine — something that exists separately from the specifics of the plot, something inside each of them that would create a problem whether they met in Maine or on the moon, though the problem certainly should be exacerbated by their situation.

After you decide where the emotional tension comes from, you can create and complicate it at will. And by manipulating that emotional tension, you're better able to keep your reader involved and happy from start to finish.

Emotional versus intellectual conflict

Without the surrounding context of a plot, the distinction between emotional and intellectual conflict is easy to make, yet writers continually struggle with it in their manuscripts. Simply put, an *intellectual conflict* is a conflict of ideas, while an *emotional conflict* is one that grows from feelings.

The temptation to use an intellectual conflict — and even to mistake it for an emotional one — is understandable, because intellectual conflicts are obvious — and everywhere, and many are fascinating. The morning paper and the news are full of debates over important concerns like foreign and domestic policy, the economy, and the environment, and smaller issues, like uniforms in public schools and lawn-watering restrictions.

What makes an intellectual conflict intellectual is the fact that it starts out in the mind. People's feelings about an issue can be very strong, and arguing them into seeing another point of view may be impossible; but even so, every argument has two sides, and intelligent people can make a case for either side. Intellectual conflicts can be interesting, but in the context of a romance novel — where the intent is to engage the reader's heart, not her head — they're counterproductive if they appear front and center.

Emotions, unlike opinions, don't need to have a logical basis and can't be reasoned away. They come from inside and simply *are*. They're not up for discussion or argument. Your emotions are an intrinsic part of who you are. They're not something you decided on one day after you took a course, read a book, or saw a news special; they come from your genetic makeup, the way you were raised, and your experiences in life and love. They affect how you see yourself, your family and friends, and — maybe most of all — who and how you love.

An emotional example

You can't build every plot completely around the emotional conflict, but every plot needs to highlight that conflict whenever possible. The more complicated your plot is, the more threads you have going on at once; however, emotional tension should underlie everything that's happening. The emotional conflict should always be in the characters' and the readers' minds. Here are a couple of sample heroines and a sample scenario that shows you how to create an emotional conflict for each of them:

- ✔ **Heroine 1:** Born to a single mother, abandoned to the foster-care system, and shuttled from family to family, she's likely to be self-contained, independent, distrustful, wary of forming close bonds, low in self-esteem, and practically incapable of believing that she deserves love.

- ✔ **Heroine 2:** Raised in a large, tight-knit family, the only girl among six children, doted on and cherished, encouraged in safe directions but protected — even overprotected — from risk, she's likely to have a bright, open personality and to make friends easily. But she's also likely to doubt her ability to operate independently and fear being smothered by love, especially romantic love.

Intellectually, in a debate over cocktails, these heroines may be identical, but in every way that counts, they're polar opposites and always will be. They approach life in completely different ways. And although both may be wary of love, it's for totally different reasons, which means their emotional hot buttons are different, and they're drawn to and wary of completely different characteristics in men.

Their choices in life are driven by their inner selves, the emotional human beings that they are:

- ✔ **Heroine 1** may choose a way of life that lets her remain aloof from others — maybe as a researcher in a high-tech lab or a computer programmer — because that's how she protects her tender emotional core, the part that's always felt abandoned and is afraid to love because she's sure she'll only be abandoned again.

- ✔ **Heroine 2** may be busy making her way in the police department, proving to her big, overprotective family (and, not incidentally, herself) that she can go it alone and cut it as a beat cop in a tough neighborhood.

Enter the hero, a police detective working on a case. He shares the same views on politics, religion, and all the rest, so he can't argue with either woman on that score. Like Heroine 1, he was raised in foster care, but he had a younger sister who was raised with him, and from the time he was a little kid, he's been her protector. He joined the force to protect even more people. Plus, when his parents died, he was old enough to remember what being part of a loving family was like, and he wants that again.

Both heroines see a murder take place and need to be put into protective custody until the killer's apprehended, tried, and — with the benefit of their testimonies — sent away for life. One of the heroines lucks out and gets the hero as her watchdog at the safe house. The story plays out differently depending on which heroine the hero is assigned to:

- ✔ **Heroine 1:** If she gets the hero as her protector, she's going to resent him spending the long hours they're confined together trying to connect with her on the subject of their shared backgrounds, because she doesn't want to bring up all those painful memories. And she certainly doesn't want to find herself hooked on this incredible guy who can — even in her present scary situation — make her laugh, get her talking about everything under the sun, even when she keeps telling herself to shut up, and who's sexy beyond belief, besides.

  For the hero, it makes him nuts that she continues shutting him down and withdrawing just when he thinks he's getting close to her. But even though he knows keeping his heart uninvolved would be smart, he can't help being drawn to her, so much so that he has to remind himself that he's on the job and pull back — just as he's about to kiss her. She feels rejected, all the old hurts of her childhood rise up, and they're on the outs with each other and neither one knows why. And I've set up an emotional conflict without any effort beyond creating complex characters and letting them react believably.

- ✔ **Heroine 2:** If she gets locked away with the hero, she's going to react differently for different reasons. She's going to bridle at his protective side, point out that she's a cop, too, and is more than capable of taking care of herself, and think his fantasy of having a big, happy family would make her crazy, because she'd end up lost in the ruckus, taking care of everyone in that traditionally female way that she's sworn isn't for her.

  He can't believe she doesn't understand the value of family and is fighting to break away from hers. He respects her professional abilities plenty, but in the circumstances, she *does* need to be protected, and why can't she see that he's just the guy to do it? They keep butting heads, but they're also attracted, challenged, and in no way ready to write each other off.

Plot — the need to lock the hero and heroine together in a safe house — puts them together but doesn't provide the conflict. Plot gives the hero and heroine the opportunity to be in conflict, but the conflict itself is emotional. It comes from within, from a clash between who they are, not what they think.

In any romance novel, the emotional conflict needs to affect the hero and heroine's relationship, to have romantic ramifications, so that they're irresistibly drawn toward each other, while simultaneously feeling that a relationship can't possibly work between them.

Taking care with intellectual conflict

You can use elements of intellectual conflict in your book, too, but you have to be careful. Keep these two tips in mind:

- ✔ Intellectual conflict can never be substituted for emotional conflict.
- ✔ Relate any elements of intellectual conflict to the characters' emotional conflict as much as possible.

To clarify the second bullet point, here's an example I always use at conferences to demonstrate this strategy. He's a developer; she's an environmentalist. He wants to use a piece of property to build housing; she wants to preserve it to save the rare spotted squirrel. Arguments about the housing needs of people versus the need to preserve the environment ensue. Any reader who's stayed awake long enough to make it to the end finds out that they compromise and build cluster housing on one section of the property and maintain the rest as legally protected woodland. The characters thought their way to a mutually acceptable solution. Everybody wins, and now the two of them can act on their mutual attraction. As a plot, it's an exercise in mental gymnastics and nothing more. The story has no heart.

However, the story could have heart. Maybe the hero's not just an in-it-for-the-money developer but is someone who has a mission: providing reasonably priced housing for people who may otherwise never get to own a nice home in a place where they can raise their families. Perhaps he was raised by a hard-working single mother who barely made the rent on a cheap apartment, and this is his way of giving back to the world in her memory. The heroine was raised in the inner city, and the only time she ever saw the country was on a city-sponsored summer program. She's determined to save a little piece of the wild within spitting distance of the city so less fortunate kids will always have a place they can get away to and meet nature.

This plot isn't the most compelling one on the planet, but at least now it has an emotional component, and you can see how the two types of conflict can work together. But I'm not recommending this approach — taking an intellectual conflict and adding an emotional element to make it a book — because it works backward. By the time you start writing, your idea should already be an emotional one, even if it started from an intellectual point.

Internal versus external conflict

Another (and related) way to look at conflict is as internal versus external. *Internal conflict* comes from the characters themselves; it's whatever they bring to the story, both emotionally and intellectually. *External conflict* comes from the plot and circumstances, or is created by other characters.

Emotional conflict is always internal. This kind of conflict finds a way to manifest itself whatever the circumstances are. Going back to my example of the heroine from the big family and the protective hero, these two people are going to have issues no matter how or where they meet, simply because of who they are.

An example of external conflict is your hero and heroine arguing over the best way to handle the case. Any two cops — including two men or two women — can do that. You can't substitute external conflicts for internal ones, but you can enhance emotional conflicts by using externals to provide a context that gives your hero and heroine a chance to be together and seemingly at odds against one thing (how to handle the case, in the example above) while what they're *really* arguing over is something else entirely, in this case his tendency to protect — or overprotect, as she sees it — her.

Your hero and heroine can't spend the entire book talking about their emotional conflicts, otherwise your story ends up reading like a long session at a psychotherapist's office. An external conflict lets your characters talk about something concrete with their emotional issues as a subtext — a subtext that you can clarify by getting into their heads for a point-of-view look at what's going on, which I talk about in Chapter 9.

Personal versus situational conflict

One final way to talk about conflict is as personal versus situational. *Personal conflicts* are conflicts that grow from the innate issues and insecurities that everyone has. You carry around certain feelings inside yourself that are personal to you. In most of your day-to-day relationships, they don't raise their heads, but with the people who matter most, your personal issues are important. Your family and friends — these are the people whose opinions count and who have the ability to make you feel great or horrible. Those people who are close to you matter on a personal level, and with them, your deepest feelings come into play. This situation is the same with your hero and heroine; they can touch each other on the deepest, most personal levels.

A *situational conflict* arises from place and plot. In the safe-house example, the situational conflict comes from locking the hero and heroine up where they can't get away from each other, which forces them to deal with their internal, emotional issues or else spend the entire book in separate rooms. As with intellectual and external conflicts, situational conflict can work with the key emotional tension your hero and heroine have to deal with, but situational conflict can never substitute for emotional conflict. Situational conflict can provide the hothouse atmosphere where tension can grow, but the novel's deeper issues are always the characters' personal and emotional conflicts.

The best romances are built around a complex emotional conflict that's played out in an equally interesting and tightly connected context — one that forces the characters to deal with each other and their issues.

Handling Conflict Effectively

Coming up with the right idea and creating characters whose emotional makeup allows for conflict isn't enough. You still need to use that conflict to drive your story. Your idea and the basis of the tension between your hero and heroine form the beginning of the story. Working with that tension drives your story through the middle and on to the end.

Keeping them together

Your plot is your best tool for keeping your hero and heroine together, which gives them the opportunity to focus on their emotional issues. Your hero and heroine need to be together for the bulk of your book, which may seem obvious, but I long ago lost count of the number of manuscripts I've seen where the hero and heroine don't even meet until the end of the first chapter or later. Or where they're apart for 20 pages as the book progresses, going about their solitary, even if somewhat related, business.

A strong romance plot puts the hero and heroine together early on and, no matter how much difficulty they may be having connecting emotionally, the plot physically separates them as infrequently as possible. Close proximity allows the characters an opportunity to externalize their internal, emotional conflicts. Here are some of the most common issues romance characters face:

- **Trust issues:** What if a cop hero has problems trusting women? Maybe he messed up on a case because he fell for a witness who wasn't as innocent as she pretended to be. Now he's falling into that nightmare all over again, investigating the heroine, who's under suspicion of murdering her husband. She insists she didn't do it, and the hero believes her. But why? Because she really *is* innocent, or just because he wants her to be? Either way, he's putting his entire career at risk by falling for her. The investigation keeps them together and gives them something to talk about while they work out their emotional issues, which provide the subtext for every conversation.

- **Control issues:** What if your heroine comes from a wealthy, pampered, but ultimately confining, background? She's worked hard to prove herself, to get out from under her tycoon father's thumb and build her own business from the ground up. She's not about to give up calling the shots — and then along comes the hero, who engineers a hostile takeover of her company. The battle of wills has begun. The overt fight is for control of the company, but the real fight is for control of her heart.

- **Self-image issues:** What if your heroine, despite being the youngest daughter of an earl, was always gawky, awkward, and more at home in the stables than learning to paint delicate watercolors? She still dresses in drab colors and oversized dresses, and now her father has offered her in marriage to a duke — the most handsome man she's ever seen, and one who deserves a beautiful wife. She can't believe she's grown into a woman who could catch his eye, so when they argue over her preference for horseback riding over hosting tea parties, what they're really talking about is her inability to believe he could possibly love someone like her.

Letting conflict complicate your plot

Just as your plot offers the context for the romance to play out, the romance and the conflict that complicates it should drive the plot forward, creating an inseparable whole. Take, for instance, the example from the previous section: The cop hero who has trust issues because he was burned after falling for a woman who was involved in a case he was investigating, now finds himself drawn to the heroine, a suspect in the murder of her husband.

Logic demands that an investigation occur and that clues be followed up on, but the developing relationship and the tension between the hero and heroine should motivate as much of the action as possible. The hero hopes that the heroine's innocent, and maybe even sits on evidence that seems to indict her (difficult divorce proceedings, for instance, that would have left her with very little, but now she stands to inherit quite a lot) while he looks for information to clear her. And all the while he's furious with himself for falling for another woman who's undoubtedly only using him.

The heroine is covering for a younger brother who she's afraid has followed up his spoiled childhood by getting mixed up with embezzlers, ending up involved in her estranged husband's death. By nature, the heroine's open and honest, but she has to fight these natural inclinations and lie to the hero, putting her reputation and freedom at risk — even though she's attracted to him and wants to level with him and see where the attraction might go.

With both the hero and heroine drawn to, but also distrustful of, each other, their decisions are based not just on logic and a desire to get at the truth, but also on emotion and a desire to figure out the dynamics of the romance.

Basing key decisions on the characters' emotions and not just on logic is a tactic that works with any story line and is the key to creating a compelling romance novel. And convincing emotional motivations are an outgrowth of believable, complex characters.

Taking two steps forward and one step back

Timing plays a key role in the tension of your novel. In real life, as I point out in the "Using romance to create suspense" section earlier in this chapter, relationships tend to run smoothly, with emotional and physical intimacy building on each other. Couples have setbacks along the way, but they usually talk things out and keep going, moving along the path together — ideally until they realize they want to spend their lives together. Romance novels build toward that same happy ending, but they follow a much rockier road.

The progress of the romance, in terms of both emotional and physical intimacy, creates the suspense necessary to hold your reader's attention. Instead of progressing smoothly, move your romance like a dance: two steps forward and one step back. Your hero and heroine should always be making progress, but slowly, and far from easily. Here are some tips you can use when you move your romance two steps forward and one step back:

✔ **Follow every success with a reversal.** The key is in not letting an exchange of confidences and intimacy lead to more closeness. There will be times in the book when the characters will grow closer emotionally, when they'll trust each other, maybe confide in each other, and when they'll also get closer physically. But when they're done talking, when the embrace is over or when they wake up in each other's arms after a night of blissful lovemaking, make their relationship take a backward step. Going back to the cop/suspect example, maybe the hero pushes what he sees as his advantage after a night of lovemaking, asking her for information, proof that he can use to clear her or knowledge that may lead him to the real killer. Suddenly realizing how close she's come to giving up her brother, she withdraws emotionally, refuses to say anything more about the case, and maybe even leads him to believe she made love to him only to secure his sympathies. He feels he's been used again, and he's angrier with himself than he is with her.

✔ **Play the scene from another angle.** You could play that same scene from the other character's perspective. You could make the heroine realize that she's let herself be seduced — literally — by the hero, and recognize how easily she could let herself rely on him, love him, and just tell him the truth. Then she could help her brother through the investigation and trial with the financial resources she inherits. But she stops herself, feeling selfish and disloyal to her brother, and immediately treats the hero coldly. And once again, the hero feels used and betrayed.

Both scenarios work, and both have the same result: The hero and heroine are left in conflict, unable to trust each other and follow up on their attraction. Yet neither of them is able to forget their moments of intimacy and honesty on every level, and those memories underlie all their future interactions. They've tasted what could have been, and they've had to back off, wanting more and feeling that a relationship is impossible.

Repeat that pattern of progress followed by a step back throughout the course of your novel, each time making staying apart harder for your hero and heroine. The closer they get, the more they long to stay close. Each conversation, kiss, and time they make love is a reminder of what they want and can't have, because each intimacy is followed by a reversal.

The wedges you use to drive your couple apart must be as believable as their growing feelings for each other are. Years ago, heroes and heroines of romance novels were driven apart by misunderstandings more often than anything concrete and believable (see the "Cutting the Other Woman out of the picture" sidebar in this chapter), but readers these days expect real conflict, not something that could be solved with one simple conversation.

Using sexual tension to deepen conflict

Both emotional and physical intimacy can help you create and work with conflict, but sexual tension lends itself to additional discussion and strategies. Sexual tension begins the moment your hero and heroine lay eyes on each other, and it continues throughout the manuscript, whether they never share so much as a chaste kiss or engage in sexual athletics to rival those in any adult film. Sexual tension comes from sexual longing and, at least in the world of romance novels, sexual longing never wanes when a couple is truly meant to be together.

Cutting the Other Woman out of the picture

Not too many years ago, simple misunderstandings were a common tool to create conflict, and none was more common than the Other Woman. A sample scenario: The heroine would call the hero while he was away, and the Other Woman, who was really only his assistant, would answer the phone. (The Other Woman and Other Man were such common character types that they were always capitalized and rarely had much personality beyond being unpleasantly clichéd.) But the Other Woman wanted to be more. While the hero was otherwise engaged and didn't know the heroine had even called, the Other Woman would imply that all sorts of intimacies were going on and that he was right there and unwilling to waste time talking to the heroine.

The heroine, instead of reaming the hero out the next time she saw him and asking just what

game he was playing, immediately and without a word packed a suitcase (always including one uncrushable evening gown, just in case) and ran off to the Outback or somewhere else suitably remote. Or she simply refused to talk to the hero, and the two of them shared smoldering looks and angry remarks but no actual conversation, because if they'd actually talked, the truth would have come out and the book would have been over.

I'm glad to say that those days are over. Neither heroines nor readers are satisfied with such transparent plotting and meatless conflicts. A modern heroine, even in a historical romance, has too much backbone to avoid confrontation. Current readers are looking for much more convincing and interesting plotting, so steer clear of using simple misunderstandings.

Simply by its existence, sexual attraction and the struggle that comes from the couple's inability to satisfy their desire (no matter how often they indulge in it) adds to the effect of the emotional tension. Friends can share all kinds of confidences, but physical intimacy is reserved for a lover or a spouse. Physical intimacy is what sets a couple's intimacy apart from everything else. It's the ultimate prize. The hero and heroine's sexual longing reminds them of what they want and can't have — what they're being deprived of by their inability to sort out their emotions: true emotional intimacy.

Because their emotional issues threaten to separate them at any point, their lovemaking feels all the more poignant, because each time may be their last. For more on using love scenes — and the different ways men and women react to physical intimacy — to create tension, check out Chapter 11.

'Twas but a dream

Your reader should long for the love scenes just as much as the hero and heroine, and one trick for satisfying her and increasing her longing (as well as at least one of the character's) is through a dream. The hero and heroine may not be able to make love in actuality for plenty of reasons. For instance:

- **Physical impossibility:** Your plot may have a point that dictates your couple be in separate places (but not too often). Or one of them could be ill or injured, so they can't follow up on their desires. These obstacles can help build sexual tension, so long as you make sure they're in each other's minds even when they can't be in each other's arms.

- **Emotional separation:** As the conflict waxes and wanes, your plot likely has points where, no matter how physically attracted your hero and heroine are to one another, they're so upset with each other that love-making would be a betrayal of their own feelings and integrity.

- **Timing:** The timing may be too early in the relationship — particularly in a historical romance, where social mores dictate the behavior of the sexes — for the couple to physically get together without undercutting them as characters.

- **Subgenre restrictions:** In some romance series, as well as the entire inspirational romance subgenre, showing the characters making love or, in the latter case, being sexually intimate at all, is inappropriate. With certain caveats, though, a dream sequence can be an allowable way of making the reader feel the characters' romantic longing for each other, though without getting graphic.

In any of these circumstances, a dream can help build the sexual tension and add dimension to the conflict. In all but the last instance, a dream allows your hero, heroine, and reader to indulge in essentially guilt- and tension-free sexual enjoyment, fulfilling the need for them to get together and providing a hint of what their relationship *could* be like. At the same time, because their love-making was just a dream, you increase the reader's desire for the characters to make love for real — not to mention the characters' own desire. Lastly, a dream adds an edge to all their future encounters, because whichever character had the dream feels an awareness, even embarrassment, and a sense of intimacy that's simultaneously both real and imaginary, but still powerful.

If you face subgenre restrictions, you need to make the dream far less explicit. In the case of an inspirational romance, the dream can't be explicit at all; stop it with a kiss, at most, and include few details. The characters' longings, and the subsequent dream, need to be more romantic than sexual. The dream may involve a wedding ceremony, and then stop at the bedroom door on the wedding night. Or it may feature the hero and heroine as a married couple sharing breakfast, with a warm, satisfied look and the touch of one hand on another. These dreams imply sexual fulfillment in an acceptable context: marriage, but the terms are entirely emotional and romantic.

Saving "I love you" for the right moment

The quickest way you can diffuse both sexual tension and the power of your emotional conflict is to have your hero and/or your heroine confess their love. From then on, all suspense is gone. Your reader's wish is fulfilled, and all that's left is for the hero and heroine to talk out their problems in a rational (read: boring) way — and your reader's not interested in that conversation.

Part of maintaining emotional tension throughout the book, even if the characters make love, is withholding those three longed-for words: I love you. However, the hero and heroine can separately realize how they feel, and the reader can be privy to their thoughts. So long as you maintain the fiction that your hero and heroine won't be able to overcome their problems, you add tension to the story, because readers know how much is at stake: real love that may never be given a chance to flourish.

Every rule has an exception. In some successful romance novels, the hero and heroine confess their love early, and then face legitimate obstacles before they can fulfill that love. This trick is difficult to pull off, however. I see far more writers who try this plot fail than succeed. So my advice — especially when you're still perfecting your craft — is to follow the usual path of saving the confession of love for the climax and resolution.

If you make sure your hero and heroine don't suspect each other's feelings, they're free to recognize their own feelings at any point in the book. Making their feelings believable is important. Let the reader see the characters' feelings develop in the course of the story, and they become part of the development and step-by-step solution of the emotional conflict. As an editor, I see two main mistakes that writers make:

- ✔ **The unmotivated realization of love.** Too often I see characters who realize out of the blue that they love each other. Up to that point, they've done nothing but argue and feel a strong attraction, but they haven't been growing closer or felt genuine emotional longing as they dealt with their issues. Love that comes out of nowhere isn't believable. You need to build up to love in ways that let the reader, and sometimes even other characters, recognize it before the hero or heroine does.

- ✔ **The unmarked realization of love.** In an unmarked realization of love, the heroine realizes that she loves the hero (or vice versa), and then just moves on with whatever thought she was having, not even noticing that she's just reached a milestone. Whether she tries to talk herself out of the feeling, is amazed that she feels so much for such an unexpected person, or is thrilled, or whatever it is that she feels, she needs to react. And the hero needs to react, too, when he first realizes he loves the heroine. This moment is key and can't pass unnoticed.

And They Lived Happily Ever After

The words "happily ever after" rarely (if ever) appear in romance novels anymore, but they're still a powerful force in the characters' and the reader's minds. Happily ever after represents the ideal end to every romance — in real life as well as fiction. The biggest difference between the two worlds is that in a well-constructed romance novel, the promise of happily ever after is fulfilled, unlike real life, where 50 percent of marriages end in divorce.

Every romance exists to fulfill the reader's expectations (see Chapter 2). The final expectation every reader has when reading a romance novel is that it will end with the hero and heroine expecting to spend their lives together and face any future trials as one. Timing is the key to making your reader believe in your hero and heroine's happily ever after. How you build up to the climax and the mutual confession of love, and the support you give to the resolution, determine whether your reader believes in your happily-ever-after ending.

Not every romance novel needs to end with the actual marriage or even a formal proposal. (The one exception is when you're writing an inspirational romance, where the explicit commitment to marriage is crucial.) In some romances, the author shoehorns those proposal and/or marriage scenes into the final chapter or adds them as an unnecessary epilogue. As an editor, my recommendation is to cut them, because they make the storytelling feel awkward or drag the book on past the natural finale. Assuring the reader that the couple is emotionally committed to each other is what's important. Without that assurance, you may have a wonderful piece of women's fiction, but you don't have a romance novel.

Making your reader believe

As you build toward resolution and happily ever after, you need to be sure to bring your reader along with you. At this final stage of the book, every single element comes together. Any flaw can draw your reader out of your novel's world and back into the real world. And once the fantasy is broken, you may lose her forever — not just for this book, but for every book you ever write.

When you hit this final stage, you've written the bulk of the book, and you're down to the last chapter or two. Your reader ought to be turning pages more quickly than ever at this point, being carried along by:

- ✔ **Her belief in your characters:** Your reader's belief in your characters is probably the single biggest factor in her reading enjoyment and the biggest motivator in getting her to turn the pages. At this point, because of her identification with the heroine, your reader should feel that her own happiness depends on the couple finally overcoming your carefully built tension and confessing their feelings.

- ✔ **Her feeling that the tension has reached a make-or-break point:** She feels this way for two reasons. The first is simply that she realizes the book doesn't have many pages left, so if the conflicts aren't resolved now, they never will. The second reason is that if you've effectively built the tension by moving forward, backward, and then forward again, your characters are at a point where they don't have any options left except solving their problems or watching the entire relationship end.

- ✔ **Your pacing:** As you build toward the climax and resolution, speed up your pacing using short, intercut scenes, mini-cliffhangers, and active prose to carry the reader forward. (Read Chapter 10 for tips on all these pacing techniques.) Don't use long, leisurely descriptions at the end of your novel; instead, use broad brushstrokes that tell the reader what she has to know and keep her moving forward.

With these elements working together, you're ready to take your characters and your reader to the next step: the climax. Then you can move on to the resolution, so your hero and heroine can get on with living happily ever after.

Climax: Timing is everything

It's as true in romance fiction as it is in sex (especially romance-novel sex): When it comes to reaching climax, timing is crucial. In a novel, the *climax* is the moment when everything comes to a head. The climax always comes right before the end of the book: All the threads of the story combine to reach a make-or-break point. The tension — on all levels — is at its highest peak, and it's now or never for finding a solution or giving up in defeat. If you're into diagramming your story, it's the top of the tension mountain. The climax is the characters' last chance to solve everything — not just the emotional tension (so the romance is free to go on unencumbered) but also any remaining external, intellectual, and situational tension, and any plot issues.

Real-world relationships frequently develop without drama and major confrontation. But a romance novel needs to build to a dramatic payoff. It's part of the promise of a romance novel, and it paves the way for the happily ever after. Your reader expects it, so building up to it is crucial.

At that climactic moment, the characters break through their emotional walls. Even if they don't have a chance to admit how they feel and that they're committed to making things work between them, the reader's left in no doubt that that moment's coming — and usually the characters are pretty sure of it, too. They may sort out some of the specifics, or they may save those for the resolution, which follows closely — sometimes so closely that it's really part of the same scene.

The *resolution* is characterized by an easing back of tension that comes from knowing everything's going to be okay, and it's the scene where everything gets figured out. The climax is often over quickly — especially in books with a lot of action or suspense, where events are moving as quickly as emotions and there's no time for a lot of talk. The resolution is the characters' chance to figure out details, tie up loose ends in the plot and their emotional conflict, and talk about the future they plan to share. As its name implies, the resolution resolves whatever's left to be resolved.

Don't get too hung up worrying about where your climax ends and your resolution begins, or exactly what plot point or revelation goes where. The line between them is often so blurred that they end up being the same thing. They're really only points on a continuum, and so long as a reader feels like she got everything she wanted from your book, she's not going to care how the scenes were broken down.

A lot of writers and, especially, writing teachers are very big on analyzing the rise and fall of the elements of a novel. You may have heard people talk about mini-climaxes leading up to the main climax, or the "black" (or "dark") moment when everything seems impossible and the characters despair, and you may wonder why I haven't mentioned them. It's because I'm not convinced of the necessity of those elements, at least not in such intellectualized terms. Two steps forward and one step back is, I think, enough of a structural technique to keep your reader engaged while not losing sight of a key point: If you're too strict about outlining your story structure, you work against the more important goal of letting your characters drive the story by behaving naturally and believably, based on who you created them to be (see Chapter 7 for a step-by-step guide to outlining your romance).

However, if you find that a more formal approach works for you, go with it. When you're writing a romance, the key is simply to make it work. When an editor reads your book, she won't know or care how you got the manuscript to the stage she's seeing; she'll only care whether it works. So long as you've satisfied the reader's expectations and gotten the book to the crucial moment of climax, that's all that counts.

After the reader has read the climax, she will breathe a huge sigh of relief (even if only metaphorically). If your hero and heroine haven't out and out admitted their love yet, your reader knows that they will, and any major plot difficulties that were hanging over their heads have also been dealt with. That leads you to the final stage of your novel: the resolution.

Resolution: Endings made easy

Underestimating the importance of the resolution is easy to do, and I often see authors rush through it or even leave it out altogether, thinking that the climax takes care of everything. But that thinking is just not true. In fact, the resolution is crucial in sending the reader off feeling satisfied and eager to see more of your work.

The climax often passes by in a rush. The hero and heroine may not have time to do more than acknowledge their feelings. In a romantic suspense novel, the action may be so intense that the characters don't even get that satisfaction, especially if one of them gets hurt. In a case like that, your use of point of view tells the reader how they feel, but they aren't able to tell each other (see Chapter 9), so the resolution is even more crucial to your story.

The resolution can be an extension of the climactic scene or it can be a separate scene, but the function of the resolution is always the same: to provide the couple with a chance to talk out their emotional conflict in light of the fact that they've finally mutually confessed their love. In some cases, the resolution is also the scene that first lets them voice their feelings.

Real emotional issues don't go away just because two people fall in love. That holds true in real life, and it's also true in your romance. If you've created complex characters and a complex source of emotional tension, that tension isn't going to go away as if it never existed, so you need to give your hero and heroine a chance to confront their remaining issues.

But don't devote pages to a detailed psychological discussion of where their issues came from and how they're going to cure each other. For one thing, you will have dealt with some of those issues incrementally in the course of the book, as you let your characters move two steps forward and one step back. In addition, a long discussion would just get boring.

Letting your hero and heroine talk in emotional terms is important. They've finally admitted their feelings for each other, and new love is a heady thing. You want to cover just enough territory to let the reader know that they recognize what their issues have been, and that they're more than capable of dealing with them.

The resolution is also your opportunity to tie up any loose ends: where the hero and heroine will live, job issues, kid issues, mystery-related questions, and anything else.

Sometimes a story may have remaining issues that require an epilogue to resolve them. For instance, if your story has a question such as whether the heroine can bear a child, or if she's pregnant when the book ends and there's a question about the baby's health, an epilogue is the perfect vehicle to convey that information.

Too often, though, the real story ends with the last chapter, but the author adds an epilogue just to show that the characters got married and their lives are going fine. In this case, I find adding an epilogue anticlimactic, but I also know that some editors disagree with me. You need to decide for yourself what works best for your book. Even if the epilogue issue is a problem for an editor, she won't use it as the deciding factor as to whether she makes an offer on your book, so you can't go too far wrong either way.

Chapter 6

Setting the Scene

. . . .

. . . .

*H*ave you heard that the three most important things to think about when you're buying a house are location, location, location? Well, location may not be the *most* important thing to think about when you're writing a romance novel, but it definitely counts for a lot. The right setting can tempt a reader to buy your book, while the wrong one can turn her off. The locale that you choose can show off your characters' best traits or provide a challenge that brings out their undiscovered strengths. You can use place to prime your characters — and your reader — to feel romantic or to keep them on edge and looking over their shoulders.

Your romance novel isn't only set in a particular place; it's also set in a particular time. The term *setting* refers to both the place and time in which your story takes place. You may be writing a book set in what I call the *eternal present,* which makes the reader feel as if she's reading a book that could be happening at that very moment. Or you may choose a particular period in history: the Regency period, the Gold Rush, World War II, or the Vietnam era. The *when* of your book is just as important as the *where* in terms of determining what the world is like and how your characters fit into it.

Before you start writing, take some time to think about where and when your story's going to take place and how you can use your setting as you write — it definitely makes the novel-writing process smoother.

Sometimes you just know without even thinking where you want to set your novel. Your decision may be based on the simple fact that you grew up on a ranch in Montana, so Montana ranch life is what you want to write about. Maybe you've always harbored a secret wish that you'd been born in Medieval England, so you naturally gravitate toward that period for your romance.

If you already have your setting in mind, you're lucky, because you've already made an important decision. But keep reading to see what you still have to think about in order to effectively use your setting. If you haven't already got a setting in mind, you have to make a conscious decision, and this chapter can help, because I talk about how to choose your where and when, and how to use both to your best advantage.

Deciding Where Your Story Takes Place

Just as having a romance without a hero and heroine is impossible, so is telling their story without knowing where the action is taking place. Readers want to know where things are happening, just as a matter of curiosity. More importantly, the setting has implications for your characters and plot.

Your setting can set your plot apart from similar story lines. The same basic plot — a marriage of convenience, for example — looks very different set in a small European principality versus small-town U.S.A. And some plots only work in certain settings. For example, stranding your heroine with a stranger in the middle of a crowded city is pretty difficult to pull off, but stranding her with a stranger in the Rocky Mountains is relatively easy. The same principle holds true when you're talking about characters. A cop hero comes across one way in a small Midwestern town and quite another in New York City.

Following the lead of your characters and plot

Most of the time, before you start looking for a setting, you already have either your hero and heroine or your basic plot in mind — and sometimes both. (Check out Chapter 4 for the ins and outs of character development and Chapter 5 for the essentials of constructing a plot.) Look at what you know about your characters and plot, and use that information as your starting point for deciding where you want your story to take place.

- ✔ **Characters:** If you've chosen a cowboy hero, you're most likely thinking of using a western setting, while a hard-driven CEO heroine may have you thinking more of a big city.

- ✔ **Plot:** If you have a particular plot in mind, certain settings lend themselves naturally. Corporate espionage is more likely to have a city setting, and a hunt to save the world from a deadly terrorist could easily be set overseas against an international background.

But you may have multiple possibilities open to you. For instance, a runaway princess story may have you thinking of settings as diverse as the Australian Outback, a small town in Kansas, or Los Angeles, simply because she could get lost in any of them.

After you consider basic character and plot implications, you can start to narrow the geography down and choose a specific locale, not just the Midwest but Chicago or Peoria, not just Europe but London, Paris, or the Spanish countryside.

Narrowing down the geography

With a general idea of your setting in mind, ask yourself questions to help narrow down your options until you know exactly where you want to set your romance. The following are some sample scenarios that show you how to zero in on a setting. In each case, the more questions you ask, the closer you get to figuring out your ultimate answer — where you want to set your book.

- **Western:** You know you'd like to write a western, so the setting has to be (you guessed it) out West. But your story can take place anywhere from downtown Denver to a pueblo in New Mexico to a reservation in North Dakota to a ranch in Wyoming, Montana, Texas, or several other states to the slopes of the Rocky Mountains. Is your hero a cowboy and your heroine the sheriff who's investigating cattle rustling on his land? Scratch Denver and the Rockies. Is your hero or heroine Native American? If not, scratch the pueblo and the reservation. A ranch with a nearby town or a small city (for the heroine's base of operations) sounds like what you need. So what state? Have you recently read an article on cattle rustling out West? Where was it taking place? That may be a good state to use. Or are you already familiar with a particular state? Are you interested in finding out more? The answer to that question could solve your problem. If you've read a dozen books about ranches in Texas but none set in Wyoming, why not choose Wyoming and stand out?

- **International intrigue:** Your plot description already tells you to set all or most of your book outside the United States. Are you looking for a plot ripped straight from the headlines? In that case, the news of the day is your map to an answer. Are you interested in a mystery with its roots in World War II, a Cold War conspiracy, or palace intrigue among the British royal family? Are you a Francophile who takes any excuse to discover more about Paris, your favorite city? Is your plot about money laundering? (If so, the Cayman Islands are known as banking havens.)

Digging even deeper

Every book takes place in a country, a state, a city or town, or a jungle, a desert, or any other climatic region you can think of — but your setting isn't only a particular geographic point. If you're writing a medical romance, your setting is also a hospital, a free clinic, or a doctor's office. Perhaps your setting is a ranch, the headquarters of a multinational conglomerate, a haunted house, or a tropical resort.

Give as much thought to creating and describing the immediate environs as you do to the larger world around them. In fact, some books are set in such a limited locale — in a hospital or mountain cabin or on a cruise ship — that the big-picture geographical setting, although mentioned, is less important and needs less attention than the immediate environs.

Joining the real world or living in your imagination

Most romance novels are set in real places, at least as far as countries go. And so far, I've never seen anyone make up a 51st state. But you may find it easier to make up a town rather than choosing a real one.

- ✔ When you're looking for a big city, finding information on a real city like Chicago, London, or Sydney is easy, and each one lends its own cachet to your work.

- ✔ If you choose a real small town, getting accurate information is often hard, and there's no excitement boost from choosing Grants, New Mexico, or Homer, New York, because most readers haven't heard of them before.

With small-town settings, choosing a real place provides few advantages, but you get one huge advantage from creating a fictional locale: complete control. You can design the town to be exactly what you need it to be, and that aspect can be a big help as you write. You can place buildings where you need them to be and set your town alongside a lake or in the mountains or wherever you want, even if a real town isn't anywhere nearby.

Sometimes creating an entire country even makes sense. Fictional countries let you avoid

- ✔ **Alienating readers due to political or ideological differences:** If you want to set a book in Northern Ireland, you run the risk of alienating some of your potential readers, because of differing political sympathies. The same holds true for any hot spot, such as the Middle East. If your story requires that all readers share a certain point of view, you may find it easiest to create a country so you can stack the deck in your favor.

- ✔ **The research hassles that complex royal lineages present:** If you want to deal with royal characters — not just duchesses and earls, but kings, queens, princes, and princesses — creating your own kingdom and monarchy is almost certainly easier. Not only does it give you complete control of your characters and the specifics of their rule, but it also lets you create whatever lineage best serves your story.

Keeping your setting in check

Setting is important; however, it's not the point of your book. Travel guides are popular, and readers who buy romance novels buy plenty of travel guides, too — *but for entirely different reasons.*

Romances are about people, not places. Your setting's role is to provide a context for the central romance. A well-chosen setting can enhance the romance, and a poorly chosen one can detract from it. Never let your setting take (bad pun alert) pride of place over your characters. Too much time spent on setting means too little time spent on characters. Here are some tips (bad pun alert #2) for keeping your setting in its place:

- ✔ **Be sparing and sporadic.** Instead of writing large chunks of description about your setting and dropping them into your text almost as interruptions to your story, work in a sentence here and a sentence there. Mingle the description of your setting with the rest of your text so it feels like a natural part of the novel, not a digression.

- ✔ **Don't fall in love with your setting.** No matter how much you love the setting that you've chosen, save your emotional energy for your characters. Wax rhapsodic about the beauty of your heroine, not the beauty of the tropics. Be descriptive without being doting.

- ✔ **Choose telling details.** Tell the reader what she needs to know to get a clear picture of the setting; then go on to include only details that enhance the story, relate to the characters' experiences, move the story forward in some way, or are otherwise germane. Don't waste time on the area's history, a tour of Main Street, or anything else that doesn't have direct relevance to your characters and plot.

- ✔ **Let your characters do the work.** Whenever the opportunity presents itself, use your characters' points of view, their reactions, and even dialogue (as long as it sounds natural), to describe your setting. Because the description comes from the characters, the reader will feel more interested in it than if it comes via straight narration.

Telling Time

Contemporary or historical, the time period you choose for your manuscript is part of your setting, too. However, because your reader is living in the same time period as a contemporary, she tends not to think of it as an era in the same way she thinks of a Regency, Medieval, or World War II romance. In a contemporary romance, your reader doesn't have to wonder how people dress or get around, or what the social mores are, because they're second nature. You don't need to explain anything extra about the period. But in a historical romance, you need to think more consciously about the when of your story and its importance for the characters, as well as what you need to tell the reader about the period.

Just as you need to define and describe the physical setting of your story for the reader, when you're writing a historical romance, you need to define and describe the era. The guidelines to keep in mind are pretty much the same as those you use to keep yourself in check when you talk about the physical setting because, just as a romance novel shouldn't become a travel guide, it also shouldn't become a history text or even a historical novel (which places much more emphasis on the history than you should in a historical romance):

- ✔ **Remember that you're writing a romance.** All sorts of fascinating and historically important things may have gone on during the period: the Napoleonic Wars, the Industrial Revolution, or the Gold Rush. But don't hit your reader over the head with history. Mention events to indicate the time period and create a sense of the societal concerns and tensions your characters are living with. But keep the reader's attention on your characters and work in the historical details when and where they're important to the characters or necessary to the reader's understanding of the story. As you begin the book, use period details as background, not as ends in themselves. As you continue to write, don't remind the reader with every sentence that she's reading about the past.

- ✔ **Don't fall in love with history.** As you research, you find out all kinds of fascinating things, and often times you feel tempted to drop them into your novel so the readers can share them, but you need to resist the temptation. Unless you can justify including a piece of information based purely on storytelling grounds, leave it out. History isn't the story, it's part of the context for your story. And remember, more character and more story is always better than more history.

- ✔ **Use your characters to work in historical details.** Keep your characters at the forefront from the very beginning, and work in the historical details through their experiences and points of view. Don't just describe a muddy street, the sound of carriage wheels and the squawking of geese being carted to market; instead, describe your heroine as she holds up the hem of her dress to keep it out of the mud, dodges to avoid the wheels of a rich man's carriage, and thinks the squawking of the geese is making her pounding headache even worse. That way you're getting across your characters and the reality of their world at the same time — and in a way that's the most effective for your reader.

  On a related note, you also have to make sure you keep your characters consistent with the times. Everything about them — the way they dress, act, think, speak, and so on — must mesh with the era. Check out Chapters 4 and 9 for more information.

Using Your Setting to the Fullest

In some ways, setting is the unsung hero of your book. If you use it well, the reader will hardly even notice, and she almost certainly won't comment. (If you don't, trust me, she'll say something.) Yet setting can very effectively help the reader understand your characters and sometimes even operate as a character of sorts itself. The key is knowing how — and when — to make that happen.

Illuminating your characters

If you were to visit my office, you'd be able to get a good idea of who I am: a confident professional woman who's comfortable with a cluttered desk that doesn't get in the way of her ability to do her job. You'd also see someone who likes to personalize her workspace with pictures of her favorite actors *du jour,* several ridiculous salt and pepper shakers, and a lot of monkeys. But that's not the only me. At a conference, I can be confident but all business, no touches of whimsy allowed. With my family, I'm just a daughter and sister, and my concerns have nothing to do with business. Or take me completely out of my comfort zone and watch my confidence go south. Inside, I'm always myself, but on the outside, that self comes across in different ways.

Your setting can offer your characters the same opportunities to express the different sides of themselves, to face and master challenges. You can use setting to illuminate and enhance your characters in three key ways (see Chapter 4 for more on developing characters). Use one, two, or even all three of the strategies I provide in the following section in every book you write and in relation to both your hero and your heroine. In every case, a change of scene leads to challenge and success — and romance.

To decide the best strategy (or strategies) for using setting to deepen your characters, ask yourself these key questions:

1. What do I want the reader to know about my character?

2. How can my setting help?

Demonstrating competence

Showing that your hero and heroine are strong and capable is important, because that's what makes them admirable and worthy of their roles. One simple way you can demonstrate these qualities is by showing your characters operating successfully in their natural settings. For example:

✔ **Show your heroine, a successful pediatrician, deftly handling an office full of patients.** Calm, cool, and collected in the face of crying kids and nervous parents, she has an especially powerful effect on the good-looking single father whose little girl has taken a bad spill off her bike. And of course, his subsequent dinner invitation is only to thank her for how well she soothed and treated his daughter, right?

✔ **Show your cowboy hero sitting tall in the saddle and cutting an unruly cow from the herd.** Whether your heroine is an expert horse-woman herself or a total greenhorn, she's going to feel her heart beat a little faster at the sight of this ruggedly handsome man handling his horse as if born to the saddle.

✔ **Let your fireman hero pull a child from a burning school.** And let the news photographer heroine document the rescue. Better yet, let him pull *her* child from the flames, and then finish the scene with a hug that starts from relief and gratitude but ends with a frisson of physical awareness.

By showing your characters at their best in their normal settings, you let your readers see how the characters' strengths can be admirable and complementary, and sometimes sexy and emotionally stirring, as well.

Uncovering vulnerabilities

Characters need strengths, but your hero and heroine also need to be flawed, to have normal human vulnerabilities (see Chapter 4). Setting can also help you bring those vulnerabilities to the surface.

Suppose your heroine is cool, calm, and collected as she goes about her day running one of North America's most successful home-shopping dot.coms. Her business savvy convinces everyone that her heart's made out of the same cubic zirconia that her company sells so successfully. It's not true, of course, and you need to convince your reader of that before she decides the heroine is someone she can't possibly identify with. Simple. Take her out of her office, where everything's under control, and put her somewhere where she's not in control and her vulnerabilities can come through. For example:

✔ **A wilderness team-building exercise for CEOs:** Suddenly she's the lone woman, and everyone seems to know more than she does about everything from building a fire to pitching a tent. The hero could be a rival businessman whose company is trying to take over hers, but in this new setting they must become temporary allies. Now that he's seen her at what she considers her worst, that experience changes everything when they're back across the negotiating table from each other.

✔ **A family reunion on a cruise ship:** Families aren't like employees; family members don't have to listen to you or do what you say. And just what is a driven CEO — who normally has every minute scheduled and the phone glued to her ear — supposed to do lying on the lido deck out of cell range? Suddenly she has time to think, to inventory what's missing in her life — like the kind of life her sister has with her husband and kids. Even so, she's not really thinking seriously about the handsome, witty, single dad who's brought his kids on the cruise to take their minds off the anniversary of their mother's death. Or is she?

- ✔ **A hospital bed:** She's worked herself right into a bad case of walking pneumonia, so bad that she's not even up and walking anymore — she's in a hospital bed. Not only is she unable to give anyone orders, but she also has to take them from other people every minute of the day. Her brain feels fuzzy, she's sick and unhappy and knows she looks awful — and here comes Dr. Gorgeous.

In each case, taking the heroine out of her everyday setting and putting her in a new setting that catches her off guard makes her think about things she normally ignores, showcases her weaknesses instead of her strengths, and lets people — hero and reader alike — see past her carefully constructed in-charge persona, which helps make her into the imperfectly perfect heroine I describe in Chapter 4.

Bringing out the best

One way to let your characters grow is to challenge them and let them rise to those challenges (see Chapter 4 for more on character growth). Your setting can be a key part of that process. After you've used the setting to demonstrate your hero or heroine's flaws, show them standing up to whatever difficulties have been thrown in their way. For example:

- ✔ **Strand your hero and heroine in a mountain cabin when a mudslide closes the road.** She's a city girl all the way, so the prospect of spending some indeterminate amount of time without electricity or (gasp!) indoor plumbing doesn't fill her with happiness, to say the least. The hero, a rancher who ended up taking shelter in the same cabin, can't believe he's going to have to put up with Miss Priss for who knows how long.

  Things don't start off well, but before too long her natural optimism has reasserted itself and she's pulling pictures out of a magazine and nailing them to the wall for décor, mixing up an improbable combination of canned goods from the cupboards to create a surprisingly tasty meal to cook over the fire the hero set, and tempting a lost puppy out of the woods with the leftovers. As much as he doesn't want to get involved with a woman whose normal life is so different from his, the hero soon finds her impossible to resist.

- ✔ **A tough-talking CEO is forced to take time off to play Mr. Mom when he inherits his late sister's baby.** No more boardroom table and contentious shareholders' meetings. Now it's nursery furniture and a fussy newborn for this hero, and he couldn't feel any less competent if he tried. Stuck at home with a baby whose idea of communication is crying loud, louder, and loudest, he can't change a diaper to save his life. Mixing formula means mixing a mess, and every time he tries to bathe the baby, he's the one who gets wet. Being stuck inside the house is making him crazy.

He doesn't know what to do, other than thank heaven for the single mom next door who takes him under her wing and teaches him that parenthood can be paradise. Before long, even midnight feedings don't faze him, although he likes daytime better — when his neighbor's around. But just so he can get advice, or so he tells himself.

✔ **Put your ranch-bred tomboy heroine in silk or satin and watch for sparks.** As a working rancher, she's as at home on horseback as any cowboy, but she's definitely out of her element when she has to dress up and play hostess for the nearest town's annual Christmas fundraising dance. She has trouble keeping her balance in heels, keeps tugging at her skirt and wishing she were wearing denim, and the makeup she let herself get talked into wearing feels like a Halloween mask. So why does that gorgeous guy keep staring at her from across the room?

She has no idea that he's a Dallas tycoon looking to buy a ranch-country getaway and that he thinks she's a wonderful contrast to all the sophisticated, even jaded, women he deals with all the time. He can't help admiring the way she has a smile and a cheerful word for everyone, even though she obviously wishes her dress weren't so mouth-wateringly tight or her heels so high. He thinks that more women should have her selflessness and her ability to laugh it off when they can't manage a two-step in three-inch heels. Right there and then, he vows that this is a woman he has to get to know better.

Making your setting a character

Most of the time, you won't need to (and shouldn't) use the suggestions in this section because, most of the time, you won't want to (and shouldn't) draw a ton of attention to setting. You won't have a reason to make setting function as a secondary character.

But you may face occasions when atmosphere is *so* crucial that the setting takes on added importance and functions almost like a character, with its influence directly felt. Usually this occurs when you want your setting to indicate menace and a sense of deepening threat. Sometimes you only need that added effect for a scene or two; other times you want to keep the feeling through the book. A few examples where setting takes on added importance:

✔ Your story is a suspenseful one, so as the villains close in on your hero and heroine, every shadow, cracking twig, or rustling of leaves sounds like a threat.

✔ You're writing a Gothic or a romance set in a haunted house, in which case the house itself is part of the threat.

Whatever the reason, here are some tactics you can utilize to milk your setting for extra effect:

✔ **Take more time describing your setting:** Don't simply use longer chunks of narration; a subtle interweaving is still the most effective road to take, just do so more often and in more detail. Don't say it's a moonlit night in the woods and leave it at that. Take time to describe the way the moon casts shadows, and, later, comment on the way the light shifts when a cloud crosses the face of the moon. Does the sky look darker and the stars brighter when the moon is full? Do sounds from the forest seem scary in the strange brightness of the night? Mention those details, too. The ongoing accumulation of detail builds atmosphere and starts to draw the reader's attention to the setting. And the extra attention you pay to setting indicates its importance.

✔ **Use more adjectives:** Ordinarily, you should use a minimal number of adjectives to describe your setting — just enough to get the job done. But when you want to give your setting a more active role, use more adjectives than usual to help draw attention to it. For instance, don't just say "moonlight," say "a cold light" or "a pale, thin light." Adjectives add personality to a place, just as they do to a character.

✔ **Use loaded words:** Pick words for their effects; choose words that convey and evoke emotion. Mountains aren't just high, they loom threateningly. An old house doesn't just creak, it groans like an animal in pain. Choose words that don't just tell the reader something factual but instead make her feel their effects. A house isn't just deserted; its windows stare out like animal eyes seeking prey in the forest. Again, you're personalizing your setting, treating it like a character, so it affects your heroine, hero, and reader just as another character would.

✔ **Have characters react to setting as they would to another person:** If your characters — especially your hero and heroine — react to your setting as if it's a character (getting spooked, feeling as if they're being watched, even just jumping at an unexpected noise), your reader will react right along with them. Let your characters attribute personality to the setting, even let them comment on it, and it takes on added meaning for the reader, as well.

Be careful not to let the setting take over from the characters. But in some cases, setting *can* become like a supporting character and add depth and impact to your book.

Traveling the wrong way down a one-way street

Even though 99 percent of the time your setting will literally be kept in the background, if you make a mistake, someone will catch it. If you write about New York City, where most avenues and streets are one way, be sure you have traffic running in the correct direction. If your heroine drives from Los Angeles to San Diego, be sure it takes the correct amount of time. If your couple embraces passionately while watching the sunset, be sure they're somewhere that faces west. In other words, do your research, even on the smallest details. The following suggestions are a geographic supplement to the general research advice in Chapter 13.

- **Surf the Internet.** Use one of the many available search engines, making your query as specific as possible, and chances are you'll find what you need. But be careful: A lot of misinformation is out there, so consider the source and, wherever possible, get confirmation from a second and independent source. Some examples of the most reliable information:

- Official Web sites set up by state governments, chambers of commerce, and departments of tourism

- Driving directions that tell you how long it takes to get from Point A to Point B

- Airline schedules that give you flight routes, departure and arrival times, and durations

- Travel bulletin boards and Web sites

- Maps and photographs

- **Read travel brochures.** Travel guides are available from a variety of sources, including travel agencies and official departments of tourism.

- **Read travel guides and travel memoirs.** Any general bookstore has a whole selection of these, whether you're looking for a particular country, state, or even city. If you're buying a guide, be sure you get the most up-to-date version you can find.

- **Read travel magazines and newspaper travel sections.** Many times past issues and articles are also archived online.

- **Look at maps and atlases.** As with travel guides, be sure you get the most current version.

- **Talk to family, friends, and friends of friends.** You never know who's just taken a vacation to your locale of choice or grew up in the area that you're focusing on.

Chapter 7

Outlining Your Romance

. . . .

In This Chapter

▶ Knowing what an outline can do for you

▶ Creating a successful outline

▶ Letting creativity flourish

▶ Keeping your eye on the prize

. . . .

*I*f I had a nickel (okay, a quarter) for every author who's told me "I can't write an outline" or "Writing an outline ruins the story for me," I'd be a rich woman. Unfortunately, no quarters have been forthcoming, and I probably would have to give them all back anyway, because 99 percent of those authors did learn to write an outline.

But for most aspiring (and even published) authors, outlining remains the most daunting step, at least in the creative process. (Sending your manuscript off to an editor is probably at least as daunting.) The most common complaints I hear are that knowing what's going to happen until it actually does is impossible, and that outlining the story destroys creativity.

Despite those fears, outlining is a valuable, even crucial, step in the process for most writers. In fact, outlining can make your life immeasurably easier when you know how to do it. In this chapter, I address the common fears about outlining and teach you strategies to demystify the outlining process.

What's an Outline?

An *outline* is a *synopsis* is an *outline.* Editors tend to use these two terms interchangeably. The important thing to know is that both terms refer to prose documents that give an overview of your book. When an editor asks you for an *outline,* she's not asking for one of those highly formatted A-B-C-i-ii-iii things you did in high school to outline a paper. She's asking for a *synopsis* — a straightforward piece of prose that tells the basics of your story, with a focus on the development of the romance. For the purposes of this chapter, I use *outline/outlining* to refer to what you create for your own use, as you're planning the book. In Chapter 15, I use *synopsis/synopsize* to refer to what you create for an editor to see when submitting, but things aren't so clear-cut in real life, so be forewarned.

You're almost certain to run into several types of synopses during your writing career. This chapter focuses on one of them: the outline you put together to guide yourself as you write.

Many of the tips I give you for creating a useful outline also apply to creating an effective synopsis, so though I discuss them here in relation to your outline, you can expect to see some overlap when you read Chapter 15 for insights on how to use a synopsis when you submit.

Mapping Your Way to "The End"

An *outline* is the road map you use as you write. It's a document-in-progress, one you create before you start writing and often find yourself revising, even re-creating, as you go. Your outline can be as long or as short as you need it to be, and neatness doesn't count, so feel free to scribble notes in the margins. No one has to see your outline except you, so you can be as freewheeling as you want — which should already make you less afraid of writing one.

I use the term *road map* to describe an outline because I really do think that the purpose of your outline is to help you map your way through your story. Not only does the idea of a road map sound a lot less intimidating, but more importantly, the term is also an accurate description of the planning process — a process that can help you write.

Just as you wouldn't drive from New York City to Los Angeles without looking at a map and planning out your route, so you shouldn't start writing Chapter 1 without at least some idea of how you're going to get to The End. But just as you can change your route along the way in order to avoid construction or visit an interesting landmark, you also need to stay open to revising your outline as you go.

You start your book knowing who your characters are, a bit about their journey (where the book takes place, and maybe a couple of big plot points: a kidnapping, a corporate takeover, and so on), and your ending (happily ever after). But the actual route's a mystery — until you create your road map. Your outline gets your characters started on their journey and provides a basic route for them to follow, but they're not locked into anything. The road map simply gives you touchstones along the way.

Your outline helps you keep your focus and makes you think about what's most important about your characters, your plot, the emotional development of the relationship, and the way those elements fit into the book's imaginary world.

What can an outline do for you?

As intimidating as it may feel to start planning out your characters' story before you've started writing it, there are a lot of advantages to figuring out as much as you can ahead of time. Having an outline helps you

- ✔ **Streamline the writing process.** I won't kid you — nothing can ever make writing a book easy. Writing a book is time-consuming, draining, and difficult, and writing a romance, especially, lays all your emotions bare. But if you've written your outline and have an idea of where you're going, and if you've taken care of the basic facts, your creative side is free to focus on the more emotional and artistic side of the process.

- ✔ **Pitch a project.** Admittedly, you probably won't run into an author or agent at the grocery store. Although, I've been on vacation and met aspiring authors who recognized me from conferences. And conferences certainly do provide opportunities for talking about your book. Even if you haven't snagged an appointment with an editor or agent, you may find yourself in conversation with one. If you have an outline, you have an answer to "What are you writing?" Instead of stuttering your way through a disjointed series of scenes, you have a coherent — even intriguing — story to talk about. And you never know when a simple conversation can turn into an invitation to submit.

- ✔ **Guesstimate your manuscript's length.** After you have an idea of your story, you can get a general (very general) sense of how long your finished book will be. If you have a complicated plot with lots of twists and turns, you can tell that you have too much story to fit into one of the shorter series books. And if you're planning on a 100,000-word mainstream romance but have a relatively straightforward plot, your outline can tell you that you need to aim for a shorter format or build in some additional complications. (For more on the different types of romances and their needs, see Chapter 2, and check out Chapter 5 for plotting info.)

What belongs in an outline?

Ultimately, the answer to this question is "Anything that will help you write your book." Because no one else ever has to see it, your outline can be as detailed, as messy, and as idiosyncratic as you want. It's a tool to help you, and you can custom design it. There are certain basics, though, that you should think your way through before you sit down to do the actual writing.

✔ **Who are your hero and heroine, and what's the basis of their emotional conflict?** The answers to these questions are crucial to the setup and development of both the romance and the plot (see Chapter 5), so get a handle on those answers from the get-go.

✔ **Where — and how — will your book begin?** Chances are you're going to know a lot of background information on your characters and their story that doesn't belong in your novel, so you need to decide what goes on page one. If you choose the most effective beginning for your book ahead of time (see Chapter 12 for hints on knowing where to start), you can save yourself a lot of time, because you won't have to go back and rewrite when you realize that you've made the common error of starting in the wrong place.

You don't always have to outline before you start writing the book. Some authors find it's helpful to write a chapter or two — even though those chapters may ultimately be discarded — just to get to know the characters better and get a sense of where they're driving the story.

✔ **How will the big events of the story progress and fit together?** Instead of writing yourself into a corner where nothing makes sense and you have to go back and rethink your whole story, outline your way from point to point, making sure your story line is logical. The more complicated your story line is — and especially if you're incorporating suspense into your plot — the more crucial this step is.

✔ **How will the characters' developing relationship affect the story line and vice versa?** The emotional logic of your story has to work just as much as the plot-based logic does. By outlining, you get to work through your characters' emotional issues and make sure their behavior makes sense — and also that it makes sense when considered alongside the plot. Don't forget to include the repercussions of your hero and heroine's developing physical intimacy, too.

Start your outline at whatever point is most helpful for you. Your outline exists specifically for your own benefit. If you need to write your way through lengthy pieces of background information on your characters, their situations, or anything else to get into your story and your characters' heads, do it. Just be aware of the point where the manuscript itself will begin.

Think of the big events in the book — both the major plot points and the key moments in the relationship — as *milestones*. They should stand out as destination points on your outline, and the rest of your story involves moving from one to the next in believable, interesting ways. In fact, one way to begin writing your outline is to start by laying out the milestone events. Then you can figure out the details of moving from one to the next. That way you never lose sight of your interim goals as your characters move from point to point in the story. (Check out Chapter 10 for a full discussion of these milestones as they relate to pacing.)

You may also find it helpful to break down your outline chapter by chapter, so that you can build in effective beginnings and endings for each chapter. (See Chapter 12 for ideas on creating great beginnings and effective endings.)

Outlining additional advice

In the following sections, I cover a few more things you can do to make putting together your outline easier.

Keeping your characters front and center

You may still be getting a handle on your characters when you begin outlining, or they may be very definite personalities in your mind. Either way, your characters' needs and reactions — not your need as a writer to have a love scene here and an argument there — need to drive both your plot and the progress of the relationship. In real life, people make choices that affect their lives, and their choices are the real-life equivalent of your plot. So in order for your characters to feel real to the reader, the characters' choices need to affect their lives (which means *your* plot) in the same way.

If your characters aren't already fully developed in your mind, they should become real to you as you outline their story. The more you're still getting to know them as you outline, the more likely you are to have to go back and rethink the earlier sections of your book. That's natural, so don't be discouraged.

Setting goals

Just as a traveler sets out with a destination in mind, you have certain goals in mind when you sit down to start your romance novel. The most obvious goal is getting to happily ever after, but the journey is never as simple as it looks. Where does the emotional tension between your characters come from? Issues of dependence and control? Inability to trust? Fear of facing the pain of loss again? You want to devise a plot that lets you explore those themes via your characters, and your outline helps you conceptualize your goals and then gives you the chance to explore what works and what doesn't, without writing an entire book as an experiment.

Retaining a real feel

All romances must unfold in a logical manner. Your reader needs to buy into the story's reality and believe in it throughout the novel (even when you're writing a paranormal romance or using a fictional country as your setting). As you write your outline, keep the rules of the world — the one you're creating *and* the real one — in mind and follow them. Think about the whys, hows, and whens as you plan, so they're all taken care of and make sense when you sit down to write the book itself.

You need to think out the realities of your characters' jobs and lives, the timing of events, the ways their lives intersect, and how their relationship moves forward. These elements become the structure of your outline — the milestones, plotwise and emotional, on your hero and heroine's journey toward love. The events of your story must be believable, and they must happen in a sequence and over a period of time that makes sense. (They shouldn't happen on a rigid schedule, though.) As you develop your outline, ideas will occur to you that you didn't think of before. You can fit those ideas in and take care of any repercussions while you're still at the outline stage — a much simpler task than revising a manuscript when new ideas occur.

You may have heard of the concept (which applies to fiction in general, though I'm going to talk specifically in terms of romance novels) of willing suspension of disbelief. Simply put, the *willing suspension of disbelief* means that your reader knows that she's going to read a romantic fantasy, so some elements won't be totally realistic and some may even be totally *un*realistic — vampires, for instance, if you're writing a vampire romance — and she accepts that fact when she starts reading. The willing suspension of disbelief also means that after you've set up the parameters of your fictional world, everything that happens within it has to make sense. Logic still applies to your characters' behavior and the way the world runs in general, otherwise you'll lose your reader's trust and her interest not only in the book at hand, but also in your future work.

Working in research

Despite your best efforts, you may find yourself facing unanticipated questions as you write, which will force you to break from the creative process to look for answers. But if you do your research ahead of time, you improve the odds that you won't have to start and stop during the writing process. As you write your outline, you're thinking about your book on every level, and a lot of questions occur to you: the specifics of the legal system of 18th-century France; which way the traffic runs on Fifth Avenue in New York City; the psychiatric definition of narcissism; which weekend in May is the running of the Kentucky Derby. Get your answers right away and account for them in your outline, and you ultimately streamline the writing process. Check out Chapter 13 for all your research needs.

Questioning everything

I often say that one of my most important jobs as an editor is to ask questions, because readers are always thinking and asking mental questions as they read. If I can read a submission and ask all the questions, letting the author answer them before the book is published, the reader can stay so captured by the novel that she can't put it down and looks forward to the author's next novel. And, as an editor, I love receiving a submission where the author has anticipated all my questions and answered them.

To avoid later problems, you should begin that process of asking yourself questions as you write your outline. Question everything. Why are your characters the way they are? How did they get involved in whatever you, as their creator, have decided to involve them in? Do your hero and heroine's responses to events make sense? Do other characters' responses to your hero and heroine make sense? Have you checked and double-checked all your facts? Have you contradicted yourself somewhere along the way without realizing it?

You should question your characters and the way you've woven your plot throughout the outlining process. But questioning everything again at the end — when it seems all put together — is crucial. A day or so after you've finished your outline, go back and reread all of it, asking questions about your story as if you were seeing it for the first time. A little distance lends perspective. As you reread, mistakes and omissions you didn't see in the heat of writing, and contradictions you missed the first time through, jump out on a second viewing.

Using Your Outline Effectively: Write, Write, and Then Rewrite (Maybe)

After you've created your outline, the next step is to move forward with your writing, remembering that your outline is there to help you, not hinder you, both as you write and once you've finished your manuscript.

Listening to your creativity

Talking about listening to your creativity in a chapter devoted to outlining may seem odd, but an outline truly gives you a framework where your creativity can flourish. It frees you from thinking about the mundane details, so you can focus on characterization and emotion, without stressing over the basic logic of your plot.

Because you aren't worrying about plot mechanics, you're able to get deeply into developing your characters, giving them the freedom to take over and make your book stronger because the emotions are so genuine (the key drawing card for the reader). The trickiest or most unique plot in the world means nothing if your characters and their romance don't resonate with readers. If you're busy worrying about how to get people from Napa to Nevada or about the legal technicalities of a custody battle, you aren't free to focus on characterization, and your hero and heroine won't get to break free to be themselves. Your outline lets your creativity shine through.

Your outline includes key plot points and emotional transitions: the moment when the heroine first realizes she loves the hero, and vice versa; the first kiss; the first time they make love (assuming they do); major disclosures, like a secret baby or an undercover existence. Any of these are subject to change as you write. Characters usually become more real the longer you live with them, and as they become real, they sometimes take over. They just don't do what you meant them to. The key moments of the relationship are suddenly in *their* control, not yours. For instance, you may have expected them to hold off from getting hot and heavy until Chapter 5, but suddenly in Chapter 2 they can't keep their hands off each other. That kind of change is okay as long as they hold off confessing their love and planning for a future until the end, and you can easily slot these new developments into your outline and your book.

Remembering the marketplace

Writing a novel is a funny business, because you have to balance the importance of letting creativity and emotion shine while keeping an eye on the marketplace and the readers' needs. Again, your outline can help you.

When you start writing the outline, you're thinking intellectually at least as much as you are emotionally, maybe even more so. At this stage, you're fitting puzzle pieces together until they add up to a romantic, story-based picture. You're also trusting yourself to make the emotional development work and determining the best places to put those scenes, without locking yourself into a structure you can't break free from. Additionally, you're making sure you fulfill the readers' expectations for the story that you've chosen to tell. Later, when you're writing the actual manuscript, you're thinking much more emotionally and creatively, letting the characters have their heads and drive events themselves. At this stage, your outline serves a valuable purpose as a reality check, so you don't let emotion run away with you. Refer back to it periodically as you write, to see where you're on track and where you've gone off track.

Going off track isn't always bad. Sometimes the changes you make as you write make the book stronger. Compare and contrast your changes with your outline, then go with whichever avenue works better for the book.

Your outline is a concrete reminder that, for instance, as opposing attorneys, your characters can't say to hell with the world and flaunt their relationship openly. Not only would their careers be destroyed, but the romantic tension that is the key component of every successful romance novel would also be diffused. Your outline also lets you double-check your facts. In the flush of writing, you may forget some of your research or the logic of your story. Your outline pulls you back to an intellectual mindset long enough to tell you that the turn you've taken is the wrong one, and you're saved from writing an entire book that ultimately doesn't work.

Avoiding the rewriting trap

You must be open to rewriting, doing several drafts, then polishing and getting things right. At the same time, rewriting can be a delaying tactic — a way of keeping yourself safe by not sending your book out into the world, where rejection is a definite possibility.

You can get caught in the rewriting trap without even realizing it, because every time you go over your manuscript, you *will* find something — even if only a typo or a missing comma — to fix. Or maybe you realize how crucial it is to get your opening right, so you can't let go of Chapter 1, because another approach may make it just a teensy bit more compelling.

Your outline can help pull you out of the rewriting trap. After you've written the book, let your outline show you how much you've gotten right. You thought deeply about all kinds of questions related to your characters, their story, and their world, because the outline *made* you think about them. Now you can reap the benefit of all that effort as you let your outline tell you whether you still have work to do or if it's time to take the risk of submitting your book.

If you find yourself endlessly polishing, revising, rewriting, and second-guessing, take another look at your outline. Read through it as objectively as possible. Pay attention to how much sense it makes, to how well you thought through not just the mechanics of your plot, but also the development of your characters. Just as your outline helped you before you ever wrote a word of the actual book, it can help you at the final stage when every word's been written. Analyze your manuscript in light of your outline to see how many of the elements you have right, how well the actions are motivated, what consequences those actions have, and how everything works together to not only drive your plot forward, but to also further the course of the relationship. If your book lives up to your outline, if you've thought through any major changes and decided they make the novel stronger, if you've written the story you set out to tell, then your outline's sending you a message: It's time to stop rewriting your manuscript and take the next step: submission.

Part III
Putting Pen to Paper

The 5th Wave   By Rich Tennant

"It had an interesting emotional arc and some nice plot twists, but the heroine and subsidiary characters were unconvincing within the historical context."

In this part . . .

When your plot and characters are clear in your mind, you can turn your attention to writing. So it's time for the subjects I talk about in this part — voice (both your own and your characters') and pacing. In addition, I pull back the covers and talk about writing love scenes, from sweet to sexy.

Chapter 8

Finding Your Own Voice

*I*n a romance novel, the characters' voices — especially the hero and heroine's — are key (as I discuss in Chapter 9), because it's their relationship that the reader's interested in. But, as the author, your voice matters, too. The way you tell the story is as important as the story you tell, even though, if you do your job right, the reader may never even notice your style and voice, because she's paying attention to the characters and events. A reader doesn't pick up a romance to marvel at a pretty turn of phrase or to compliment the author's use of metaphor. A reader picks up a romance novel for the emotional fulfillment that comes from seeing two right-for-each-other people get together. Everything you do as a writer should illuminate that romance and its emotional conclusion, not draw attention to your own abilities. In this chapter, I talk about what to do and what *not* to do, so that the *telling* part of *storytelling* leaves plenty of room for your *story.*

Speaking Up for Yourself

You probably don't plan out every sentence before speaking or listen closely to yourself when you're telling your husband or best friend what went on at work or the funny thing that happened when you were walking the dog. But the truth is, we're all natural storytellers, and we practice our craft every day when we tell the people in our lives what we've been doing. We talk about not only *what* happened, but also *who* was involved, *what* they did, *what* they said, *where* the event took place, and *how* it ended up. We talk our way through what happened, and our audience laughs, groans, cries, or offers us hugs when we tell our stories well. As you write your romance novel, you want your story to have the same effect.

You need to tell your story in a way that makes your reader react the way you want her to. You need to write effectively without calling attention to the writing itself. If your reader pauses to admire your prose, then you've pulled her out of your story and away from your characters. Everything you do as a writer needs to keep the reader intrigued and foster her identification with the characters, because that keeps her turning pages. And successfully using author voice can help you in these areas. Finding your *author voice* involves recognizing and going with your own natural bent — whether that's to be funny, dramatic, atmospheric, or anything else — and then developing an awareness of your own language, rhythms, and vocabulary. As a writer, you need to find your own voice, and then keep yourself from taking too loudly.

The most effective author voice serves the story, not the other way around. Keep that tip in mind as you work, and your own voice will become stronger and more effective.

Revealing where readers hear your voice

Asking where readers hear your voice is a natural question because, technically, you're writing the whole book. But a large part of what the author does (as I discuss in Chapter 9) is give voices to her characters, creating the illusion that they're speaking for themselves. Your voice comes into play in between the characters' conversations and thoughts.

Romances are occasionally written in *first person* (in which case, the entire book reflects a single character's voice), but they're generally written in *third person* (with the focus moving from character to character but staying mostly on the heroine and, secondarily, the hero). A romance novel rarely uses true *omniscient narration,* a literary device in which the narrator is a separate voice, divorced from any character's thoughts and feelings, that often delivers information no character is capable of knowing.

Because romance novels are all about emotion, which is entirely personal, the impersonal omniscient viewpoint, even if used only as an occasional interjection, works against the book's nature. Likewise, avoid foreshadowing: Let your reader experience events as they occur, because they'll have much more impact. Don't interrupt the flow of the story with an omniscient aside like "If she'd only known what the morning would bring, she wouldn't have fallen asleep with a smile on her lips."

You should tell every scene in a romance from a particular character's point of view, though not every element of the scene involves dialogue or directly reported thoughts, both of which showcase the characters' voices. The other elements — description and narration — showcase the author's voice.

✔ **Description:** Descriptions, whether of a person, place, or thing, are rarely done in dialogue because they usually sound awkward — sort of like those ridiculous soap opera scenes where two characters sit down over coffee to rehash the history of a relationship they both know very well. They're talking about it for the viewers' benefit, which makes the scene artificial. The same thing happens in a book when dialogue is the outlet for description. For instance, one character is unlikely to describe to another the office where they're meeting or the local landscape surrounding the ranch where the story takes place.

Descriptions give you a chance to use your authorial voice to show the reader where the characters are and what's going on. Also, use your own voice when describing a character. Even if your heroine describes the hero to a friend, she's going to do it in normal conversational terms. His hair is merely black, not jet black, for instance, and she won't hit on every detail of his appearance. By using your own voice, you can go further with your description, making it more effective and complete, while still making the heroine's feelings about him clear.

✔ **Narration:** In every romance novel, there are times when you need to tell the readers what someone is doing and why she's doing it. Keep such sections brief and interspersed with "personalizing" elements. For instance, if you have your hero climbing a sheer cliff face in search of the heroine, who's trapped on a ledge above, you need to tell readers something about the mechanics of how he makes it up. But you can mingle the "right hand here, left foot there" bits with his feelings about what he's doing: fear that he's too late, determination to make the climb despite fatigue and pain, and fantasies of what they can do after they're safely at the bottom.

For the purposes of this chapter, and to differentiate the description of actions and thoughts from the description of a person, place, or thing, I use the term *narration,* not only to refer to the complete act of telling a story, but also to the ways you describe the characters' *actions,* or the things that your characters do. A related term, one that groups description and narration together to include everything that's not dialogue or a character's direct thoughts, is *narrative,* and I use this term frequently in Chapter 9, when I discuss your characters' voices.

I provide all kinds of additional information on description and narration later in this chapter (see the sections "Description: Putting the Show in Show and Tell" and "Narration: Telling It Like It Is").

Your voice and your characters' voices often intertwine in everything except dialogue (see the "Mixing what you say with what your characters know" section later in the chapter). Don't try too hard to separate one from the other. Concentrate on giving the reader what she needs, and don't get lost in analyzing your prose.

Making the language your own

The first thing every romance writer needs to do is tell a story her way, which means finding a personal way of handling language. But you've already done most of the work: We're all storytellers every day; all you need to do is listen to yourself and discover the storytelling style you've developed over your lifetime. Then adapt your own natural conversational style and make it the basis of your writing style. You don't need to start from scratch, just take what you already know and do, and build on it.

Do you like to make people laugh? Or are you in your element creating drama in the everyday? When you talk about what happened at work, do you put words into people's mouths and act out each person's part? Or do you love to delve into the nuances of description, creating a sense of atmosphere so your listeners feel as if they're in the middle of the scene? How you answer these questions will help you decide not only what kind of story to tell (a humorous or a dramatic one, for instance) but also how to tell it.

We all overuse certain words, like a piece of current slang, an all-purpose response ("Brilliant!"), or a favorite descriptor ("beautiful"). As a writer, you need to be the most articulate version of yourself, so vary your word choices. Not only does it get boring, even irritating, to hear the same words — especially adjectives — used over and over again, they also stop having any meaning. If everything's beautiful or big or great, how can any one person or peril stand out?

If you're most comfortable using dialogue, don't make yourself crazy trying to write long, beautiful descriptions. Instead, stick to the basics and be straightforward, without getting lost in long metaphors. On the other hand, if you love to create an atmosphere with long descriptions, use your skill, but don't go on too long before allowing your characters to speak, too.

If you're a plain speaker, not given to lots of adjectives and adverbs, nothing's wrong with being a plain writer, too — just not *too* plain. Readers need details about people and places, but don't feel you have to describe every little thing. Decide what's truly important and spend extra time and words on that subject only. The very fact that you've spent extra time on a detail will stand out to the reader and emphasize its importance.

Choosing your words wisely

As an author, the decisions you make affect how your reader sees your characters and their story. The words you choose provide the reader's only knowledge of what's happening, where, and to whom, so choose wisely.

You can't write clear descriptions and narration (and make your reader see what you want her to see) without using adjectives and, to a lesser extent, adverbs. For example, a house, a big house, and a mansion are vastly different. And not all mansions are created equal, either. Is your hero's mansion made of glass walls and angular rooflines, modern and stark? Or does he live in an ivy-covered Norman construction, forbidding and gray?

And characters going up a hill can walk slowly, breathing hard, or sprint to the top. A soldier walking wearily up the path toward home after a year fighting with the Confederacy is very different from a soldier, shiny in his new uniform, walking smartly up the path to his girlfriend's house to propose before shipping out to a distant land.

But effective prose doesn't shout, "Look at me! Look at me!" Effective prose does its job without attracting the reader's attention, whether because something's wrong *or* something's right.

Too many adjectives and adverbs can get in the way of what counts: your characters and their romance. Keep the phrase "less is more" in mind when you write. Too much of a good thing is still too much, and overwriting is a far worse thing than underwriting. I've read manuscripts where even the adjectives had adjectives, and no character just walked without doing so arrogantly, stiffly, or primly. Most of the time you just want to move someone from one place to another, and how he or she gets there doesn't really matter. You don't want the reader to wonder how many more ways you can describe walking and forget all about what the characters are feeling.

And although the reader may care how the heroine's dressed, getting the details of every character's wardrobe probably isn't important. Use a general phrase whenever one will serve, such as "well-dressed" or "sloppy."

Even when you describe something in more detail, don't go overboard. The heroine's dress can be silky, ankle-length, with flowing lines, and in an emerald shade that reflects the color of her eyes. But don't describe it in such detail that a reader's eyes glaze over and you sound like you're quoting a fashion column: ankle-length, cut on the bias, with sleeves ending 3 inches above the wrists, and a skirt that moves with her but is narrow enough to make climbing stairs a challenge, and a shade of green that's like a deep emerald crossed with the shade of a forest in full sunlight, and on and on.

Mixing what you say with what your characters know

Your authorial voice is filtered through a character's point of view, usually the hero or heroine's. What you're really doing when you describe a character or place, for example, is describing what your heroine sees and, often, personalizing it with her reactions. Her thoughts and feelings are threaded through your description. When writing, be sure that the tone of your description is in keeping with who she is and what she knows, which can be a very fine line to walk.

Here's an example: Your hero is a cutting-edge physicist and your heroine is meeting him for the first time in his lab to ask him to participate in a local bachelor auction. In this case, you need to describe the hero and the lab. But because the heroine isn't a scientist herself, she's not going to know what all the equipment is, so be careful that you don't describe it all by name, which implies that she does.

> *Leah took a look around the room. Easily the most noticeable thing in it was the man himself. Marcus Whitford was 6'2", at least, and as far from the stereotypical science nerd as a man could be. His thick, mink-brown hair made her long to reach out and touch someone, and his whiskey-colored eyes held both intelligence and humor. And he was built like someone who climbed mountains or herded cattle for a living, strong and well-muscled, without looking like he had corn flakes with a steroid chaser for breakfast every morning. Afraid she was staring, she looked away and noticed that a Amegamagmamometer stood next to a stainless steel apoplectimeter, and a gleaming countertop held a minimicrotiptopper.*

Nothing is wrong with the first part of the previous paragraph, which shows you how to mix your voice with the heroine's reactions. But you lose your reader with the last couple of sentences. She knows that your heroine has no way of knowing what all that equipment is, so your reader loses her connection to your character and your story. In these situations, generalities can serve you well: Your heroine can simply notice all the equipment and how impressive it looks, even though she has no idea what any of it does. You can also use dialogue so the hero can explain some of the equipment to her, although you can run into pitfalls here (see Chapter 9 for more on dialogue).

Use the same caution in narration, as well, and don't let your characters demonstrate more knowledge than they can believably possess. For example, your heroine may get a chance to watch the hero work in his lab, in which case, unless he tells her about the process he's demonstrating, she's not going to know exactly what he's doing, just that it's complicated, time-consuming, and other nonspecific things.

Putting the Show in Show and Tell

Readers hear the author's voice the most in descriptions, mainly because descriptions are usually presented in chunks, without being broken up by a lot of dialogue or action. But as long as your descriptions are presented effectively and don't go on too long, they don't stop the reader in her tracks, or pull her attention away from the world of your story and back to the real world. In this section, I give you a few key points to remember when you're writing descriptions (in addition to the general rules of good writing that I discuss in "Speaking Up for Yourself").

Knowing what you need to say, and then saying it

You need to know going into a description what information is important and what's not. Knowing what you want to say keeps you from getting carried away by how clearly you see the scene in your mind and how much you enjoy writing about it. You may be tempted to fill in every detail, to paint as complete a picture as possible. However, you need to avoid this temptation.

In writing, the medium is linear, and your reader's progress is dictated by the words you choose and the order in which you present them. You're never able to describe every detail, and attempting to gets in the way of your real goals.

Avoiding lost readers

If your description goes on too long and is too complex, your reader just gets lost. As you write, you see the scene in your head, so the details are all clear to you. But the reader's trying to paint the picture as she reads, and her perfect picture quickly turns into a confused scribble when she has too many details to focus on.

Only details that either provide a sense of the overall picture or play a role later in the novel matter, so focus on them and let the others go unspoken.

Preventing boredom

Descriptions that go on too long make your book drag, and slow pacing (as I discuss in Chapter 10) is a problem that can literally put your reader to sleep. Keep your descriptions to a paragraph or two, not something you can count in pages — which means you should focus on only what the reader needs to know. Often, you get a chance to fill in more details later in the book, creating your description piece by piece, rather than in one hard-to-digest chunk.

For instance, if you're writing a Regency romance, your hero probably lives in a manor house, which the reader needs to be able to visualize. As your heroine's carriage drives up the tree-lined approach, your reader sees the house for the first time, so start your description with the stately façade and a general sense of the landscaping, perhaps mentioning the terrace and garden bordering the east side of the house, the gazebo on the small rise to the west, or how the property slopes to meet the sea to the south. As the heroine walks inside, you can describe the foyer and perhaps the bedroom that she's led to.

Instead of giving the heroine and the reader a room-by-room tour of the house, end your description there, let the book move on, and describe other rooms later, when the action takes the characters into them. And if the heroine never sees all the rooms — the kitchens, for example — your reader never needs to see them, either, even if they're mentioned at some point in the book.

As for the garden, the gazebo, or the sea, you may not need to describe them further, unless they become key to the action. If the hero dances the heroine out onto the terrace and then leads her into the garden to steal a kiss, that's the time to talk about statuary and the romantic scent of roses by moonlight.

Speaking metaphorically

Use metaphors in moderation. Incorporating a lot of metaphors in your descriptions can be tempting, because they give you a chance to be creative and stretch your skills. Do your best to resist the temptation, though. Too many metaphors — just like too many adjectives — get in the way of your real goal: involving the reader in your characters' relationship. When used sparingly, metaphors add to a description; so each time you're tempted to add one, make sure that it contributes to the overall impact of your story. If you're just showcasing your own skills, cut it.

Describing your characters

Character descriptions are subject to the same cautions as all descriptions (see the "Choosing your words wisely" section earlier). You want to give a complete and compelling picture of your hero and heroine, and your major supporting players also require enough description to make them individuals in the reader's mind — just not so much that they rival your main characters in importance. Describe minor characters fully enough to fulfill the reader's need for information, but no more (see Chapter 4 for character development).

The amount of time spent describing a character is a signal to the reader about how important the character is, so keep the amount of detail appropriate to the role.

Making every word count

Choose loaded words, not neutral ones, so that every word counts. As much as possible, use words that do more than describe the basics. Use words — or add an extra, if the payoff's great enough — that convey feeling and affect your reader. A canyon isn't just deep, it's dizzying. A mountainside isn't just rocky, it's jagged. Your heroine's hair isn't just soft, it's silken. A sideboard isn't just loaded with serving dishes, it's groaning under the weight of them. The air isn't just thick, it's swirling with dank tendrils of mist. Know what effect you want to create and choose the most effective words. One well-chosen word is worth more than a dozen that don't quite hit your mark.

Don't get lost in your thesaurus. A thesaurus can be a great tool when used sparingly and with knowledge. It can also mark a writer as a rank amateur who hasn't mastered either vocabulary or the tenets of good writing (for more on the problems presented by overusing a thesaurus, see Chapter 14).

Talking too much

Make sure that you don't talk too much, whether in your description or narration. This idea is key and is really an extension of knowing what you need to say. Describe something because, and only because, the reader needs that knowledge to fully enjoy your book. As the author, your job is always to give the reader what she wants, and what she wants is interaction between the hero and heroine and their eventual happy (and romantic) ending.

To keep the reader happy, you need to keep the book moving. To keep the book moving, you have to keep your descriptive passages to a minimum and make them as brief as possible (see the section "Moving right along" later in this chapter). Don't describe things that are interesting but unimportant. Even if your reader shares your interest, the book ultimately loses its ability to compel her to turn the pages, because you're taking too many side trips into territory that isn't directly related to the events in your story. She may finish the novel, but she's unlikely to look for more of your books in the future. And readers who don't find your digressions interesting lose patience even sooner and put the book down for good.

Don't use your book as a soapbox. Romance novels are popular because they entertain readers and because they offer an escape from real life into a world of romantic fantasy. So don't use your book as a pulpit from which to preach your views on politics, world peace, ecology, the economy, or anything else. Your characters are welcome to have opinions of their own, but when you forget the rules of good characterization and put your own opinions into your characters' mouths or slip them into your descriptive or narrative passages, the reader knows she's really hearing you preach to her — and she'll resent it.

Telling It Like It Is

Much of the action in any book can easily be described in minor phrases, often interspersed with dialogue. For instance, the heroine walks across a room while talking to her best friend, or the hero shuffles papers on his desk while talking on the phone to the heroine. Other times, just a few straightforward lines are enough to explain a character's actions: The hero saddles a horse and rides off across the pasture, or the heroine puts a pie in the oven and then sits down to read while it bakes. The tips in this section apply to even these minor examples, but they're most handy when you need to spend an extended amount of time talking about what a character is doing, and you don't want to confuse your reader or slow down your story.

Keeping your writing clear

One advantage that the movies have over books is in clarity. Watching something happen on-screen is the easiest way to understand what's going on, what even a complex process entails. In the absence of visuals, authors have to describe what are sometimes complicated actions so the reader understands what's occurring. The following tips can help you maintain clarity:

✔ **Simplify, simplify, simplify:** The more complicated the action is, the more confusing it is for the reader. Simplify as much as you can. For example, if your hero's a doctor and your heroine's a nurse, and you have a key scene set in the operating room, focus on the interaction between the two of them — which is what the reader really wants to see — and not the by-the-book details of the operation. Tell the reader enough so she can follow how the operation is progressing, paralleling the progress of the operation with what the characters are *really* thinking about, but not so much that she feels like she's operating herself and doesn't have time to worry about a romance going on in the background.

✔ **A little tech talk goes a long way:** Every profession and hobby has a specialized vocabulary and, when used judiciously, pieces of that vocabulary can give your book the ring of truth. But when you load a scene with too many specialized words that most readers don't understand, you confuse people, slow the book down, and even cause some readers to put your book down in frustration.

As you describe what the characters are doing, choose words whose meanings are clear enough from the context so the reader doesn't feel like she's missing something without a definition. Say that your heroine bridles her horse, not that she slips the egg-butt snaffle into his mouth, adjusts the martingale, and tightens the throat latch.

✔ **Summarize when you can:** If your hero and heroine are in a car, racing through the narrow streets of a small Italian village with a killer on their tail, don't map out every twist and turn of the route. Use a sentence or two to say that they're going at a breakneck pace, sending pets and pedestrians scattering, passing the small hotel where the heroine stayed, and blindly rounding corners. Spend the rest of the scene on what counts: their conversation and how they feel about what's going on.

You can use these same techniques to get across hard information that you turned up in your research. Stick to what the reader needs to know, break the information into manageable chunks and insert it as necessary. Mix the chunks of information with action, and remember to be as clear as you can. You want to teach the reader what she needs to know without her realizing she's just gone back to school.

Moving right along

Don't get so caught up describing what the characters are doing that you lose track of the emotional side of your story or slow your pacing. Being clear and concise always helps maintain your story's emotion and pacing, but the following strategies can also help.

Mixing action with dialogue or thoughts

A step-by-step explanation of what's going on can be dry and unemotional, and your reader isn't looking for an instruction manual or a textbook. If you mix dialogue or a character's inner responses with the more cut-and-dried description of unfolding events, you not only break up the potentially dry part into easier-to-digest pieces, but you also add emotional resonance to it. If you have your couple investigating a case, examining reports and clues, let the heroine notice the concentration in the hero's eyes as he reads through the case reports. Let the hero see how vulnerable she looks when he asks her about her missing sister. Intersperse their reactions to each other with the action, and the action automatically becomes more interesting to the reader.

Writing prose that moves

Some scenes move quickly just because of what's happening. A car chase has its own momentum, and a life-and-death operation keeps people reading quickly so they can discover the outcome. But what if your characters are mucking out stalls? That's not a dramatic activity and certainly isn't an intrinsically romantic one.

 You can make any scene move by using longer, flowing, active sentences instead of short, declarative ones. Notice the difference between the following two paragraphs. Nothing different happens in the second paragraph than in the first, but the prose moves more quickly because the sentences run longer and are more active, so the reader isn't constantly being pulled up short.

> *Rick lifted a forkful of manure. He tossed it into the wheelbarrow, and then looked over at Melanie. She had almost finished the first stall. She didn't look happy, though. He hoisted another forkful of dirty straw, then another. Soon he had filled the wheelbarrow. He would have to pass by her on his way to the manure pile. He hoped she wouldn't toss a barbed remark — or worse — his way.*

versus

As he tossed a forkful of manure into the wheelbarrow, Rick looked over at Melanie. Despite having almost finished the first stall, she looked anything but happy. He went back to heaving dirty straw, and soon he'd filled the wheelbarrow. As he wheeled it past her, he found himself hoping she wouldn't be tossing any barbed remarks — or worse — in his direction.

Another part of writing prose that moves is using contractions. Romances are popular fiction, and even the narrative passages should feel informal and move quickly. That means contractions aren't only fine, they're preferable.

Making life interesting

Make sure that something interesting — emotionally, plotwise, or both — is happening. You may have your characters mucking out stalls for a good plot-related reason — maybe someone's been doping racehorses and the heroine's about to uncover a syringe in the straw — but the scene always moves faster when something emotionally important is also hanging in the balance. Maybe the hero's trying to figure out how to ask the heroine on a date, but first her bad mood gets in the way, followed by the discovery of the syringe. He's lost his chance, but your reader hasn't lost a step, because so much has happened that she hasn't had time to be bored by the characters mucking out stalls.

Breaking up the action

Breaking up the action is a technique that works well when you need to talk about something that's not very exciting (like mucking out stalls). The technique works even better when you're talking about something that *is* exciting. Start the action, and then cut away to something else — like a scene that's occurring simultaneously elsewhere, or a flashback, a memory, or a daydream. If the action you're leaving isn't exciting by its own nature, then your reader will enjoy the break. And if the action you're leaving *is* exciting, she'll read quickly so she can get back and see what happens. Essentially, you'll have built a mini-cliffhanger into the middle of your scene.

Chapter 9

Hearing Voices: Letting Your Characters Speak

....

....

*Y*ou have two kinds of voices in a romance novel, and both are important. The first is your own author voice, which I discuss in Chapter 8, and the second is the subject of this chapter — your characters' voices.

Your voice should, for the most part, go unnoticed. Your reader *should* hear your characters' voices and feel that your characters are the ones actually carrying the story. In your reader's mind, real voices make for real people, and real people (as I explain in Chapter 4) create the kind of identification and emotional involvement that make a reader happy with your book and can propel you to the top of her must-read list.

You have three techniques at your disposal for conveying your characters' voices — dialogue, point of view, and internal monologue. Once you master these three techniques, you can feel confident that you're doing all you can to let your characters carry the story and, in the process, deepen your reader's involvement in what's going on. In this chapter, I talk about using all three of these approaches to give your characters their own voices, as well as how to use those voices effectively. I also help you avoid some of the traps new writers often fall into, so you can make your book and your characters strong enough to please an editor.

Giving Your Characters Voices

The best possible thing that can happen to you is for your characters to become so real in your own mind that writing dialogue feels almost like taking dictation. Their voices should become so real that the reader feels like she's eavesdropping on their lives.

Your characters' voices come across most noticeably and obviously in dialogue, which is literally their chance to speak. But the totality of any character's voice is a conglomeration of dialogue with his or her thoughts and feelings. The lines between the various components of character voice are often fuzzy, but their role is always to present a particular character's words, thoughts, and feelings, so you can always recognize character voice by its function, even when it's hard to determine the specific technique being used.

Making every character unique (and real)

Just as you wouldn't make two characters look the same (unless they're twins or your plot depends on the similarity in their looks), you don't want to make any two characters sound exactly the same. Even though people from the same part of the country or members of the same family may sound a lot alike (sharing speech patterns, vocabulary, and even expressions), they don't sound identical to each other, and neither should your characters.

The reader must connect with your characters, and for that to happen, your characters must feel real. And to make every character, even the secondary ones, feel real, you have to give each one a voice of his or her own. (For all the ins and outs of characterization, see Chapter 4; also see the "Meeting the secondary-character challenge" section later in this chapter.) You can do a lot of things (and you can also avoid doing some things) to make every character sound unique.

Reining in your own voice

Don't let your own voice come through for every character. Your heroine, especially in your first book, may sound a lot like you. That's okay — just be sure every heroine you ever write doesn't also sound like you, because you don't want readers to think you can't actually create a character. And even if your heroine sounds like you, make sure nobody else in the book does, or all your characters will end up sounding like the same person.

Listening to your own voice objectively and then avoiding replicating it over and over can sometimes be hard, but you can do two things to help yourself:

- Compare your speech patterns to those of other people (friends and family who live far away included, to account for regionalisms) and see whether you have certain words or phrases you use constantly that others don't. Then avoid having all your characters use those phrases.

- Make a conscious effort to create unique voices for your characters, comparing their speech patterns to each other and varying them.

Bringing up backgrounds

A character from the South talks differently than one from New England, not to mention one from Merry *Olde* England. Don't go overboard highlighting regional differences, but don't ignore them, either. Education and social standing also affect the way people, including your characters, speak. Word order, cadences and pronunciation, and colloquialisms can help differentiate characters' voices. (Check out the "Using dialect and accents effectively" section later in the chapter for more on matching backgrounds and dialogue.)

Separating the sexes

Men and women talk differently. Women are more likely to focus on feelings, and men on problem solving. It's a cliché, but it's true, so don't make your men — especially your hero — too sensitive and girlie. Your hero shouldn't be a caveman, but he should be a *man*.

If your hero's dialogue seems to be having a gender-identity problem, eavesdrop shamelessly — but not obviously, of course — whenever you're in the vicinity of men talking together. You'll pick up on male speech patterns and "guy shorthand" that'll make your hero sound like a manly man.

And a strong, proactive heroine should still sound like a woman, not one of the guys. If circumstances demand that she talk tough — for example, if she's in the military and giving orders to a bunch of hard cases who can't believe their commanding officer is a woman — be sure you use her point of view to counter the impression her words give. (For tips on that, check out "Point of View: How to Choose and How to Use" later in this chapter.)

Avoiding clichés

Not every waitress snaps gum while she talks, and not all single women in their 30s are bitter about men. Even if a character shares an aspect of the cliché, that aspect shouldn't be the sum total of his or her personality, so don't make that thirty-something friend drag her bad experiences with men into every conversation. Let her talk about other things, too.

Spoken clichés can be just as off-putting. Unless it's part of someone's character to always reel off a cliché at any difficult moment, try not to use more than a few and make sure that you use them effectively — as a way for your hero to avoid revealing his real emotions, for instance. But don't let clichés substitute for a character's real voice.

Speaking up

Remember that dialogue represents spoken English. People speak informally — sometimes even ungrammatically, depending on their backgrounds — so don't let your characters sound like examples from a grammar text. Even if speaking in perfect English informs your character, be sure he or she still sounds like a person, even if an uptight, snobby, or pretentious one. And don't make everyone informal in the exact same way.

To see just how real your dialogue sounds, read it aloud. Read it into a tape recorder, if at all possible, and play it back. Even the act of reading it aloud tells you a lot. Do the words flow easily, or have you placed them awkwardly, so that they trip you up? Are your sentences so long that you can't even complete them without pausing for breath? Are there so many asides that you forget where you are? Is figuring out where to pause or what to emphasize impossible? If you answer "yes" to any of these questions, go back and rework the dialogue until it sounds like spoken, not written, English.

Working out the quirks

Use quirks sparingly. You can set someone's dialogue apart by giving them a verbal quirk or a difficulty in pronunciation: a tendency to pause a lot, to cut themselves off and correct themselves as they go, a lisp, or a stutter. Used sparingly, such a noticeable speech pattern can help to create a character's voice, but remember that a little goes a long way. Don't insert the quirk into that character's every line. Use (or mention) it often enough to let the reader know it exists, but don't bash her senseless by emphasizing it. You also shouldn't give every character a quirk or a problem, and you probably want to steer clear of giving them to your hero and heroine at all. They're on the page most of the time, and you can drive yourself — and your reader — nuts if you have to work something so noticeable into the bulk of your dialogue.

Giving every character a consistent voice

After you create a unique voice for each character, you need to keep that voice consistent and not let one character's speech patterns start leaching into another's. Depending on your own writing preferences and how real each and every character has become to you, you may find that keeping voices unique is easy to do as you write, but no matter what, you should pay special attention to voices as you do one of your later reads of the story.

You may even want to devote one pass solely to looking at dialogue, if you start catching a lot of problems as you go. Think about the voice you intended to create for each character and make sure you stayed true to your vision all the way through. That's the key to keeping the reader's belief and involvement unbroken. Make sure you aren't overusing certain words or expressions, putting them in everyone's mouth. Make sure a character who normally speaks in short, declarative sentences doesn't suddenly launch into a long, self-involved soliloquy (unless that dramatic change is important to your story). Make sure a character who's not too bright and never graduated high school doesn't suddenly start using the word "soliloquy."

Speaking historically

In addition to everything else you need to keep in mind, if you're writing a historical romance, you also need to think about the vocabulary and speech patterns of the era you've chosen. At the same time, you're writing for a contemporary audience, so make sure your reader can understand your dialogue. Avoid *anachronisms,* words and phrases (and facts) that are inappropriate to the time. To avoid using words that are too modern for your setting, use an etymological dictionary to tell you when a word came into general use in the English language. On the other hand, don't immerse yourself so deeply in the past that your reader doesn't understand anything your characters are saying.

Also avoid using stiffness and formality as a way to indicate that you're writing about the past, especially for lower-class characters in what was almost certainly an extremely class-conscious society. Historical dialogue still has to flow and sound smooth to a contemporary reader's ear; if the dialogue's too stiff, it won't sound natural, and the reader will lose interest in your characters and their story. Don't rely on words like *thee, hath,* and *canst* over and over. Don't use them at all unless they're appropriate for the particular period you've chosen. Even if these words are historically correct, don't load up every sentence with them, otherwise your dialogue gets in the way of readers actually getting to know and care about your characters as people.

Meeting the secondary-character challenge

Usually, the task of writing dialogue is relatively easy with your hero and heroine, because they're your most fully realized characters, so you may not even have to think very hard about how they sound. In fact, if you're writing a contemporary romance, the heroine of your first book will quite often sound a lot like you, so she's very easy for you to create.

It's often a trickier proposition to make the secondary characters sound unique, because they're not on stage as much — sometimes only for a single scene or a single line — so the temptation is to hurry through their bits, have them play their parts (giving information, acting as a sounding board for the hero or heroine, and so on), and then move on with your main story. As a result, they often sound like clichés: the supportive best friend, the hound-dog male co-worker who comments on every woman, the amusingly bitter single friend, the Cockney coachman. (For more on this subject, see the "Avoiding clichés" section earlier in this chapter.)

But don't try so hard to make every character stand out as witty, wise, exceptionally quick- or slow-witted, or anything else that may distract your reader from the central romance for too long. Think of them in the Hollywood sense — they're characters, not extras, but they also have a specific job to do. They're meant to support your hero and heroine and *their* story, not shout, "Look at me!"

You can also get trapped in writing secondary characters who don't have any character at all, whose dialogue is so plain that a reader forgets it and the characters as soon as she reads what they have to say. With truly minor characters, this trap is less problematic, even a positive, simply because they're less important. But for any character who has an actual role to play (as opposed to a line like "You can catch the 4:07 on platform nine if you hurry"), dialogue without character leaves a vacuum in your book. Your story comes to life when your hero and heroine are on the page, but the reader's mind wanders whenever anyone else is talking — and your reader's quite likely to put down your book for good.

Writing Great Dialogue

No matter how beautifully you write *narrative* — which includes everything that represents your voice (the subject of Chapter 8) rather than your characters' voices — no matter how clever your plot, no matter how complex and interesting an emotional conflict you set up, if you can't write dialogue, you can't write a good romance. Good dialogue is one of the make-or-break elements every editor looks for, so I spend some time in this section giving you all the ins and outs.

Supermodels are beautiful, but they're just pictures without a personality. Actors are often just as attractive, but in the viewer's mind, they take on the attributes of the characters they play, and that — not just their looks — makes them interesting and turns viewers into fans. Actors get to speak, not just pose. In the same way, dialogue makes your characters exist for the reader. They, too, get to speak, to step off the page and into the reader's mind and heart. Your story is the stage, your characters are the actors, and no one goes to the theater to see the pretty sets.

Using dialect and accents effectively

Part of creating unique character voices comes from knowing your characters' backgrounds and incorporating that knowledge into their dialogue. That often means writing dialect or an accent — one of the trickiest things to do right, and getting it wrong sends up a red flag to an editor, telling her that you're not a pro.

Here's the short and simple thing to remember: Whether you're dealing with your hero, heroine, or a secondary character, don't spell out dialects and accents phonetically. It looks ridiculous:

> *"Eeze zat true?" Pierre asked. "Eeze Emeelee really meesing?"*

or

> *"Ah juss doe know, shuguh," May-Ellen said. "Whah don' you go ask yer pappy?"*

This dialogue is hard to read, for one thing. So many words are misspelled, even if they're written out phonetically, that the reader gets pulled right out of the world of the book. The dialogue is also so self-conscious that it's laughable, which may be fine if you're writing romantic comedy and a character's overdoing things for effect, but if you're writing romantic suspense and trying to build up a menacing atmosphere, it isn't so great. Instead, follow this advice:

- ✔ Just use an occasional "misspelled" word and let that stand in for the rest, and occasionally describe the way the reader should be hearing the words. Definitely mention an accent the first time a character speaks, which is also a good time to misspell a word or two, and then remind the reader of the character's quirks every so often as you go on. Not every time the character speaks, though, otherwise the reader will feel like you're smacking her over the head with the info. This strategy also holds true if you want to indicate any kind of verbal quirk, such as speaking slowly, with frequent pauses. Inserting ellipses every few words looks awkward; an occasional reminder to the reader is much more effective.

- ✔ Instead of writing *just* (or *juss*), write *jus'*, letting the apostrophe stand in for the missing letter. Although this rule seems to contradict the dialogue strategy I previously advise you on, using an apostrophe to indicate a dropped letter is one case where you should be consistent. If you drop the final *g* in a character's dialogue, do so each time he or she speaks. If the character says *runnin'*, then he or she also says *goin'*, *smilin'*, and *sittin'*. Because the apostrophe makes for such an unmistakable visual, I recommend avoiding a need for it in your hero and heroine's dialogue, because they'll be speaking so often during the course of your book.

- ✔ You can also use word order to indicate an accent. English *syntax,* the normal patterns of speech and sentence structure that govern the way nouns, verbs, and other parts of speech are organized, is different from the syntax of other languages, so use the character's native syntax, along with a mention of his or her accent, to tell the reader how to hear the character's speech. Be careful, though — don't jumble up the word order so thoroughly that sentences become impossible to follow. As with so many other things in written dialogue, a little goes a long way.

✔ An occasional regionalism or tossed-in foreign word (one that the reader can easily understand in context) can also indicate where a character's from and give a unique edge to his or her dialogue without getting in the way. You want to flavor the dialogue without overwhelming the reader.

Keepin' it cool: A word about slang

You can use slang as a wonderful way to differentiate characters, to tell the young from the old, Yankees from Southern belles from Aussie jackaroos. But a little goes a long way if you're writing for a general audience. (A hip-hop flavored romance is going to lean much more heavily on slang, but it's also going to have a narrower target audience.)

Using slang has pitfalls, though, even when you don't overuse it. You need to be aware of these pitfalls so you can decide how to avoid them. By its very nature, slang ties itself to a specific time period — often a very brief one — and sometimes even to a specific place. If you get it wrong, you risk looking foolish and, worse, making your characters look foolish. This risk isn't just a part of historical romances, where you don't want contemporary expressions like "cool," "it blew me away," or "radical" to intrude.

Don't use last year's slang in a contemporary romance, a book intended to take place in what I always call the *eternal present,* because your reader should feel as she reads that your story could be taking place that very minute, even though you may have written it a year or more ago. Passé slang makes your book sound dated, as does setting a book in the '90s and having your characters all speak like refugees from the '60s. Writing a book set in the '50s and using '60s slang isn't any better, because readers will certainly pick up on the inaccuracies.

Ultimately, you need to decide for yourself just how current and time-sensitive you want your language to be. But when I'm asked for advice, I always suggest keeping slang to a minimum (the youngest characters usually use the most slang in their speech, just like in real life) and steering clear of really trendy phrases in favor of those phrases that have stood the test of time. *Cool* will probably be with us forever and, well, I'm cool with that.

Another reason to steer clear of too much slang is that slang makes translating your book for sale in foreign markets more difficult. Translation is generally more of an issue with series books, because so many of them are published overseas, than for all but the most popular mainstream authors. But because your goal is to be popular, sell a lot of copies, and be available all over the world, you may want to keep this particular slang issue in mind even if you're writing mainstream romances.

Using dialogue to convey information naturally

Most people don't lecture for a living, and the same is true of most characters. Even when your character's an expert in his or her field, putting long, fact-filled speeches in his or her mouth still doesn't read well. Having long passages of spoken explanation or the recitation of endless facts plunked down in the middle of the story is simply a turn-off (and, generally, a real drag on pacing), no matter who has the floor, you or one of your characters.

I'm not saying that you can't use your characters to convey necessary pieces of information, whether that info is a description of someone or somewhere, a plot twist, or details of your research, but I *am* saying that you need to be very careful in how you do it. As I discuss in Chapter 13, you have to first accept the fact that your research will uncover a lot more info than your reader needs or wants to know. Before anyone starts saying anything, pare down the information so that you know which bits need to go into the book and which bits don't. Apply this same strategy when you want to convey a detailed description of something or a complex piece of plotting. Dialogue may help you get the basics across, but it's not the place to put every detail or twist, even those you feel are necessary.

After you've decided what info you need to include, think about the best way to explain the necessary bits to the reader. You may decide narrative is the way to go, in which case, take a look at the section in Chapter 8 where I talk about narrative writing. The techniques I discuss in Chapter 8 apply to conveying any kind of information. If you decide to let your characters get the information across for you, here are some tips to keep in mind:

- **Break it up:** A long lecture really stops your story's momentum. Deal with the information piecemeal, letting your characters explain only what's necessary — and only *when* it's necessary.

- **Use natural language:** Don't make a character who usually talks in a normal, realistic way suddenly get all stiff and formal, as if she's quoting an instruction manual or addressing a grad-school seminar. Keep her speech patterns normal and avoid as many technical terms as you can.

- **Don't forget that you're writing a romance:** Along with conveying information, convey characterization, whether through tone of voice or the characters' behavior — for example, the hero's inability to focus fully on what the heroine's telling him because he can't stop looking at her lips, or the heroine momentarily losing her train of thought when she notices how handsome the hero looks when he's listening intently.

✔ **Use conversation:** Alternating between questions and answers lets you follow these tips simultaneously, and it's especially helpful if you have a fair bit of information that you have to convey all at once. This technique breaks things up and gives everything a normal, conversational feel (if you do it right). Using conversation also lets you build your characters while you convey information, because you show them reacting to each other. You can even convey emotional subtext while your characters talk about whatever cold, hard facts you need to convey. Just don't let the Q & A session go on so long that it feels like an interview.

Avoid having two characters talk about something they both know simply because the reader needs to know it. I see this mistake all the time. The reader gets irritated because the conversation feels so artificial. If you're in a position where you need to tell the reader something and the characters can't talk about it naturally, you can always drop into someone's point of view or use internal monologue, which I talk about later in this chapter.

Putting dialogue on paper

Writing good dialogue involves more than just knowing what your characters need to say and how they'd say it. You also need to know how to put it on the page so that it works for an editor and a reader. Some editors feel more strongly than others about various formatting points, but you can't go wrong if you take all the tips in the following list to heart:

✔ **Don't use semicolons or colons in dialogue.** Semicolons and colons are written punctuation. In speech, meaning dialogue, people either pause (a comma) or stop and start another sentence (a period). Punctuating your dialogue that way better reflects real speech and sounds more realistic in the reader's mind. Plus, the dialogue doesn't look so written, even though it is.

✔ **Don't use parentheses in dialogue.** Like semicolons and colons, parentheses are written punctuation. Set off an aside with dashes or ellipses, both of which reflect natural speech patterns.

✔ **Avoid exclamation points.** You don't need to avoid them all the time, just 99 percent of it. An exclamation point indicates that a character yells a piece of dialogue or speaks with strong emotion, and most people don't speak at the tops of their voices all the time. If you emphasize everything with an exclamation point, nothing stands out after a while. It's like the boy who cried wolf. When you finally really need to have someone shout something important, like yelling, *Get down!* when bullets start flying, the exclamation doesn't register on your reader as any more important than *I'm going to the store!* and *We're out of fabric softener!*

✔ **He said, she said.** You don't need to use characters' names all the time in dialogue attribution. After you establish who's speaking, you can use pronouns most, if not all, of the time. Text reads as self-conscious and awkward when you see names everywhere, and it feels repetitive in a way pronouns don't.

✔ **Be conservative with dialogue tags.** In an effort to sound different from everyone else or to clarify how a piece of dialogue should sound, authors sometimes ignore the perfectly serviceable (and usually preferable) *said* in favor of words like *groaned, hissed, chortled, cried, giggled, sighed, shouted, laughed,* and so on.

All of those descriptors are fine — occasionally (okay, except maybe *chortled,* which describes a sound that I just don't think most people make). Like exclamation points, save them for when you really need them. Most dialogue is simply spoken, and the words and context give all the necessary clues as to how it gets said. Save extraordinary tags for extraordinary circumstances. If every line has a unique tag attached to it, the tags start drawing attention to themselves at the expense of what your characters are actually saying.

✔ **A dialogue tag has to indicate sound.** You speak dialogue, so any tag attached to it has to involve noise. Dialogue can't be smiled or grinned or seethed, or, worse yet, acted out. For example, this sentence is wrong: *"Hi there," he walked across the room.* If you need to get across something beyond the sound of a line, go with something like:

- *"Hi there." He walked across the room.*
- *"Hello," he said with a smile.*
- *"I can't believe you did that," she said, seething internally.*

✔ **You can't hiss without an *s*.** Hissing, by definition, requires an *ess* sound. You can hiss *yes* or *I hate Christmas* (though only if you're very, very mean), but you can't hiss *no* or *I hate my birthday.* Unfortunately, I don't know of any way to describe that way of speaking that's a cross between a hiss and a whisper in a single word, so if you want a character to deliver a line in that unfortunately indescribable tone, you have to do your best to indicate it in some way other than calling it a hiss.

✔ **Be careful with unattributed dialogue.** If two characters are talking, you don't have to identify the speaker of each line, so long as the reader knows who's speaking. Pages and pages of unattributed dialogue will almost certainly confuse your reader, though, especially if the speeches are brief and don't give you a chance to use voice to establish character. I've been confused more than once, and I've counted speeches from the last attributed line and discovered that the author got confused, too, having the same person say something and then provide the response.

✔ **Three or more speakers require extra care.** You can't just say *he said* and *she said* when your conversation has three or more speakers, because you're going to have at least two characters of the same gender. That's the time to use names or descriptions *(the older woman, the heavyset man)* to identify the speaker. And never use unattributed dialogue in scenes with many characters.

✔ **The rules of logic apply.** In real life, conversations are often elliptical, and people answer questions or refer to things that someone said several sentences back. In written dialogue, though, responses need to follow logically on what was said immediately beforehand, not a line or three back. Written dialogue needs to feel real, rather than be real. Be sure that one character's response follows logically from the last thing the previous character said, and don't put too much narrative or description in between, diverting the reader's train of thought.

Point of View: How to Choose and How to Use

Even when your characters aren't speaking to each other, they can still speak to the reader via your use of point of view (or POV, the common abbreviation for point of view) and internal monologue (a way of revealing a character's innermost thoughts). Most popular fiction deals heavily in POV, but romance is especially reliant on it, because romances are all about emotion, and the best way to communicate emotion — or build a reader's identification with a character — is through POV.

Point of view, as it's used in this book and in terms of popular fiction, generally means describing the action as a particular character experiences it, complete with thoughts, reactions, and emotional responses. Using a character's point of view doesn't mean dropping into first person, though you can use first person for brief periods (usually only a line or two, as a character talks to herself or himself silently; see the "Is there a place for first-person point of view?" sidebar in this chapter).

What are they thinking?

Most of the time, you should use point of view in small doses — a line or two attached to a piece of dialogue or mixed in with the action of the book. As I say in Chapter 8, your narrative voice and your characters' thoughts often become so intertwined that one can't even exist without the other. Your voice tells the reader what's happening in terms of place and plot. Point of view lets you clarify what's going on inside your characters' minds, telling the reader what your characters can't tell each other, and clarifying why things are happening and what they really mean.

Articulating the attraction

Because a writer builds a romance around two characters falling in love but not being able to talk about it (as I discuss in Chapter 5), your characters very often say and do one thing while thinking something else entirely. Because of that, you need point of view to describe what's really going on. Otherwise, the reader can't understand your characters' inner lives, which are the most important sides of things in a book that's ultimately all about emotions.

Your hero and heroine may be having a knockdown, drag-out fight about something plot-related, and if the reader only sees their dialogue, she thinks they hate each other. By getting inside your characters' minds, you can give the reader the real story. You can show her that they're actually incredibly attracted to each other, even when they're making each other furious — that your heroine hates being at odds with your hero, that he loves to watch her eyes snap with anger and wonders if they'd spark equally hot with passion.

You can do the same thing during action scenes. Even as you put most of the focus on the externals, on what's happening, a few economical but well-placed lines of POV, even just a word or two, can keep the romance front and center in your reader's mind, adding emotional depth to the simplest actions.

Feeling the love

One of the most important places where your characters' thoughts can illuminate what's really going on is in your love scenes. Your characters can't let each other know how they feel, but your reader needs to know they're not just indulging in a purely physical one- (or two- or more) night stand, and that they're developing real feelings for each other. Point of view is crucial because it lets you make the characters' feelings, not just their actions, clear, and the reader cares about their feelings. Your characters' feelings make them come alive as sympathetic people deserving not only of making love but of feeling it.

Getting practical

Other times, you may need to drop from dialogue or action into a key character's point of view for practical reasons, because you can convey a piece of information the reader needs most easily that way. Having two characters discussing the details of something they both already know sometimes feels artificial, but you can use one character's POV to give the reader the information in a subtler, more natural way. Other times, you don't have anyone else on the scene, so your character's thoughts are the only way to get information to the reader and still keep the story moving forward.

Knowing whose voice to use

To use point of view effectively, you need to decide whose head to get into. Authors of romances, especially series romances, used to tell the story exclusively from the heroine's POV. The hero's thoughts often remained a great mystery right up until the end, when he finally broke his silence and admitted to the heroine that, all indications to the contrary, he loved her. Those days, I'm very happy to say, are gone.

These days, almost every romance uses both the hero and heroine's points of view, but romances don't generally use a lot of points of view besides those two, or use them frequently. As a general rule, if the heroine or the hero is present, use one or both of their points of view, not the POV of any other characters on hand. Jumping into minor characters' heads simply because they're there is, at best, self-indulgent and, at worst, lazy and amateurish. You can't go wrong telling a romance only from the heroine and hero's points of view (or even just the heroine's, though keeping the reader in the dark as to the hero's thoughts can prove tricky in terms of building up understanding and empathy).

In romantic suspense, you may get the villain's point of view, and important secondary characters in any romance sometimes have points of view, as well (mainly when they have crucial insights into the hero and heroine's relationship or when they're involved in a strong secondary romance). For more on using secondary characters, check out Chapter 4.

Series romances limit the number of points of view more strictly than mainstream romances do, in large part because of the constraints of length. So knowing your market (something I talk about in Chapter 2) also helps you determine how free you can be in choosing point-of-view characters.

Avoid using so many points of view that the book, and the reader, loses focus. A romance, by definition, tells the story of a single relationship that ends happily, and too many points of view get in the way of that, turning the book into women's fiction or a relationship novel, both of which are related to romance fiction but not synonymous with it (see Chapter 2).

Determining where to begin

I strongly recommend beginning with your heroine's point of view because the story is hers, and your reader needs to identify with her. But you can begin with the hero's thoughts, if you want, without too much worry, because your reader needs to fall in love with him, so the sooner the better, right?

You just need to be sure to get them together (in the same scene, not emotionally) quickly and make sure that they focus on each other, even though the tension between them should be quite high early on in your story. You definitely don't want to write a long excursion into one character's POV, focusing on all kinds of non-romance-related things, and then write a similar excursion into the other character's POV, before they finally start to think about what's supposed to be going on in the book — their relationship.

Starting from a third character's point of view is tricky and usually ineffective, though a brief prologue that sets up the danger can sometimes be effective in romantic suspense. It helps, though, to include one of the main characters in such a prologue, either as part of the action or as the subject of the baddie's plotting. (See Chapter 12 for more info on starting your novel effectively, including tips to keep in mind when using a prologue.)

Moving from scene to scene

As you continue with the book, tell every scene, to a greater or lesser degree, from one (or more) character's point of view, not from your own as the author. Sometimes choosing whose point of view to use is easy, because your scene features only your hero or heroine (or a key secondary character who can provide necessary information that the hero or heroine can't). But, in many cases, you can choose between at least two points of view — the heroine's and the hero's.

As with so many things, I'm not big on rules. I rarely analyze whether a book uses 50 percent or more of the heroine's POV as compared to the hero's or anyone else's. I'm more concerned with whether the book works, meaning whether the writer made the most effective choices for her characters, her story, and the intended readership. But if you're aiming for a particular editor or a particular series, and they *do* have preferences, even requirements, regarding POV, listen to them and not me, because you have to give your particular editor what she wants.

There are two schools of thought on using point of view within a scene:

  ✔ **Single point of view:** This more formal school holds that you need to choose a character — for example, the heroine — and stick with her point of view for the duration of the scene or, at the very least, for a substantial portion of it. To switch POV, you need to insert a time or scene break. Editors who subscribe to this outlook usually require writers to revise scenes that employ multiple points of view so that those scenes reflect only one POV.

✓ **Multiple points of view:** I, not surprisingly, belong to this less formal school, which sees nothing wrong with what's commonly (and rather disparagingly, unfortunately) called *head hopping,* but which I prefer to think of simply as using multiple points of view. This school says that moving back and forth between your characters' points of view within the scene is fine as long as the reader doesn't get confused as to whose head she's in at any given time. We less formal sorts have no problem with writers using single or multiple points of view, leaving it up to the author to decide which works best or feels more comfortable for her.

If you're gearing a book toward a particular editor, you may know how she feels about point of view, either because she's talked about it at a conference or in a newsletter interview, or because you can make an educated guess based on reading work by the authors you know she edits. The same holds true, at least to a certain extent, if you're aiming for a specific line of series romances. By reading books from that line — something you should be doing in any case — you can at least see what's generally allowed in the line, although you may not be able to gauge a specific editor's preferences.

In the absence of either a specific target or any reliable information about an editor's or house's feelings, you can only handle point of view in the way that feels most natural to you and to the book, knowing you may turn off some editors or be asked to revise later.

If you opt for the multiple-points-of-view approach in your scene, you don't have to worry about whose POV to choose, but if you decide on the more formal approach, each scene requires you to decide whose head to enter. Ask yourself who — your heroine or your hero — has the most at stake, the most to learn, the most to tell the reader, or the most interesting take on things. Then choose his or her point of view for that scene. If you can't decide, opt for the heroine's POV, because she's your reader's way into the story.

Don't show the same scene twice, once from the heroine's point of view and again from the hero's. Too often, authors simply use this approach as a way, and an ineffective one, to lengthen a book that doesn't have enough going on. Sometimes, though, the characters see things in different ways, and you may need to show that to further your story. If you're not using multiple points of view, tell the scene from one character's point of view, say the heroine's, and then, later, let the hero reflect on that same scene. Don't retell the entire scene — just use a key moment to spur the hero to reflect on how he felt or to recall the key piece of information you need the reader to know.

Internal monologues and how to use them

An *internal monologue* is basically point of view writ large, or at least long. Most of the time, you convey your characters' thoughts and feelings in brief, even subtle, ways. But sometimes you need to stay inside someone's head longer to convey an important point, and that extended trip is an internal monologue. No formula says that "If it's over *x* number of lines, it's an internal monologue." But trust me, you'll know one when you see one. Internal monologue isn't only helpful, it's almost required, in two basic instances (both of which can recur in your book): times of emotional stress and revelation, and points when you need to convey a larger-than-usual amount of information.

The most important use of internal monologue is at moments of great emotional stress and revelation. I'm always amazed at how often I'm reading a manuscript, as caught up in the characters' difficult romance as any reader, and I finally reach the welcome point where one of them (usually the heroine first, and the hero later — maybe much later) realizes he or she loves the other. This revelation is huge, key to everything else that will happen . . . and the author simply mentions it as casually as if she were saying that the heroine loves fresh-baked chocolate chip cookies and then moves on.

A moment like that is the time for an internal monologue. The reader wants — *needs* — to know how the heroine feels about her sudden realization. Is she furious with herself for falling in love with someone who can never love her back? Furious with the hero for showing her his vulnerable side and making her fall for him, when he's the single most unsuitable man on the planet? Relieved to know she can feel love again, when she'd thought she was dead inside? Afraid, because she knows she and the hero can never work things out, so she's bound to get her heart broken in the end?

Whatever she feels, those feelings are dramatic, complicated, and fascinating, and you need to spend some time inside her head to tell the reader all about them. Your heroine needs to marvel at her feelings, analyze them, and try to figure out what they mean for her future. Your reader needs and wants to see all of that, and you need to give it to her by writing an internal monologue.

Your book has other emotional points, though usually somewhat less dramatic than a realization of love, when having your characters think about their feelings and the developing relationship makes sense, and you can also use an internal monologue in those places. Any place where a real person would take a breather and think about the big stuff going on in her (or his) life, or where some new development has just changed the picture and the character needs to do a little rethinking, lends itself to an internal monologue, even if it's only a paragraph.

The second use for internal monologue is a more practical one. You can use an internal monologue to convey information — explaining how something works, what motivates a character, what a character thinks motivates someone else, or any other type of information that doesn't comfortably fit in conversation and needs more than a line or two of explanation or clarification.

Is there a place for first-person point of view?

Probably 99 percent of all romance novels are written in third-person point of view, but some romance novels — both series and mainstream — are handled in the first person. If you want to try first-person POV, you need to know it's risky for several reasons.

✔ **The me-me-me syndrome:** A lot of first-person narration falls into the trap of sounding self-important or too self-involved. You may have trouble making someone entirely sympathetic when she's spending several hundred pages essentially talking about herself, so think long and hard about whether you, and your heroine, are up to the challenge. The fact that she's the only point of view character puts extra pressure on her, because the reader gets no respite from her; so even if she's not actively egocentric, you may want to put extra work into making sure that readers will find her interesting and appealing.

✔ **Limiting reader access:** Although you get to tell the reader everything your heroine knows, she's not going to know everything that's going on in her world, so getting across all the details of the plot can be tough. And you have to convey other characters' thoughts and feelings entirely through their words and behavior. In other words, first person can be quite limiting in ways that many writers (and some readers) find frustrating.

✔ **Going it alone:** Though related genres, like chick lit (see Chapter 2), often feature first-person POV, it's still a relative rarity in romance, so you're setting yourself up for a harder sell — not impossible, if your book is good, but definitely harder.

Check out these tips for writing effective internal monologues:

✔ **Remember your character's voice:** People think pretty much the same way they speak, so even though you're not using first-person POV, you still need to keep your character's voice in mind and let it flavor the internal monologue. Internal monologue should feel conversational, even though no actual conversation is going on, and true to the character as you've created him or her.

✔ **Use action or dialogue when it can do the work:** Too often I see manuscripts where the characters spend a lot of time thinking about what happened between them, but the author never actually shows them together or doesn't show them together often enough. Internal monologues can show the reader important details, but she still wants to actually experience the action of the story, not just hear about it.

✔ **Keep it short:** There's no hard-and-fast rule, but most of the time, devote only a page or two, max, to an internal monologue. Often you only need a paragraph or two. You may find an exception, but if your internal monologues go on for pages every time, you have a problem. You're probably repeating yourself and can cut out a lot of what you've written. If you can't cut it down, try to find a way to break it up into smaller, more manageable pieces.

Chapter 10

Pacing: The Secrets of Writing a Page-Turning Romance

. . . .

In This Chapter

▶ Using plot to support your pacing

▶ Avoiding the "sagging middle"

▶ Showing versus telling

. . . .

A great story badly (especially boringly) told fails as a story. That's not a cliché, but it should be, because it's as true as any cliché I know. The best romances are constantly referred to as page-turners, and that term refers directly to pacing.

You undoubtedly have a friend or acquaintance who can take the most interesting events and turn them into a foolproof cure for insomnia. Somewhere between "I was cashing my paycheck when two masked gunmen ran into the bank" and "Then the cute policeman asked me if I wanted to go to dinner" lies a wealth of boring detail ("It was 3:14 p.m., well, really 3:17 p.m., but my watch is slow") and digression ("I was wearing that great dress I bought when Lisa and I went shopping two weeks ago, the blue one with the cowl neck. She thought I should have gotten it in red, too, but . . .").

In real life, you can nudge your friend to keep moving: "I know the dress you mean" or "What about the policeman?" In a book, your reader is pretty well stuck. She can skim, but the point of reading a romance is to immerse herself in a world of emotion, not hunt for pieces of interesting information. If a reader ends up skimming big chunks of your book to get to the good parts, she's going to feel she didn't get her money's worth, and she's not going to waste time and money on you again. And that's assuming an editor didn't get bored and reject the book long before a reader ever saw it.

Pacing, knowing what to say, and when and how to say it, is what keeps your story moving and your reader moving with it. I touch on pacing in Chapter 8, as the subject is closely linked to author voice, but I go into a lot more detail in this chapter. Using the techniques in this chapter, you can tell the story you decide on in the best possible way.

I frame this discussion about pacing in terms of your entire book, but you need to think about how to pace individual scenes, especially key moments involving action and emotional revelations, and also love scenes, which can be slow and sensuous or intense and fast-paced. The general pacing techniques I provide for your manuscript are just as applicable to individual scenes.

Pacing Doesn't Mean Racing

"Don't eat too fast or you'll choke." You should take that warning to heart when you write, too. Overall, you want your book to move along at a good clip, but that doesn't mean you have to race for the finish line (or the final page) or that every paragraph has to move quickly.

For one thing, if your pacing is all the same — whether that's fast, slow, or somewhere in between — your book gets boring. To quote another applicable cliché, variety is the spice of life. Your book benefits if you vary the pace. Slow things down occasionally, not to a crawl or a dead stop, but just enough so that the reader feels the difference.

Nonstop excitement ends up feeling like the normal state of affairs, so it's no longer exciting. If you slow things down to a more usual pace, your reader's adrenalin starts pumping again the next time the action and the emotion pick up.

You also need to give your reader an occasional breather, especially when you're writing action or adventure. Even if you only have her, and your characters, perched on an emotional high wire, she needs a break occasionally so that she can pull herself together. After you've revealed a key piece of information or allowed the characters a moment of emotional or physical closeness, let them, and the reader, enjoy that moment. Give them time to reflect on what it means and then move forward toward the next milestone, the answer to the next question. Just be sure you never bring the book to a halt. Vary the tempo, but don't stop it in its tracks.

Pacing and Plotting: Two Halves of a Whole

The first thing you need to know is that pacing and plotting go hand in hand. Your plot is concrete, made up of events that move in succession and create your story. *Pacing* is a technique — a key technique — for both structuring those elements and writing about them. If you have a strong, interesting plot, the reader already wants to turn the pages. (See Chapter 5 for all the details of constructing a plot.) And if you know the tricks of successful pacing, you can make her want to turn those pages even faster. First, you need to figure out how to recognize the key elements of your story, which are the building blocks you use to create pacing that works.

Good pacing is, in my opinion, more about structural decisions than about your actual writing. A lot of would-be authors don't know that. Now that you do, you're a step ahead because you can — and should — think about pacing from the moment you start conceptualizing your story.

Knowing what readers care about

If the only things that made readers turn pages were action, action, and more action, things would get really boring really quickly, because everything would be the same. Your characters don't need to be running around doing exciting things all the time in order for your book to move. Even if you do write a more action-oriented romance, you still need to break up that action.

Mystery, suspense, and adventure plots, or any kind of a search (for treasure, for the truth about someone's past or a child's parentage, for a cure or other scientific discovery, or for the answer to a secret) have a built-in momentum. But to achieve effective pacing, you need more than an exciting plot. You have to be able to recognize what you're working with before you can use it effectively.

Recognizing key plot points

Your plot should include certain key events, what I call *milestones* when I discuss outlining in Chapter 7. With a few major exceptions, the specifics vary from book to book, because your story is never exactly like anyone else's. Those few exceptions are crucial, though, because every romance needs to contain certain important events, whether internal or external.

The three basic kinds of key plot milestones are

- ✔ **Key setup points:** The couple's first meeting and the seeds of their emotional tension need to come out quickly.

- ✔ **General romance-novel developments:** These include the basic progression of any romance: the back-and-forth progress of their growing physical and emotional intimacy, including the realization (and eventual admission) of love.

- ✔ **Book-specific points:** These are the key events only you can decide, because they relate only to your book and your characters, not to anyone else's.

You can use all of these points, large and small, general and specific, to pace your story. What they share lies in the reader's attitude toward them — anticipation. She wants to see each milestone reached and handled.

In the order they normally occur, the milestones that all romances share are

1. **The first meeting:** Whether they knew each other before the book begins or are literally meeting for the first time, the scene in the book where your hero and heroine see each other for the first time is the first milestone you reach — and the first one the reader is dying to reach with you, even before she's read page one. It's also the one time you shouldn't delay in giving her what she wants (for more info on choosing a starting point for your novel and creating that all-important first meeting, see Chapter 12).

2. **Confrontation:** At least once, and often several times throughout your book, your hero and heroine need to talk or, more likely, argue about the external issues keeping them apart, the external tension that creates a structure for working out their internal and emotional issues (for more on this subject, see Chapter 5). They may also discuss their emotional conflict at some point, but be careful: Discussing it can conceivably lead to solving it, which can't happen until the end of the book.

3. **Physical attraction:** Whether these scenes contain only a meaningful touch of the hand or a chaste kiss (the most you're likely to find in an inspirational romance), fully consummated lovemaking, or anything in between, the reader's expecting to find love scenes in your book. And that expectation keeps her turning pages.

4. **The realization of love:** This realization actually happens twice, once when the heroine realizes she loves the hero and once when he realizes he loves her. She's usually the first to figure it out, but the order is up to you. Go with what works for your characters and their story.

5. **The mutual confession of love, The End:** Although the confession may not literally be the end of your book — you may need an epilogue to tie up loose ends, for example — you should keep it as close to the actual end as possible. The moment when the hero and heroine admit their feelings, talk out the last of their issues, and assure each other (and the reader) that happily ever after is in the offing presents everything that your reader has come for — and everything you've paced the story to reach.

In many cases, your book follows one of the well-known romance plot types, which I list in Chapter 19, and each of those plot types comes with one or more milestones of its own. Table 10-1 contains some major milestones associated with (but not limited to) specific plot types.

Table 10-1	Common Setups and Related Milestones	
Plot Type	*Milestone*	*Comments*
Pregnant heroine	Baby's birth	If your heroine's pregnant, your reader's going to be waiting eagerly for this moment.
Marriage of convenience	The wedding	If you set up a marriage-of-convenience story, you want to show the wedding — and the wedding night. Whether everything happens between them or nothing does, the tension — both sexual and emotional — is bound to be high, so use it to your advantage.
Amnesia	Memory regained	Ninety-nine percent of the time, an amnesiac character regains his (or her) memory, or at least he discovers his past, even if his actual memory never returns. Your reader is as eager to know the whole story as the characters are, giving her an additional reason to turn the pages.
Woman in jeopardy	Danger and escape	A successful suspense plot involves putting your heroine in genuine jeopardy and then getting her out of it. And unless you're writing a series of books built around the pursuit of the same bad guy, you want to either kill off your villain or bring him to justice, too.
Secret baby	Parentage revealed	The fun of a secret-baby plot lies in knowing that the secret of "Who's the daddy?" doesn't stay secret forever. At some point, the hero finds out, and the reader knows all sorts of hell will break loose then and looks forward to seeing it.
Mystery	Key clues revealed	If you're building your plot around a mystery, you need to dole out clues as the book progresses and effectively time the solution for the greatest effect.

In the course of your own story, though, you set your reader up to expect all sorts of very individual milestones. I can't pretend to know all the milestones you may want to put in your story, but here are some examples, which I've made reasonably specific, just so you have an idea of what I'm talking about:

- ✔ **Who wins?** If your hero and heroine are rival Thoroughbred trainers, both hoping to win the Kentucky Derby, your reader needs to know how the race turns out. The same principle applies to any kind of contest: Let your reader know who wins.

- ✔ **The outcome of a legal case.** If you write about a custody case and your hero and heroine are opposing counsel, you need to tell the reader how the case turns out.

- ✔ **A holiday or family gathering.** The simplest things can create the most stress, and your reader wants to know how your characters fare when they meet each other's families or celebrate the holidays — always an emotional time. You can add that stress to the emotional tension they're already dealing with.

- ✔ **Can the ranch be saved?** Can the business stay solvent? Will the restaurant go under? If you ask the question as part of your plot, your reader expects you to answer it.

But plot-related milestones are only part of the picture. Your characters' emotions and the slow dance of the developing relationship provide the other piece.

Reaching key emotional moments

Every step in the development of the romance is like something out of a dance — two steps forward and one step back — until finally the music stops and your hero and heroine end up in each other's arms. (For more on this two steps forward, one step back approach to plotting, check out Chapter 5.)

The biggest steps — the characters recognizing their own feelings, love scenes, the final declaration of love — are so big that they operate as plot points. But throughout your book, you have all kinds of smaller developments that don't act as turning points for the plot but are still important.

Every encounter between the hero and heroine should have the development of the romance as its subtext, and the reader is looking for that development in their scenes together. If they had a fight, how does it affect them the next time they see each other? What happens the next time they have an opportunity to make love? After they've made love or just shared their first kiss, how do they react to each other the next time they meet in public?

Every action has a consequence, and nothing matters more to the reader than emotional consequences. Just as she looks forward with anticipation to seeing each plot point settled, she anticipates with even more eagerness seeing each new development in the romance. So keep each emotional step in mind. Those steps, combined with the milestones of your plot, are the building blocks of your pacing.

It's not only what happens, it's when and where (in the book)

After you can recognize the key elements, both external and internal, of your plot, you're ready to start thinking about pacing. Everything's in how you present your key elements, both when and where.

Pace yourself and you pace your book. Don't be in a hurry to tell the reader everything you know or everything that's going on. Be stingy, keep her wanting more, and she'll love you for it. By introducing elements as you need them, when and where they can do you the most good, you give the reader reason to keep going, because something's always happening and she always wants to know more. *Key exception:* The first meeting. You definitely shouldn't make your reader wait for that. But from that point on, you, as the author, should be doing the same two steps forward, one step back dance that the hero and heroine do.

Even though your reader knows the book's going to end happily, she pretends that she doesn't know. And she certainly doesn't know every step of the journey she, along with the heroine, takes to get there, so don't spoil the surprise. Imagine picking up a book and reading this first paragraph:

> *Melanie woke up and stretched, and then looked down at her sleeping husband. Her brand-new, gorgeous, sleeping husband. To think she'd once thought he was a killer in an angel's body. Instead, he was one of the good guys, the DEA's top agent. He'd saved her life, and now, as she lay back down beside him and cuddled up against his muscular chest, she realized that he'd saved her heart, as well. She sighed contentedly and thought back to how it all began.*

Okay, I'm exaggerating, but don't take away the reader's fun. Don't rush through things in the mistaken impression that hurrying equals pacing. Take all the key elements of your plot and your romantic development, and introduce them one at a time in ways that make logical sense. Let each element act as a question, a case of "What happens next?" or "How can this problem be fixed?" Then delay answering that question.

I'm not advocating that you diagram every chapter (unless that works for you, in which case . . . go for it), but I can lay out the beginning of Melanie's story the way it should be told in the following list so that you can see what I mean:

✔ **The meeting:** Melanie, who's just been downsized, is at the bank, depositing her final paycheck, when masked and armed robbers burst in. A teller is killed. The cops come and round up two of the robbers; the third gets away, taking Melanie hostage. He forces her, at gunpoint, to drive him away in her car. When he takes off his mask, she realizes he's gorgeous — but he's also tough, and the situation's terrifying. The day has just gone from bad to impossibly awful.

✔ **Confrontation:** Melanie wants out, offers him the car, and promises not to say which way he was heading. But he's not buying it. They retreat into silence. She's terrified, but at the same time, she doesn't feel in any physical danger. Rafe (the hero) wishes he could tell her the truth, which isn't specified, but he knows she'd be in even more danger if he did.

✔ **Physical attraction:** They're forced to spend the night in the car. Rafe ties her to him with some rope he finds in her trunk. Sometime in the chilly night, they end up snuggled together for warmth. When they wake up in each other's arms, they're both embarrassed and awkward — and strangely attracted. The next day, as they drive, the conversation is far-ranging and fascinating, and she finds herself wishing he were a normal man, not a criminal and possibly a killer. And she keeps remembering how good it felt to wake up in his arms.

✔ **Suspense:** Melanie tries to escape when Rafe stops for gas and a phone call. He drags her back into the car, but not before she overhears him talking to someone about "what he should do with her." Suddenly really scared, she withdraws as they continue to drive. He feels terrible because earlier, when they were talking, he'd found her the most interesting — and attractive — woman he'd ever met.

✔ **The kiss:** That night, he finds a cheap motel, barricades the door with his bed so she can't escape, and they warily get ready for bed. She asks him again to let her go and tries a little flirting to sweeten the discussion. They kiss, and both get carried away, but then she remembers it's all an act, and he reminds himself that she has ulterior motives, so they break it off, both breathless, both wishing things could be different.

That's probably two or three chapters, at least, and I parceled out information and introduced complications (plot-related and emotional) to keep the reader interested throughout. Here are the tools I used that you can use, too:

✔ **Start the action with a bang.** Begin at a point that intrigues the reader, that involves her emotionally or makes her want to see what happens next. I started with the heroine having a lousy day, something every reader can identify with, and then getting caught in a life-and-death situation, making the reader want to see what happens next.

✔ **Withhold information.** Instead of revealing right away that the hero's DEA (Drug Enforcement Administration), I hid that fact, not only from the heroine but from the reader. I made it clear that there's more to him than meets the eye, but I didn't say what he's hiding, so the reader keeps reading because she wants to figure it out. Many authors would explain right away, to the reader and possibly even the heroine, that the hero was DEA, but revealing his real position gives away a useful tool for pulling the reader along through the book.

✔ **Create sexual tension.** I made Melanie and Rafe clearly attracted to each other, but I didn't pay off on the sexual tension right away. And when I did let them get close, I cut it off at a kiss and left them both wanting more — and thinking more is impossible.

✔ **Taking two steps forward and one step back.** I let Melanie and Rafe talk and enjoy themselves, developing a level of intimacy between them, and then introduced additional suspense, which made her reassess the situation and back off, just as I let them kiss and forced them to stop.

You can cram all those things and more into the first chapter. It would be an extremely fast-paced first chapter, and the reader would be completely caught up in it — but you can't keep up that level of pacing. The reader would end up feeling let down, as if your book had suddenly dragged to a halt.

Knowing what to tell and what to leave out

Understanding the structural side of pacing your book doesn't only involve knowing how and when to introduce information; you also have to know what information to include and, just as important, what to leave out.

You're telling a story, and your job is to take away everything that doesn't contribute to that story. Everything that's left is what belongs in your novel. And if you make sure that everything you include has a purpose and structure the book according to the precepts I discuss in the section "It's not only what happens, it's when and where (in the book)" earlier in this chapter, your pacing can work for you, not against you.

That friend who can't tell a story because she can't stop digressing? She doesn't know what to leave out. A good storyteller picks and chooses what to tell, and she chooses everything she does because it serves the story and because it moves the story forward. Including any one of the following items is a problem, and many novice writers indulge in two or even all three, which makes getting published impossible:

✔ **Factual digressions:** Whether a piece of information you want to include is really interesting or not, if the story doesn't need it, cut it. Be ruthless. Yes, the farming practices of 16th-century France and the state of 21st-century genetics are fascinating (well, to some people), but if information you turn up in your research doesn't move the story forward, it goes (see Chapter 13 for the complete scoop on avoiding information overload).

✔ **Every thought and feeling:** Unedited, stream-of-consciousness writing doesn't belong in a romance novel. Real people's thoughts go all over the map. They're momentarily distracted by sounds or smells, and they go off on long mental digressions about childhood and favorite meals. To make their characters seem real, many aspiring authors include all those digressions in their books, stopping the action dead and making the reader lose interest. The reader puts the book down, and suddenly pacing is a dead issue. (I detail the dangers of wandering minds in Chapter 9.)

✔ **Too much description:** You absolutely need some description. Description sets the scene and helps the reader enter the world of the story. But too much description — passages that go on too long or descriptions of every single outfit, room, or minor character — slows the book down. The reader stops wondering what's going to happen next because, from her point of view, nothing ever happens at all. (See Chapter 8 for more on the dangers of description.)

Never fall in love with your own prose. That's a sure way to forget what matters and slow your story down to the point that it gets lost in a welter of pretty but ultimately useless words.

Avoiding the Dreaded Sagging Middle

One of the most common problems aspiring writers run up against is the sagging middle, when a strong beginning and a compelling ending bracket a central section that can be slow, at best, and boring, at worst. This problem is one of the biggest that you can have, in terms of pacing, because it can go on for a hundred pages or more. Some readers may be willing to forgive a paragraph or two that go off on a tangent, but no one's willing to skim the entire middle of a book in hopes that things eventually pick up at the end.

Recognizing a sagging middle

As you walk down the street, you can easily recognize the people whose middles are sagging, and it's not a lot harder when you're reading someone else's book. But seeing your own sagging middle can be tough, because you like your characters and your story, so everything that happens interests you. You need to make yourself look at your novel objectively and see if your story has any of the telltale signs:

✔ **A lot of time with the hero and heroine apart:** Because your hero and heroine are apart, the romance can't move forward, so the reader sees them leading their separate lives rather than working through their issues so that they can lead a life together.

✔ **Lack of tension:** The reverse of having the heroine and hero apart is to keep them together and essentially dating. They spend a lot of time in each other's company and getting along just fine; any tension is dealt with or, worse, forgotten.

✔ **Much ado about nothing:** Everyone seems busy, but nothing's really happening. People are shopping, eating, rounding up cattle, negotiating contracts, renovating houses, hosting parties . . . all kinds of busy work, but nothing's moving the story forward, and the romance is static.

Maybe the hero and heroine are never alone together in the middle of all the pointless action, or maybe they're just too busy with the mundane details at hand to deal with anything important. Either way, it's like sleight of hand, with all the fuss trying, whether consciously or subconsciously, to divert the reader's attention from the fact that the middle of the story tells her nothing important.

✔ **A lot of recapping and repetition:** Characters either spend a lot of time talking about things the reader has already seen earlier in the book or the same kinds of scenes and conversations recur, so that the story and, more importantly, the romance never move forward.

✔ **Sudden focus on secondary characters:** All of a sudden, secondary characters move into the foreground, and the focus shifts from the central romance to the secondary characters' lives and relationships.

Basically, if your book suddenly seems to lose momentum, if you lose your focus, the middle's sagging.

Stopping the sag before it starts

Because you may find fixing a sagging middle difficult, if not impossible, after the fact, the best thing you can do is keep your book lean, mean, and moving from the get-go. As you write, you can and should keep some strategies consciously in mind. (This advice is especially applicable early on in your writing career, when you use the process less intuitively than you may after you have a few manuscripts under your belt.) By keeping these strategies at the top of your mind in relation to Sagging Middle Syndrome (hereafter SMS), you increase your chances of avoiding the problem:

✔ **It all starts with plotting.** The single biggest cause of SMS is poor plotting. You simply don't have enough story to support the length of the book. You don't have enough happening, and you haven't added enough complexity to the emotional issues. And this problem is as common in submissions for shorter series like Harlequin Presents and Silhouette Romance as it is in 150,000-word mainstreams. I recommend outlining your romance mainly because of this problem. An outline can help you make sure you have enough happening to fill your chosen word count (see Chapter 7 for more on this topic).

✔ **Keep the action incremental.** After the first few chapters, it's easy to feel as if you need to tell the reader what's going on and make your characters hurry up and deal with things, both emotionally and plotwise. Don't do it. Keep things moving piecemeal and remember all the lessons of pacing that this chapter offers. Those lessons apply throughout the entire book, not just long enough to get the reader hooked. Effective pacing not only makes her start reading, but it also keeps her reading until she's reached the final page.

✔ **Make sure everything that happens matters.** Because you know the middle of your book is a danger zone, keep an especially tight rein on yourself during the crucial central section of your book. Consciously focus on the key elements of the romance and the plot, and don't let yourself get sidetracked by your research, your secondary characters, or anything else.

✔ **Stay flexible about your goals.** Some romances can't possibly be satisfactorily told in 75,000 words (in which case, SMS is never going to be the problem), while others can't be made to fill 100,000–150,000 words, no matter how talented a writer you are. In some cases, you may set out to write a 125,000-word mainstream book and then realize that the story you're telling, and already emotionally involved with, just isn't big and complex enough. In that case, you have to decide whether to abandon it or rethink your goals and aim for a shorter length and, often, a different market. Your idea may be perfect for series romance, and a well-told series romance trumps a sagging mainstream any day.

Dealing with it

Sometimes, despite your best efforts, you end up with SMS anyway. You may not even know it until a critique partner or an editor tells you that your book's sick and you need to get it to the ER (Editing Room), stat. The situation may be critical at that point, but it's not necessarily fatal.

You have a couple of things to consider. Truthfully, they don't always work. Some books, despite the author's best intentions, will never be publishable. If that happens with a manuscript of yours, you need to look at it as a learning experience and move on. But before you reach that point, here are a couple of operations, er, options you can consider:

✔ **Major surgery:** Despite being the most dramatic-sounding option, this procedure is actually the simplest. You may find that you can simply delete whole chunks of your book, sometimes whole chapters at a time, write transitions to stitch together the remaining important pieces, and end up with a shorter, tighter romance that works.

✔ **Grafting:** If the problem is with a lack of complexity in the emotional tension or the plot, you may have to start rethinking from the beginning and create believable complications that let you replace the sagging section with chapters that work.

You may have more problems with grafting than with the surgical option, because it's much more complicated and requires a lot more rewriting. You need to go all the way back to the beginning of the book and start threading in the new information little by little and in a lot of places — conversations, thoughts, and events. You can't just drop it into the story in big chunks, or it feels clunky and artificial, and the book still doesn't work. If you do it well, though, you can effectively save a book that wasn't working otherwise.

And if neither major surgery nor grafting can save it? Don't consign it to the garbage or use it to light your next fire. Put the manuscript at the bottom of a drawer, at the back of the file cabinet, wherever it will be out of sight and mind. Get it out again in a year or two, and you may be surprised to find that you've learned so much that now you can fix it. At the least, you'll see how much your writing skills have improved.

Show It, Don't (Always) Tell It

More than just structural considerations related to plot and conflict control pacing. The storytelling choices you make also have a strong effect. I fully discuss the two key aspects of your writing — your voice and your characters' voices — in Chapters 8 and 9, but I talk about them now specifically in terms of pacing.

Do keep the writers' adage of "Show, don't tell" in mind when you're thinking about pacing, but be aware that it's an oversimplification. Both showing, through dialogue, and telling, through narrative, have a role to play.

Harnessing the power of dialogue

Generally speaking, *dialogue* (which, for the purposes of this chapter, means the characters' true spoken words, not point of view and internal monologue) moves more quickly than narrative does. The rhythms of speech flow. Spoken sentences are generally shorter than the more "writerly" ones you create for the narrative sections, which means those shorter sentences have a momentum of their own. One character's dialogue leads naturally into the next, so the reader doesn't stop to think or get distracted. But at the same time, you also have to avoid the trap of using too much dialogue.

Speeding up the pace

The more dialogue you can include, the more quickly your book moves. Some readers even flip through a book before they buy it to see whether it has a lot of dialogue because, whether consciously or subconsciously, they're looking for a fast read, and they know a dialogue-filled book gives it to them. Written dialogue, if it sounds natural, makes for quicker pacing for a number of reasons. It

✔ **Feels like a real conversation:** Like a real conversation, the reader doesn't want to turn away, to stop paying attention even for a moment, because she may miss something. The dialogue isn't going to disappear if she looks away, but the illusion works. You're in much less danger of your reader putting the book down while she's reading dialogue than when she hits an extended narrative passage.

✓ **Provides a direct link with the characters:** Dialogue creates an immediate "you are there" feeling. Instead of observing a scene, the reader feels as if she's right in the middle of it. Her identification with the heroine increases, making her feel as if everything that's happening to the heroine is really happening to her. That sense of identification makes her read more quickly — she has something personal on the line.

✓ **Looks easy to read.** Dialogue also works to power your pacing in a purely visual way. As I discuss in Chapter 9, good dialogue sounds real. Most of the time, people speak briefly — short sentences, short paragraphs. Then the next person speaks, and then back to the first, and so on. Because of that natural back-and-forth pattern, dialogue makes for a lot of white space on the page, which looks a lot less daunting than long, dense paragraphs of narration. In a way, this pacing tool is purely psychological, because words are just words, however they're arranged, and a reader reads each individual word at the same rate, but dialogue-heavy pages do read faster than pages filled with prose, simply because they contain fewer words. The quicker the page reads, the more quickly the reader turns it. And the very act of turning pages quickly is exciting for a reader, making her speed up even more to keep turning them.

Avoiding the pitfalls

Over-using dialogue as a pacing tool has its pitfalls, though.

✓ **Dialogue has its limits:** Using dialogue as a way to describe a scene, relate action, or convey a character's thoughts is often a mistake. As I discuss in Chapter 9, having two characters sit down and deliver a bunch of explanation disguised as dialogue is awkward. You can have one character explain to another what's going on at times, but those times are few and far between, and you need to keep the explanation relatively brief. Otherwise, the speaker stops sounding like a real person. The minute that happens, the reader's pulled right out of the book and back to the reality that she was trying to escape by picking up a romance in the first place.

For the same reason, having your characters talk about their feelings endlessly, or describe what they're physically doing at every moment, doesn't feel believable. It's stiff, fake, and turns readers off.

✓ **Too much of anything gets boring:** I love lobster, but I don't want to eat it for every meal. Readers love dialogue for a lot of good reasons, but a steady diet of it bores them. Hundreds of pages that look and, essentially, sound the same can be a turn-off.

✓ **All your eggs are in one basket:** Excessive dialogue means your dialogue-writing skills have to be note perfect. With a book full of dialogue, the reader has no other elements to fall back on if she's turned off by a particular character's voice or can only take so much of "listening" to a particular person. You run the same risk if you tell a story from the first-person point of view, which is relatively uncommon but not unheard of in romance novels. If the reader likes the character's voice, you win, but if not . . . you lose.

A book that relies too heavily on dialogue ends up one of two ways. It's

- ✔ **Too little:** The story may sound shallow and incomplete, because you have to leave out so many things that the reader wants to know.

- ✔ **Too much:** The characters explain every detail, making your story sound false and uninvolving. This situation is worse than the first pitfall, in my opinion.

Telling it like it is: Using narrative effectively

Narrative is just as much a part of good pacing as dialogue, even though writers frequently don't think of it that way. In fact, it seems to me that many writers think that narrative gets in the way of good pacing, but I think too many writers tend to think of pacing as something speedy and nothing else. Plus, authors misuse narrative more often than dialogue. Overall, readers are more likely to complain when they think a book is boring, which often means slow, rather than too exciting or too fast-moving. (It's also much more common to see books that move too slowly than books that move too fast.)

Narrative allows you to compensate for what dialogue can't do. As I discuss in Chapters 8 and 9, narrative and internal monologue let you do everything from laying out the basics of what's happening to letting the reader know your characters' most secret thoughts. All those things are crucial to creating a great romance novel, but in order not to trip up your pacing, you need to know how to use narrative effectively.

Here's the key: As much as possible, break your narrative sections into bits. Tactics include:

- ✔ **Avoiding long paragraphs:** Pages filled with long paragraphs of densely packed prose look off-putting, even intimidating. Don't make your paragraphs too long. Just from a visual standpoint, shorter paragraphs are more approachable, more manageable — and read more quickly. I often see paragraphs that fill an entire page, and I immediately know that if I go to contract on that book, I'm going to break that paragraph into three or four. *Bonus tip:* If you do have a lengthy paragraph, follow it with one that's only a few lines long, almost as a reward for the reader.

✔ **Cutting off a scene before it's actually over:** This tip goes along with what I say in the section "It's not only what happens, it's when and where (in the book)" earlier in this chapter. Don't end every scene with things resolved. Sometimes you can leave the reader hanging without telling her how things turned out. She wants to know what happened, so you're forcing her to keep going eagerly — pacing at its most effective.

✔ **Moving between points of view:** Whether you're using full-blown internal monologue or just dropping into different characters' points of view for a line or two, if you move between different characters' minds, you're creating the kind of variety that keeps a reader interested (see Chapter 9 for more on using multiple points of view).

✔ **Punctuating narrative with dialogue:** Instead of paragraph after paragraph of description, action, or internal monologue, break up narrative with dialogue. You may be able to add just a line, or you may have room for an exchange of several speeches, but however long your dialogue, it makes the page look more readable and keeps the reader directly connected to the characters and the reality of their world.

If true dialogue isn't possible, if only one character's on scene, you can always have her talk to herself. Be careful that you don't overdo it, though. It can start to seem self-conscious and awkward, even silly.

✔ **Working narrative into dialogue tags:** As much as you can, break the narrative bits down into small, discrete pieces that you can attach to a line of dialogue. Rather than just using *she said,* go for *she said, picking up her suitcase and heading out the door.* This small change camouflages the narrative bit, slipping it under the radar, and gets the information across without calling any attention to itself.

Working together, the last two points in the preceding list can really help your book keep moving without giving short shrift to getting across the necessary information.

But you also want to use narrative for the important task of slowing things down when you want to give the audience a breather or time to think, or to vary the pacing to keep the reader fresh.

As with dialogue, you may encounter some dangers in over-using narrative. You're probably already aware of the first — and biggest — danger: Too much narrative, no matter how interesting the subject, can bring your book to a screeching halt. A second danger, one that you may easily overlook, comes with the temptation to put things into narrative that you can put into dialogue simply because it's so easy to just keep going and explain things in what's essentially your own voice.

As a general rule, if you can put something in dialogue, you probably should.

Finding the balance between showing and telling

To create successful pacing, you need to reach the most effective balance between showing and telling. That balance is different for every book you write, so you need to make conscious decisions as you go. It's not just a matter of deciding on a ratio of x percent this to y percent that, or of creating some kind of diagram that you can apply to every manuscript.

First, you need to think about the ideal pacing for the story you're telling. Here are a few examples:

- ✔ A suspense or adventure plotline probably moves more quickly than a more intimate, family-oriented novel.

- ✔ The pace of life in the era you've chosen influences a historical romance. If it was a time of high tea and leisurely social calls, that needs to be reflected in your storytelling.

- ✔ A sexy book feels driven by the characters' passion for each other, which adds intensity and a push to the pacing.

- ✔ An inspirational romance probably makes room for slower-paced, thoughtful scenes as the characters consider faith and its place in their lives.

After you've decided on the ideal tempo of the pacing, you need to keep that in mind as you write, making sure that, overall, your pacing fits with the kind of story you've chosen.

As you write each individual scene, think about its role in the overall story. Does it galvanize things? Or does it slow them down to provide a breather? Does it give the reader key information? Maybe it lulls the reader into a false sense of security. Does it make her think? Shock her? After you answer the question of each scene's purpose, you know how to pace that scene and how it fits into the whole.

After you know the pacing you want to achieve with a scene, you can look at the practicalities of that scene — whether it consists mainly of conversation, action, description, or whatever — and figure out the most effective way to execute it.

You can figure out where you can, and where it makes sense to, use dialogue, point of view, or internal monologue to tell your story, which all have a more personal feel. But remember that you need narrative, too, and use that narrative thoughtfully, for effect. Ask yourself which style works better in every scene and at every moment.

Vary the proportions of one style to another, always being conscious of how each comes across to a reader. Not only should you make every word in your book the result of a conscious decision on your part, you should also plan out your bigger choices. Your awareness of everything you do pays off in the end. To the reader, everything feels smooth, natural and seamless; she never sees the work you put in and the way you're pulling strings all the way through. She only knows that the book works — and moves.

During your final read-through of your manuscript, pay special attention to your book's pacing to see whether you've achieved the overall effect you set out to capture.

Prose That Goes and Prose That Slows

The most important parts of getting your pacing right involve the big decisions: structuring your story properly (not to mention making sure that you have enough story there to structure) and determining what to tell the reader through dialogue and what to tell through narrative. If you get those decisions right, you've already done 90 percent or more of your work.

But you can tweak your prose to support your goal, whether that's making things move faster or slowing them down. Here are some techniques to keep in mind:

- **Choose prose that moves.** Instead of saying: *He didn't take time to think. He just ran to the car and jumped inside, then took off in pursuit of the kidnappers,* use gerunds. Make the reader participate in the action, and say: *Without taking time to think, he found himself running to the car, jumping inside and taking off in pursuit of the kidnappers.*

- **Avoid the passive voice.** Passive-voice constructions, by their very nature, distance the reader (and the characters) from what's going on. In an active-voice construction, the character does something: *Rachel felt unhappy with her new job. The attacker hit Jake over the head.* Passive voice involves something being done to the character: *Rachel was made unhappy by her new job. Jake was hit over the head by the attacker.* It puts everything at a distance and makes for a much less effective way of telling a story.

- **Short sentences move faster than long, complex ones.** This tip especially relates to dialogue, where short sentences in sequence reflect a quicker, more clipped way of speaking. They create a faster rhythm, whether a single character is saying several brief things in quick succession or two characters are exchanging quick speeches. In narrative, however, too many short sentences in sequence can end up sounding choppy and off-putting.

By the same token, longer, more complicated sentences — spoken or in narrative — slow the pace, in part because the reader has to take longer and put more thought into reading and interpreting those sentences. Their rhythms are different, more flowing, so they pull things back. You can let your reader know that she can breathe again after any kind of an intense scene by shifting the rhythm of your prose from quick and short to medium-length sentences, and then to slower and more thoughtful ones.

✔ **Short words pack a punch.** If you want to make a scene move or create intensity, go for short, sharp words, which have a different impact from longer, smoother ones. This distinction is like the one between short sentences and longer ones, only on a mini-level.

✔ **Punctuation affects pacing.** Ellipses create pauses, and dashes indicate sharp breaks. Commas, which authors frequently don't think much about and often misuse, represent pauses that are shorter than those pauses indicated by ellipses. Because of that, I'm a big fan of using commas inconsistently, leaving them out when you want your prose to move more quickly, putting them in when you want the reader to slow down. Exclamation points reflect excitement and intensity, and that speeds up the pacing.

✔ **The more adjectives, the slower the pace.** Description slows your story down, so don't interrupt a scene that you want to move quickly for a long description of something. In almost every case, no matter what's going on in your story, you only need one adjective, maybe two. In breakneck scenes, even one adjective may be too many. Be sparing. Describe only what's absolutely necessary, especially in fast-moving scenes.

As you write, your mind has to be multi-tasking to the max: focusing on characterization, logic, narrative versus dialogue, and every single word choice. Don't worry if you don't get it right every time, because that's what you use revisions and multiple drafts for. If you need to dedicate a draft to each part of the process, do it. It's time-consuming, but it may also be well worth it. Polishing your prose to get the desired effect can be the icing that may help you sell the cake.

Chapter 11

Taking It All Off: Writing Love Scenes

In This Chapter

▶ Creating characters through love scenes

▶ Using love scenes to support tension, not diffuse it

▶ Writing love scenes that fit your book's style

A man and a woman who enjoy each other's conversation and company are friends. Add sexual attraction, tension, and, ultimately, lovemaking or the promise of it, and you have a romance. In this chapter, I talk about the key component of any romance, written or real: love scenes. I give you tips on where to place the love scenes in your novel, how to let those scenes help you create your hero and heroine's characters, and how to write the steamy moments so that they contribute emotionally to your book, instead of reading like purely physical asides.

Comparing Sex and Romance

Though sex and romance have a strong and crucial bond in romance novels, they're not the same thing. At its most basic, sex is a purely *physical* act. Romance, by definition, involves *emotion*. Although not every romantic act (flowers on a special occasion, breakfast in bed) is physically sexual, every sexual act in a romance needs emotional underpinnings. In a romance novel, a love scene involves just that: *love,* even if the characters don't realize it yet.

Emotion mixes with the physicality of sex, and the proportions of each vary based on the specifics of your intended market, your characters, and your plot. Ultimately, no lovemaking scene is ever purely sexual, even though it can be highly sensual, physical, and erotic. Even the most erotic romances (which aren't the same as pure erotica) are still romances, and the sexual encounters between the covers lead to a romantic conclusion.

The focus of a romance novel is on the developing relationship — both emotional and, in most cases, sexual — between one woman and one man. Whatever their romantic pasts, your hero and heroine should be monogamous in the course of your book, because the idea that they're meant to be together and just aren't interested in anyone else is part of the fantasy the reader brings to the book. (And, yes, there are exceptions, but I strongly recommend that you don't set out to break this rule, especially with your very first book.)

Knowing Where and When

You have to know where to place the love scenes in your book to make them really effective. Even a beautifully written love scene jars the reader when you put it in the wrong place, making her question the characters — and stopping the book in its tracks. Place the love scenes properly — and after the proper build-up — and half your job is done, because the reader will want your characters to get together just as much as the characters themselves do.

Creating sexual tension

A well-written, well-placed, and effective love scene is the result of the sexual tension between your hero and heroine, which slowly builds in the course of your novel. Sexual attraction and tension should begin the minute your characters meet and should be components of every subsequent scene between them, building alongside their emotional tension (which I discuss in Chapter 5), so that by the time you finally write that first full love scene, your characters and your reader are ready.

Simply put, *sexual tension* is the inevitable result of making your hero and heroine physically attracted to each other but unable to act on that attraction. As I discuss in Chapter 5, the reasons why they can't act are limited only by your imagination — you can place physical, circumstantial, or (best of all) emotional barriers between them. They want to act, but they can't. Sometimes they get a taste of what they're missing (a touch, a kiss, or even the beginnings of lovemaking) before they pull back. And that tease only makes the tension worse.

Think of a kid in the days leading up to Christmas, looking at those presents under the tree, shaking them, trying to read through the wrapping, but unable to open them until Christmas comes. Your hero and heroine should feel that way about each other — only they're not sure that Christmas will ever come. For all they know, they may never be together fully and physically. Every time they see each other, every time they talk, you need to make sure an undercurrent of unresolved sexual tension hums between them.

Here are some helpful ways to ramp up the tension on the way to a love scene and throughout your book:

- ✔ **Make it obvious.** They may fight it, but your hero and heroine need to be undeniably attracted to each other. A sidelong glance, a casual touch that leaves heat in its wake — subtle signals like these are extra effective precisely because the characters are fighting their attraction. These signals demonstrate the strength of that attraction because they override common sense and the characters' own intentions. And don't just let the reader know; let the characters know, too, adding an extra edge to their encounters. Even when they're at odds, keep the physical awareness humming in the background.

- ✔ **In or out of sight, but always on their minds.** They may not be happy about the fact that they can't stop thinking about and being attracted to each other, but they can't do anything about it. The longer the book goes on, the more they want each other — and the more the reader wants them to get together, too. Right in the middle of a contract negotiation, the hero is assaulted by thoughts of the heroine. And she's thinking of him right then, too, as she tries to call a fractious class of third graders to order. It doesn't always have to be in a positive "wish he were here" kind of way, but they need a gut-level awareness that just doesn't go away.

- ✔ **Make 'em wait.** Don't let them act on their attraction right away, even — or especially — if the circumstances seem perfect: a moonlit night on the beach, or a hot summer day and a pond just right for skinny dipping. Frustration feeds tension, so let them feel frustrated and drawn to what they can't have.

- ✔ **Let 'em start and then make 'em stop.** Whether you end a kiss abruptly or allow it to go on for long, slow, wonderful minutes but never let it go any further, give your characters a taste of how good they are together but don't let them go all the way until they just can't stand to be apart (and the reader can't stand for them to be apart, either) anymore.

- ✔ **Leave 'em wanting more.** Whether they share a kiss or they spend all night and half the morning tangled up in the sheets — and each other — never let them feel satisfied. The more they have of each other, the more they want.

Hitting the sheets before sharing their hearts

Here's one of those "Yeah, but . . ." instances. In the "Creating sexual tension" section in this chapter, I stress that good love scenes are the natural conclusion to increasing sexual tension. But sometimes sex comes before the sexual tension. Or rather, sometimes sex follows immediately after sexual tension becomes evident. For example, the common romance plot of sex with a stranger doesn't work with a long build-up of sexual tension. In a case like that, the sexual tension often follows, when the strangers discover they need to spend time with each other and

can't stay strangers. In some of today's most sensuous romances, the hero and heroine are looking for no-strings sex, which they think they've found with each other, so it's only after they get sexually involved that their emotions get involved, too, and sexual tension grows. In both these cases — and quite possibly in others that you can think of — the sexual and emotional development of the relationship turns the usual pattern on its head, following the hero and heroine's sexual involvement rather than preceding it.

Deciding when the time's right

Everything in a romance should be character-driven. Your love scenes especially need to follow this rule; those scenes should feel like the characters' decision, not yours. The reader should never see your hand because, to be blunt, no one should be forced into having sex. If the timing doesn't feel natural, you lose the larger sense of romance, of two people being perfect for each other.

As I discuss in the preceding section, sexual attraction and tension should build from the start. Despite that, every time the characters have the chance to act on that tension, they don't (or not all the way). So why now? I can sum up the answer in just one word: motivation. Your characters' motivations should be the true drivers of every aspect of your plot (see Chapter 5), and motivation plays an especially crucial part when it comes to love scenes.

When your characters finally get sexually involved, you (and they) need a reason. That reason can't be simply that *you've* decided it's time for a love scene; it has to be *their* reason. That reason is rarely as cut and dried as "(S)he's cute, let's get it on," because most of your readers don't think that way about getting sexually involved, so they don't want the characters to think that way, either. The reader wants to know that the hero and heroine's feelings for each other are involved in their decision, not just their hormones.

Because you're writing a romance, and because nothing's more intrinsically tied to romance than *love*making, your characters need an emotional basis for their decision to make love. And, in fact, they may each have their own reason, or even multiple reasons (because people are complex and your characters can be, too).

✔ **Hero:** Usually the hero is much less conflicted about making love than the heroine. He may hold back because he doesn't want to hurt her or feels he can't offer her a future, but guys connect the physical act with emotion much less than women, and that holds true in romance novels, just as it does in real life. Generally speaking, he doesn't realize that his heart's on the line until later — often much later — in the book.

✔ **Heroine:** Your heroine is most likely the one with the most doubts about making love, usually stemming from the fear that a relationship can't possibly work out with the hero, so she's afraid of being hurt beyond repair when the inevitable collapse comes. For that reason, she needs to have a definite reason for thinking *now* is the right time.

As the book progresses, sexual tension grows, and emotional conflict (which I discuss in Chapter 5) slowly moves toward resolution. Her decision to make love should come at a point when the tension feels irresistible and the conflict has progressed to a stage where she recognizes this man's importance to her and is willing to risk the inevitable pain of a breakup for the sake of storing up memories to live on later. Because of that, she's now willing to take the emotional risk of making love to him, leaving herself totally vulnerable. So long as you explain that decision to the reader, who's already feeling the sexual tension and longing to resolve it, she'll find the timing of the love scene just right.

Using love scenes to increase the tension

Love scenes, properly placed, help build the tension in your book. They add an extra edge to the emotional tension that's a key component of the relationship and, contradictory as it sounds, love scenes can also help build the sexual tension. Just as a number of factors meet to lead *into* your love scene, you can take real benefits *out* of the scene as you move forward with your story.

Upping the emotional ante

Your characters should move into the love scene thinking, on some level, that making love can resolve things between them. Having made the decision to take their sexual relationship to the next level, they expect exactly that conclusion: a leveling out of the situation, including the emotional roller coaster they've been riding with each other. Instead, they need to discover that nothing's been settled at all. Instead of bringing relief from emotional turmoil, lovemaking leaves things more stormy and confused than ever.

In fact, just as the heroine has to do the most soul-searching going into the love scene, the hero often feels the most confused coming out of it. Heroes, as I discuss in Chapter 4, usually consider themselves impervious emotionally. Your hero most likely thinks that making love with the heroine can be a wonderful, sensual experience that will leave him untouched on any other level. Imagine his surprise to find that his heart's become involved in ways he can't deny. Because that's the last thing he wants is to own up to that — the reality that love makes a person vulnerable, and he's not about to let himself be vulnerable — he has to find ways to hide what he's feeling. He can be angry, curt, condescending, reduce their meaningful interaction to the level of a joke, or anything that fits with his character and doesn't let the heroine know what he's really feeling: that life without her feels emptier than he wants to admit.

Whether in reaction to his behavior or because she's afraid of being hurt and decides to make a pre-emptive strike, the heroine doesn't let on about her feelings, either. So the characters end up feeling more for each other than ever, yet they keep pulling even farther apart.

The result? The act of lovemaking, which should bring two people even closer together, instead ups the ante on emotional tension and creates more problems for them to spend the rest of the book overcoming.

You can use the couple's emotions to your advantage both during the love scenes and afterwards, by shifting into one or both characters' points of view, letting your readers see how much lovemaking means to them, how deeply their emotions are engaged, and how much not being able to confess their true feelings hurts them, building a sense of what's at stake for the hero and heroine and, through them, the reader.

Sexual tension feeds . . . on sex?

Sounds contradictory, doesn't it? If you build sexual tension chapter after chapter, until the hero and heroine finally make love, then their lovemaking should release that tension. And it does — for as long as it takes them to exhaust themselves making love. After that, the tension starts building all over again — and it can become even stronger, because now they know how great their lovemaking can be.

Suddenly every accidental touch is filled not only with imagined potential, but also the memory of how wonderful lovemaking was — and increased longing and sexual tension. Their relationship is still a mess, so they can't be like any normal couple and make love whenever they want to, but want to they do. After all, one chocolate chip cookie can't satisfy, and making love with the perfect partner is a whole lot better than cookies. The problem is that cookies are pretty easy to come by, and their feelings don't get hurt. Your characters need to be painfully aware that making things work with the perfect partner is a little tougher.

Using love scenes to support your pacing

After they make love, your characters are still emotionally messed up and filled with sexual tension, the very things that drew your reader eagerly into your love scene in the first place. Because your reader still wants resolution, you haven't lost any steam by letting your hero and heroine — and your reader — have a little fun.

Your reader, like your characters, lands back on square one, still hoping everything can work out, still turning pages waiting to see how things end — and hoping for some more lovemaking along the way.

That's the beauty of love scenes. Because they don't resolve anything, you can ratchet up the tension, diffuse it temporarily with another love scene that brings your characters closer for a moment and shows them how wonderful things could be, and then ratchet it up some more and take the whole roller-coaster ride all over again. Your book keeps moving, and your reader keeps turning the pages.

All my advice for effectively timing love scenes, and using them to keep your tension high and your book moving, also applies to any scene involving sexual contact: kissing scenes, unconsummated love scenes — even dreams of lovemaking.

Writing the Scene

After you figure out where to place your love scenes for best effect, you still need to write the scenes themselves. Remember to keep your market and the readers' expectations in mind when you progress to the writing itself.

Knowing your market

As I discuss in Chapter 2, the romance market is a varied one, and just as you don't want to mix Regency mores with a contemporary mystery, you don't want to put a sexy love scene in an inspirational romance or have your Medieval characters using the birth control pill. In other words, even readers who read a wide variety of romances — from contemporary romances to western historical romances to romantic comedies to inspirational romances — have varying expectations regarding the frequency, content, and sensuality level of love scenes based on the subgenre they're reading.

Readers who specialize are even stricter in their expectations, so you need to know what's appropriate for the sort of book you're writing. Readers of inspirational romances want a very low level of overt sensuality and no premarital sex. Highly sensual series, like Harlequin Blaze, draw readers who expect a lot of love scenes, a high level of sexual tension, and characters who are inventive when they make love. Mainstream contemporary romances and historical romances have room for varying levels of sensuality, based on the particular characters and plot, so you have a whole continuum along which you can find a spot that feels comfortable for you and your characters. (Check out "Suiting your language to the market" later in the chapter for more on market considerations and choosing appropriate love-scene language.)

What are the best ways to gauge the readers' expectations for love scenes?

✔ **Read:** As I say throughout this book (and can never say too often), you need to read. Even if you, like many successful authors, don't like to read within your field while you're actively writing, you need to do your homework before you start. You should read enough that you have a good sense of what your readers are looking for.

✔ **Get the guidelines:** Not every publisher has guidelines for aspiring writers, and some guidelines talk only about what romantic subgenres the publisher is interested in or what length manuscripts they want to see, without addressing levels of sensuality. Other guidelines, however, are more specific. Series publishing, because of its nature, often has very specific sensuality requirements, and series publishers do provide guidelines outlining what's appropriate.

If a publisher has guidelines (also known as *tip sheets*) available, you can send a request and a self-addressed, stamped envelope, so the publisher can send those guidelines to you by mail. You should also check out the publisher's Web site — publishers often post submission guidelines online. I list other types of writers' resources in Chapter 3, and many of those resources can tell you good sources for guidelines.

It's not what they do, it's how you say it

Here's where everything I talk about previously in this chapter comes together: in actually writing a love scene. Most writers think of love scenes as the difficult part, but I think that writers who struggle with love scenes often have trouble because they're thinking of the scene in isolation.

Instead, think of a love scene as an outgrowth of the characters' needs and feelings, and a key step in the development of the relationship and the pacing of the book. Keep these ideas in mind, along with your readers' expectations, and the actual writing becomes easier, because you have the emotionally motivated basis for your scene already figured out, and you don't have to count on the act of lovemaking alone to carry the weight of the scene.

Because you can feel fairly sure that everyone in your audience has a pretty good idea of the mechanics of sex, that frees you up from having to describe the whole "Tab A into Slot B" thing. You need to indicate what's happening, but not in clinical terms — in emotional ones.

Focusing on feelings

Don't just explain what the characters are doing but focus on how they feel about what they're doing. What goes through the heroine's mind as the hero strokes the soft skin of whatever body part you choose? She's aroused, of course, but use her point of view to give emotional weight to the act, as well.

✔ Is she a virgin? Perhaps she's surprised that a man — especially this man — can make her feel a pleasure she never dreamed possible.

✔ Is she a total tomboy? Feeling so feminine, so much a woman, may amaze her. And she also can be amazed by finding a man who appreciates her strength yet sees into her vulnerable heart.

✔ Is she divorced from a man who made her feel inadequate in every way, especially in bed? How delightfully shocking to find out he was wrong, because *this* man clearly finds her a total turn-on, and yet how sad to think it can never last.

The same idea holds true for your hero, who finds your heroine both physically exciting and unexpectedly emotionally affecting. Be sure to include his point of view and feelings, as well.

As I discuss earlier in this chapter in the "Deciding when the time's right" section, everything grows from your characters, so think about what each of them needs and how you can fulfill that need via their lovemaking. So long as neither confesses it to the other, you can even use lovemaking as a catalyst for one or both of them to realize that they're in love and that they want this — the lovemaking and the relationship — to go on forever, in and out of the bedroom.

Matching language with the moment

You're writing about a sensual moment in the relationship, so use words that go beyond the basics and have sensual implications. The hero can just touch her, but even better, he can stroke her or slide his palm along her flesh. She can kiss him back, or she can nibble his earlobe and tease her lips along his jaw line to his mouth. And though I'm a big proponent of "less is more" when using adjectives and adverbs, a love scene is a good place to loosen up on that rule a bit. Kissing, caressing, and lovemaking are a lot more interesting to the reader than any landscape, so she's won't mind spending some extra time on both what's going on and how the characters feel about it. In addition, love scenes are all about building up feelings and connections and an atmosphere that's conducive to both, and extra descriptors can be a big help on that score.

Feel free to use words with emotional implications. Your characters can't say that they love each other, but they can love what they're doing to each other. Their hearts, not just their bodies, can respond to each other. They can exalt, celebrate, triumph, and more. The feelings they can't admit to themselves, much less each other, out of bed can surface during lovemaking, and even though they can't be expressed openly, those feelings color everything that follows.

You don't want to use an adjective or an adverb to modify everything, but carefully used, they can bring an extra dimension to the scene. No "wham, bam, thank you, ma'am" here. Even if your hero and heroine are so excited that they practically race to the finish line, they do so because they feel an insatiable hunger for each other, so sounds (like the quick rasp of a zipper)

shiver along the heroine's aroused nerve endings. Or maybe seduction happens slowly. Sensations are soft, textures are silky, and heat rises in waves along the hero's skin.

Suiting your language to the market

Here's where all that reading comes in handy. If you know your market, you know how far you can go not only in terms of what the characters do (see "Knowing your market" earlier in this chapter) but in terms of how explicit you can be in describing it. Sometimes you need to stick entirely to euphemisms and vague descriptions, but in other cases, you can be as explicit as you want in naming body parts. Most of the time, you find yourself falling somewhere between those two extremes (sort of the way movies show breasts and butts but not full frontal nudity, even though they make it clear what's going on). But don't try so hard not to call a spade a spade (or a penis a penis) that you resort to euphemisms that sound sillier than they do sexy.

Using all five senses

Lovemaking is a sensuous experience, so use the characters' senses to add effect. Naturally you want to rely on touch, because the scene is all about how your characters are touching each other, but don't forget the other four senses.

- ✔ How does her hair smell when he wakes up and leans over to kiss her?
- ✔ How does the light fall across his face, highlighting his cheekbones and deepening the shadows around his eyes?
- ✔ Is he further aroused to hear her moan in abandon as he parts her thighs?
- ✔ Is his skin salty as she runs her tongue across his chest to his nipple?

Don't just stick to what's going on when they're together, either; use sense memory to bring them closer by recalling feelings later on. The scent of gardenias reminds him of her signature scent. The feel of a denim jacket as she throws it over her shoulders makes her fingers itch to unzip the jeans he always wears. Let them infiltrate each other's lives on such a basic level that it seems they can never be free of each other.

Letting your setting work for you

Setting can do more than just identify locale; it can work for you in bigger and better ways. (See Chapter 6 to find out how to set the scene.) The setting you choose can also work for you in smaller, more intimate ways, and setting is especially important in a love scene. Your setting can heighten the experience by working in tandem with the hero and heroine's responses or by providing a striking contrast.

- ✔ **Work with the moment:** Start with a big, airy bedroom; a king-size four-poster bed with a sheer canopy; satin sheets; candles burning and adding light to the moonlight streaming through the windows; and the scent of roses from a vase on the dresser. Add a hero and heroine slowly exploring each other's bodies and learning each other's responses, reveling in each sensation. Fill the room with sensual cues to enhance your characters' feelings and make the moment sensual on every level.

- ✔ **Create a contrast:** Contrast the sensuous magic of lovemaking with an anti-romantic setting, like a cheap motel room with bad lighting, a squashed double bed, threadbare covers, and the sound of a TV from the room next door coming through the thin wall. The heat of passion and the private paradise two people can create can override the handicap of such an unlikely setting, even transform it into something romantic and wonderful, proving the power of the hero and heroine's feelings for each other.

Birth control: necessary or not? You don't have a problem if you're writing historical romances, but you need to think about contraception of some kind if you're writing contemporary romances. Some people feel very strongly that you have to mention condoms, but I think that you need to stay true to your characters and yourself — and also the realities of the situation. If your characters are on the run in the jungle, neither one probably has any condoms on them. But if your hero plans a romantic evening, he can logically stash a few in the drawer of the bedside table. So decide for yourself what you and your characters feel comfortable with and let that be your guide.

Part IV
Putting It All Together: Mechanics Count, Too

The 5th Wave   By Rich Tennant

"Saaay, I have an idea. Why don't we turn down the lights and parse a few chapters on conflict resolution from my romance manuscript?"

Part IV

Together

In this part . . .

Romance writing is a creative undertaking, but it has its practical side, too. In this part, I talk about how to start your book, and how to start and stop each chapter and scene, because it's not just what you write that counts, it's also how you put the parts together. Getting your facts straight is another practical concern with far-reaching consequences, and in this part, I tell you how and where to do your research. And you wouldn't want to send your manuscript out full of punctuation errors, grammatical inconsistencies, and improper margins, because, well, that would be unprofessional. So, I provide a quick review of all the little stuff.

Chapter 12

Starting and Stopping

*T*he single most important section of your romance novel that you'll ever sit down to write is the beginning. (Pressure, much?) If your opening doesn't capture an editor's attention, your book probably will never see the light of publication. Even if it gets published, if the beginning doesn't work, you'll lose readers while they're still in the store, before they've paid a penny for your work.

If you haven't spent time hanging out in a bookstore and watching the way readers shop, give it a try next time you're shopping for books yourself. The process is similar for all fiction, but because romance readers tend to buy a lot of books, and because they tend to be extremely knowledgeable about what they like and how to find it, watching them in action is a real education.

Almost every romance reader has a favorite author whose name on a book cover guarantees a sale, but most of the time, book buying comes only after book browsing. A reader stands at the romance rack and looks around to see what grabs her attention. A cover (which I discuss in Chapter 18) catches her eye and makes her pick up a book to see whether it's worth taking home. Next, she checks the back-cover copy to get a general sense of the story. And then she probably opens the book to Chapter 1 and starts skimming.

If she's caught up in the story after reading the first page (or even the first two or three), she realizes that she either has to stand there for hours and read the whole book or pay her money and take it home. That's the power of a great beginning in action.

You want to write a beginning strong enough to force a reader to spend her money, but the pressure's not off, even after you get the opening right. You need to keep your reader's rapt attention on every page, and one of the best ways to do that is to start and stop every chapter with enough punch to hold her interest and keep her eager to see what happens next. And even within each chapter, you need to structure scenes to create mini-cliffhangers and maintain your hold on the reader's attention.

In this chapter, I talk about all the aspects of starting and stopping, wherever you are in your book, paying particular attention to the all-important opening, as well as chapter endings and beginnings.

Starting with a Bang: Mastering the Winning Beginning

Any form of entertainment needs a great beginning, and that beginning is never more important than when you're talking about a novel. A movie viewer has already paid for her ticket before she sits down in the theater, so she's not likely to walk out unless the movie's really, *really* bad. TV comes right into the viewer's living room, so she can just stay on the couch and keep watching easily enough. But a novel has to sell itself *before* a reader pays for it. And a compelling beginning is your best tool for making her reach for her wallet.

The opening of your novel gives you an opportunity to introduce your characters in the most intriguing way, to highlight your plot's most fascinating twists, and to immediately demonstrate your abilities as a storyteller, all of which combine to convince the reader that she can trust you to hold her interest all the way to the last page.

If you blow the beginning, you may lose your only chance to win a fan. Ace it — and follow through — and you have a fan not only for that book but quite possibly for every book you publish.

When you first sit down to write, page one may look very intimidating to you. But for your reader, page one should seem like the exciting beginning of a great adventure. You want to involve your reader from the very first line so that your book stands out in her mind, even if she's not quite sure why your book seems so much more interesting than every other book she's seeing.

You know your story better than anyone, so you're the best judge of its strengths and which hooks can most likely get — and keep — a reader interested.

You need to begin with a bang, not with a slow buildup but with something that grabs your reader and refuses to let go. You need to engage your reader's attention right from the get-go, both intellectually (in terms of what's happening with your plot) and, more importantly, emotionally, because romances are all about feeling — your characters' feelings and what those characters can make your reader feel.

How to hook your reader

A lot of elements need to come into play right at the beginning of your book, because your reader is looking for an immediate introduction to as many of the key components of your novel as possible — character, plot, sexual and emotional tension, and writing style.

Here are the two top techniques to hook a reader right off the bat (I explain the actual mechanics of these techniques at length in the "Putting Theory into Practice" section later in the chapter):

✔ **Choose an exciting place to begin your story.** If you start your novel in the middle of the action, when something interesting is already happening, your reader wants to keep going to see how it turns out. If the book begins with the hero and heroine in the middle of an argument, for instance, the reader wants to know who wins. Emotional excitement and plot-based excitement are both effective, and a combination is more than the sum of its parts.

✔ **Involve the reader right away.** If you make her care about what's happening, she has a vested interest in your story. If you start with your hero and heroine on a sinking ship, you engage your reader on a gut level because you've put her in the middle of a life-or-death situation. She tries to stay afloat right along with your characters — and she keeps reading to be sure everyone's safe. You can't make every situation literally life or death, of course, but you can make every situation *feel* like it is. If you start inside a character's point of view as they deal with something that matters to them, you can make that thing matter to the reader, too.

Opening night without the stars

There are exceptions to every rule, and some books begin with a prologue or a scene that doesn't feature either the hero or the heroine. That can be tricky to pull off, so if you try it, be sure to keep two points in mind:

✔ You need to choose an exciting moment to start your story.

✔ You need to get your reader personally involved in the outcome.

Often, even when the hero and heroine aren't on the scene, one or both of them will somehow be the focus of what's going on.

You're writing a romance, so the hero and heroine — and sparks — should figure prominently from the very beginning. Not every book can or will begin with both the hero and the heroine in the scene together, but whether one or both are present, you have to provide compelling characters from the start. All the advice I provide in Chapter 4 on developing strong characters is particularly applicable to your hero and heroine in the beginning — if you don't grab the reader's attention now, she won't give your characters the chance to win her over later, because she'll stop reading. Here are a few points to keep in mind:

- ✔ **Make the reader empathize with your heroine.** Get your reader to identify with your heroine from the start and you increase the likelihood that she'll keep turning pages (and plunk down her money for your book).

- ✔ **Make the reader fall for your hero.** Romances are all about falling in love. When you give your reader a reason to care about your hero from the start (beyond his undeniable good looks), she'll be his 'til the end — and will keep reading to get there.

- ✔ **Make sure your hero and heroine are attracted to each other.** Even though your hero and heroine should be at odds — often quite dramatically — from the beginning, the minute they're together, there should still be an unmistakable spark between them that tells the reader these two people belong together — and assures her that she's going to enjoy watching them fall in love.

From beginning to end, make your reader ask questions. Design your opening so that the reader wants to know the answers to questions like: What's going on? Why is she mad at him? What's he rescuing her from? Questions and curiosity get your reader involved and keep her reading.

How to bore your reader

Right along with beginnings that guarantee you can hook a reader, there are beginnings guaranteed to turn her right off. You want to avoid these opening techniques, because if you turn a reader off at the start, you've probably turned her off forever.

- ✔ **Don't recap the background.** Your reader doesn't care about the details of the Battle of Hastings or the trials of modern-day ranching when she's reading a romance. She'll just move on to another book that gives her the emotional excitement she's craving. Don't start with long descriptions of scenery, the political situation, or what in the heroine's life made her end up in this place at this time. All that information can come later. At the beginning, it just gets in the way of the good stuff.

- ✔ **Don't create a laundry list of character descriptions.** Finding out who your characters are, not what they look like, makes your reader care about them. Instead of providing boring descriptions, use dialogue, character thoughts, and piecemeal details to tell your reader the basics of what a character looks like while also explaining who the character is. Writing *Sabrina's green eyes snapped with anger as she strode into Drake's office* engages the reader much more effectively than writing *Sabrina had bright green eyes*. The first sentence makes the reader ask why Sabrina is angry at Drake. The second sentence is a narrative dead-end that doesn't encourage the reader to find out more.

✔ **Don't spend time on unimportant info when you have a story to tell.** Nonessential information only delays your reader from getting to the elements that keep her reading. If you start out with a heroine who's a police hostage negotiator in the middle of a life-or-death situation, no one cares that she has a sister and two brothers, all younger, along with a dog named Murphy — unless one of them is a hostage who she's negotiating for. The reader just wants to know whether the hostages can be saved — and where she can find the hero. Get in her way and she puts down your book and picks up (and pays for) someone else's.

The cute meet: Necessary or not?

Writers often ask me at conferences whether starting with the cute meet is necessary. This question is usually followed by someone else asking what a cute meet is. A *cute meet* means that you begin your book by introducing your hero and heroine in some unique, memorable, and often humorous way. The possibilities are endless, but here are some examples:

✔ Your heroine accidentally backs her car into a handsome stranger's luxury SUV in the company parking lot, and then goes up to her office and discovers that he's her new boss.

✔ The hero and heroine are both in law enforcement, and they're investigating the same case, but neither one of them knows it. Approaching from opposite sides of a building, they round the corner and end up aiming their guns at each other.

✔ Your hero's furious because his son has been suspended from school and storms into the principal's office to complain — only to find out that the principal's the woman he was flirting with at a party the night before.

✔ Strangers Julie Denton and Blake Denton are assigned to share a cabin on a sold-out cruise because someone mistakenly assumed that they're husband and wife.

✔ Heroine Jaimie Dickson reports for her first day of work on an oil rig, where her good-looking new boss is shocked to discover that he's hired a woman, not the man her name had led him to expect.

Should you start your romance novel with your characters' own cute meet (which I hope you can make more original than the examples I just gave)? Ultimately, only you can answer that question. A cute meet has both pros and cons, so you need to weigh both sides of the equation.

First, here are the pros of using a cute meet:

✔ **It starts with action.** Action involves the reader immediately, which is one of the two things that a good opening scene does (see the "How to hook your reader" section earlier in this chapter).

✔ **It helps define the characters.** By showing how they react in an interesting, unexpected, and even stressful situation, your characters stand out as individuals right away. That gives your reader an immediate chance to identify with the heroine and fall for the hero.

✔ **It can immediately introduce the source of tension.** Even if additional complicating factors show up as the book goes along, the cute meet gives you an opportunity to immediately set up at least part of the conflict the hero and heroine need to overcome, which lets the reader get right to the heart of the story.

✔ **It's memorable.** Because a good cute meet is unique, the characters and their situation stand out in the reader's mind. A reader wants to follow a story line that's memorable and more than just the same old, same old.

And here are some potential pitfalls to using a cute meet:

✔ **The cliché factor.** The first and last examples I give earlier in this section really *are* clichés. These days, you really can't use those examples in a book and make your characters seem unique and their story worth reading. To use a cute meet, you have to work hard to make sure that it's something readers haven't seen before.

✔ **The contrivance factor.** Cute meets often feel contrived, like something the writer's forcing the characters into, not something real people would ever do or a situation they'd ever find themselves in. If the meeting feels contrived, the reader never believes in the characters. And if she doesn't believe in the characters, she won't care about them or their story.

✔ **It undercuts your characters.** Instead of showing your characters as well-rounded, admirable, interesting people, the cute meet can make them come off as shrill, selfish, sexist, petty, just generally unpleasant, or even stupid. In short, a cute meet can show them as exactly the kinds of characters no reader wants to get to know any further.

✔ **It sets the wrong tone.** As a word, *cute* implies a certain lightness, and many cute meets *are* light and humorous in tone. That tone works perfectly if you're writing a romantic comedy, but your opening may mislead the reader if the rest of your book is suspenseful or dramatic. She'll either expect a different kind of story than she's going to get and be disappointed if she buys the book, or she won't realize it's actually going to turn into a book she'd like, and she *won't* buy it.

✔ **It misrepresents your conflict.** Sometimes a cute meet tries so hard to be as cute as the name implies that it makes the conflict seem as if it has no depth, because the characters end up arguing over something minor and silly. Instead of introducing the real — and compelling — source of conflict that occupies the rest of the book, the cute meet puts something silly front and center, which can turn off a reader looking for substance.

After you've weighed the pros and cons in relation to the characters and story you have in mind, you have to ask yourself one all-important question: If I had never met these characters before and had no idea what their story was going to be, would a cute meet make me more or less likely to continue reading? If the answer is "more likely," then you definitely want to go for the cute meet.

Putting Theory into Practice

After you realize that you need a sense of excitement to capture a reader's interest, you can decide what point in your story makes for the most effective beginning and how to handle that beginning. You can also create the necessary sense of connection in the reader, making your story matter even more to her.

In the hands of a capable writer, watching paint dry can be exciting. Although I don't recommend that scene for the opening of your romance novel, it does make the point that an exciting scene doesn't have to involve running, driving fast, gunfire, or karate.

Finding your starting point

The best way to make something — anything — exciting is to start in what writers call, thanks to the ancient Romans, *in medias res* (translated as "in the middle of the thing"). Don't start your story at the beginning, because beginnings often move slowly and don't seem very interesting until events reach critical mass. You can always go back later and fill your reader in on the details (see "Backtracking to the background" later in this chapter). Start your romance novel in the middle, when something interesting is already going on.

The *real* beginning of a story — not the place where a novel *should* begin — is often slow, a buildup of details that may seem unimportant and unrelated, even just plain boring, at first. If your romance novel begins at this beginning, you're probably looking too far back in time. Even when you communicate relevant and necessary background info, the reader is likely to find it uninvolving and way too time-consuming, so where *should* you start?

You need to choose an exciting moment, a moment when something is happening that lets you show off your characters and their situation to best effect. Think of it as the beginning of the story the characters share together, rather than the beginning of the entire story.

Suppose your heroine is sure that her brother has been framed and sent to prison for a crime that he didn't commit, and she thinks that the hero is the one who framed him. She decides to confront the hero with her suspicions. That scene's bound to be exciting and full of fireworks, along with the first hints of sexual tension. So why not start with the moment when she walks into his office, ready to bombard him with her suspicions?

Be sure you have a handle on your heroine and hero so that they seem real to you — and therefore to the reader — as soon as they're introduced (see Chapter 4 for more on building characters). Then let your story rip. Get the reader involved — emotionally, intellectually, any way you can — from the first line. Drop her into the action, get her adrenalin flowing, make her care about your characters, and she's turning pages as fast as she can.

Here are a couple of alternate takes on the scene I just described, where the heroine walks in on the hero, gunning for metaphorical bear. These examples demonstrate not only why this is an effective place to begin a book, but also two techniques for writing that beginning: narrative and dialogue.

You can start with a line or two of narrative:

> *Melody Smith knew she was treading on thin ice when she marched into Derek LaMott's office unannounced, but she was past caring. This man had ruined her brother's life and, by extension, her own, and there was no way on earth she was going to let him get away with it. Derek LaMott was about to pay for what he had done.*

I make a point of staying inside the heroine's point of view to add immediacy to the scene and to create a connection between her and the reader.

You can also start with dialogue and mix in some narration to give your reader a bit of context:

> *"Did you really think you could get away with it?"*
> *Derek LaMott looked up from behind his impressive walnut desk. Against her will, Melody Smith found herself momentarily mesmerized by the deep blue gaze he turned her way. Then she caught herself and remembered why she was there: for justice.*
> *"Get away with what?" LaMott asked, his deep voice shivering its way up Melody's spine.*

Both those approaches work, though I prefer the one that uses dialogue, because I think dialogue adds immediacy to the scene. I also think that you can best get to know someone through the way he or she speaks, and that fact is as true of fictional characters as it is of real people.

Both approaches immediately draw the reader into the story, which is why they both work. They start in the middle of "the thing" and put the reader in the heroine's head so that she cares what happens next. Both approaches also get the reader asking questions: How did Derek ruin Melody's brother's life — and hers? What does she think he got away with? What kind of justice is she looking for, and how does she plan to get it? If the reader is asking questions, she's going to want to keep reading to find out the answers.

The second example also introduces a few salient points about each character and establishes the beginnings of sexual attraction. And because every romance needs that element of attraction, the sooner you demonstrate that your hero and heroine feel it for each other, the better.

Both openings avoided the time-wasting — and interest-killing — traps I point out in the section called "How to bore your reader" earlier in this chapter. Instead of force-feeding details to the reader (whatever Melody's brother supposedly did, full descriptions of Melody and Derek) before she cares about the characters and their situation, these openings hit a few key points and save the specifics for later, when the reader has the time and interest to deal with them.

Backtracking to the background

After you choose the best place to open your story, you're almost certainly left with information your reader needs to know. But that information would be out of place in the beginning, so your job is to figure out where and how to get the relevant info to your reader.

Suppose your heroine just quit her job in the wake of her boss's unwanted advances, and then went home, hoping for a good cry, and found her fiancé in bed with another woman. Luckily for her, the heroine recently inherited a ranch from an uncle she hardly knew, so she heads out West and makes a new life for herself, far away from the bad memories. The smart place to open the book is with her arrival at the ranch, where she immediately meets the hero. But the reader will wonder why she's there. What was bad enough to make her leave everything she knew behind and start a whole new life?

Those questions need to be answered or your book won't make sense. Your next challenge is filling in the blanks in the background, without stalling the story's forward momentum. You can use three tried-and-true techniques to do that. The first method involves taking a moment relatively early in the story to *briefly* review necessary background. Or you can dole out information piecemeal throughout the book, so the reader's never stopped in her tracks for a history lesson. The third technique involves the use of a flashback, which takes the reader back in time for (usually) a few paragraphs or pages, or (sometimes) even a chapter or more.

Picking a quiet moment

After you start your novel at an exciting and involving point, you can fill in the background later, where doing so doesn't take much time or get in the way of your story. A lot of aspiring writers think that they need to actually show everything — including all the relevant background — or, at least, provide the reader with all the details. Not true. Most of the time, an overview works just fine. Often a paragraph or two, or even just a couple of key sentences, can do it. In the preceding section, I fit most of what a reader needs to know about the heroine's background into a few sentences (the boss's advances, the fiancé's philandering, the uncle's ranch). Fleshed out with a few details to give it weight and lend interest, that background can still fit into a paragraph, and you can frequently fit a paragraph like that into a quiet moment shortly after the book gets going. For example:

- ✔ The heroine arrives at the ranch and runs smack into the hero, the foreman who's been running the place since her uncle's death (and, truth be told, for the last few years before he died). They immediately get into a run-in, based on a combination of her not belonging on a ranch she hasn't ever visited — which he sees as an insult to her uncle, a man who was like a father to him — and her attraction to him, which makes her distant, even rude, because she's in no mood to think well of *any* man at the moment.

  After their set-to, she wanders around the ranch, feeling at loose ends, maybe meeting some of the secondary characters, seeing the hero again from a distance and again tamping down her interest, or having another run-in of some sort, before finally collapsing on her bed (a bed in a room and a place that feel totally foreign to her), reflecting briefly on what led her to make the trip to a new life.

- ✔ You can also use the alternate approach of making one of the secondary characters someone friendly and welcoming who gets her to talk, and the whole story of the sleazy boss and even sleazier ex-fiancé comes spilling out.

Either approach lets you present the basics of the background briefly and in one go. Later, if the reader needs more information, you can write in a line or a paragraph containing the necessary bits and include it in a similar way, where it doesn't call attention to itself or interrupt the flow of the narrative.

Doling out details as you go

You can also take your time and dole the facts out slowly, one at a time. The heroine may reflect on quitting her job but not reveal why she left until several pages or more later. You can even leave the whole story of the ex-fiancé as a mystery, using her point of view to indicate that something major happened but never specifying what, until it all comes out in an emotional scene with the hero.

Saving key facts and hinting at their existence without revealing them is especially effective when you're dealing with a romantic mystery or suspense plot. By withholding information and making the reader try to figure out what's going on, you're essentially presenting additional clues — whether those clues deal with the plot or the characters' emotional state — to the reader, who's already in mystery-solving mode and primed to enjoy the additional challenge.

Making use of flashbacks

Flashbacks get a bad rap, I think, because too many writers tend to overuse and just plain misuse them. When they're handled properly, though, they can be extremely effective. The key lies in knowing when and how to use them.

Sometimes you really need to include a crucial scene in its entirety for full emotional effect, but it happens before the true action of the book begins or just doesn't have the right characteristics to be an opening scene. That scene can become an effective flashback.

How do you know whether a scene is worthy of a flashback or not? Most of the time, you need to base your decision on whether or not it features the hero or the heroine (usually both) and strongly impacts the relationship. Occasionally the flashback isn't relationship related but features one or the other of your main characters and is necessary for the plot. In either case ask yourself whether the book would be weaker without it. If you answer "yes," you have a flashback on your hands.

Authors most commonly use a flashback to fill in the past relationship between a hero and heroine who knew each other before the book began. Don't use a flashback if they only knew each other as passing strangers or business acquaintances, though. You should use a flashback if they were lovers, spouses, or otherwise romantically involved. Their past relationship colors everything that happens in the present and forms the basis of your book, so just saying that they used to be involved doesn't get across the emotional impact you want.

You can, and should, have the two characters talk out their issues at some point in the course of the book. But because they're talking about a shared past, it feels awkward if they go so far as to recount every detail of what happened, because they don't need to remind each other of events they lived through together. (I talk more about this issue in Chapter 9, when I discuss natural and believable dialogue.) This situation just begs to be dealt with in flashback.

Choose an appropriate point — usually following an encounter between the two of them, often an emotionally intense one, and maybe even after the first scene — and have one of the characters think back to how things used to be, how everything fell apart . . . whatever makes sense for the story. You just need a sentence or two of transition, and then you can present the flashback in the same tense (simple past) as the rest of the book.

Depending on your story and how much of the past you need to show, you can use a series of flashbacks or even one long one that's comprised of multiple scenes and can go on for a chapter or more. The bottom line lies in something I say all the time to writers: It's all in the execution. I've seen romances where more or less half the book was a flashback. If it works, I'm fine with it. I also see books with one brief flashback that doesn't work — the scene itself is unnecessary or the placement is jarring, for example — and I'm *not* fine with that. It really isn't what you do, it's how you do it that counts.

How should you format a flashback? If you're lucky enough to get feedback from an editor, she may have a specific format she'd like you to follow, but if you're working in the dark, you have several possibilities. You can italicize the entire thing (much like a dream), but personally, I find that awkward and hard to read (especially for multiple flashbacks or flashbacks longer than one page). You can also present it as part of your text, without any special spacing or other formatting, but to me, the clearest approach is to set it off with time/space breaks (see Chapter 14 for a description) before and after the flashback.

Opening lines that work

Because the first page, especially the first paragraph, and even the first line, of your book can be so important, you should put some extra time into thinking about what makes an opening work and what practical techniques you can use to make sure yours is a winner.

Going solo

Visually speaking, a single, relatively brief line really catches the eye. If you can craft a strong opening line, one that intrigues the reader, you can increase its impact by letting it stand alone. A few examples off the top of my head (and believe me, I'm sure you can do better):

The man in the corner wouldn't stop looking at her.

It wasn't until the arrows stopped flying that she realized she'd been hit.

There she was, the woman he loved and hadn't seen in six months — and she was nine months pregnant if she was a day.

Each of those sentences puts the reader right in the middle of a situation where the stakes are high, whether in terms of curiosity (the first: Why is the man looking at her? Is he the hero?), suspense (the second: Will she live?), or emotionally (the third: Is it his baby? Why didn't she tell him before he left?). Each opening line makes the reader ask at least one question that's interesting and important enough to make her keep reading.

Shorter is better

Even if you can't come up with a single line as an opener, or if your story doesn't lend itself to such an abrupt beginning, try to avoid starting with a long, dense paragraph, especially one that takes up all or most of the page. A big chunk of text, whether it's description, internal monologue, or anything else, looks intimidating. Try to make your first paragraph relatively brief, and follow it with several manageable-looking ones, not one that takes up the rest of the page. That makes your book look more inviting to the reader.

Talking the talk

Don't start with just any dialogue — start with something exciting that puts the reader right into the scene and a key character's head. Use a brief, punchy line — one that makes the reader wonder what's happening and where things are going. Here are some dialogue examples:

> *"What the hell are you doing here?"*

> *"What do you mean, it's my baby?"*

> *"I'm going to get out of here, and when I do, Mr. Kirkland Martin the Third is toast!"*

Any one of those lines can stand alone, but you can also add a dialogue tag or an ensuing line of description. Here are the expanded versions:

> *"What the hell are you doing here?" She knew she was shouting, but she couldn't stop herself. She'd traveled 2,000 miles to get away from him, and now here he was, standing on her doorstep, as large as life and even more handsome than she remembered.*

> *"What do you mean, it's my baby?" he growled, moving to stand threateningly over her and the tiny blue-clad bundle she was cradling in her arms.*

> *"I'm going to get out of here, and when I do, Mr. Kirkland Martin the Third is toast!" She felt stupid talking to herself, but after three days locked in a bank vault — damn long weekends, anyway — she was desperate for the sound of a voice, any voice, even her own. Besides, threats always sounded better aloud.*

Asking questions

Two of the previous examples ask a question. You want to make the reader curious, to get her asking mental questions about what happens next. If you can find a natural way to ask a question for her, which makes her try to think of the answer herself, so much the better. Just be sure that the question sounds natural; you don't want the reader to hear your voice talking to her, only your character's.

Setting deadlines

This technique doesn't work for every storyline, but time pressure in your book can work on your reader the same way that time pressure works in real life —increasing a sense of urgency — which makes her even more eager to keep reading. You can work in a built-in deadline easily if you're dealing with suspense, but you can make it work just as well in nonsuspense stories. For example:

> *Five minutes. Five minutes, and then, if the stick turned blue, her life was going to take a ninety-degree turn straight into booties, babies, and boy, was she in trouble.*

> *Lisa tapped her foot impatiently and checked her watch. Again. She would give him another 30 seconds, and then she was going hunting for another husband.*

Bucking conventional wisdom

How you approach this option is up to you. Sometimes you have an idea so good that you just have to toss the rules out the window and go with it. If you think that's happening to you, commit it to paper, let it sit for a day, and then go back and read it, asking yourself one question: If you went into a store, picked up this book and, knowing nothing about it, read this opener, would you want to know more? If you can honestly answer yes, go ahead and give it a shot.

Constructing Can't-Miss Chapters

Just as the opening of your book is crucial to getting a reader interested in the first place, every chapter — the ending of one and the beginning of the next — needs to keep her interest high and get her to keep turning pages instead of putting the book down and going off to do something else.

A reader is most likely to put down a book at the end of a chapter, a natural and logical break, and any time a reader puts a book down, she's in danger of never picking it up again. If that happens, she ends up looking at that author as a waste of money and avoiding her in the future. For that reason, the end of every chapter you write needs to leave her at a point where she's dying to know more.

You can't guarantee that a reader will *never* put your book down — some things, like the call of a crying baby or the need to finish lunch and get back to work, have to take precedence. But you *can* do your best to ensure that she picks it back up again the minute she has a chance.

Treat your chapter openings with as much care as every chapter's ending. For one thing, a lot of readers cheat and sneak a peek at the opening of the next chapter, in large part to see whether the action that ended the previous chapter continues, because the reader wants to know how it turns out. In addition, when a reader picks the book back up, you have to lock her back into your story as quickly as possible so that real life doesn't beckon her away.

Aim to keep each chapter at about 20–25 manuscript pages. This length keeps the book from feeling choppy, as if it's been broken into too many sections, and minimizes the number of chapter endings, each of which poses the risk of your reader putting down the book for good. But at that length, each chapter also stays short enough not to be daunting, so if your reader's tired or only has a little bit of time to read, she feels capable of managing "just one more."

Viewing every chapter as a new beginning

Think of every chapter opening in the same terms you think about the opening of your romance novel itself. You don't introduce your characters every time, of course, and the physical attraction between them should be clear even by chapter two, but you can always reveal something new about them or emphasize and deepen the attraction.

The beginning of every chapter needs to grab the reader's attention right away. Whether you pick up where the action of the previous chapter left off or switch to another scene (or another character's point of view), make sure that what you're doing is exciting and interesting.

As with the opening of your book (see the section "How to hook your reader" earlier in this chapter for my tips on how to start), you may want to start right in the middle of something. But because you have the weight of your book behind you, which already gives the reader the impetus to go on, you can also start at the beginning of a scene, so long as you make the beginning interesting.

Avoid opening a chapter with a long period of setting the scene or introspection that doesn't also raise questions in the reader's mind that she wants to see answered. You've worked hard to keep your book moving up to this point (see Chapter 10 for more information on pacing), so you don't want to slow it down — much less bring it to a halt — now. Give the reader a good reason to go on, and go on she will.

Leave 'em wanting more: Effective chapter endings

Many aspiring writers succumb to the temptation to finish every chapter as if they're ending a mini-book. They sum up what happened, wrap up the action, and leave the reader with a sigh of relief. Big mistake.

If the reader's feeling good, as if she's gotten a payoff, she has no incentive to keep reading. She's more likely to put the book down and bask in her happiness (and the characters' happiness) for a while. That may be great for her, but it's lousy for you. That kind of feeling may even make her put the book down when she doesn't have to — when real life isn't beckoning, when she's wide awake and not struggling to read "just one more page" — and that's a dangerous situation. If your chapter ending doesn't give her a reason to read on, you've failed. As you can see in the following sections, you have more than one option for making chapter endings work for (not against) you.

Hanging by a thread: Cliffhangers made simple

The easiest way to force a reader to keep going (and best of all, she'll be so caught up in the story that she won't even resent it) is to end your chapter with a cliffhanger. Whether you use a literally life-or-death scenario (the heroine hanging off the side of a cliff and hoping that the hero arrives in time to rescue her) or you only make it feel that way (the hero has just stormed out of the bedroom, accusing the heroine of betraying him by not telling him he has a son), you can get the reader's heart racing, her brain whirling, and her fingers turning pages by breaking away from the action at a crucial point.

Some plots lend themselves to cliffhangers more readily than others. Any kind of suspense, mystery, or adventure plot is a natural fit. Historical romances, because they often take place at a time when day-to-day life was more exciting and demanding, also often lend themselves to cliffhanger endings. Any action-oriented scene creates an easy opportunity, but you can make anything in your story feel important enough to build a cliffhanger around.

Is your heroine waiting for word on the outcome of her child's operation? Does the fate of the ranch hang on how well the cattle sell at market? Has the power gone out in the lab just as the hero was about to complete the last crucial equation? Have the horses left the starting gate but not yet reached the home stretch?

Even without an earth-shattering plot twist, every romance has the perfect ingredients to create a cliffhanger: a man, a woman, and romantic tension. Every romance reader wants to see the ultimate happiness of the hero and heroine. Get the characters to an emotionally fraught point and then cut the scene short. Leave them without resolution (even send one of them storming away), and you have a cliffhanger no reader can resist. (For tips on when to resolve cliffhangers, see the "Keeping transitions fresh" section later in the chapter.)

Romances have an advantage over every other form of fiction when it comes to cliffhangers — the extreme importance that the romantic relationship holds for the reader. No other form of fiction can promise that kind of emotional involvement on the part of the reader. Romance novels have access to every kind of cliffhanger in fiction in general — plus guaranteed access to one more.

Sending mixed messages

You can also keep your reader reading by giving her satisfaction on one level at the end of the chapter but withholding the total happiness she's looking for. To do that, get to a point in the plot or even emotionally that seems to offer satisfaction, and then use your hero or heroine's point of view to show that things aren't really as simple or on as even a keel as they look. Another option is to get to what seems to be a resolution, and then throw a monkey wrench into the works by introducing another complication. Just be sure that whatever you introduce feels believable — an emotional issue that's been simmering under the surface or an unexpected but still logical plot twist, for example. Out-of-the-blue contrivance — the hero's teenage daughter *who's never even been mentioned before,* for instance — is a surefire way to irritate a reader.

By creating a partial sense of satisfaction, and then adding doubt and tension, you give the reader reason to hope that she may eventually get everything she wants. And you also give her a specific reason to keep reading: to see what effect the newly introduced or otherwise unresolved issue has on things. You can use this approach with a purely emotional scene or by using action.

- ✔ **Playing on emotion:** Throughout the entire course of every romance, the reader is hoping for one thing — to see the hero and heroine get together. In most cases, that means physically, through lovemaking (or, at least, kissing and other physical intimacies). In every case, the reader's hoping for emotional intimacy and for the characters to settle their differences.

  You can give the reader a great partial payoff at the end of a chapter by letting the couple get closer physically, whether it's a first kiss or actual lovemaking. But then withhold the full emotional payoff by using one character's point of view to show trouble in paradise, a secret that can break them up, an emotional complication that he or she thinks can't possibly be overcome . . . anything that lets the reader know that these characters still have plenty to resolve in the relationship.

✔ **Wrapping up the action:** You can wrap up something active or sus-penseful (the opposite of creating a cliffhanger), letting the reader breathe a sigh of relief. Nonstop action can be tough. You have to give her a break sometime. Then you can undercut her relief by getting inside a character's head to reveal more trouble — whether plot-related or emotional — to come.

Maybe the hero's just rescued the heroine from a group of South American revolutionaries, and she's fallen into his arms in gratitude. But then the hero hears the sound of approaching footsteps and the snick of the safety being released on a gun. Or maybe the hero and heroine have just finished a tough negotiation with a rival company. Their side won, so they're laughing and happy, and he's giving her a preview of just how much happier he plans to make her in bed that night. The reader's happy, too — until the heroine thinks to herself that soon she'll have to start making excuses not to go to bed with the hero or he'll notice that she's pregnant and starting to show.

As a variation on this approach (less effective because it's less immediate, but still viable), you can leave an important issue unresolved earlier in the chapter and then provide a payoff for something else at the end of the chap-ter. The reader enjoys the resolution you do provide, but she'll keep reading in search of a resolution for the earlier issue, too. Just be sure that the unre-solved issue is important enough to stay in the front of the reader's mind, so she's still thinking about it even at the end of the chapter when you're wrap-ping up something else.

Packing a punch

The hardest type of effective chapter ending to talk about is what I call *ending with a punch.* I'd be rich if I had a nickel for every time I've told an author she needs a punchier line for the end of her chapter — and I'm not talking about the punch line of a joke.

Sometimes the punch comes not in what happens but in how you say it. That concept can be difficult to explain: It's both vague and frequently subjective. Essentially, it means ending the chapter at a moment of high emotion or excitement, so your prose is still moving, and not tacking on a final line that slows things down and wraps them up. Keep the reader's adrenaline flowing; don't give her a chance to relax and pull away from the book.

✔ **An ending with punch:** Picture a wonderful, emotional, sexy love scene with a lot of intense description as the hero and heroine create never-before-seen forms of foreplay. Finally, the moment comes, and to end the scene, you say something like: *He pulled her tighter, stared deep into her eyes and, with a groan torn from deep inside, plunged home.*

✔ **An ending that falls flat:** I often see an author who has the right end line, but she's tacked on something extraneous that ruins the pacing and deflects the punch: *He pulled her tighter, stared deep into her eyes and, with a groan torn from deep inside, plunged home. He had never felt so right, so complete, so at peace.* That one extra line slows the pace and makes the scene feel finished in a way the first version didn't, and that makes it less likely to draw the reader forward.

You can use this technique with any kind of scene, not just a love scene. If you end a chapter without a cliffhanger or mixed message (the other techniques I cover in this section), take a look at what you've written and think about each of the last few lines, or maybe the last few paragraphs. Experiment by cutting the last line or paragraph, especially if it seems like you've wrapped things up, and see if you can make the chapter end with a bigger bang.

Keeping transitions fresh

As you move between chapters, you need to vary the way you do it. If you end every chapter with a cliffhanger, your reader starts to find things predictable, and eventually your cliffhangers become increasingly less effective — especially if you immediately solve each one at the start of the next chapter. By working variety and unpredictability into how you handle your chapter openings and endings, you keep the reader interested and on her toes — and eagerly turning pages to see what happens next.

A good technique for moving from chapter to chapter while keeping the reader involved is to end one chapter on a cliffhanger and then start the next chapter with something completely different but also interesting. This strategy keeps the reader's interest on two fronts. She wants to know how the cliffhanger turns out, so she keeps reading for that reason alone. But because you've also started the next chapter with something interesting in its own right, she also wants to know more about what's going on right in front of her.

You can also end with a cliffhanger and then dial things down at the beginning of the next chapter. You can't dial them so far down that the reader gets bored or skips the boring bits in a search to see how the cliffhanger turns out. But, if you keep the writing interesting, you *can* vary the pace, maybe get inside a character's head for some explanation or move into a flashback (see the "Making use of flashbacks" section earlier in the chapter). You don't always need to move from action to action, and in fact, you shouldn't. As I discuss in Chapter 10, the best pacing involves varying the tempo.

Moving from Scene to Scene

Moving from scene to scene is very much like moving from chapter to chapter, just on a smaller scale. Every word you write should be geared toward drawing your reader forward from page to page, so beginnings and endings — whether on the macro- or micro-level — are key components of your writing and one of the elements of pacing.

Stringing scenes together

Look at scenes as tiny chapters and then use the same techniques to move between them that you use for moving between chapters:

- ✔ **Start with something interesting.** Your book has no room for anything that doesn't earn its keep. Don't think a reader doesn't notice or mind if you sandwich a filler scene — however interesting you may find the info or however poetic the description — in between two interesting scenes. Other than a fire, an earthquake, or a crying baby, you can't find a surer way to get her to put your book down in the middle of a chapter.

  Just like the beginning of your book or the start of every chapter, the beginning of every scene has to interest her, even if it's not deeply emotional or actively exciting. An individual scene is a smaller increment than a full chapter, so you can paint it on a smaller, less dramatic canvas. In fact, it makes sense to save most of the big-bang stuff for transitions between chapters, where the risk of losing the reader is greatest.

- ✔ **End with something intriguing.** You have more flexibility here than with chapter endings, but overall, you should employ the same techniques as you do when ending a chapter — cliffhangers, mixed messages, and punch (as I discuss in the "Leave 'em wanting more: Effective chapter endings" section earlier in the chapter). With scene endings, though, you can also end with a genuine wrap-up of that small piece of the action, whether plot-oriented or emotional.

- ✔ **Vary your methods.** As with chapter transitions, don't rely on the same technique every time. You don't want your reader to be able to predict your every move, so mix them up.

Although you generally don't want an entire action chapter to move into a chapter made up solely of introspection, single scenes can have a single tone because they're shorter. But if you end one scene on a calm note, start the next scene on a different note — exciting, suspenseful, humorous.

Seeing scene endings as mini-chapter endings

The way you end each scene is particularly crucial. In addition to employing the same techniques that you use to end any chapter (see the section "Leave 'em wanting more: Effective chapter endings" earlier in this chapter), watch out for one pitfall that I rarely see with chapter endings but frequently see with scene endings: trailing off.

Sometimes, a writer is so focused on making every chapter ending dramatic that she loses sight of her individual scene endings. Each scene may be important, but instead of ending effectively, some or all of them just sputter away. Here are a few examples:

- ✔ Characters finish the relevant part of a conversation but keep talking, moving on to other subjects, saying extended goodbyes. Real-life conversations do move in that way, but in a romance novel, that kind of conversation is counterproductive. It bores the reader and takes the focus off what she's supposed to take away from the scene.

- ✔ Don't let the action go on too long. The reader rarely needs to see the follow-up to the important parts. If the heroine's been trying — and failing — to saddle her own horse every day for a week, end at the moment when she finally succeeds. Readers don't need to see her mounting up and riding away.

- ✔ Know the point of your scene. Characters often reach key conclusions and revelations about themselves or what's going on during action scenes, sometimes even during scenes of mundane everyday action. The point of a scene like that almost always lies in the character's progress, not the action itself. So after you've hit that high point, wrap up the scene and move on to the next.

Intercutting scenes

If you end a scene with a mini-cliffhanger or with the reader in doubt as to how things will work out, don't always be in a hurry to relieve her suspense or answer her questions.

You can follow what's essentially the chapter pattern: Break off the scene at a key point, cut to something else entirely (the equivalent of opening the next chapter without picking up where you left off), and then resolve the cliffhanger a scene or more later. But because scenes are so much shorter than full chapters, you can alternate between two scenes in a way that you'd have a lot more trouble doing successfully if you were working with chapters.

You can follow the film technique of *intercutting* two scenes (moving back and forth between them) so that you break each down into three, four, or more bits. This technique works most effectively when each scene is compelling in its own right, so that the reader is equally interested in how both of them turn out.

Each time you cut away, pick an exciting moment, even a mini-cliffhanger, and each time you cut back, re-enter the action *in medias res*. (Check out the section "Finding your starting point" for a description of that $10 phrase.) Don't recap, just keep things moving, going back and forth until you resolve each scene.

Don't overuse the technique or you dilute its effectiveness. But when you have the raw material, in the form of two compelling scenes happening simultaneously, don't be afraid to maximize the excitement by intercutting them.

Chapter 13

Getting Your Story Straight: Doing Research Right

*A*bout the only time that you can get away with absolutely no research is if you're writing a contemporary romance that's set in your own area and deals with realities — jobs, settings, and character types — that you already know. You might also be able to get away without doing any research if you're a historian and writing about a period that you know inside out. But if you don't need to do any research, you're one of the lucky ones — and your book is a relative rarity. Most books require research, even if only a little, to make them accurate. And your book *needs* to be accurate, which makes research crucial.

Few people would question the need to research a historical romance, and most contemporary romances include at least one or two aspects outside the author's personal experiences or knowledge. Even futuristic and fantasy-based romances usually require some research, depending on the world you create, because those worlds still need to feel believable and logical to the reader. This fact is especially true of any story based on current scientific developments.

In this chapter, I talk about everything research related, starting with how to recognize what you need to know more about. I also give you some ideas on where to find the facts that you want, how to organize the facts that you find, how to use information to make your book stronger, and what to do about getting legal permission when you need it.

Getting It Right: Priority Number One

Everything — selling an editor on your work and then selling readers on your talents — depends on one thing: Getting your readers so wrapped up in the story that the characters' lives, emotions, and the world you've created for them feel real. To make that happen, you have to make the illusion perfect. You can't let anything break the spell — and nothing breaks the spell like running smack into some sort of mistake, whether it's a western saddle on a Thoroughbred racehorse or a Medieval heroine zipping up her wedding dress.

Factual missteps can turn off readers, but if an editor catches a lot of mistakes, your manuscript likely will never even see a bookshelf. As an editor, I need to know I can count on a writer to get things right, because I don't have time to check and fix all the details, though I keep an eye out for everything I can. So if I don't feel I can trust an author to get the facts straight, I'm just not going to take her on.

Your editor counts on you for accuracy, because she can't double-check *every* fact in your book, although she will question or correct everything she can (Chapter 18 explains the publication process and talks about who does what on your manuscript). Sometimes, though, despite everyone's best efforts, factual mistakes make it through all the way to publication, and most of the time, readers *will* catch those mistakes, even if it's only one reader in 10 or 100. And every reader who catches you in a mistake may never pick up another one of your books. What she *will* do is tell all her friends (not to mention everyone who reads the who-knows-how-many romance-related Internet message boards). She could even be a reviewer who tells thousands of people what you did wrong.

Ultimately, sales are the lifeblood of every author, and if your sales suffer because you aren't careful with your research, your career can disappear before it ever gets fully started. Wherever and however you do your research, check and double-check everything you can. Making absolutely sure that you have things right can never hurt.

Making Research Work for You

Research is important, but diving headfirst into the Lake o' Facts without thinking the process through can be counterproductive. Having a plan before you actually start looking around for information can help you focus on finding what you need, rather than wandering off on tangents that, however interesting, probably just waste your time.

Efficiency is the name of the research game. You want to spend your time writing your book so that you can get it in front of an editor as quickly as possible. Being prolific — whether that means writing two or three series books a year or one mainstream book every nine to twelve months — can help you become successful. So you don't want to sabotage your own chances by getting distracted. Real life provides enough unavoidable distractions, so why add more if you don't have to?

Figuring out what you need to know

Most editors question everything they can. I'm forever asking my authors (and asking other editors to ask their authors) to check their facts. Even so, there are some things I never even think to question, and plenty of very good editors focus on the bigger-picture aspects of editing (characterization, story structure, and so on), leaving the details in the hands of the author and, secondarily, the copy editor. That's why it's your job, as the writer, to do your research and stay one step ahead of any possible questions an editor might — or, more problematically for your book, might not — ask.

Whenever I ask a question, most of the time my authors can quote me chapter and verse to back up what she put in her book — but not always. And I catch a lot of mistakes in submissions from aspiring writers. Some types of mistakes (in police procedure or in historical fact, for example) can sink an entire book. So if you're one step ahead of an editor and ask yourself all the questions as you write — and then answer them accurately — you've gone a long way not only toward looking like a pro but also toward looking like someone who any editor can trust.

Starting with the basics

In doing research, you first need to figure out what questions you need to ask and what answers can make your book stronger. Certain kinds of research are a starting point for almost any romance novel, even if all you do is think for a moment and decide you know everything you need to, so no research is necessary after all. These basics include:

- **History:** Obviously, this research topic comes into play with any historical romance, but sometimes history even affects a contemporary romance (if a character needs to know information for a plot-related reason, for example) or a paranormal novel (if the modern-day lovers are reincarnations of past lovers, for instance).

- **Professions:** Most of your characters do something other than what you do at your day job — and they probably aren't romance writers, either. Get your facts straight about whatever jobs they hold, whether their profession is ranching, medicine, the military, or anything else.

✔ **Geography and locale:** Whether your characters travel to the Grand Canyon, New Orleans, Paris, or the Amazon Rain Forest, you need to accurately portray the locations you choose for your book. That not only means getting the landscape (or the cityscape) right, it means getting the local flora and fauna right, too. And don't forget the weather, either.

Finding the devil in the details

Within any of the larger categories listed in the preceding section, you can find a whole world of information, some of which will clearly be necessary for your purposes. But realizing which smaller facts matter isn't always second nature.

You need to sensitize yourself so that you're aware of every fact, however small, that you use. And you need to question every detail you put on the page (Do I know this for sure or not?) and commit an item to print only when you're 100 percent certain of its accuracy. The bad news is that this can be pretty time-consuming, especially when you're writing a long book or one that has a lot of hard facts in it. The good news is that the longer you keep at it, the more it becomes second nature to ask (and often answer) the questions, which helps to streamline the process.

As an editor, I want to know whether a piece of slang that sounds too contemporary to me was really spoken during whatever era the book is set in, whether DNA tests can really come back within a particular period of time, and whether cowboys really brand their livestock in the spring. These are the same sorts of questions you should ask yourself, whether you ask them before you write, during the writing process, or after you complete your first draft.

Watch out for mistakes as seemingly simple as having your heroine take a New York City taxi uptown on Fifth Avenue — which runs downtown — or sending your hero north on Interstate 82 — north/south interstates have odd numbers. Streets and highways may not seem like research-worthy subjects, but assumptions like that lead to mistakes. Take nothing for granted and, when in doubt, check. The smallest facts can trip you up:

✔ Is 100 acres large enough for a ranch? If you live in a city, 100 acres sounds like a lot of land, but the answer is no.

✔ Do you want an English saddle, a western saddle, cavalry, racing, side-, or some other kind of saddle on your hero's horse? Be sure that you have the right one for the right use.

✔ When were zippers invented? I don't know, but if you're writing a historical romance, you need to, so you don't put one in the back of your Regency heroine's dress.

✔ Does the Canadian postal service deliver mail on Saturday? Not the last time I talked about it with a Canadian.

- Are sparkling wine and champagne the same thing? Laymen call a lot of sparkling wines champagne, but a vintner hero knows which ones really are and which aren't.

- What time does the evening news come on? Viewers in the Eastern and Pacific time zones get the news at a different time than those who follow Central or Mountain time.

- When did CDs start replacing cassettes?

- When did VCRs become popular, and when did DVD players start succeeding them?

- When did England do away with primogeniture?

- Does mincemeat really contain meat?

Avoiding information overload

You not only have to decide what you need to know (and get it right), but you also need to recognize what you *don't* need to know. Too much information creates problems of its own.

Weighing down the reader

Too much information can stop your story in its tracks. You end up boring a reader or, even if she finds the information interesting, reminding her that she's reading a book, which breaks the spell a romance tries to cast. You want to provide enough information to make the world of your story feel complete and to accurately portray every locale and profession — but no more.

Just because something interests you, it isn't necessarily interesting and/or useful to a reader. An interesting tidbit belongs in your book only when it contributes something necessary in terms of characterization, plot, or setting. It's up to you to scrutinize every detail and decide whether including it serves a purpose — if it's necessary for the reader to really enjoy the book or if, like Mount Everest, it's just *there*. You're going to find out all kinds of things that your reader doesn't need to know, so be ruthless as you pick and choose what to put in the book. Save the rest for writers' get-togethers and cocktail-party trivia. Check out these examples:

- If you're writing a historical romance, you probably need to describe a typical meal at some point, but you probably don't need to describe every detail of what the kitchens are like, how many cooks and servants are needed to prepare the food, or how long the meat hangs to cure before it's cooked. Any of these things may play into your story, and if they do, you should include them — but *only* if that information is relevant to your plot.

✔ If your hero and heroine are doctors, you need to use — and use correctly — enough medical terminology to make them seem real, and you may need to correctly identify an operation or other procedure, possibly even mention a detail or two about how they do it. You don't need to describe the operation in detail, though. (And, unless you want a large portion of your readership to get terminally queasy, you also shouldn't describe it too graphically.)

✔ You can describe a landmark building, but the reader almost certainly doesn't need to know who the architect was, how he or she designed the building, and how a particular construction company built it.

✔ Does the hero drive an SUV? You may want to mention the color, the make, and the fact that it has 4-wheel drive (if that's going to be important later on). But the size of the engine, every detail of the interior, and how much it cost . . . not so noteworthy.

You can easily avoid giving too much information — especially of the "how things work" variety — by cutting away from describing the specifics of the action to another scene and then coming back when the characters have finished that action, whatever it is. Or you can cut away from description to how your hero or heroine is feeling and what he or she is thinking, which the reader is much more interested in knowing, anyway.

Delaying your writing progress

The more you can decide ahead of time what you need to know and what you don't, the more time you can save yourself as you research — time that can be better spent actually writing your romance.

Discipline yourself as you research so that you're capturing the information you need but not going beyond the necessary. You're bound to be tempted at some point by all kinds of fascinating stuff, no matter how much you try to narrow your focus only to what you need. Sometimes you'll succumb, so don't beat yourself up. Just cover your eyes, and resist as much as you can.

You'll thank yourself later (and me, for telling you to be tough on yourself) when your book is done and on its way to an editor, while your writer friends are still having fun researching and stumbling across all kinds of interesting but ultimately useless trivia, their books still unwritten.

You may come across information that falls into the "maybe" category: info you may end up needing later in the book, depending on how things develop, or that spurs an idea for another story. I don't want you wasting time later retracing your research steps or losing an idea for the next bestseller. So save it, either as a note for your current book (in the following section in this chapter, I talk more about organizing your research) or in your idea file (see Chapter 5), so that you can go back to it later and follow up.

Getting Down to Business

Before you ever crack open a research book or log onto the Internet, taking a few minutes to get yourself organized is worth your time. You need to choose the best spot in the writing process for doing your research, or at least the bulk of it, and you need to know how you plan to keep track of what you find out, so you can pull the necessary facts out of your hat (or filing cabinet) when you need them.

Timing is everything

When should you do your research? Try to do your research ahead of time — after you've outlined the book (so that you have a good idea of what you need to know; see Chapter 7 for the scoop on outlines) but before you start actually writing. You can work more efficiently that way because, if you research before you write, you can have most of the information that you need already in front of you. That way, you never (or rarely, anyway) have to leave your creative zone.

Almost inevitably, though, you'll realize as you write that you need to know something else. If you only need a small detail that doesn't have any repercussions for your characters or your plot, you can probably just make a note and check it out later. If, however, the answer to your question is going to affect how the rest of the book plays out, you have no choice but to check it out right away. As frustrating as pulling yourself away from a manuscript is when you're really into the writing, it's a lot better than having to go back later and redo everything because you made an assumption that turned out to be wrong.

Doing your research and getting it all organized ahead of time sounds like a lot of work and a big investment of time, and I suppose it is. But the investment pays off as you write and saves you time in the long run. That investment can also make the difference between selling your book or not, and that's the best investment of all.

Organizing like a pro

You can organize your research in whatever way works for you. The key lies in organizing it at all, so that you don't find yourself muttering, "I *know* it's here somewhere," as you turn over every inch of your office and comb your hard drive, wasting time looking for something you know is there. Somewhere.

If you organize your research as you go, accessing it as you write becomes easier for you, streamlining the process — and, in case you haven't noticed, I'm all about efficiency. I want you to get your book written and on my or another editor's desk. As long as your book is still at your house, it can't sell.

File everything the minute you get it. I know firsthand the perils of the "I'll put it in this pile and deal with it later" approach to filing. It either never gets done at all (I usually end up having to go find the information all over again), or it gets done in a big rush at the least convenient time, because that's when I simply *have* to have some particular thing I just *know* is in there. Somewhere.

Backing things up

I recommend saving hard copies of your research somewhere because, as much as I love computers, I'm very aware of their fallibility. I've been through several crashes myself, with the resulting loss of information I would much rather have kept.

Saved documents and URLs are vulnerable in a crash, not to mention that URLs seem to change with the wind. At the very least, download and save your research on a floppy disk as well as your hard drive. Not only are you protected in case of a crash, but it also makes things easier if you upgrade to a new computer, because you already have your important info separated from all the nonsense every computer hard drive seems to amass, and you're ready to load it onto your new machine.

When you save hard copies of information that you get off the Internet, you're making things easier on yourself, because you probably don't do all your research online. And, as you can see in the next section, having all your research organized and in one location makes life easier.

Keeping info handy

In the course of your research, you may end up with articles saved from magazines and newspapers, photocopies of relevant bits from books, stories printed from the Web, and even pictures you pulled from catalogues or took on vacation (for advice on finding resources, see the "Finding the Facts" section later in this chapter). To save your research, subdivide it into related groupings, for example:

- ✔ Geographical/locale-based information
- ✔ Job-related information
- ✔ Historical facts
- ✔ Miscellaneous

The "Miscellaneous" group can be broken down into as many smaller specific categories as you want. Include things specific to your book, such as fashion, news stories that relate in some way to your plot, and so on.

Store your research materials in a filing cabinet, a multipocket expanding file, individual folders, manila envelopes, or whatever works for you. One exception: If you use entire books in your research, they're most likely to end up on a shelf somewhere.

If you organize everything except books together, you can find a particular piece of information more easily when you need it, because you only have to look in one place, not two dozen. Whatever storage method you use, you need to develop a system that's logical for you, and keep things clearly labeled and accessible. (Make files on your computer for any information you save there, too, and name them something that will make sense to you later when you go looking for a fact or a figure.)

As you're working, you may find keeping some of your research around you especially useful if you know you'll be needing it frequently. (A historical timeline, a list of military ranks, or specific technical terminology may fall into this category.) This list of necessary facts can also include pictures — your hero's estate house, for example, or just landscape photos that help you stay in the right mindset for the book. In Chapter 3, I talk about setting up your home office, which involves giving yourself space to tack up papers and pictures or paste sticky notes.

Completing the project

After you're done writing a book, save your research. To make room so that you can start on the next book, you may need to box up the research or rubber band it into a stack and put it under the bed. But don't get rid of it. For one thing, if an editor asks you to revise, that research may come in handy for rewrites — or for answering her pesky questions when she wants to know if such and such is really true. For another, it may be useful for another book someday, so why go through the effort of gathering it all again?

Finding the Facts

You can do your research in all kinds of places, and many writers use several different methods for each book. In fact, one method can lead you to another. An article cites a book, a book leads you to another book, an online site leads you to another site or yet another book, and any one of those sources can give you the name of someone you want to talk to personally, if you can. Even family and friends can be sources, often in a six-degrees-of-separation kind of way, that lead you straight to the horse's mouth.

Surfing the Net: Great information — and misinformation

The newest entry in the "Where to Find It" sweepstakes has quickly become one of the most used — if not *the* most used — research tools out there. The Internet is wonderful, and you can find pretty much everything in the world there — if you know how to look for it, and you're skeptical enough not to believe everything you read. To use the Net for research (something you almost certainly will do, at some point) keep the following in mind:

✔ **Narrow your search parameters.** Whether you choose a search engine that works with key words or lets you pose an actual question, experiment with different words and combinations of words, or with asking your question in different ways, so that you get a list of results that can actually help you. If at first you don't get what you need, rephrase and try again. Over time, the process will become more intuitive, and you'll go through fewer trials, make fewer errors, and waste less time before finding what you want.

✔ **Consider the source.** Not all opinions are created equal. One of the things that gives the Net its richness and makes it so interesting is that anyone who has something to say can have a voice. But the complete lack of censorship, the fact that no one has to offer proof of what they say, and the ability of "facts" — unproven though they may actually be — to spread in literally moments if they catch the interest of enough people, means that all opinions can *look* equal, even though they aren't.

Before you accept something as the truth and use it in your romance novel (or anywhere else), take a look at the credentials of the person who said it and the site where you found it. Make sure you're not looking at the result of axe grinding but at unbiased, accurate reporting. Check and double-check — and be sure that your backup sources aren't just quoting the original and each other in an endless round robin.

Basically, look at the Internet as if it had "Researcher Beware" stamped on its metaphorical forehead. If you do, you can find it a fabulous resource in every way.

✔ **Check the date.** Errors can live forever online. Books tend to go out of print as they — and the information they hold — become dated. Magazines and newspapers carry obvious dates. Online, you often have to look harder to find out the age of a piece of information. Look around the site to see if you can find the date when the site's creator entered the information. If you can't find one, getting independent confirmation, with a date attached, becomes even more important.

If you're writing a Regency historical romance, a site that hasn't been updated in years can be just as accurate as one updated yesterday. Because the Regency period ended in 1820, nothing about it has changed in a while. But even when dealing with historical periods, it pays to keep track of any new theories and discoveries. The older the period and the less well-documented it is, the more likely this is to be true. Scholars of ancient Egypt, for example, seem to rewrite history with the discovery of each new tomb. And if you're checking into cutting-edge medical treatments, artificial intelligence, the political situation in the Middle East, or anything else where timeliness counts, definitely be sure that the information you use is both accurate and as up-to-date as possible.

You can also use the Internet as a great source for hard-copy research materials that you can't find anywhere else: out-of-print books, or even old magazines and newspapers. I strongly recommend buying new copies of texts whenever you can. Other writers need their royalties just as much as you hope to one day need yours, and newspapers and magazines need to make money or they go out of business. But sometimes you can't find something new, only a used copy. When you can't find a source anywhere else, the Internet turns the world into your marketplace.

Supporting your local library (and bookstore)

With the Internet available from the comfort of your own home and offering everything you can possibly want, you can easily forget that you have all kinds of other research available to you. For in-depth information, the Net can't compare to a good book (though it can often steer you toward one). You will find times when you need to know more about a certain topic. At those times, you need a good, old-fashioned book.

Look to a book for an in-depth exploration that lets you get the full experience. You can't beat a book when you're writing a historical romance. And don't worry so much about immersing yourself in the grand history of the time but rather in the rhythms and events of the day-to-day life of the period you've chosen. Doing so allows you to write from the same position of comfortable knowledge that an author writing a contemporary book can (as long as you know that you can resist the siren call to include every fact you've discovered). Frequently, you can find books — sometimes even firsthand accounts — that let you enter the past. You can rarely find that kind of extended sojourn online, where you're more likely to see summaries of what life was like in other times or top-line lists of information.

You can use basic textbooks (not the complicated grad-school kind but text-books geared for high school or even junior high students) as a great research resource. They contain as much information as you usually want or need, and they present that information clearly and concisely and in easily understood language: You won't need to do research to understand your research. Be sure that you have a current edition, though.

Which books should you borrow and which should you buy? Glad you asked.

- ✔ **Head to the bookstore:** You should probably buy any book that you think you'll need for a while — whether for an extended length of time as you write this book or later, for another book. Bookstores are useful when the book is relatively easy to find.

- ✔ **Check out the library:** Research often involves a lot of books that you read once and don't need again or books you'd love to own but that just aren't available anymore. To get hold of these books, start at your local library. What your library doesn't have, it may be able to get on inter-library loan. And because libraries are a threatened species these days, anything you can do to keep yours busy and prove its worth is a good thing. If you're lucky enough to live near a public university, its library (or, often, libraries, because individual departments often have in-depth research collections) is another resource to look into.

Developing a nose for news

To find the most up-to-date information, magazines and newspapers are a terrific source to use. Whether you subscribe to a newspaper or magazine or buy what interests you on the newsstand, you can find plenty of ideas to spur twists in your current book or entire plotlines for future romances. And if you're looking for information on a specific topic, you can often find the most timely developments written up in newspapers and magazines.

Even when you don't need cutting-edge knowledge, you can find a lot of specialty magazines that can give you information — maybe all the information you need or, at least, information enough to help you formulate additional questions and figure out where you can go to find the answers.

If you can't find the kind of magazine you need even at a big newsstand or your library (and the more specialized or scholarly the magazine, the less likely you are to find it just lying around somewhere), your library has a periodicals directory that can help you track down what you want so you can order it directly.

The unlucky seven: Places *not* to do your research

Plenty of pitfalls are waiting to trap you if you don't do your research carefully and thoroughly. Plenty of unreliable sources exist, and even reliable sources can sometimes fail you. Maintain a healthy skepticism about everything you discover, double-check every fact, and you can't go wrong. Here's a sampling of places and sources to avoid, or at least to treat with extreme caution:

✔ **A friend of a friend:** Urban legends always supposedly happened to a friend of a friend. Rumors follow the same chain. Distrust anything that comes to you this way. Most of the time, the info is so off base that it would be funny — if so many people didn't believe it. Check, double-check, and triple-check any fact or story you hear second- or thirdhand.

✔ **E-mail fun-facts lists:** These lists claim that a duck's quack doesn't echo, a swan is the only bird with a penis, and all sorts of other weird but not outrageous information that *could* be true. But most of it isn't. E-mail warnings about terrible things that happen to women in mall parking lots, kids in public restrooms, and the like fall into this same general category. The stories are usually exaggerations, at best, and fabrications, at worst, so don't refer to one as reality in your romance unless you have independent confirmation that it happened.

✔ **Spoof sites:** Some online sites look incredibly real — but are total nonsense. They may be parodies of official sites (like the FBI) or created to look as if they represent the voice of reason, and they often contain well-faked photos. Be amused, but don't be taken in. If something looks too funny, freaky, or generally unbelievable to be true, it probably is.

✔ **Tabloids:** Whether they deal in celebrity gossip or Bigfoot sightings, no tabloid practices what's called mainstream journalism. Take what they offer with a grain, or pound, of salt. They're designed to entertain more than to report, so be entertained but check everything twice.

✔ **TV dramas and the movies:** Some TV shows and films are scrupulous in their own research, others extrapolate from real-world information or fudge a few details, and still others may as well be set on Mars. I can almost always tell when an aspiring author has based her research into police procedures, for example, entirely on Hollywood's version of reality. You can find useful information on TV and in the movies, but consult other sources to sort the wheat from the chaff.

✔ **Other novels:** Fiction can spread misinformation just as effectively as TV or the Internet. I'm forever reading published books that are filled with major errors — and I can only imagine how many mistakes get published that I don't know enough to catch. Fiction is for fun; nonfiction is for research. Don't be guilty of spreading others' errors.

✔ **Memory:** The mind is unreliable. Your recollection of something you read, heard, or saw in the past may be 100 percent accurate — or a mile from the truth. Before you build a book around something you remember, check to be sure your memory isn't playing tricks.

As for newspapers, most of them end up recycled or under the litter box after a day or two. But many newspapers (and magazines) archive their stories online, so depending on how old the article you want is, you may be able to find it by checking the paper's Web site.

Libraries are a great source of old newspapers (especially local papers that you can't find anywhere else), usually saved on microfilm or microfiche. Several CD-ROM sources are also available for newspapers, so see whether your library has them on hand. Depending on how far back the records go, you may even find old newspapers helpful when you're writing a historical romance, especially one you've set locally.

Taking time to stop, look, and listen

TV and radio, as well as documentary films, can be another great source of information. News magazines, made-for-TV documentaries, documentary films, and even the plain old nightly news . . . all of these sources can give you great information. Record what you think may interest you, if you can, but you can also get a lot of these sources on video or DVD. You can even buy transcripts of many news magazines and interview shows directly. Stay tuned after a show to see if it offers a transcript service.

Entire cable channels are devoted to all kinds of special interests, so check into what's available to you (or to your friends and family, so that you can beg them to record a show for you) and see what's on the schedule. Look for nonfiction videos and DVDs, too. You may run across all kinds of things that you never knew existed.

However, be sure that the broadcast material is of the nonfiction, news variety. TV police dramas, infomercials, and last summer's blockbuster action movie don't count as credible sources. (For more info on avoiding less-than-stellar sources, see the sidebar "The unlucky seven: Places *not* to do your research" in this chapter.)

You can find good sources of information in news radio, talk radio, and public radio, but be sure you don't mistake one person's opinion for absolute fact. This problem comes into play most in talk radio, which is an open, uncensored (other than a several-second delay so that censors can bleep out profanity) forum, so anyone can talk and say pretty much anything.

Traveling for fun and profit

You can use travel — whether to the museum in the center of town or overseas — as a great method of researching everything from locale to culture to history to anything else you can think of. Travel can also cost you a pretty penny (but see Chapter 3 for some basic information on writing off your costs), so don't go broke running around the world.

When you *can* travel, though, take full advantage of the opportunities it presents. Take all the pictures that you can (wherever you have permission for picture taking), talk to anyone who can help you (locals, experts at historical sites, tour guides), and buy research material (postcards, books, newspapers, whatever looks helpful) that you don't have access to at home.

Most people are happy to talk to a writer, so ask questions wherever you go — as long as the person, the locale, and the situation seem safe. Do be careful in any situation that looks dicey. Trust your own instincts and don't take chances.

If you can't get up and go, become an armchair traveler. Read articles and books by people who've been there, especially firsthand accounts that give you that "you are there" feeling. Check out coffee-table books, which usually have great pictures. Read travel guides and look at maps — including street maps of major cities you plan to include in your book. Get to know everything you can about a place or time, just as if you were really planning to go. Just be careful not to sound like a tour guide when you start writing.

Talking to experts: Firsthand is the best hand

Nothing beats talking to someone who actually walks the walk and talks the talk, especially when you're trying to uncover the ins and outs of a particular profession — not just how to do the job but what life is like when that's how you make your living. An expert in any field (history, science, or whatever) is always a helpful resource, especially when you need in-depth information or a real-world sense of things.

Here's a quick step-by-step guide to landing and conducting an interview:

1. **Find an expert.** In the course of your online, print, and broadcast media research, you may come across names of people — or the people themselves — who can help you. Talk to your family and friends, too, because any one of them may know just the person you should talk to.

2. **Ask the expert for his or her help.** After you've identified a possible contact, don't be shy. Introduce yourself, whether in person, or through a call, letter, or e-mail. Explain what you're looking for and ask for help. Not everyone has the time or inclination to oblige, but a lot of people do.

When in doubt, pick up the phone and make a cold call; you'd be amazed how many people are happy to talk to you about their specialties. Pity the poor expert, who often has no one to talk to in detail about his or her specialty, family and friends having long ago tired of hearing the details of how to run a candy company or research the space-time continuum. Imagine how happy they'd be to talk to someone who really wants to know what it's like.

3. **Conduct the interview.** When you're interviewing someone, be polite and respectful, friendly but not in an imposing way, and don't take up any more of the expert's time than you need to. Take careful notes or, if your expert's willing, record your conversations. In the end, you probably have a lot more detail than you need, but you also get an irreplaceable sense of reality to bring to your writing.

4. **Follow up after the interview.** After you're done, don't just write a thank-you note. Let your expert know that you'll send a copy of the book if it's published, and be sure that you do. You should also publicly say thanks for the help in your dedication or an acknowledgment if you sell.

You can also, in some circumstances, actually live your research, at least to a degree. If you're writing a police procedural, call your local police department and ask to go on a "ride-along." Talk to your local firehouse about hanging around and watching life at the station. You may be able to spend time on a working ranch, go out on a commercial fishing boat, or spend a day watching your local veterinarian in action. Sometimes insurance regulations and legal concerns make things impossible, but you never know 'til you ask, so it can't hurt to give it a shot.

Getting Permissions

When you're writing a romance novel, you're much less likely than a nonfiction writer to need legal permission for anything you want to put in your book. Still, from time to time, permissions may be an issue — whether you want permission to use a quote from a song, a script, a poem, or another book, or because you're using proprietary information from any source, or you want to reference a particular person or business by name in your book.

Determining when permission is necessary

When you sign a contract with a publisher, something I talk more about in Chapter 17, one of the clauses almost certainly deals with *warranties and indemnification*. Basically, that clause says that you, not your publisher, are legally — and financially — liable if someone sues because you quote a source without permission, use information without permission, base a character on a real person without their consent, *libel* a person or business (meaning you defame them in writing), or leave yourself open to legal action in any other way through something you say in your book.

Bear in mind as you read this section that I'm not a lawyer. I'm giving you a layman's advice, albeit a layman who's been in the publishing business for a long time. My basic recommendation always comes down to being cautious, not taking chances you don't have to. Whenever possible, avoid writing anything that may require getting legal permission. And if you're not sure how much of a chance you're taking, or if you don't want to do something that you think may cause trouble, get legal advice. It may cost you, but undoubtedly less than losing a lawsuit would.

I'm sure I can't think of all the possibilities that put you at risk, but here's a list of things to avoid if you can — and how to avoid them:

- ✔ **Don't name real people.** Other than historical figures (Abe Lincoln, Geronimo, and so on), you're better off avoiding the issue of real people altogether. For example, if you're writing a contemporary romance with a political setting, make up the name of the president and other officials.

- ✔ **Just the facts, ma'am.** If you must use a real person, contemporary or historical, stick to the known facts about that person. Don't speculate on people's personal lives, sexual kinks, or anything else you can't support with research.

- ✔ **Don't base characters on real people.** You want your characters to feel real, but base them on traits and qualities you compile from various sources. Don't write about your ex-boyfriend, your neighbor, or your best friend from college, making them fictional just by giving them a new name. By the same token, don't base a business, whether a giant corporation or a local restaurant, entirely on a real business.

- ✔ **Avoid direct quotes wherever you can.** Refer to *a popular love song* instead of quoting one directly, for instance.

Or stick to sources that are in the public domain: Shakespeare rather than Neil Simon, for example. *Public domain* refers to works that are no longer covered by copyright, but the laws governing when a works falls into the public domain are complex and are based on the type of work — song, book, and so on — and when it was created. Something hundreds of years old, like Shakespeare's plays, won't be a problem, but a specific translation of an ancient work may be, as may more recent works, so you'll have to research the work you'd like to use. You should also look into the laws governing *fair use,* which allows excerpts of a certain length and of certain types of work to be used in certain circumstances. Again, the laws are complex, but you can use the same skills that help you research facts for your book to research these legalities.

✔ **Don't say anything negative about a real person or business.** This mistake is the biggest taboo of all. If your characters eat fast food and get food poisoning, don't name — or in any way describe so that the reader can identify — a particular restaurant or franchise.

Books in every bookstore undoubtedly do everything I've just told you not to. That fact doesn't matter. Whether you end up in legal trouble or not, you have absolutely no need to take the chance. Let someone else make headlines — and take legal chances — for writing a scandalously tasty page-turner; you're writing a romance, and that's something else entirely.

Even if you do everything you can to avoid needing to get legal permission, sometimes you may find it unavoidable. You may not see any way around using a quote or mentioning a real person in a way that's completely neutral or even complimentary. Or, if you talk to an expert, I recommend getting permission to use the information he or she gives you. Depending on the specific circumstances, you may or may not need it, but when in doubt, play it safe and get permission. You can't go wrong covering your assets.

After you're under contract, feel free to ask your editor if you're unsure whether you need to get permission for something or not. She has access to her company's legal department and can get you a specific answer, one no general book (like this one) can provide.

Filling out the paperwork

Every publisher probably requires something different, even if only slightly, in terms of an acceptable permission, so when you're unpublished and need to come up with something for your source to sign, you're really flying blind.

I recommend that you come up with a basic letter for your source (or whoever) to sign. The specifics of what you're asking (to use a direct quote, to use information, and so on) vary, but you're asking to be allowed to use whatever it is in your book at no cost and to be released from any future legal action. You may find a cost is involved in using a quote or other material that requires permission, and you need to decide whether the quote is worth it or if you're better off doing without it. That letter may or may not be good enough to satisfy your publisher if you sell the book, but it gives you a starting point. And your editor can tell you what else she needs if and when the time comes.

Chapter 14

Neatness Counts — and So Does Grammar

. . . .

. . . .

*A*fter all your hard work, after all the creativity you've poured into your novel, you don't want to think that you can trip yourself up with the mechanics, but you can. Mechanics can't make a sale, but they can break one, for sure. If your writing makes understanding your story impossible, or if your formatting makes the story a headache to read, your novel might as well not exist.

To be a successful romance writer, you need to be a storyteller, but you can't be *only* a storyteller. You need to get all the mechanics right: grammar, punctuation, spelling, formatting, word count . . . every detail plays a crucial part in getting your story past an editor to the reader. If your manuscript has mistakes that are obvious as soon an editor picks it up, she won't even read your work; other kinds of mistakes can stop her dead in her tracks before she's read more than a few pages.

Never forget that you need to make your manuscript as perfect as possible in every way before it ever lands on an editor's desk. Her job isn't to teach you to write or to fix all the "boring" details you don't want to be bothered with. Her job is to take a good book and make it better. And the mechanics are easy enough (even if a nuisance sometimes) for every author to get right, so the editor can spend her time offering you her expertise where it counts.

In this chapter, I not only talk about what you need to know about grammar and punctuation and where to get your questions answered, but I also give you some specific pointers and let you in on some editorial pet peeves. And I talk about how to format your manuscript so it looks professional and doesn't raise the red flag in an editor's mind.

Minding Your P's and Q's

You can find several different explanations for the origins of p's and q's, including one that has particular relevance here. Supposedly it provided a warning to schoolchildren (and typesetters) to get the lowercase letters *p* and *q* right, because those letters are pretty much mirror images of each other. As a writer, you need to get your p's and q's right, too — along with a whole lot of other things, starting with grammar.

Grammar's not in the kitchen baking cookies

In a romance novel, editors consider good writing as writing that helps tell the story, instead of getting in the way of it. And that means the language can be more colloquial than in many other types of fiction. But that doesn't mean the rules are nonexistent or that you can flout (not flaunt! — see the sidebar "Avoiding common mistakes" later in this chapter) them at will.

Handling grammar in fiction, especially popular fiction, can be tricky. You need to look at grammar in different ways depending on what part of the book you're talking about.

- ✔ **Dialogue:** You can use the language a lot more freely in dialogue than you can in narrative. Even university professors (and editors) have been known to misplace the occasional modifier or split an infinitive when speaking, and most people are a lot less formal — and a lot less accurate — when they talk.

- ✔ **Narrative:** Even in narrative, editors apply the grammar rules much more loosely for popular fiction than for literary fiction or most nonfiction, especially of the scholarly sort.

But before you can play fast and loose with the rules of grammar, you need to know what they are, and you can't always count on your ear to tell you what's right or wrong. You may have grown up or gotten used to hearing regionalisms or particular quirks of particular people (your parents' speech patterns probably influenced you more than anyone else's) that aren't technically correct, even though they sound fine to you. Those peculiarities of language can be useful to you in dialogue, but they can really trip you up in narrative.

The first thing you need to do is get a good grammar book and keep it where you can refer to it whenever you need to. You can find several good ones out there, some serious and at least one that takes a lighter, quirkier approach. Any grammar guide is fine, as long as you have one. Pick one that you feel comfortable with and that you can use to quickly find what you're looking for.

My favorite is that quirky one, Karen Elizabeth Gordon's *The Deluxe Transitive Vampire: The Ultimate Handbook of Grammar for the Innocent, the Eager, and the Doomed* (published by Pantheon).

But the biggest problem most writers face isn't finding an answer when they have a question. It's knowing when they should be asking a question at all. I don't have a surefire way to teach you that skill, but you can do a few things to get yourself started.

After you've figured out the mistakes you tend to make and become sensitive to them, you can be on the lookout for them as you write. Then you can catch and correct them before they ever meet an editor's eyes.

Plugging into grammar programs

A lot of word-processing programs have a built-in grammar-checking capacity, and you can also buy separate programs that check grammar for you. Before you write an entire book and find out you've made the same mistake(s) over and over, grammar-check a chapter and see what your program points out to you, and then consult your grammar book to see how you can fix your mistakes.

One caution: Grammar checkers are strict taskmasters, and sometimes they point out grammar mistakes that don't really cause a problem, at least when and where they appear in your manuscript. The rules of language sometimes lag behind common usage, so don't blindly follow where they lead you, or you can end up with a book so stiff and formal it can never cut it as popular fiction.

For instance, proper English usage has a whole prohibition against dangling prepositions, but sometimes you can't avoid them without sounding ridiculous. Technically, it's wrong to say "That's something I won't put up with." But wrong or not, it's preferable to "That's something up with which I will not put." Most of the time, you're not going to run into anything quite so extreme (or silly), but it still pays to think about every example and not just accept what an impersonal program tells you.

Taking a course

Take a grammar course or, if one's not available locally, a writing course that focuses not just on storytelling but on mechanics. You can even ask your instructor to focus on grammar when she reviews your work. In-person courses aren't your only option, though. Look online for a course available from a college or writers' resource site, or get a grammar workbook so you can focus specifically on understanding the rules and then applying them to your romance-novel-in-progress.

Asking a friend

You can also ask a friend for some input. If you have a willing friend with the right expertise, ask her (or him) to look over some of your work and mark it up specifically for grammar.

Making a point with punctuation

Grammar involves not just word order and sentence structure but also the use of punctuation. I want to discuss punctuation separately, because all too often I see books where I can tell the writer has no real idea of how certain punctuation marks function and how to make punctuation work for her.

I'm not going to talk about all the rules of punctuation (look at the grammar book I tell you to get in the previous section for the nitty-gritty punctuation details), but a few things make such a difference that I feel bringing them up is important.

Choosing your commas carefully

An awful lot of writers don't seem to realize that a comma used inside a sentence (rather than at the end, just before "he said") represents a pause. I see them peppered all over the place in ways that make no sense, something the author would realize if she read her work aloud, pausing at each comma.

Comma placement can literally change the meaning of a sentence. This instructional example circulates on the Internet periodically. A professor writes the following words on the chalkboard and then asks the students to make sense of them: *woman without her man is nothing*

> ✔ **A male student comes up with:** *Woman, without her man, is nothing.*
>
> ✔ **A female student comes up with:** *Woman. Without her, man is nothing.*

Biiiiig difference.

Most of the time, your comma usage isn't a weapon in the battle of the sexes, but commas can still help or hinder your prose. I'm a big believer that it's better to use commas inconsistently but for effect rather than use them strictly (bad pun alert) by the book. Punctuation really is a tool, which means you control it, not vice versa. Think carefully about your commas, because if you get them right, they can really enhance the way your prose flows. If you get them wrong, though, they can make it stutter along like a leaky balloon.

Pausing to consider ellipses and dashes

One of the biggest mistakes I see is writers who use one of these punctuation marks, either an ellipsis or an em dash, when they should use the other.

An ellipsis represents a pause if it comes in the middle of a sentence, or a trailing off if it comes at the end. An em dash in the middle of a sentence marks an abrupt change or denotes emphasis; at the end of a sentence, it shows that the dialogue has been cut off, often mid-sentence or even mid-word. You should use ellipses as part of slow, thoughtful moments; em dashes usually come when a character's angry or upset. Em dashes can set off a phrase the same way commas can (though they imply greater emphasis); ellipses can't.

Here are some examples of the correct use of ellipses:

> ✔ *She thought she could like him, but maybe . . . maybe that was just too much wine talking.*

> ✔ *"I can't even think how you could . . ." She let her words trail off, unsure what to say next.*

> ✔ *"Would you . . . I mean, could you . . . could you ever love me?" she asked slowly.*

If you use an ellipsis to indicate that a full sentence has trailed off, you need to end your sentence with a period, followed by the three-dot ellipsis. If only a phrase trails off, the three-dot ellipsis alone is correct.

Here are some examples of the correct use of em dashes:

> ✔ *She immediately thought — though she had no idea why — he was the man she was destined to marry.*

> ✔ *"I can't — I won't — I refuse to — to —" She stopped speaking abruptly, unable to put her thoughts into words.*

> ✔ *"I'm so furious I could —" Afraid she would say something unforgivable, she turned away without another word.*

You should set off only one phrase at a time with em dashes:

> ✔ **Correct:** *He was the most irritating — the most infuriating — man she'd ever met.*

> ✔ **Incorrect:** *He was the most irritating — the most infuriating — the most incomprehensible — man she'd ever met.*

This rule holds true even if what you're setting off comes at the end of a sentence:

> ✔ **Correct:** *She was ready to spring into action the minute she got the word — and he was going to get what was coming to him.*

> ✔ **Incorrect:** *She was ready to spring into action the minute she got the word — and he was going to get what was coming to him — and she was about to become his worst nightmare.*

Used within a sentence, em dashes should come in pairs (as in the first correct example above). I often see writers using them in threes, which makes it impossible to see which phrase is actually being set off and emphasized. For example:

✔ **Incorrect:** *He was making her crazy — infuriating man that he was — crazy enough to scream — and she had to get away.*

✔ **Correct:** Rephrasing is almost always the only way to correct this sort of error: *He was making her crazy enough to scream — infuriating man that he was — and she had to get away.* Or you can break one sentence into two: *He was making her crazy — infuriating man that he was — crazy enough to scream. She had to get away.*

Breaking the rules (after you know them)

Even though you know the rules of grammar and punctuation, you may sometimes find yourself choosing to break them. In fact, as an editor, I'm a firm believer that you may find, on occasion, that you not only *can* break the rules, you *should.* The key is in knowing the rules first and respecting them where they're helpful, only breaking them when you know why you're doing it. You can't just write freely and think your text makes sense just because you want it to.

Dialogue generally offers the most compelling reason to break the rules, so your characters sound both natural and like the individuals they are. (I talk in more detail about this license to break the rules in Chapter 9, when I discuss the entire subject of giving your characters voices.) Very few people speak as if they've walked straight out of the pages of a grammar book — and most of those people do tend to live in grammar books or language texts. You don't want to make your characters speak so ungrammatically that the reader gets a headache trying to decipher what they're saying, nor do you want to ladle on the colloquialisms, regionalisms, and everyday sloppiness so your characters sound like constructs, not real people.

But you do want your characters to sound informal and conversational. Because of that, when you're writing dialogue, your ear for speech (not the analytical part of your mind that handles the rules and regulations of grammar) should take charge.

Even in narrative, you may find it helpful to think of yourself as *telling* a story as much as *writing* one. A romance novel needs to move, to carry the reader along, so your language needs to have a casual quality to it because that keeps the book moving. Don't stop your reader dead in the middle of a paragraph too ponderous and stilted to stand up to its own weight.

Unless you're writing in the first person, your narrative should be less conversational than your dialogue, but you can and should feel free to bend, even outright break, the occasional rule when following it makes your novel read like a scholarly lecture on the nature of love, not the actual experience of it.

Reining in the runaway thesaurus

The wrong word choice can ruin even the most grammatical (in an appropriately informal sense, of course) prose. Part of the reason to play just a bit fast and loose with the rules of grammar involves creating a tone that sounds comfortable and natural to the reader, because that familiarity pulls her in. If you punctuate that natural prose with strange word choices — even if that word accurately describes what you're after — you break the mood you've worked hard to create on every level with both the creative and the mechanical aspects of your book. (I touch on not relying on your thesaurus too heavily in Chapter 8.)

Choosing a ten-dollar word when a cheap one will do

Sometimes writers try so hard to vary their vocabulary that they end up replacing common words that don't — and shouldn't — call attention to themselves with outlandish choices that yell, "Look at me! Look at me!" The reader may even laugh at them because of their silly, awkward, or inappropriate appearance.

A car is a car is a *car.* Maybe it's a *sedan,* an *SUV,* or a *pickup truck.* But you rarely need to call it a *vehicle,* even though, technically speaking, it is one. And by the time an author starts talking about her character's *mode of transport* (or just *transport*), I'm pulling out my pencil in frustration and writing in *car.* And that example isn't even particularly extreme!

Thesaurusitis really becomes a problem in descriptions, where fewer adjectives are usually better anyway, and normal, comprehensible ones are almost always better than the incomprehensible exotic variety. As a general rule, make a cliff *steep,* not *declivitous;* your room *well-lit* rather than *refulgent;* and your hero's background *secret,* not *recondite.*

In popular fiction, you never want your reader to have to consult the dictionary. Make the meaning of any unusual word, including technical terms, clear from context, or explain it unobtrusively in the text.

Selecting incorrect synonyms

I find another kind of thesaurus trouble writers get into even more irritating to read than the high-falutin' word syndrome, because it's not only intrusive, it's incorrect. The writer chooses what she thinks is a synonym based on the thesaurus, but the word she chooses really isn't a synonym — at least, not for the word as she uses it.

The English language not only features inconsistent rules of grammar and pronunciation, but an awful lot of words — even common ones — have multiple meanings. Too often, an author tires of a common term or just decides to have a little fun with language, but because she doesn't really think about multiple meanings when she grabs her thesaurus, she doesn't come up with a synonym at all. Moving with *easy* grace isn't the same as moving with *elementary* grace, much less *commodious* grace, but both of those ten-dollar words turn up in a thesaurus as synonyms for *easy.*

If you absolutely have to consult a thesaurus and you choose an unfamiliar word, double-check it in a dictionary to make sure that it means what you want it to mean.

Proofreading: Its knot two hard too reed yore own work

I think that this heading may need the smallest amount of explanation of all the headings in this whole book. Technology is your friend in many ways, and spell-check can be great, so don't misunderstand me. I'm not telling you never to use it. (Although I admit that I've never loaded it on my own computer.)

But spell-check is quick and easy. In fact, it's too quick and easy. Every editor I know says the same thing: We see way (not *weigh*) too (not *two* or *to*) many books that an author has clearly spell-checked but not proofread.

Whether you proofread chapter by chapter as you write or save your proofing until the whole romance is written, it's crucial that you proofread your entire book at least once, because your eye can catch errors no spell-check program can.

When you're on a roll and the story is really working, I'm guessing that, like most writers, you type as quickly as you can to get your thoughts down on paper. As you write, you're very likely to type a *homonym/homophone* (typing *boar* instead of *bore,* for example) rather than the word you had in mind. Because you're racing, you're not even going to notice what you've done, much less stop to correct yourself, and you *shouldn't* stop. Giving your muse her head at that point is much more important than worrying about spelling.

Later, though, you need to correct those mistakes, and if you typed a real word (just the *wrong* real word), spell-check can't help you. Spell-check catches true typos — *insted* for *instead* or *mybe* for *maybe* — but it can't catch homonyms. To catch those words, you have to go back and read through the book as if you were your own proofreader, looking carefully at every word to be sure it's the write, er, right one.

In the rush of writing, you can easily make word-choice mistakes, like typing *with* for *will.* Spell-check doesn't help you catch those errors, either — but proofreading does.

Avoiding common mistakes

An awful lot of people get a number of common expressions and words wrong. The following list contains some of the mistakes I see most often.

✔ **To the manor born:** Even though *to the manner born* makes a certain amount of sense, the correct version uses *manor*. If you were born in the manor house, you've been brought up with the correct manners and everything else.

✔ **A hair's breadth:** The width of a hair is very thin, and that's what you're talking about: the smallest possible distance. It's not *a hare's breath,* though I'm sure a bunny's breaths are pretty small, too. And *a hair's breath* doesn't even make sense, not that lack of sense has stopped an awful lot of people from writing it.

✔ **Soft pedal:** This phrase means to play something down. It comes from the music world and refers to using the soft pedal on a piano. Don't use *soft peddle* by mistake, because the soft sell is something else altogether.

✔ **Flaunt versus flout:** *Flaunting* something means to show it off, and *flouting* means to ignore or go against. For example: *He flaunted his ignorance as he flouted the law.*

✔ **Hardy versus hearty:** If someone or something's hardy, they're sturdy, durable, and healthy. But if they're hearty, they're enthusiastic and unrestrained. For example: *Luckily she was hardy or his hearty hug might have crushed her.*

✔ **Heart-rending versus heart-rendering:** If something's *heart-rending*, it's heartbreaking. *Rendering* is a butcher's term for getting fat from flesh, so . . . ewwww. For example: *It was a heart-rending story about the victim of a heart-rendering serial killer.*

✔ **Incarnation versus incantation:** An *incarnation* is a life (hence reincarnation), or a version of something that personifies an ideal. An *incantation* is a ritualized formula or statement. For example: *In his incarnation as a wizard, he was given to reciting mysterious incantations.*

You can really trip yourself up by not eyeballing your manuscript. If the book's great, an editor may still buy it. But — I can't believe I'm typing these words! — no editor's perfect, and even though a copy editor and a proofreader see your book, they're not perfect, either. Everyone who works on your book catches some of the spelling errors, but some may still sneak through. If you proofread your manuscript first, you're going to catch a bunch of those mistakes yourself, leaving fewer for everyone else to find and, ultimately, fewer that stand a chance of making it into the published book.

Formatting for Success

Even if your book's insides — the story and the mechanics of how you've told it — are perfect, you still need to put the manuscript into an acceptable format before you present it to an editor. Looks do count, and for very good reasons.

Margins are more than marginally important

In your finished manuscript, you need to make your *margins,* the blank spaces around the printed area of your pages, consistent throughout. Here are a few guidelines:

- ✔ Margins should be at least 1-inch wide, and no more than 1½ inches, on the sides and at the bottom. At the top of the page, most editors like a margin of 1½ inches because it leaves room for a running head (which I talk about in the "Remembering a running head" section later in the chapter).

- ✔ Set up your margins so you have the same number of lines on every page, counting the extra spacing between scenes, called *space breaks,* as lines. The exceptions to this rule are the first and last pages of every chapter: You should establish layout rules to make all your first pages the same, but your last pages vary and can't be predicted.

- ✔ Don't make your margins too large. Every editor is on to that trick and knows it's just a way to make a book look longer than it really is.

You don't use margins just so your book looks nice or to prove that you've read the rules and want to look professional. Margins also make reading your manuscript easier on the eyes. More importantly, margins provide vital space for the editor to use as she edits. They allow room for her to pencil in changes, write notes to the copy editor (asking to have a fact confirmed, for example) and, most important, write notes and questions to you. I'm a big believer in making use of the margins. I ask my authors questions so they can make revisions and clarifications, and I also let them know if a particular passage has made me laugh or cry, or if it has just called to mind something I can't resist telling them.

On top of that, your manuscript's going to get photocopied any number of times in the course of the publishing process, and every photocopy changes the dimensions slightly. (I've been told that photocopiers are set to do this for legal reasons, so that you can always distinguish an original contract from a copy. Sounds good to me, though I've never looked into the truth of it.) If you've written right up to the edges, text starts getting lost each time someone photocopies the manuscript.

Using the right fonts and spacing

Double-space your book. It really is that simple. You may have places where you need to single-space a particular section — if you're quoting a letter a character has written, for example — but you almost certainly want to double-space 99.9 percent of your book. If I get a manuscript that's single-spaced, I send it back unread and tell the author to format it correctly before resubmitting.

Your editor and copy editor need the space between lines to do their jobs. If you've spaced the lines too tightly, your editors don't have room to write anything. Plus, your editor can read your manuscript a lot more easily when you haven't squashed all the lines together.

Be sure your printer has dark ink, and use medium-weight white paper. Take pity on the poor editor, who reads all day, and make your manuscript crisp and clear, so you don't drive her toward either the aspirin bottle or the optician.

As for your font, choose something clear and unfussy. Times New Roman is the standard and by far the best, because it's easy to read. Whatever you do, avoid anything fancy, too thin, heavy, scripty, or compressed. A whole manuscript in these types of fonts makes your editor's eyes spin and her head pound.

Size matters, too. Go for 12 point because it's big enough to be clear and easy to read, but not so big that it looks like large print.

Don't use an *italic* font to indicate italics. Instead, <u>underline</u>. That way, if your editor wants to change a word or passage back to standard format, she can make that change easily with a single pencil stroke.

Breaking your story up

Paragraphing is a key piece of formatting. When I get a submission that's improperly paragraphed, I send it back unread and tell the author to format the book correctly before she can submit it. Paragraph a romance manuscript just like a published romance novel. Don't put an extra space break between paragraphs (unless you're indicating a time or place break, which I get to in just a second), and make sure you indent the first line of each paragraph. Don't follow the format of this book, because nonfiction is a different animal altogether.

You can indicate a time or place break in one of two ways:

- ✔ **Double-space:** You can just include an extra blank line to alert the reader to this shift.

- ✔ **Double-space, type — # — and double-space again:** Because simply double-spacing can look like a mistake to an editor, I recommend using this method.

Don't simply add four or five (or more) spaces, leaving a large gap, to indicate a break. That technique looks unprofessional and wastes space unnecessarily.

You can find books that give you exact rules on how to format, and that's fine. I tend to be fairly easygoing in the formatting department, as are most editors I know. I just want clear text and easy-to-spot chapter openings.

When you start a new chapter, be consistent. For chapter openings, I recommend spacing about a third of the way down the page, and then centering and typing *Chapter [Whatever]*. Space down from there to the page's midpoint and start the text of your chapter there.

Remembering a running head

A *running head* is the strip of identifying information that runs across the top of every page of your manuscript. You need to include this information on every page because it can prove helpful if a page gets separated from the rest or if the manuscript falls and someone has to reassemble it.

A running head should contain your name (first and last, or just last), the manuscript title (or a shortened version of it), and the page number. Always put the page number in the top right-hand corner. You should put your name flush on the left, and center the title.

Feel free to choose a slightly different format for your name and the book's. Some authors like to include the chapter number, as well. I strongly recommend that you always number your pages at the top right, though. Editors (and everyone else) automatically look there for page numbers, so make it easy for them.

Always leave an extra space between your running head and your text so that the running head stands out as something separate. That way, your editor doesn't turn every page and start editing the running head, thinking it's part of the book.

Number your pages in order, from first to last. Don't number each chapter separately. Your editor should be able to look at the final page of the manuscript and know the exact length of the entire thing.

Counting your words accurately

The word count of your manuscript, though not necessarily something you pay a lot of attention to as you write, ends up being important when you reach the end of the writing process. If a book is too long or too short, you're going to have a hard, even impossible, time selling it. The details vary a bit:

> ✔ **Series:** If you're writing a series romance, word count is crucial, because you need to be sure you fit within your chosen line's parameters. Every series has a set range, with the shortest series currently running at about 55,000 words and the longest contemporary series at 85,000–90,000 words, and one historical series at 100,000. (See Chapter 3 for information on obtaining tip sheets, which set out the editorial needs and requested word counts of different series.)

✔ **Mainstream:** If you're writing mainstream novels, word count ultimately translates to page count. And because paper costs keep climbing, an extremely long manuscript ends up becoming an expensive book and is much harder to sell to readers who don't know the author and are less likely to take a chance on her. The upper end of what most publishers like to see is 125,000–150,000 words. (See Chapter 2 for a review of the various types of romance novels.)

For some reason, the question of word count gets writers upset the way nothing else can. Despite the fact that your heart may already be racing at the mere thought of the subject, you need to know how to come up with an accurate count, because you have to know the length of your book.

First, forget whatever your computer tells you your word count is. Your computer's counting actual words, but for the purposes of taking a word count and translating it to a published page count, actual words don't, well, count. That's because a one-word line of dialogue takes up as much space as a twelve-word line of description, and the first and last pages of a chapter count as full pages, even though they have a shorter actual word count. You're looking for a functional count, not the real thing.

Second, don't count on the various formulas that purport to tell you how many words you have per page (usually 250) based on margin width, number of lines, and so on.

The only truly accurate way to determine word count is by hand, with the help of a calculator. (Unless you're a math whiz, in which case paper and pencil — or just your brain — may be all you'll need.) Follow these steps to determine the manuscript's *total functional word count* (the count an editor needs to know):

1. **Write down the number of lines you get per full page.**

   Each page of the manuscript, except for the first and last page of each chapter, should contain the same number of lines. (Time and place breaks count as full lines for this purpose.)

2. **Count the number of words in ten representative full lines that you choose from throughout the manuscript.**

3. **Average out the number of words per line.**

4. **Multiply the words per line by the number of lines per page to get a words-per-page count.**

5. **Multiply the number of words per page by the total number of pages in the manuscript for a total functional word count.**

Your functional word count is always — at least in my experience — longer than anything your computer tells you.

After you've written a chapter, or at least a few full pages, you can get your words-per-page count. And based on that, you can use long division (intended total functional word count divided by words per page) to figure out how many pages you should write to reach your desired total functional word count.

Creating your cover page

The cover page is the first manuscript page an editor sees, but I've left its creation 'til last. Your cover page needs to include your word count, so you can't create it until the end, anyway. Printing out your cover page also has a final and almost symbolic feeling about it, as if it formally marks the last stage of the writing process.

Some writers skip the cover page, and its absence isn't going to cost you a sale. But it adds a professional look to a manuscript and gathers all the relevant information in one place so that the editor can always find it.

You can easily find and should feel free to use a template for a cover page — check the Internet and your local bookstore. I'm looking for clarity and an attractive format, not rules. As long as you include the necessary information, you don't need to worry about how to make your editor happy.

A typical cover page should include:

- ✔ **The manuscript title:** The title should be the top-most element on the page, centered, and quite possibly done in bold, a larger font, or all caps.

- ✔ **Your name:** Center your name a few lines below the title. If you're using a pseudonym, you should also indicate *w/a* (writing as) and your pseudonym.

- ✔ **Your address:** In the lower left corner of the page, stack your name, address, and phone number. You may also want to include your e-mail address.

- ✔ **Word count:** In the lower right corner, even with your name on the left, type the total functional word count (see "Counting your words accurately" to find out how to get that total functional word count).

- ✔ **Additional information:** Depending on circumstances, you may also include information like your agent's name, address, phone number, and e-mail address. You may also want to include a line regarding your book, such as *A contemporary romantic suspense novel* or *A Silhouette Intimate Moments novel.*

Reviewing the Manuscript Preparation Checklist

Before you send your book off, you should read and reread it for content, making sure you have all the creative elements in place. Also look over your hard copy to make sure you have all the practical, mechanical details under control:

❑ **Proofread the entire manuscript with an eye toward grammar, punctuation, and spelling.** You can do this step (and only this step!) on-screen, if you prefer. But personally, I think that you find errors on the hard copy you don't see on-screen.

❑ **Eyeball every page for clarity.** Go through the hard copy and make sure every page is legible, with no blurred, distorted lines, no faded spots, or other printer-related glitches.

❑ **Eyeball your margins, time breaks, chapter heads, and so on.** Be sure everything looks clean and clear, and that your on-screen formatting translated correctly to the printed page.

❑ **Count the pages.** Literally go through from page one to the end, looking at page numbers to make sure you haven't included duplicate pages or numbered blanks (which sneak in more often than you'd expect).

❑ **Check all your chapter numbers.** Finding two different Chapter 3's, for example, isn't uncommon, so page through and find all your chapter heads, making sure you haven't duplicated (or left out) a number.

❑ **Check and double-check your cover page.** Be sure you've included all the necessary information and check extra carefully for typos, because you can miss them in words you know by heart (and thus don't read too carefully), like your own name and address.

Part V
Submitting Your Manuscript — and Making the Sale!

The 5th Wave   By Rich Tennant

"Oh, Will— such passion, such pathos, such despair and redemption. I've never read a more moving grocery list."

In this part . . .

After you've finished writing your book, the creative process gives way to the business end of things. In this part, I talk about targeting the right publisher and editor for you, submitting your manuscript — including how to write query letters and synopses — dealing with rejection, making the sale (every writer's dream), and working with your editor on the stages from page to press.

Chapter 15

Targeting the Right Publisher (and Editor)

. . . .

. . . .

*A*fter you finish your manuscript and polish it until it shines, you're ready to start looking for a publisher — probably the most daunting point you'll ever reach in your writing career, especially the first time. The bad news is that selling a book is hard. But I have good news, too: You can significantly increase your chances of getting published by knowing who's who in the business — publishers and editors — and how to tailor your submission so that it's strong and as close to what they're looking for as possible.

At this point, with a completed manuscript in hand, you also need to decide whether you need an agent — something you already may have been thinking about, and maybe even doing something about. If you haven't thought about the agent issue or taken the steps to find an agent (if you decide you need or want one), now's the time.

When you've decided on the most appropriate publisher, maybe even a specific editor, you've taken the first step, but you have more to think about. Each publishing house has its own submission procedures, so you need to know how to tailor your submission to suit the requirements of each publisher. *Query letter, partial, complete* — you need to understand these terms and know how to meet expectations. In this chapter, I give you tips on negotiating the publishing maze, figuring out the most appropriate publisher to target (and even how to choose a specific editor), answering the question of whether you need an agent, and creating a query letter, synopsis, or partial manuscript that does justice to your book.

Researching the Market

When you're submitting your novel, you first need to research the market with an eye toward who's publishing what, so you don't submit your manuscript to publishers who aren't interested in your kind of book. I've spent my entire publishing career working on romance novels and general women's fiction, but despite that, I've seen autobiographies, illustrated science fiction, self-help books, and all kinds of other totally inappropriate submissions — even a coloring book. Those submissions weren't only a complete waste of my time, but they were also a waste of the author's time.

When you submit your romance novel, you want to make the process as brief and painless as it can be, so you can get your book published and on the racks quickly. Even if the book's fate is rejection, you're better off knowing that sooner rather than later so you can move on. The uncertainty of waiting for an answer isn't something you want to prolong.

Always be working on a new manuscript. Nothing can make you forget that you have a book sitting on an editor's desk somewhere or that you're waiting to hear back for permission to submit, but you can help distract yourself by working on your next book while the current one's out in the world trying to prove itself. Whether the worst (rejection) or the best (a contract) happens, you'll be glad you started working on another project. If your current book doesn't sell, you'll be ready that much sooner to submit another and continue trying to build your career. And if your first manuscript *does* sell, your editor will want to see your next book as quickly as possible. You'll be that much closer to making her happy if you have a new manuscript well on its way.

Finding out who's who

When you first look into the market to figure out the appropriate areas to apply your talents (see Chapter 2 for more information on the types of romance novels), you're thinking creatively. Now you have to think analytically, because you're entering into the business side of your career.

You can get an idea of who the different publishers are and what they're looking for in plenty of different ways. I recommend using as many of the following sources as you can to make sure you don't miss any relevant info.

  ✔ **Bookstores:** Head to a large bookstore with a large selection in the romance section. Look at all the titles that are similar to what you've written in general terms, like historical romances, and, where you can, specifically, like Civil War historicals. Start your search from A and work your way through the alphabet. Check to see who publishes each book, and eventually you'll have a useful list. You'll see that one publisher has published a dozen similar romances, another only one, while a third checks in with eight, and so on.

✔ **Online bookstores and searches:** You can go to one or more of the big online bookstores and search by subgenre, if your book easily fits into one, and see what publishers are represented. Plus, the Internet is wonderfully searchable.

✔ **Publishers' Web sites:** I list a number of publishers' Web sites in Chapter 3. (But doing an online search can help you find additional publishers that have entered the marketplace since this writing.) Every site is set up differently, so you need to look around, but most sites give you a sense of what the house publishes, either by listing the month's offerings (go back to the site for several months to get a full sense of their needs) or by providing a more extensive online catalogue.

✔ **Tip sheets:** Some publishers put out *tip sheets,* one- or multi-page handouts that talk about their editorial needs, including information on the types of books they want to see, preferred word length, and sometimes on manuscript preparation and submission procedures. You can often find these handouts online (on the publisher's site or general writers' sites) or at conferences, or you can send a request and self-addressed, stamped envelope (SASE) to the publisher, assuming the house offers a tip sheet, and have one sent to you.

✔ **Romance-based Web sites:** A number of writers' and readers' sites exist, and you may even find sites from specialty booksellers. All these sites have a lot of easily accessible information available, and many of them — as you may already have discovered in the course of your writing — also have bulletin boards and mailing lists, where you can ask questions of and get guidance from other writers.

✔ **The Literary Market Place (LMP):** The LMP is a vast publishing reference that comes out annually and is available in most major libraries. You can also visit the Web site at www.literarymarketplace.com. An entire section is devoted to publishers, many of whom specify the types of books they publish and their submission requirements. Registration is required to search the site, and some information is available only to paid subscribers.

✔ **Special-interest magazines and newsletters:** Writers' magazines, romance-specific magazines, and magazines that cover the publishing industry in general are all good sources of market information. Many writers' groups put out newsletters, which usually contain market news and other relevant information (see Chapter 3 for helpful specifics).

✔ **Writers' organizations and conferences:** Whether you're a member of a writers' group or only attend a conference, you can find out a lot of information just by listening to speeches, panel discussions, and the conversations going on around you. You may also be able to set up a one-on-one appointment with an editor or purchase tapes of speeches and workshops you weren't able to attend.

✔ **Personal contacts:** Chances are you've gotten to know other writers, both published and unpublished, in the course of writing your manuscript. Any one of them can be a great source of information.

To e- or not to e-

Electronic publishers, or *ePublishers,* are a recent phenomenon in publishing, including romance publishing. ePublishers differ from traditional publishers in several ways, starting with the format of the book itself. Some ePublishers make books available only for download, and some make books available for download and in print. ePublishing contracts are different from traditional publishers' contracts, and frequently they're quite different from each other. As of this writing, ePublishing is still a very small part of the industry, and for most authors, traditional publishing is still the first-choice route, with publishing an eBook as a fallback plan. Like so many instances where technology's involved, things are subject to change, so you need to research for yourself — in all the places I suggest in the "Finding out who's who" section in this chapter — to see what the state of ePublishing is when you're ready to submit your manuscript.

Tracking the elusive editor

When you have a general idea of which publishers are likely to be interested in your book, you're ready to target a specific editor. This step isn't required, because you *can* just submit to a publisher and let whoever receives all the unsolicited and general submissions decide where to route your manuscript, but I think targeting a specific editor is a smart move. You can do very little after your manuscript has left your hands, but you can at least try to maintain some control over who decides its fate. Whether you've come up with one possible publisher or half a dozen, the next step is finding out who, at each house, may be especially receptive to reading — and acquiring — your book. You can get this information from

- ✔ **Other authors:** If you know who an editor works with, you can get a sense of her tastes. If you write romantic comedy, for example, knowing who edits other romantic comedy authors can be helpful to you. Check out writers' Web sites and industry-related magazines for interviews with writers, because many writers mention their editors by name. You can probably also ask some authors directly, if you've gotten to know them or if they participate in online discussions and bulletin boards that you frequent.

Look inside other authors' books at their dedications. Lots of authors dedicate a book to their editors somewhere along the way, and those dedications can be a good source of information for you.

- ✔ **The editor:** The best way to know what an editor is looking for is to hear it from her own lips. You can find editor interviews online at romance sites, in special-interest magazines and newsletters, and live or on tape at conferences.

Many conferences offer attendees a chance to meet one on one with an editor (or an agent), but knowing beforehand that you're meeting with an editor who's likely to be interested helps, so you don't waste her time or your own. Instead of leaving things to chance, try to figure out ahead of time which editor can be most helpful to you, and then try to get an appointment specifically with her.

Leave room for a wild card. You may hear of an editor at a publishing house you weren't considering (maybe because she's only just started acquiring your sort of book, so she never made it onto your radar) who sounds like she'd love your work. Often she's the perfect person to approach, because she's probably receiving fewer submissions (at least along the lines of your novel) than many of the other editors who you're looking into, because other writers will have overlooked her in favor of the more obvious possibilities.

Aiming for the top: Yea or nay?

One concern many aspiring authors share is whether to aim straight for the top, submitting their manuscripts to a big-gun editor, or try their luck with a more junior editor. Both options have pros and cons. Many submissions, no matter whose desk they land on first, end up in the hands of other members of the editorial staff anyway. Still, because you can control who sees your book first, you need to think about your options. Basically you have to decide which matters more to you: power or accessibility, because that's often what your choice comes down to.

- ✔ Top editors often have more power to make a decision independently, while an editor with less seniority may have to go through one or more editors — sometimes, depending on the house's policy, an entire editorial board — to get the okay to go to contract.

- ✔ On the other hand, newer and less senior editors are often hungrier, looking to build an author base, and are therefore more willing to work with aspiring authors to revise their manuscripts for publication. Finding information on junior editors can be harder, so choosing one isn't always an option anyway.

If you've made a personal contact and gotten a request for your manuscript — perhaps you met an editor at a conference or she judged your work in a contest — that's absolutely the editor to follow up with, no matter how lofty her title is or isn't, because an editor's request to see your book is like gold.

Entering contests: Pros and cons

Writing contests geared toward romance authors are extremely common and have become an increasingly popular way for aspiring writers to get their work in front of an editor. Many times editors judge the final round of these contests, after the top-ranking submissions have been chosen by a panel of judges that often includes published authors.

Romance Writers of America's Golden Heart Award was created for unpublished authors and is broken down by subgenre. A complete manuscript is required to enter. Many of the organization's local chapters hold their own contests, as well, often for the first chapter or synopsis, rather than a complete manuscript. Some writers' conferences also sponsor contests, as do some publishers. Details can be found in various industry-related publications and by searching the Internet.

The obvious plus of entering contests is the possibility of getting your work in front of an editor, and that can be a very big plus. I've bought at least three authors I can think of offhand because I read their work when I judged a contest. Plenty of other authors have gotten their starts that way, too.

The downside to entering contests is that for some authors it becomes a career in itself. They endlessly polish the same opening chapter or synopsis. Often they place in or even win contest after contest. But they never complete a book, so they never actually submit a manuscript. Or an editor asks to see the complete manuscript, based on the first chapter she judged, and the rest of the manuscript turns out to be nowhere near as good, because the author lavished all her attention on the opening chapter and never brought the rest of the book up to snuff. Even though the novel's complete, it never sells.

Submitting Made Simple

After you figure out which publishers and editors are most likely to be receptive to your manuscript, you've made it to the nitty-gritty of the submission procedure. You need to figure out what each house's procedures are, and then target your pitch to be exactly what they're looking for. After that, all you can do is wait, but waiting can be a lot less daunting if you know you've come as close as you possibly can to giving them what they want.

Figuring out what a publisher or specific editor is looking for is step one. You're looking for the answers to three key questions:

✔ **Are unsolicited submissions accepted?** An *unsolicited submission,* also referred to as a *slush* or *over-the-transom submission,* is any submission that hasn't been specifically requested by an editor and/or isn't represented by an agent. If the house doesn't accept unsolicited material, you can try to get your manuscript in front of an editor via a one-on-one appointment at a conference or through a contest. (See the "Tracking the elusive editor" section earlier in the chapter.) The most reliable option, though, is to look for an agent (which I discuss in the "Deciding Whether You Need an Agent" section later in this chapter).

✔ **What form should a submission take?** There are three basic ways of submitting a novel:

- Query letter

- Partial manuscript

- Complete manuscript

I discuss these options later in the chapter, but every house makes its own decisions as to which form it wants to see and from whom. Some houses accept unsolicited submissions only in the form of a query letter, while they look at partials or completes from an agent or by direct request.

What about electronic submissions? Most publishers still ask to see hard-copy submissions, but as technology advances, that may change. Unless a publisher specifically says that it accepts submissions via e-mail (or on disk instead of on paper), you're safest assuming that it doesn't and making contact via snail-mail.

✔ **Does the house accept multiple submissions?** A *multiple submission,* also known as a *simultaneous submission,* involves sending the same project to several publishers at once. Some houses allow multiple submissions, while others want to see a project exclusively. Either way, you should submit your manuscript to only one editor at any given house or *imprint* (a subdivision within the house). Even publishers who are willing to compete with other houses don't want their own editors fighting over a book.

To get the answers to the questions I pose, you can consult many of the resources I advise you to rely on throughout this chapter, including

✔ **Publishers' Web sites:** A publisher's site is the single best place to find information on submission procedures, because other places may not be as up-to-date or may operate on rumor as much as hard info.

✔ **Tip sheets:** Tip sheets often contain information on submission procedures and manuscript preparation.

✔ **Market updates:** Market updates often appear as an annual overview in romance- and general industry-related publications and newsletters, and these sources often feature monthly columns that update changing info.

✔ **Writing Web sites, e-mail lists, and bulletin boards:** Many sites geared toward helping writers also contain information on various publishers' rules and regulations. But because these sites aren't official, they may not be completely up-to-date, and e-mail lists and bulletin boards can be prime sites for rumors that end up not being true.

✔ **Writers' conferences:** Editors who attend conferences are a first-class source of current information, but don't wait until you can get to a conference before you look for info. But, if the timing works out so that you're at a conference just when you need to find out a publisher's procedures, you can't go wrong asking an editor from that house.

After you know what "your" publisher's looking for, you need to know how to give it to them. There are three basic types of submissions: complete manuscript, partial manuscript, and query letter. The first and last are the most likely approaches for an unagented writer to take, and I discuss all three below.

There are exceptions to every rule. Though most publishers and editors prefer to see either a query letter or a complete from a new author, some are open to seeing partials. It's crucial that you find out exactly what the publisher or editor you've targeted is willing to consider or specifically asks to see.

Writing a successful query letter

A *query letter,* or *query,* is the briefest form of submission, required by some publishers (and also some agents). It's also the most common form of submission for unpublished and/or unagented authors.

Your first approach to an agent is also likely to be through a query letter. The basics are just the same, though you may need to tweak things slightly, since you're asking the agent to consider you as a client, not publish your book.

A query letter consists of three basic parts:

- ✔ Cover letter
- ✔ Two-page synopsis
- ✔ SASE

A *synopsis* is similar to the outline you create for yourself before you start writing (see Chapter 7), in that it's a summary of the story. But this time, it's for someone else — usually an editor or an agent — to see, so she can get an idea of your story and decide whether she wants to see more or even offer a contract. You create it after the book is complete or, in some cases, partially written. Synopses take various forms, depending on whether they accompany a complete or partial manuscript, or are included as part of a query letter.

The most common question I hear about queries is "How can I get an editor to buy my book if all she has to go on is a two-page synopsis?" Not to worry: You can't. But the point of a query letter isn't to get an editor to buy your novel; the point is to get her to ask to see more — a partial or complete manuscript — and invest some time in seeing if it's right for the house.

Another common question is "If a house accepts queries, should I complete the manuscript before I submit?" No hard-and-fast rule applies to this situation, but I recommend having at least a substantial portion of the book written and the rest clearly outlined before you query, for three reasons:

✔ An editor's job isn't to vet your ideas.

✔ Until you've actually started writing, you aren't going to know whether your story will really work the way you think it will.

✔ If the editor asks to see your book, you want to be able to get it to her quickly, so it helps to be well into the writing process, even if the novel's not complete yet.

The SASE component of a query letter is easy, but what about the other two elements?

Crafting a cover letter

Your cover letter should be a professionally written business letter and should include

✔ **Your name and address:** I feel as if I shouldn't have to say that you need to include your name and address, but I've seen enough letters without this information that I'm saying it anyway.

✔ **Editor's name and address:** Be sure you spell her name right (I see a *lot* of strange variations of my name), and if you use the same basic letter more than once, be sure you change the "Dear Whoever" section to the right name. Nothing tells me more clearly that I'm seeing a multiple sub- mission (something I can't accept for my house's category lines) or at least that I was second choice than seeing my name and address, and then being referred to as Dear Ms. Someone-I'm-Not.

✔ **Brief summary of your book:** *Brief* means a line or two, maybe a very short paragraph. Your attached synopsis (see "Reviewing your novel — in two pages" later in the chapter) will take care of the details. All the cover letter should tell me is that you've written a marriage-of-convenience story set in the Victorian era or a romantic suspense set in Central America, with a Navy SEAL hero and a hostage heroine.

✔ **Manuscript status:** Is the manuscript complete? If not, how soon do you expect to finish it? How many words long is it/do you expect it to be?

✔ **Professional credentials:** List any previous professional writing experi- ence, membership in writers' organizations, attendance at conferences, contest wins, and so on.

✔ **Additional relevant information:** Are you ex-military and have written a military romance? Are you a history teacher who's written a Medieval romance? In your cover letter, establish any credentials that are relevant to the book you're pitching, so the editor knows she can trust you to have your facts right.

✔ **Targeted series:** This final point applies only if you're writing a category romance, in which case you should tell the editor what series your book is intended for.

If you know the editor particularly likes the sort of book you've written, per-haps because you heard her say so at a conference or know she edits several authors who write similar stories, you can add a line to highlight that fact. Just don't go on and on telling her how great your book is and that she'll like it even better than Betsy Bestseller's work.

Your cover letter should *not* include

- ✔ **Typos:** Proof, proof, and proof again — and don't just spell-check, because as I explain in Chapter 14, plenty of mistakes can slip past your computer. If you want an editor to believe you can write an entire book, don't undercut yourself by writing a sloppy letter.

- ✔ **Irrelevant information:** Got three kids and six grandkids? Raise collies as a hobby? Run marathons? Unless those things are relevant to the book in some way, they don't belong in your cover letter, because the editor's just not going to care.

- ✔ **Cute prose and quirky info:** Don't tell me that the minute I opened the envelope, your guardian angel slipped out and is sitting on my shoulder as I read. And I don't want or need to know that you wear sexy lingerie to get you in the mood to write love scenes. (You can do it; just don't tell me about it.) I'm a professional, and your letter should tell me that you are, too.

Tuning up your two-page synopsis

The heart of a query letter— and the part that strikes the most fear into aspiring writers' hearts — is the synopsis. In two single-spaced pages, which gives you more room than you'd think, you need to synopsize your story from start to finish, focusing on the following:

- ✔ **Brief introduction to your main characters:** Focus on what the editor needs to know so she can understand your plot and the basis of the characters' conflict, not on background and appearance. One or two lines apiece for the hero and heroine, and fewer lines for any subsidiary characters that are important enough to make an appearance, should be all you need.

- ✔ **Plot basics:** Hit the high points. You don't have room — especially if your book is long or your plot is complex — to detail every twist and turn or delve deeply into everyone's motivation. You're just giving an editor an overview of your story line, enough to tell her you have some-thing interesting to say and that in general terms it makes sense. The milestones you created in your outline (see Chapters 7 and 10 for more information on these) can provide a good starting point.

- ✔ **Source of emotional conflict:** This point is key — to an editor and even-tually to a reader — so don't forget to include it because you're busy talking about plot. You need to explain where the emotional conflict comes from and how it plays out in the course of the story. And if the characters make love at some point, don't forget to tell the editor when, as well as how that affects the relationship.

✔ **How your story ends:** Never finish a synopsis by saying, "And if you want to know more, you'll have to ask to see the book." Wrap things up, both the romance and the plot. Especially if some kind of mystery is going on, you need to explain whodunnit or whatever the solution is.

Stylewise, make your synopsis straightforward. Don't worry about flowery prose, lots of description, or building mini-cliffhangers. Just go from beginning (often pointing out exactly where the book itself begins) to end. If you can do that and still give the editor a sense of your voice, that's great, but those extra elements are gravy. At this stage, the editor's not reading for style. She's reading for character and story, so give her what she wants.

Coming up with a complete

Some publishers are willing to consider a complete manuscript right off the bat, but more often publishers would rather start with a query letter (see the previous section, "Writing a successful query letter"), then move on to a complete if they like your query. There are a few things to remember if you submit a complete manuscript, whether from the get-go or in response to an editor's request.

✔ **Include a cover letter and a SASE with adequate postage.** The guidelines for writing a successful cover letter in the "Crafting a cover letter" section earlier also apply when you're submitting a complete. The only change is that you don't need to discuss the manuscript's status, since the editor will be holding the complete in her hands.

✔ **Include a synopsis.** This synopsis should be brief, 2–3 pages in most cases, and provide a top-line overview of your entire book. I recommend double-spacing it for ease of reading. Because the entire manuscript is there with it, you don't need to cram in every detail.

✔ **Make sure your manuscript is in perfect shape.** Chapter 14 gives you (bad pun alert) chapter and verse on how to format your manuscript. Make sure yours is (yet another bad pun alert) letter perfect before you send it off.

Preparing a partial manuscript

A *partial manuscript* consists of several chapters — usually three — and a synopsis. A partial manuscript allows an editor to get a sense of both your storytelling skills and the full plot of your book. But because a partial manuscript is substantially shorter than a complete manuscript, it takes her less time to consider.

Sometimes a first-time author can sell her book based on partial manuscript, but most authors need a complete manuscript the first time. However, many editors prefer to consider a partial first, since it takes them less time to read, even though they ultimately ask to see a complete before considering going to contract. Every house — and often every editor at each house — has somewhat different requirements, so you need to be prepared for any eventuality when you enter the submission maze.

Putting it together

All the do's and don'ts that make a good query (or complete) cover letter also make a good cover letter to accompany a partial manuscript. And just as you need to include a cover letter with your query or complete, you need to include one when you submit a partial, as well as a SASE that's large enough to hold the partial manuscript and bears sufficient postage. When you're putting the chapters together for a partial manuscript, remember to

- ✔ **Submit the first three chapters:** Part of what an editor wants to see is how the book begins, so don't send three unconnected chapters that happen to be your favorites (as some writers do). And if you have a brief prologue, include that *plus* three chapters, so the editor gets to read a substantial chunk — 60 to 75 pages — of your book.

- ✔ **Read everything over one last time:** Even though you've probably read your book all the way through a dozen times, reread the chapters one last time before sending them to be sure you've caught every typo, that every transition works, and that your printer didn't glitch and mess up a page or even drop one.

Synopses made simple

The synopsis that's part of a partial is different from the one you write as part of a query letter or to accompany a complete. A good synopsis in this case is longer and needs to include all the book's key points, or *milestones* (see Chapters 7 and 10 for a discussion of these milestones).

Because you may not have finished writing your manuscript when you create your synopsis and submit your partial, some of the things you need to think about and include are still going to be your best guesses, not fact. Though your first three chapters are of course polished at this point, I recommend that you also have at least a first draft of the rest of your book, to ensure a reasonable degree of accuracy in your synopsis and also because that will speed up the submission process if an editor asks to see the entire book.

Other key points to consider when writing a synopsis as part of a partial include:

- ✔ **Size *does* matter:** The length of a synopsis that accompanies a partial varies based on the length and complexity of the manuscript itself. You need less room to describe a 55,000-word Silhouette Desire or a 60,000-word Harlequin Flipside than a 150,000-word mainstream romantic suspense novel. Generally speaking, most synopses run anywhere from 5 to 50 pages, with most in the 20 to 25 page range, in my experience, and they should be double-spaced. (Reading double-spaced pages is easier for an editor when she has more than just a couple of pages to cover.)

✔ **Synopsize the complete manuscript:** Because some editors (I'm one) prefer reading the synopsis first and then the chapters, don't just pick up the story with Chapter 4. To make reading your synopsis easier for an editor who reads the chapters first, you can break the synopsis up into two sections: *Chapters 1–3* and *Chapter 4 on.*

✔ **Hit the high points:** A synopsis takes the editor through the entire book, but you don't need to mention every single thing that happens. You're showing her the big picture, which means you need to make your major events and your characters' motivations clear. Lay out major transitions and explain the progress of both the plot and the characters' emotional development.

✔ **Choose a format that works for you:** You can start right in with the story, introducing the characters as you go, or you can start out by introducing each character separately, and then pick up with the story. Either way, if you start out by giving background information, make a point of noting where the book itself begins, so an editor knows that *you* know what makes a good opening scene.

Flexibility is built into your synopsis just as it is in the outline you construct before you begin writing (see Chapter 7). An editor who buys your book based on a partial manuscript has certain expectations for the plot that she expects to be met. However, those expectations are big-picture ones — as long as you don't suddenly move the book from Wyoming to the Sahara or turn a Medieval into a Regency, you're probably fine in making minor adjustments. *Do* let her know about any major changes in your book, because she may already be writing copy for it, and you want the copy to be accurate.

Deciding Whether You Need an Agent

If you decide, whether because you need or want one, to take on an agent, you're hiring a professional to represent you. An agent serves as your middleman (or woman) when submitting your manuscript, negotiating your contract, and dealing with any other problems that may arise.

Authors have two basic reasons for taking on an agent; one reason is a matter of necessity, and the other is a matter of choice.

✔ As of this writing, all the major mainstream houses are limiting submissions to specifically requested manuscripts (a very small portion, usually based on an author-editor appointment at a conference) and manuscripts that come in via an agent. For that reason, if you want to sell a first mainstream, having an agent is pretty much a necessity.

✔ If you're interested in writing for series, an agent isn't necessary, because unsolicited submissions can still be made via query letter. Even so, many authors prefer having an agent. Not only does having an agent streamline the submission process (skipping the query stage and going straight to partial or complete), but it also allows the author and the editor to maintain a creative partnership, letting the agent handle the complicated and occasionally contentious business details.

Understanding an agent's job

Every agent makes different arrangements with her authors (something I address in "Examining the author-agent relationship" later in this chapter), but the basic job description remains the same. Agents deal with

✔ **Manuscript analysis:** Some agents, especially those who are former editors, give a great deal of editorial input to their clients, while other agents handle a manuscript basically as is. In either case, a big part of the job is deciding on the strengths and marketability of their clients' work, so they feel confident in its salability when they submit it.

✔ **Market analysis:** Agents are always in touch with the market, keeping on top of who's publishing what and what particular editors are looking for. Your agent targets your submission effectively and gets it straight to the chosen editor's desk.

✔ **Submission:** Agents have full authority to submit their clients' work to any house, and they can choose whether to submit a partial or complete manuscript. A house won't buy a partial manuscript from a brand-new author just because it came in via an agent (it also doesn't mean that they *won't*), but they *will* look at it. In most cases, even if a book is rejected, an agent is given some basic information as to why and doesn't receive a simple form rejection (which I describe in Chapter 16).

✔ **Contract negotiation:** Agents are versed in contracts in general, and most houses' contracts in particular. They know what terms are fixed and which are open for discussion. Often they have prenegotiated changes that are inserted in all their clients' contracts. Agents take care of all the ins and outs of negotiating on your behalf: the amount and payment terms of the advance; royalties, when those are negotiable; subsidiary rights, when those are held by the house; option times and terms; and so on. As your representative (and, essentially, employee), your agent gets back to you at various points in the negotiation to get your thoughts and, ultimately, your approval.

✔ **Subsidiary rights:** When the house doesn't hold subsidiary rights, your agent is the one who markets and negotiates them. The most common are film/TV rights, serialization rights and foreign rights. Some agents handle subsidiary rights themselves or, if they work for a large agency, they hand them over to the agency specialists; others hand them off to a specialized subagent for handling. For a fuller description of subsidiary (sub) rights, see Chapter 17.

✔ **Finances:** In most (though not all) cases, the publisher sends all payments to your agent, who keeps his/her commission (check out the next section) and pays the rest to you. Your agent also receives your royalty statements and goes over them looking for problems and questions. Most agents also keep financial records on their clients' behalfs for tax purposes.

✔ **Troubleshooting:** If problems of any sort occur (contradictions in a royalty statement, author-editor issues, major problems with a cover, or anything else), your agent steps in and handles those issues for you. Don't complain about every little thing (and trust me, some authors do), because you don't want to be the author who cried, "Wolf!" directly or indirectly, but if you have an agent, you do have someone to handle the tough stuff for you if the need arises.

Examining the author-agent relationship

Just as working with an editor who you can see eye-to-eye with is important, having a good relationship with your agent is also important. Your agent is going to be your voice in many ways, so your relationship must be one of trust, and you need to feel free to be honest with her/him.

An agent works on commission, and the amount of that commission (usually anywhere from 10 percent to 15 percent) is something you work out ahead of time. Some agents ask you to sign a contract with them; others work from book to book. Some ask you to cover upfront costs (or some portion of them), like postage, phone calls, and so on, at least until your first sale. Other agents absorb those costs into their agency's budget.

Getting those business details out of the way right off the bat is crucial, so you and your agent can focus on the important aspect of your relationship: building your career. In return for the commission you pay, your agent handles all of the issues I outline in the earlier "Understanding an agent's job" section, but the relationship consists of more than those tasks.

You should feel comfortable talking to your agent about your plans and hopes, not just for each individual book, but for your entire career. That information helps your agent direct your manuscripts and strategize with your editor. And having that extra person in your corner is an additional and extremely important benefit of having an agent.

Interviewing a potential agent

The best way for you to find out about an agent is to ask questions, such as

- ✔ **What business arrangements will the two of you share?** Get business details out of the way first and be sure you're comfortable with them, so you can get down to discussing the nitty-gritty.

- ✔ **Is she on her own or part of a larger agency?** How will that affect you, especially in terms of negotiating things like foreign-language and film/TV rights?

- ✔ **What are her credentials?** How long has she been an agent? If she's new, what's her background (many agents used to be editors or other publishing professionals)? Has she sold a lot of books? Does she have additional relevant credentials? Some agents are also lawyers, for instance.

- ✔ **What's her romance-industry experience?** Does she handle a lot of romance authors? If you're a would-be series writer, how familiar is she with category romances? What romance houses and editors has she worked with on behalf of her clients?

- ✔ **How big is her client list?** Many agents handle a lot of authors, because only a small percentage need her skills at any given time, while the rest are busy writing. Still, you want to get a sense that she's able to be there for you when you need her. As a new writer, you can't — and shouldn't — expect the moon, much less constant hand-holding, but you do need to know you can reach her and will have her attention when it's important.

- ✔ **What does she think about your book?** You need to know what she sees as its — and, by extension, your — strengths and weaknesses. The two of you need to be on the same wavelength with storytelling, because she's not going to effectively represent you if she's not genuinely enthusiastic about your work.

- ✔ **How hands on is she editorially?** The only right or wrong answer to this question lies in whether her approach is what you want and need. If you're looking for a lot of editorial feedback, then you want her to be hands on. If you're not, you don't.

- ✔ **Does she have a plan?** Is she already thinking of an editor she suspects will love your book? A publishing house that's the perfect place for you to begin your career? Tell her a bit about what you have in mind for future books and the route you'd like your career to follow. Then talk to her about how she can get you there.

Most of these questions don't have a right or wrong answer. Go by whatever makes you feel comfortable. For example, a brand-new agent, if she knows her stuff and has genuine energy and enthusiasm for your book, can be a better choice than a veteran who has little time for you and may end up asking an assistant to handle everything. An agent eager to enter the romance market may be a perfect choice, because she'll work extra hard to make you a success — and herself along with you. An agent who likes to offer editorial input can be great — so long as she doesn't make you spend months revising and re-revising and never actually submits your book. On the other hand, a hands-off agent may be great for your ego but may end up sending your book out in less-than-optimum shape.

Finding an agent

The process of finding an agent has been compared in difficulty to finding a publisher. I venture to say that getting an agent really isn't as tough, but it can probably be just as nerve-wracking.

Essentially, you need to look for an agent in much the same way you'd look for a publisher. You need to figure out who the players are, and then decide who would be a good match for you and your work. The following resources can help you find an agent:

- **The Literary Market Place (LMP):** The LMP is a vast publishing reference that comes out annually and is available in most major libraries. Or you can visit the Web site at www.literarymarketplace.com, which requires free registration and/or subscription. The LMP has an entire section on literary agents. Many agents specify the types of projects they handle and their submission requirements.

- **Online sites and searches:** Writers' Web sites, as well as general Internet searches, can turn up helpful information, including insider info on different agents from authors who've worked with them. But keep in mind that just because a particular agent wasn't a good match for someone else doesn't mean she won't be a good match for you.

- **Writers' magazines:** In Chapter 3 I list a number of magazines for writers, even specifically for romance writers. These magazines are a good source of information, both primary (many agents write articles or are interviewed about their needs) and secondary (in articles about agents in general or other writing-related topics).

- **Writers' organizations and conferences:** Membership in various organizations gets you access to insider information and puts you in contact with other writers, who can be great sources of information. Conferences not only provide an opportunity to hear agents speak, but many agents also offer one-on-one appointments with aspiring writers, so you may actually pick up an agent on-site.

- **Personal contacts:** Don't be afraid to ask your writer friends — published and unpublished — for advice and tips.

When you find an agent who expresses interest in your work, set up an appointment (in person or on the phone) to discuss your work and your career aspirations, as well as how she works with authors, and make sure you ask questions (see the "Interviewing a potential agent" sidebar in this chapter).

Just because an agent offers to take you on doesn't mean that you have to go with her unless, after a searching conversation, you think she's the right agent for you. When you take on an agent, you give her a key role in your career. The right agent can help make you a star; the wrong one can stall you at Go. Agenting is a career that has very low barriers for entry, so make sure you're hooking up with one of the vast majority of highly able and professional agents, not someone who's just entered the field and has no credentials.

The Association of Authors' Representatives, Inc., (AAR) is an organization of literary agents that exists to keep its members up-to-date on developments in publishing. It also has an established canon of ethics that members adhere to. Though it exists to serve its members, not writers, its site does contain a page of suggested questions for authors to ask prospective agents, and it can also tell you if an agent you're considering is a member. You can search the site at www.aar-online.org or contact the organization at: The Association of Authors' Representatives, Inc., P.O. Box 237201, Ansonia Station, New York, NY 10003; e-mail: aarinc@mindspring.com.

You need to consider the answers to all your questions, along with your most objective sense of your own strengths and weaknesses as a writer, and decide whether the agent in question is the agent for you. If she's not, keep looking, keep having conversations, and keep your expectations realistic. Too much is riding on your choice for you to go with the first person who offers (or the second or the third), unless she's also the right person.

Chapter 16

Rejection and Revision: Don't Let Them Get You Down

*I*f I pool all the questions I've been asked in my years in romance publishing into groups, by far the largest group involves the twin subjects of revision and rejection letters. These subjects are most common because publishers buy relatively few of the books that writers submit. The rest inspire some type of rejection or revision letter, and every one of those letters becomes, to some degree, a puzzle for the writer to solve. Some letters are actually pretty straightforward — they just convey a message that no writer wants to hear. Others do require interpretation, and the plain truth is that you may never know if you're interpreting the editor's comments correctly. Still others, although not the best news (of the "Welcome to Romance Press" variety), do give good news, and after you get past the initial disappointment of not having sold, you need to recognize and make use of that good news.

You need to deal with an editor's response to your manuscript in a couple of ways. The first is practical. You need to read the letter objectively — or as objectively as you can — and decide what the editor meant, then decide how to move forward with the manuscript. The second consideration is emotional, and a lot of the writers I see aren't prepared for this one. The writing life can be an emotional roller coaster, and you need strategies to get through the rough patches without letting them stop you from working on your craft.

In this chapter, I talk about all aspects of the revision and rejection stages you'll almost certainly go through, from the practical considerations of figuring out what an editor's saying and how to revise if she asks you to, to dealing with the emotional repercussions of finding out that today isn't the day when you become a published romance writer.

What Are They Really Saying?

If your manuscript comes back to you, the first thing to do is take a deep breath and read the accompanying letter. Then, depending on what it says, you may need to grab a tissue, pick up the phone and call your best friend — or just sit down and read the letter again to decide exactly what it means.

An editor pretty much always conveys the news that she wants to buy your book by a call. So if your book comes back with a letter, you can be fairly certain that it hasn't sold — but quite possibly only that it hasn't sold *yet*. In this section, I talk about recognizing what type of rejection or revision letter you've received, and later in the chapter, I get specific about how to deal with each type.

I've broken down the whole range of rejection and revision letters into relatively few types, but, for the most part, these letters exist on a continuum — especially when you're talking about any letter that contains a book-specific critique or encouragement at any level. The range of letters you may get and phrases you may need to interpret is huge. Editors are individuals. You can't judge a revision letter's intent based purely on its length, because a particular editor may consider a one-page letter that gets into specifics about your book as incredibly detailed, while to another editor, that's brief. Another editor may mention specifics or suggest revisions of any sort only if she intends the letter to be the highest form of encouragement.

All you, or anyone you ask for interpretive help, can do is take every factor you know into account — especially if you have other letters from the same editor as a comparison — and make your best guess as to what that editor intended.

But read every word carefully and accept that the editor has said exactly what she means. The bottom line, as hard as accepting it can sometimes be, is that if an editor wants to see the book again, she says so. If she doesn't, then 99.9 percent of the time, you're better off accepting that and moving on. Do cases exist where a determined writer perseveres and the editor ends up buying that book? Yes, but those instances are few and far between, and I don't want to raise hopes that shouldn't be raised. To be a writer, you have to play the odds, using your time as wisely as possible — and that means recognizing both good and bad news for what they are. That approach increases the odds that one day you can hear the best news of all — that you've sold.

Regarding rejections

An editor can send all kinds of letters, and most are quite straightforward rejection letters. The sad truth is that most manuscripts won't — and shouldn't — be published. You're reading this book and working on your craft to improve your odds of being one of the lucky ones whose work editors consider publishable, or at least worth commenting on.. Even so, you need to know how to interpret every kind of possible response, starting with the worst.

The form reject

The so-called *form reject* can take a few similar, but not always totally unhelpful, forms:

- **Photocopied no-thank-you:** In the days before a computer was on every desk, this form used to be the standard, and some publishers still use it simply because it makes an editor's job easier.

- **Computer-generated no-thank-you.** Though it contains your name and address, and often the name of your manuscript, you need to face the hard truth: This letter is as impersonal as a photocopy, just somewhat more advanced technologically.

Neither of the above letters tells you anything, other than that the publisher found your manuscript unsuitable for publication. Slightly more helpful, but no less impersonal is the "some-common-reasons-are" version. Whether photocopied or computer-generated, this letter also contains an explicit no-thank-you, followed by a brief list of common problems that lead to rejection. These statements may include (but certainly aren't limited to):

- Your heroine wasn't entirely sympathetic.

- Your hero lacked the strength of character we require.

- The level of romantic tension was not high enough or sustained throughout your manuscript.

- Your plot was not complex enough to support your manuscript's length.

Realize that the list, whatever it contains, merely suggests general problems that the editors often find in manuscripts and that are cause for rejection. One, two, all, or none may apply to your manuscript. Unfortunately, these letters leave the burden on you to decide which (if any) apply to your work. The information this list contains is absolutely legitimate and accurate regarding the bulk of all submissions, but it may or may not apply to your manuscript.

These letters all have an unequivocal message in common: This editor or house can't publish your manuscript. Does that mean you can't get it published anywhere, or that you can never submit to this editor again when you have a new manuscript? Those questions are tough to answer, and I talk about them later in this chapter in the section "Does No Always Mean No?" But for the most part, regard such a form letter as a final response by the publishing house to this particular project.

Hope for next time

You may get a firm rejection letter for the particular project that you submitted, but that rejection may leave the door open for future submissions. This type of letter contains an unmistakable invitation along the lines of:

> *Though this project isn't suitable for our needs, I would be happy to see future submissions from you.*

Bottom line: If you find that phrase or something like it, the editor legitimately wants to see your future work, just not a revised version of this manuscript. This sort of letter often contains information on why your book didn't work, but you need to realize that it *is* a rejection letter, not an invitation to revise and resubmit. One key phrase — "Among the problems . . . " — preceding a list of specific information often indicates this kind of rejection. The editor isn't telling you everything she found wrong — information you need in order to revise — but only giving you a general idea.

On the positive side, this type of letter gives you the okay to contact this editor in the future. And if the editor does take the time to comment on your book, take a look at what she says. Aspiring authors often make the same basic mistakes in each book, so see what you did wrong and then try to find a lesson to apply to your current and future projects.

Reading about revisions

The next-best thing to selling your book happens when an editor asks you to revise and resubmit. Even if the book doesn't ultimately sell, you can — and *should* — congratulate yourself on having made a considerable step forward toward your goal, a step relatively few would-be authors get to take.

Celebrate your victories. Wherever you're on the path to publication, you can easily look at all the writers who have already gone a step further than you have or are where you're trying to go, and feel like a failure in comparison. But you need to take time to recognize your successes. If you receive a request to revise and resubmit, it's a compliment to both your talent and the work you've put into studying your craft. Accept it gracefully and with pride.

Technically, any revision letter that precedes the sale of your book qualifies as a rejection letter, but if the editor clearly requests the opportunity to see the manuscript again, it's a rejection letter of such a different — and much better — kind that it deserves to be treated separately. There are a couple of variations. Check them out, and then find out how to get down to business in the "They Like It, But . . ." section later in this chapter.

The top-line revise and resubmit

You generally get this sort of letter when the editor feels that your manuscript has potential, enough that it's worth her time to ask to see it again, but that it still needs quite a lot of work. These letters include fairly broad comments, for example:

- You need to strengthen the romantic conflict in the last third of the book.
- You don't make your heroine's motivations as clear as they should be.
- The pacing slows midway through your book and doesn't pick up again until the final few chapters.
- Your subplot became too intrusive and needs to be both cut back and related more directly to the central romantic relationship.

Sometimes the editor may also provide a few specific page references, as examples of where she noticed a specific problem.

If you get a letter like this, you can be sure the editor's interest in seeing the book again is sincere, but what happens when you resubmit depends totally on your ability to take a big-picture view of your book and her comments, and then do a pretty thorough rewrite. You still have a fair way to go to make the book publishable, but something — your characters, your plot, your ability to depict genuine emotion — captured the editor's attention, and now you have the opportunity to show her what you can do.

The detailed revise and resubmit

This letter is definitely the next-best thing to a contract offer. A letter like this can literally go on for pages, which makes it look quite daunting (even depressing). But it really is good news! It signifies that the editor thinks your book is very close to publishable, and that she's willing to invest a considerable amount of her time in writing a long and detailed letter to show you exactly where the problems lie.

A detailed letter like this probably contains general points, as in the top-line letter, but it also contains a lot of page-specific references, explanations of what does and doesn't work at particular points, and sometimes even suggestions for how to fix some of the specific problems. This letter probably also begins or ends with an emphatic request to see the book again, often "as soon as you have a chance to work on the revisions."

They Like It, But . . .

I'm going to start with the best-case scenario and talk about how to handle the revision and resubmission process when an editor suggests changes and asks to see the book again. (Check out the "Does No Always Mean No?" section later in the chapter for the less desirable but more common response.)

The revision process isn't really all that different whether you have a top-line letter or a detailed one (see "Reading about revisions" earlier in the chapter). Either way, you have to look at your book from a different angle, go back over what you thought worked, rewrite — sometimes substantially — and then go through the nerve-wracking submission process all over again.

The most important thing to know about any request to see a revised version of your book is that it's 100 percent sincere. Editors are busy people. And every editor I know is also a really nice person. But editors aren't so nice that we ask to do extra work unless we see potential for a payoff. If an editor takes the time to write a personal, encouraging letter analyzing your text and suggesting changes, then offers to invest more time in reading the revised version, you can believe that she sees potential in you and your book.

Similarly, don't ever think that an editor who sends you an encouraging letter isn't serious, and that she's really sending you the message "Put that book away and don't waste any more time on it." Editors don't put in the time on a long letter to drum your unworthiness into you but rather to emphasize how much potential you have.

If an editor asks to see your book again, it's not a guarantee that the publishing house will eventually buy it, but such a request *is* a guarantee that you've made it one step closer to your ultimate goal: publication.

What exactly do they want you to do?

I don't have a simple answer to this question, because every book is, quite literally, a different story. However, I can give you some tips that can make the revision process easier to understand and accomplish. Chances are you made plenty of revisions — large and small — while you were writing the book's various drafts. Back then, you analyzed the book yourself, and now you're incorporating someone else's analysis, but the process isn't all that different. In fact, you may find this time around easier, because someone else has posed the questions for you. You just have to provide the answers.

That's actually how I like to think of the editing process: as a matter of asking questions and making sure the book answers them. For me, it works at both the revision stage, when you're dealing mostly with structural issues, and even, later, as part of doing the line edit, when I sit down with a pencil to work on the book page by page (see Chapter 18). You can use this question-and-answer view of the editing process to your advantage as you go back over your book to incorporate the requested revisions.

When I ask for revisions, I'm pointing out places in the book where I had a problem or where something wasn't clear, didn't make sense, or took the book in the wrong direction. I'm asking the author to revise and provide a clarification, an explanation, or a turn back onto the right path. When I work with an author, she needs to fix the book in such a way that she answers my question or solves my problem.

Not every editor may think of the process in the same question-and-answer terms, but that doesn't stop you from looking at it that way as you revise, and it may be a helpful approach for you to take. If you go through the book taking the editor's notes and turning them into questions you ask as you go, you can see where you need to make changes.

✔ **Top-line revisions:** Top-line revisions are the big-picture issues, and you can turn them into questions easily. Just take what the editor said, rephrase it, and start going back through your book. For instance:

- **"Your heroine's motivations aren't always clear" becomes "Are my heroine's motivations clear in this scene?"** As you go through your book, asking that question scene by scene, you can make changes wherever you realize that you haven't made her motivations really clear. By the time you're done, you've made your book stronger and taken care of the editor's concern.

- **"Your pacing lags toward the middle of the book" becomes "Does this scene slow the book down? How can I speed it up?"** With those questions in mind, you can look at the central section of your book and use the techniques I discuss in Chapter 10 to get things moving again in scenes where the pacing slows.

You can use that Q & A approach with anything an editor says, putting it into a form that helps you with your revisions.

Page-specific revisions: Sometimes the sheer number of the revisions in a lengthier, detail-oriented revision letter can intimidate you, but remember that they're actually an editor's expression of enthusiasm and confidence. As you go through them page by page, most of them are likely to be specific and easy to deal with, but whenever something's not clear, turning it into a question can help. For instance, "The transition between this scene and the next is jarring" becomes "How can I make this transition smooth and carry the reader along?"

In addition, the editor has already done a lot of the work for you by pointing out the specific places you need to look at, so she's saved you a lot of time. You can generally handle page-specific revisions easily. Just address them in order and, even when you have quite a lot of them to wade through, you can generally be done with them relatively quickly.

Tips on technique

Sometimes thinking about rewriting an entire book can be daunting, even though you're not really rewriting everything but rather threading your revisions through from start to finish. This is true even if a lot of the changes are page-specific and relatively finite, and it's particularly true if the editor made multiple big-picture suggestions for you to keep in mind, so you have several structural considerations to keep in mind as you revise, along with any page-specific notes.

Make the revision task seem less intimidating by breaking down the job into manageable increments. You can handle a chapter at a time, reading through it, making all the changes you want, and then taking a break. Or you can look at one type of revision at a time — first pacing, then characterization, and so on — if you find focusing on and correcting problems that way easier, handling the page-specific issues as you go or as their own separate stage.

This incremental approach may not be the most time-efficient method, but if it helps you visualize the task and gets you working on the book rather than putting it off because the job seems too big, it's worth whatever extra time it may take. Also, given how busy your day can be, working chapter by chapter may actually be the best approach, because you can fit a chapter in whenever you have time, instead of hoping to find a few free hours at a stretch. You just need to find an approach that keeps you rewriting in a way that works for you.

Which works better, revising on disk or on hard copy? Ultimately, you'll make all changes on a disk so you can print out a clean copy of the revised manuscript for the editor. And you can't write your changes in longhand on the manuscript itself if they're extensive, anyway. But you may find that for your initial read, when you're figuring out where you need revisions, you can work more easily on a hard copy — which mimics the actual reading experience more closely than reading on-screen — making notes to yourself as you go. Then you can keep your revised hard copy by you as a guide when you're making the actual revisions at your computer. For smaller changes, you can just write them directly on the manuscript, if you want to, and transfer them to the computer later. The advantage of working on hard copy is that you can take it with you wherever you go and work on it whenever you have a few free minutes. But if you're so attuned to working on the computer that using the hard copy slows you down and feels counter-intuitive, don't force yourself. Find a system that works for you and stick to it.

The importance of time

Time *does* count when you're doing revisions, for a couple of reasons:

- ✔ **Every editor has a lot of projects going on at the same time.** Because editors are busy people, the sooner you can get your revised manuscript back on her desk, the more likely she is to remember it clearly, with the same enthusiasm that led her to request revisions in the first place.

- ✔ **Doing revisions on spec is kind of like an audition.** You're doing your revisions in hopes of making a sale, so no contractual deadline is involved.

But you're demonstrating to the editor that you're not only willing to revise, but also that you can do it in a timely fashion. Those are important things for her to know. If she buys one book from you, she's hoping to buy more in the future, and she needs to know she can work with you. Returning your revisions quickly tells her that she can.

✔ **Being quick may clinch the sale.** You may not know it, but when the editor asks you to revise, she may be looking at an upcoming hole in her schedule that she can fill with your book — if you get that book ready in time. Or she may see an opportunity to publish your book to tie in with a holiday or other upcoming event.

Though time is of the essence, it's equally essential that you take enough of it to revise thoroughly and effectively. If you do a slapdash job, the editor will know it, and the fact that you were quick won't be enough to offset the fact that you were sloppy. Balance out both sides of the equation, finding a way to be as fast as you can while still keeping the quality of your work high.

When great minds don't think alike

What if you totally disagree with an editor's suggestions? This question is tough, because you're giving up the possibility of a sale if you decide not to revise. Before you make that determination — and sometimes it *is* the right one — analyze the situation and why you object to the suggested revisions.

✔ **Minor points:** If you disagree only over a few relatively minor points, I suggest that you make the rest of the revisions and resubmit, mentioning in your cover letter the points you left alone and why. Be brief and don't be argumentative. A good editor is always open to discussing the need for changes, and such discussion doesn't burn any bridges.

✔ **Major points:** What if the editor's vision of your book — who your characters are, where the story should go — is radically different from yours? Her approach may be just as interesting or valid as yours, but it requires telling a different story than you set out to tell. Does that new story resonate for you? It may be worth at least trying to revise along those lines and seeing whether it works. But if the suggested new direction genuinely doesn't make sense for you, if it's just not a story you can see yourself writing, then you don't have much of a choice. Don't make the revisions. Consider approaching that editor again with a project you think may appeal to her, but direct *this* project elsewhere.

Should you send the editor a brief note thanking her for her interest, even though you've decided to take the book in a somewhat different direction? You don't want to sound like a prima donna, but you also don't want to burn any bridges by acting as if you're not appreciative of the help. So if you feel you can hit the perfect tone, you may want to go ahead and write, but it's impossible to predict every individual editor's response.

Luckily this situation is extremely rare, so if you find yourself reacting this way to every editor's suggestions on every book you write, you probably need to take another look at yourself and start figuring out how to be more open-minded and flexible if you want to succeed in this business.

Handling the resubmission process

After you finish revisions, you've done almost everything you can do to try to sell your book. Now you just have to handle the actual resubmission of your manuscript, which you may find even more nerve-wracking than when you submitted the book the first time. On the one hand, an editor read your manuscript and asked to see it again, so you have an "in," something you didn't have the first time around, which can reassure you. On the other hand, this time around — for that very same reason — you have a real shot at selling, so the pressure is turned up, and it feels as if everything's hanging in the balance, and that's *not* reassuring. Despite the pressure, you have to send the book back to the editor and then try not to stress over its fate too much.

Don't stop writing while you wait for word on a resubmission. In Chapter 15, I suggest working on another project while you wait for an editor to respond to an initial submission. Following that advice is even more important when you resubmit. Not only do you need to keep your mind off what you can't control and your creative abilities limber, you want to be prepared with a follow-up project, whether the editor buys your book or not. If she buys it, having another manuscript ready for her to look at is to your advantage, so she knows that she can count on you to be productive. Even if she doesn't buy the current book, she'll probably be willing, even eager, to see another project. So have one ready while you're still on her mind.

You need to bear a few tips in mind when resubmitting, just to make sure your manuscript has as easy a passage as possible:

- ✔ **Personalize your cover letter.** Without going overboard, use your cover letter to remind the editor that she asked to see a revised version of your book and to thank her for her interest and suggestions, which you feel have made the book stronger. (Hey, editors are only human. We're in this business because we love books and writers. We want to help, and it's always nice to know that we have.) You may also want to make a specific but brief comment or two on particular changes you've made.

- ✔ **Enclose a copy of the original revision letter.** Though you don't strictly need this copy, including it doesn't hurt. It allows the editor to refresh her memory as to what she wanted from your revisions.

- ✔ **Be sure to mark the outer envelope as "Requested Material."** Take this precaution just in case the editor has someone else opening her mail.

 ✔ **Enclose a self-addressed, stamped envelope (SASE).** You're hoping, of
    course, that the editor will buy your manuscript and won't need this
    return envelope, but you don't want to look overconfident.

The best possible scenario at this point would be for the editor to respond to
your revisions with an offer to buy the manuscript (check out Chapter 17 for
tips on handling The Call). But what can you do if your editor likes your book
and recommends it for publication, but a higher-ranking editor turns it down?
A fair number of authors find themselves in this situation, because not every
editor has the power to make the final decision about acquiring a manuscript.

If a higher-ranking editor ultimately turns the book down, the situation can go
a couple of ways, but neither one involves a totally closed door.

 ✔ The editor who makes the final decision may quite possibly ask to see a
    revised version of the manuscript, in which case you're really only
    repeating the process you've just been through.

 ✔ Even if she's not interested in seeing the book again, you now have an
    editor (without final say-so but with definite influence) who knows your
    work and feels that you're publishable. That means she's almost cer-
    tainly willing to look at future projects, and she may even be willing to
    work with you on developing story lines that work for the house.

One Editor's Insight into Common Editorial Comments

No one but the editor who wrote the letter can ever tell you exactly what she
meant by a specific comment, but a lot of top-line revision letters talk about
the same kinds of things. In the sections that follow, I outline common manuscript criticisms, my interpretations of what can spark those comments, and
what you can do to fix the problem.

Your heroine isn't as sympathetic as she needs to be

As I discuss in Chapter 4, your heroine is the reader's alter ego. She needs to
be approachable, someone the reader can empathize with. Would-be writers
often try so hard to make sure their heroines don't act like wimps that they
come on too strong. You may have made your heroine too shrill, for instance,
having her see an insult in every little thing and getting angry about it. Or she's

so capable at everything that the hero looks like a wimp in comparison. Or maybe you've just made the heroine so beautiful and privileged, without a single insecurity, that no reader can identify with her.

Chances are you know (and like) your heroine so well that you're aware of all her insecurities, for example, and you think they're right there on the page. But you need to go back and add or emphasize (to the point that you may feel as if you're exaggerating) the missing qualities that can help your reader empathize with your heroine. Or you may need to actively change plot elements to create a greater sense of equality between the hero and heroine. Most readers are looking for a relationship of equals, not a complete reversal of the traditional sex roles.

Your pacing is erratic

A lot of people have heard the sagging-middle comment (and I discuss it in Chapter 10, where I talk about pacing in detail). The sagging-middle problem is fairly self-explanatory and can often be dealt with in one finite chunk. Erratic pacing is something else. A book with this problem moves in fits and starts, like a car that keeps stalling out. Usually the author has a series of dramatic, tension-filled scenes that move well — maybe even actual action scenes, like a car chase or a fight — but she hasn't figured out how to create a similarly strong pace in the scenes that connect them. In between these scenes, she offers the reader a series of low-key dates, scenes of the heroine with her family or friends, scenes of her on the job, and so on.

If erratic pacing is your problem, you have to get rid of the filler scenes, which you can do in two ways. (You may want to do both.) You can

- ✔ **Cut the slow scenes entirely.** Replace them with scenes where something *does* happen. Not every scene has to feature high drama, but every scene does need to move the romance and the plot forward. Think of it as a workout — you warm up before the intense exercise and then cool down afterwards. Those warm-up scenes (and the cool-downs) should build on the more dramatic scenes, not exist in isolation from them.

- ✔ **Inject drama into the scenes that you already have.** Give those ho-hum scenes not just text (the relatively boring stuff that's happening) but subtext, hidden tensions and passions that the reader sees and expects to explode at any minute. These components add drama to what may otherwise be a totally uninteresting scene.

Your hero's too strong/arrogant/tough

The editor may even say he's nasty or rude. Given the popularity of the Alpha hero (who I discuss in Chapter 4), a writer often goes too far in trying to create this hero type and comes up with a guy who's just too tough and really does come off as nasty, not appealingly strong. I frequently see this kind of hero in tandem with a too-strong heroine, and the result is two people who spend the whole book fighting with, yelling at, and competing with each other — but never actually meshing. They're equals, but not in an attractive way.

If your hero is described in a negative way, you need to tone down the tough-guy stuff and create a whole different side to him. You need to humanize him, to show him having a softer, more sympathetic streak (even if he hides it from the heroine). You may also find that using more of his point of view helps you a lot, because if you show the reader why he acts so tough, he can get away with more than if his motivations are a mystery.

Your plot lacks the necessary complexity

The fact that a plot lacks the complexity necessary for the length of your novel makes itself evident in a variety of ways. A couple of examples: The romantic conflict gets settled several chapters before the end of the book, so suddenly a new — and totally unconnected — problem comes in from left field to keep the hero and heroine apart for another 40 or 50 pages. Or you give a subplot (or several) almost as much prominence as the central romance.

If you receive this comment, you first need to analyze your book to figure out exactly why the editor made it. After you've done that, you can look at various ways to solve the problem. You may want to consider whether you can get away with a shorter book. In the first example above, you can lop off the last few chapters and let the book end where the story naturally does.

But if you need to beef up your central plot to avoid relying so heavily on a subsidiary story line, you need to complicate things for your characters. If you've written a romantic suspense novel, you have it relatively easy, because most mysteries can handle another (believable) twist. Often, though, you need to look to your characters for complexity. If you deepen and complicate their conflict, you give yourself additional building blocks for their scenes together, and you give them issues that take longer to work out. Both those additions allow you the freedom to add scenes that feel dramatic and relevant, and that lengthen your book without padding it.

Your characters' motivations aren't clear

I find myself saying that a writer hasn't made her character's motivations sufficiently clear fairly frequently, and I'm sure I'm not alone. Particularly (but by no means exclusively) in books with a lot of action, like a romantic suspense novel, a lot of focus goes to what's going on but not as much goes to why. An author may explain plot developments, but she frequently overlooks emotional ones. Characters get mad or get horizontal, and the reader never gets any — or enough — sense of why. Or the heroine thinks to herself that she loves the hero, but the reader just sees the two of them at odds, even if irresistibly physically attracted to each other, so all that emotion seems to come out of nowhere.

If you're like most authors, you think you've been clear about what's going on in the characters' heads. Because you know them so well, you don't spell out what they're thinking because you're thinking it right along with them. The reader, though, is meeting these characters for the first time when she starts on page one, so she needs more to go on. You may feel as if you're hitting her over the head with a sledgehammer by spelling things out, but you aren't; you're just giving her what she needs.

I talk in more detail about using your characters' points of view in Chapter 9, but this tip can help you open your characters' minds to your reader. Let your heroine think to herself about why she suddenly sees the hero in a different light (or vice versa). Point out the small shifts in perception and emotion that ultimately lead to love. Emotions — especially love — are often illogical, so sometimes you just need to have the character ask the same question that's running through the reader's mind: Why do I like him so much? Why did I just get mad at her when I really want to kiss her silly?

Your characters seem more like types than real people

Editors most often direct this comment toward secondary characters, but heroes and heroines aren't immune. They too can feel as if the author hasn't fully formed them as individuals, instead simply assigning them suitable traits. As I discuss in Chapter 4, any character who has more than a walk-on part should feel like a real person, but often they seem to come straight from central casting: the kindly grandmother who's always baking cookies; the gay hairdresser; the surly, trash-talking teenager; the outwardly sweet but secretly bitchy — and always glamorous — other woman.

With the secondary characters, you need to go back and mix up their traits a bit. You don't want them to be so interesting that the reader pays too much attention to them and wonders too much about their lives and fates, but you do want them to seem like individuals.

If you have the stereotype problem with your hero or heroine, fixing it may be tougher than if it's with your secondary characters. You need to go back to the beginning and start thinking about your couple as emotional individuals, not just in terms of their physical descriptions and outward characteristics. Delve deeper into their backgrounds, their hopes, and their insecurities to create a more complete picture, and let their emotions drive their actions as much as possible. Emotion makes them stand out as individuals.

Does No Always Mean No?

I need to talk about a reality no would-be writer likes to think about: Most aspiring writers remain aspiring. You can definitely do things to improve your chances of success — and by using this book as a basis for working hard at your craft, you're doing one of them. Even so, there are no guarantees, so you need to really enjoy the writing process, have storytelling in your blood, and feel a real sense of fulfillment in creating characters and bringing them together.

No matter how hard you work, chances are you're going to rack up a lot of rejections along the course of your career, even if success is waiting for you at the end. Enjoying what you're doing makes rejection a lot easier to bear.

Interpreting a rejection letter

No one likes to give or dwell on bad news, and editors get into the business because we want to buy and publish books, not because we want to ruin people's dreams by rejecting them. Still, rejection is a fact of the publishing life, and it's almost certainly going to be a fact of your life if you seriously try to get your work published. Most of the time, a rejection letter isn't very difficult to interpret. No *does* mean no. If the editor doesn't suggest revisions or ask to see the book again, you need to take her at her word.

Facing up to a form reject

It's difficult for any author to accept that a book she's poured a lot of time and emotion into, and that she feels really works, has not only been turned down, but has been turned down without comment (or at least without any manuscript-specific comments). Most of the time, though, that's what happens: You get a form reject.

The interpretation of a form reject is simple: Don't send that project back to that house. I know I'm being blunt, but I'm amazed at how many times I'm at a conference and a would-be writer comes up to me and says something like, "I sent my book to Editor A, and she sent it back with a form reject. Should I revise it and send it back to her, or should I just send it to (her colleague) Editor B, instead?" Answering that question in print, rather than in person, is only marginally easier when I know I'm about to quash someone's hopes and dreams. But the answer is "Neither." If Editor A thought the manuscript had potential, she would have said so. And because it's her job to speak for the house, sending the book to Editor B wastes her time — and yours.

Your time is valuable and you don't want to waste it endlessly submitting and/or revising a project that isn't strong enough to sell. In this case, you've been told that you can't sell the project to this house, so don't invest your time in trying to prove otherwise. That doesn't mean the book may not be right for another house. I talk in Chapter 15 about how to target a publisher; use that info to figure out where you should submit your book next.

Should you revise before submitting elsewhere? The answer really comes down to this question: Do you see specific things in the book that you can strengthen, or are you revising simply to revise? Because a publishing house has just rejected your book, it's natural to feel that you can make it better. But make those changes only if you can pinpoint weak spots. If you don't have a specific sense of those weak spots, no amount of revising can help. You've made the book as strong as you know how, so let the book speak for itself.

Even in the absence of any explanation as to why the house rejected the book, try to figure out for yourself what problems the editor may have had. If you have a critique partner (a subject I discuss in Chapter 5), she may be able to help you, too. In the end, you may never know for sure what the editor's problems were, but you can still develop a new perspective on your own writing — including what you see as your strengths — and that fresh look gives you insights to use in future books.

Just as a form reject doesn't mean you can't submit your manuscript elsewhere, it's also no indication that you can't submit a different book to that editor in the future. Truthfully, given the number of submissions an editor sees, she's unlikely to remember your name. (She'd be much more likely to remember the book if you sent it back unsolicited — though not in a good way.) A form reject is book-specific, not author-specific. But, if you receive an entire series of form rejects from a particular editor or house, at some point you probably need to give up on that particular avenue and look elsewhere for a publisher. Unfortunately, I don't have a magic number; you have to make that decision for yourself if you feel you're getting to that point.

When is enough enough? For most would-be writers, a point comes with a book — sometimes, to be honest, with book after book — when you've done all you can. You've submitted to every publisher you can find, you've revised as much as you can based on general lists of potential problems, and you're still getting just form rejects. The hard truth is that you probably need to table that project. Not every book sells, and even a lot of best-selling writers have manuscripts under the bed or in the closet that never sold and never will. When that time comes for a book of yours, accept it and move on. Look at the book as a learning experience, let it go, and apply what it helped you figure out to your next manuscript.

Rejection can be encouraging

This heading may sound like a contradiction in terms, but rejection really *can* be encouraging. When a rejection letter contains feedback geared specifically to your manuscript, you've gone beyond the form reject. Although a personal rejection is still rejection, it also means you've reached a point where your work stood out to an editor, and that's a genuine step forward.

After you've read the letter once or twice, take a break from it. Give yourself a little while to adjust to the fact that they rejected your book without trying too hard to analyze the reasons, and then go back to it later, with a clearer head, to take another look. Use it as a tool, mine information from it, but don't obsess. When you find that you're not getting anything new from the letter, you're just reminding yourself that, yes, you got rejected, so put it in a file, leave it there, and go back to your writing.

A brief explanation of the problems with your manuscript doesn't constitute an invitation to revise and resubmit. Given the temptation, many authors want to resubmit, even after receiving a form reject, so you may feel understandably encouraged to take an editor's comments as a basis for sending your project back. Don't fall prey to that temptation, but do take the comments to heart. Though the editor felt your book was still too far from publishable form to suggest you revise it, she also felt you would be able to benefit from her comments. Take a look at what she said, and think about her words not only in relation to your current project but also in terms of future books.

When a rejection letter contains an invitation to submit future projects, accept it as soon as you can. Here my advice to work on a second project while an editor is looking at the first can really pay off. The sooner you have new text ready to go, the more likely the editor is to recall your earlier work and her request. So get your newest project in shape as quickly as you can, still making it strong — and if the editor gave you feedback, look over the new book in light of her comments. Then get that new book in the mail to her:

- ✔ Mention in your cover letter that she invited you to submit future manuscripts.
- ✔ Include a copy of her original letter.
- ✔ Mark the outer envelope as "Requested Material."
- ✔ Enclose a self-addressed, stamped envelope, in case she needs to return your manuscript.

Dealing with rejection, emotionally and professionally

Dealing well with rejection can not only make your life easier, it can help you make your career a successful one. It can even make the difference between having a career and giving up when you shouldn't.

Several years ago, I went out to dinner at a conference with a group of published authors. They started talking about a woman they all knew, commenting on how sad her situation was. It turned out that she was an aspiring writer they all thought had tremendous talent. She had submitted her first book, and she'd gotten back a rejection letter — but an encouraging one. The editor had explained why the book didn't work but had also asked to see her next project. Getting a letter like that is unusual enough, and getting one on a first-ever submission is even rarer. But the rejection had so devastated the author that she put the book away and stopped writing completely.

That was an extreme — and extremely sad — overreaction to rejection, but it does point out the dangers in taking rejection too emotionally. It's under-standable — even expected — that every rejection hurts. No editor doubts that every submission she sees represents someone's hard work, but despite that, most of the time our job is to tell people that their books didn't make the grade. Given how personally invested you feel in your work, you're totally justified in being upset by rejection. And no one says you have to put rejection out of your mind as if it never happened, and get back to work on your newest project five minutes after the mailman leaves.

Even published authors get rejected. Does that surprise you? Trust me, it's true. Authors who have an editor and a career still sometimes come up with a project that isn't right for the market. And if you ask them, I'm sure they can tell you that it's never easy. But because it's a fact of the writing life, they've figured out how to deal with it, and you need to figure it out, too.

After the rejection letter comes and you've gotten over your first moments of pain, give yourself some time to come to terms with the fact that this book wasn't *the* book, then deal with rejection like the professional you plan to be.

- ✔ **Expect it:** I'm not saying that the minute you mail off a manuscript, you should start mourning the fact that the publishing house will reject it, but in terms of your overall career and all the submissions you'll make over the years, you can expect to face rejection. If you factor that possi-bility in, it loses the power to surprise you when it comes, and that pre-paredness takes away a big part of its power to hurt you.

- ✔ **Analyze objectively:** You may find such analysis hard, especially the first few times, but by the time you get a rejection letter, you've probably been away from the manuscript for several months, at least. Try to think about it as if you're looking at someone else's book, and think about pos-sible reasons why an editor may have turned it down. If the editor gave you feedback, use that as your basis for analysis. You'll probably start to see flaws you didn't see when you first sent it off.

- ✔ **Seek support:** Do you have friends who are writers, or have you become part of a writers' group? (See Chapter 5 for more on this subject.) Call them, or get together for coffee, and talk about what happened. They've all probably gotten rejection letters before, and no one can offer support like someone who's been through the same thing. As an added benefit, if your letter contained book-specific criticism, they may be able to help you analyze the manuscript in light of that.

✔ **Don't stop writing:** This is probably the single most important item in the list, so maybe I should have placed it first. But I decided to put it last so it stays top of mind when you walk away from this list. If you're a real writer, not just a dabbler, you need to write the same way that you need to breathe. You may be a little distracted when you first sit down at the keyboard again, second-guessing yourself for a little while, but don't let that stop you. Keep writing, and soon you'll find yourself caught up in your latest characters and their story.

It's also important to deal well with rejection emotionally. You still have family and friends, and quite possibly co-workers, counting on you, so you don't have the luxury of falling apart. You're the best judge of how you deal with adversity, so call on your usual coping techniques to help you now. Here are a few suggestions I can offer:

✔ **It's not the end of the world:** Does that sound like a cliché? No wonder, because it is. But clichés become clichés because they're so true in so many circumstances. And, as much as you want to sell a book, you can still have a wonderful life without ever seeing your name in print. So don't exaggerate the importance of one rejection letter into a world-shattering event. It's simply not.

✔ **Go ahead and cry:** Even if it's not the end of the world, you can still feel bad about rejection. So go ahead — cry, yell, or do whatever helps. Just don't let it go on forever. (And try not to scare the neighbors.)

✔ **Remember that your book was rejected, *you* weren't:** It's easy to take rejection as a personal indictment, but that's a huge mistake. Ninety-nine percent of the time, the editor doesn't know you from Adam (or Eve). She's not passing judgment on you at all; she's judged your manuscript and nothing more. It's all too easy to extrapolate from a rejection letter and decide that you're worthless on every level of your life, but you're not — and you need to remind yourself of that.

✔ **Lean on friends and family:** Friends are for supporting you. Family, too. Don't be afraid to tell them you can use a little pampering.

✔ **Indulge yourself:** Get your mind off what happened by doing something you enjoy that may even make you feel better. Get a manicure, go to a movie (a comedy to make you laugh, a tearjerker to let you cry), or cook the kind of gourmet dinner you haven't had time to make while you've been busy writing.

✔ **Give yourself a reward:** Does this advice sound crazy? A reward for rejection? I'm not saying to break the bank and buy yourself a diamond bracelet, but it takes courage to submit a manuscript, and whatever the outcome, you've passed a milestone. So do something to commemorate it. Buy a CD you can play while you write or something small for your office, but reward your bravery and determination. Just don't stop being brave. As soon as the next book's ready, go ahead and submit it, too.

Analyzing your book in light of the rejection itself, and possibly also in tandem with editorial feedback, gives you insights as you move forward in your career. You get that knowledge — of mistakes you've made and don't intend to make again, and sometimes also of strengths you bring to the writing process — as your reward for submitting your book. It's not the reward you wanted, but it *is* something you can take forward and use.

Coping with the news gives you the composure to accept that reward, see it objectively, and make use of it. And that constructive outlook leads directly to the final step: moving on. You need to put rejection behind you. You'll probably have to deal with rejection again, but you can't let the fear of that control you any more than you can go on dwelling on the current experience. Move on, whether to the next book or the next potential publisher. Moving on may not be easy, but if you want to be a published writer, it's the only way.

Chapter 17

Closing the Deal

. . . .

. . . .

*T*here's nothing like getting the call that tells you that you've sold your first book. It's an exciting call for an editor to make, too, but being on the receiving end is where the real fun lies. When you get that call, it marks your transition from being an aspiring author to being a professional one.

If you have an agent, as many would-be writers do, the editor delivers the news to your agent, who then calls you with all the exciting details. Your agent also handles all the negotiations, consulting with you along the way, though the ultimate decisions are yours, of course. In this chapter, I discuss the process as if you're negotiating for yourself. But if you have an agent, you'll still find this information helpful, because you can be a knowledgeable, informed client when she discusses these same points with you.

As I discuss in Chapter 15, finding an agent can be difficult for new authors, so I'm here to help. Although I can't advise you in specific terms what to ask for or agree to in your first deal (every negotiation is unique), I can provide you with an overview of the contract and negotiation process, with helpful tips along the way, and steer you toward additional resources for all things contractual — and financial. This chapter helps you examine all the ins and outs and pros and cons of your particular offer and situation. It also provides you with information so you can ask intelligent questions and ultimately make the best decisions you can when you're negotiating.

I start off with the call itself and the basic information it contains. I talk about ways you can respond and questions you can ask, and then move on to tips for creating a win-win negotiation. I also give you some general suggestions for finding answers to additional questions that may come up along the way.

Getting "The Call"

Every writer's career has a few red-letter moments, and they all start with the first time an editor or agent calls to say you've sold a book. This long-awaited event leads to seeing your first line edit and your first cover, which leads to the day you walk into a store and see your very first book for sale right alongside best-selling authors whose names everyone knows. But everything starts with The Call. Without it, none of the other events can happen, and every author I know says the same thing: It's exciting every time — when you sell the second book, the tenth, the fiftieth, even the one-hundredth, but the first time. . . . Well, you know what they say: A girl's first time is always special.

Chances are you've dreamed about the moment you make your first sale, but the reality is undoubtedly going to be even better than any dream — simply because it's real. And because it's not a dream, you need to be prepared for what you're going to hear, how you're likely to respond, and what you may want to do next.

What will your editor say?

That's right, *your* editor. From this moment on, you have an editor, so take a moment and let that sink in. But what will she say? She'll probably start off by introducing herself, and at that point, you'll pretty much know why she's calling, because I don't know any editors (not that I know them all, of course) who call unpublished authors except to make an offer. So you won't have to guess why she's on the phone. Whether she starts by welcoming you to Big Bucks Books Publishing or just says straight out that she's calling to offer you a contract, she'll make her intentions clear.

After that (and after you take a minute to catch your breath), she'll probably get to the actual negotiations, going on to explain the basics of the offer: the amount of the advance, how the splits work (how payments are doled out), what rights the contract covers, whether or not they'll want you to do revisions, maybe even a potential publication date. As the conversation goes on, she may also talk about additional facts she needs from you, everything from your social security number (necessary for the contract) to information that can help in creating a selling cover.

It's okay to ask to think about it (overnight, over the weekend if you get the call on a Friday — just not forever), so that you can wrap your mind around everything that's happened, if you don't feel calm and clear-headed enough to say yes right away. Even if you ask for a little time, chances are you know you're going to accept in the end, and it doesn't hurt to tell your editor that fact, assuring her that you just need to calm down and think everything over to make sure you're not missing something or forgetting to ask any important questions. (See the "Coming Up with Questions" section later in the chapter for a handy list of questions you'll want answered.)

The minute you realize you've finally gotten The Call, grab a pen and paper so that you can take notes on everything your editor says, because your mind is going to be going a million miles a minute, and you're just not going to remember everything.

It's okay to go crazy!

Trust me, you're not likely to shock your editor, no matter what you do, so don't worry if your first reaction is to scream, cry, or swear like a sailor. I've heard all those responses and more. This is a life-changing moment for you, so go ahead and commemorate it by going just a little bit nuts. You're not risking your professionalism if you do. In fact, your editor probably expects it. I confess, I'm always surprised on the rare occasions when a new author *doesn't* react strongly.

Just don't become so incoherent that you can't manage the rest of the call. Grab a tissue, excuse yourself to get a glass of water and take a minute to pull yourself together . . . whatever it takes. Then grab that pen and paper, and get ready for the start of your career.

Coming Up with Questions

First of all, understand that asking questions about the offer is fine. In fact, before you end the initial conversation, or when you call back to finalize things, ask all the questions you can think of, whether they're about the terms of the contract (which I discuss in this section), your book, or the publishing process (which I discuss in Chapter 18). You can ask your editor questions at any time, but after the first conversation, take some time to think of all the questions you can and then ask them all at once, so you don't have to interrupt her work day too often.

There are no stupid questions. The only question you'll regret is the one you thought of but didn't ask.

Asking the money question

The first question that comes to your mind is almost certainly going to be what I always call the money question. I get asked this one in many different places and many different ways, often by aspiring authors at conferences, long before it's a relevant factor in their lives. But now that you've gotten the call and received an offer, it *is* a relevant factor for you.

Making advances — against royalties

Ninety-nine percent of the time, the advance you're offered is an advance against royalties. So what does that mean? You're getting paid *an* advance *in* advance. It's like a loan, with your book's future earnings as the collateral. Your publisher is giving you money quite a while before she can publish the book and it actually begins to earn money.

After your book is published, the various royalty rates covered by the terms of your contract kick in. Every copy sold, every foreign sale or condensation in a magazine or newspaper, or any use of the book in any other way covered by your contract, earns money for you. The first money the book earns for you, as specified by the royalty rates in the contract and up to the amount of your advance, goes back to the publisher as repayment for the "loan" they made you. After that's paid back, the money the book earns for you according to the terms of your contract goes to you in the form of royalty payments.

The schedule for paying royalties, or how often and in what months you see an accounting statement or a check, is laid out in your contract. Different publishers handle royalties in different ways, but most hold back what's called a reserve.

Because publishing houses pay royalties based not on the number of books printed or shipped but on the number actually sold, and because it takes quite a while to know how many books they can actually sell, most publishers hold back a reserve against returns for a period of time. Your contract and royalty statement should outline how much the house can withhold and for how long, and this amount determines how quickly you pay back your advance and how soon you start seeing additional money.

Note: There's no guarantee your advance will earn out and you'll see more money over time. However, given that most first-time authors don't receive huge advances (because publishers try not to offer a loan that can't be repaid), chances are that you'll eventually see additional money.

Your offer is almost certainly for an *advance against royalties,* a kind of loan against your future royalty payments from book sales. (I discuss this subject in more detail in the "Making advances — against royalties" sidebar in this chapter.) Because of this setup, the amount of money that you get upfront — especially as a brand-new author — probably won't be break-the-bank large. You're an unproven sales commodity, so the publisher probably won't want to throw tons of advance-against-royalties cash at you, because she's not sure future sales can cover a huge advance. The upside to all this? If your advance shades toward the small end of the spectrum, it's probably not the final amount you'll see on the book.

It may be a while until you see more money, so asking if there's room to increase the advance is okay. Just be prepared for the answer to be *no.* Your editor probably has little to no room to increase the offer, so don't be offended if that's the case. But it's also possible that your editor *can* go up on her original offer, and you won't know if you don't ask. So if — and only if — you feel it's warranted, go ahead and ask. Just be polite (your editor's not the enemy, despite the inexplicably combative stance some writers take) and treat her with the same professionalism you want her to show you.

Despite what you've probably read and heard about veteran authors getting multimillion-dollar advances, and new authors who make deals for multiple books at six figures per book, those instances are the exceptions, not the rule. That's what makes them newsworthy. Most advances are smaller — substantially smaller — and most are for a single book. I said *most,* because it's not inconceivable — especially if you're writing mainstream romance — that you may be offered a deal for two books, maybe even more.

I'm not going to get into specifics here any more than I do at conferences, but as a general rule, you can expect a relatively low advance (but still in the thousands of dollars) for a series romance title. Mainstream advances, even for a first book, can range from the series level to something much higher, if the editor and publishing house think they've found a star in the making and that they can sell enough copies of your book to make a profit.

If you've been offered a multi-book deal, even if there's no flexibility in the amount of the advance, you may find some in the *splits* (how much you're paid at different stages specified in the contract): signing, delivery and acceptance of proposal(s) and the complete manuscripts, and publication.

Asking about everything else

Though the money question may be the one most on your mind, it's probably not the only one. Here are some of the fairly big questions you may want to ask during that first call or a follow-up conversation:

- ✔ **How do you split the advance payments?** How much do you receive on signing, acceptance of the complete manuscript, publication, or at any other point?

- ✔ **What royalty rate(s) cover what types of sales?** Different royalty rates probably govern different editions (mass market paperback, trade paperback, hardcover, book-club edition, and so on), and rates may also escalate based on the number of copies sold.

- ✔ **What territories does the contract cover?** The contract may cover the United States only, North America, the world, or only specific other countries.

- ✔ **What languages does the contract cover?** Does the publisher plan to print your book in all English-language editions, specific foreign languages, or all major languages?

- ✔ **What subsidiary rights does the contract cover?** Subsidiary rights include everything from film and TV rights (they're glamorous, so everyone always thinks of them first) to audio rights, computer games, e-books, condensation and serialization rights, and more. How does your publisher plan to divide the income from these sources?

✔ **Does the publisher want you to take a pseudonym?** Can you take one if you want to? What strictures, if any, govern its use? For more information on taking a pseudonym, see the sidebar "Naming names: Is a pseudonym for you?" later in this chapter.

✔ **When can you expect your book to be published?** Your editor may be able to give you a specific date or just a general sense of one, but any estimate can be helpful when everyone who hears your news asks — and I promise you, they will — when your book's coming out.

✔ **How much time does your editor plan to give you to do revisions?** This question may or may not be a contractual point, but it's certainly something you want — in fact need — to know. At what point can you expect to receive a letter or a call outlining any necessary changes?

✔ **What are the terms of your option?** The option clause lays out the publisher's right to see your next work/next appropriate work, the length of time for which they get to see it exclusively, how much material (usually complete versus partial) you need to submit, and related issues.

Some of the questions racing through your head are minor enough that you may want to wait and see what the contract says. Here are some of the smaller ones that you don't need answered right away:

✔ **How many free copies of your book can you get?** Not an entirely unimportant question, because people are likely to start crawling out of the woodwork asking for signed copies. If you sell foreign rights, book-club rights, and so on, you also want to know how many copies you'll get of those editions. You should also ask about your author discount if you want to buy additional copies.

✔ **What kind of input, if any, do you have on the cover art and copy?** In most cases, you have little to no input, and you almost certainly don't have approval power. But you may be able to discuss things with your editor, at least, and she can incorporate any of your ideas that she likes. Interestingly, you often have more input with a series book than a single title (for more information on these stages, see Chapter 18).

✔ **What are your responsibilities in the editing and production process?** Will your editor give you a copy-edited manuscript to look over? A galley? What input does she allow you? (Check out Chapter 18 for a walk through the editing and production process.)

✔ **What else will your editor or your publishing house want from you?** It never hurts to ask a general question, because every house has different needs and processes.

One last thing you need to ask: What's the specific information you need so you can contact your editor? The editor who called you — *your* editor — may not be the same editor you originally submitted your book to, so you want to be sure you have the correct spelling of her name, title, exact address, direct line or extension number, and e-mail address. Just as she needs to be able to contact you, you need to be able to get hold of her easily.

Naming names: Is a pseudonym for you?

At one time, some publishers preferred that authors use pseudonyms. But these days, the decision to take a pseudonym or not is usually up to the author, so think about it and do whatever makes you happy. However, you may still be asked to take a pseudonym in these two situations:

✔ **When your name is difficult to pronounce:** When your name is extremely difficult to pronounce or spell, you may be asked to at least consider taking a pseudonym, because an easier name makes it easier for readers to ask for your book or to look for it on the rack.

✔ **When your name is too similar to another author's:** You want to stand out as an individual to the reader, so when your name is too much like — or even identical to —

another author's, especially a best-selling author, chances are you'll need to come up with a literary alias for yourself.

Some authors choose to take a pseudonym for personal reasons, such as:

✔ **A desire for privacy:** Some authors prefer living incognito, so it's not so easy for fans — and weirdos — to find them. Other times, an author who writes sexy romances may prefer that members of her church not know or want a relative to be spared "embarrassment by association."

✔ **Paying homage:** Some writers create a pseudonym from their children's names, or use a maiden or family name as a way of paying tribute to the people who've been supportive.

Sizing Up the Contract

Any contract you consider is going to be far more complicated than what's covered in this chapter, and I can't even pretend to explain every possible clause or subsidiary right. This section offers two key tips to help you check out your first contract.

Reading and rereading the fine print

I can't lie and try to convince you that reading your contract is half as exciting as reading a good romance novel. I doubt it's even half as exciting as reading a bad one. Still, you have to do it, even if you have an agent.

Your signature appears on your contract, and you're the one who's responsible for living up to all its terms. So even if you have an agent to do the negotiating for you, not to mention translate all the legalese into English when (and it most likely *will* be when, not if) you get confused, you need to read your contract yourself and know exactly what you're agreeing to. Where you have to, reread until you understand what you're reading.

Most clauses in your contract aren't negotiable and don't need to be. Don't try to prove you've read everything by asking for changes everywhere. It's perfectly possible you won't need or want to ask for any changes at all, but if you do negotiate, make sure you focus on the points that really matter.

Getting help

When the time comes to read, negotiate, and sign your first contract, having an agent really comes in handy. With an agent in tow, you have someone at the other end of the phone whose job involves answering your questions about publishing in general and contracts in particular. The good news is, after you've made a sale, getting an agent is much easier, if you want one. The bad news is that although you may find an agent in time to sell Book Number Two, the process may take too long to help you get your current questions answered.

Even if you don't have an agent, you have other resources to turn to:

- ✔ **A lawyer:** Though a lawyer who's unfamiliar with publishing can't advise you in the ways an agent can, a lawyer can certainly help you understand the legalese, and you can pay by the hour for help.

- ✔ **Romance Writers of America:** You can contact the national RWA at 16000 Stuebner Airline Rd., Suite 140, Spring, TX 77379; phone 832-717-5200; Web site www.rwanational.org. They can point you in the direction of your local chapter. And if you're a member of a local chapter, you may find that they have a library of taped speeches from previous conferences, and that tape library probably contains information that can help you. Your chapter may also have a library of back issues of the organization's magazine, *Romance Writers Report,* which has published articles, including some about specific publishers' contracts, you'll almost certainly find helpful.

- ✔ **Look online:** With the usual caveat about misinformation floating around in cyberspace, you can find a lot of good information out there, too. By checking out writers' sites, you can find helpful discussions about negotiating. You may even be able to ask questions, though I caution you against revealing specific terms (of your advance, especially), because every contract's slightly different, and the specifics of your personal and financial business really should remain *yours*.

- ✔ **Pick up *Getting Your Book Published For Dummies* (Wiley):** This comprehensive title by Sarah Parsons Zackheim, with Adrian Zackheim, takes an in-depth journey into the world of publishing in general. It contains info on acting as your own agent, finding an agent, the contract and negotiating process, selling your book, and many other general publishing topics.

Strategies for a Win-Win Negotiation

The goal of every negotiation, of whatever sort, *should* be to create a win-win result, though too often opposite sides see things as a competition, where one side wins and the other has to lose. But if you go in with the goal of getting to a win-win outcome, one that leaves both parties happy, you're much more likely to end up that way than if you start out standing in your own metaphorical corner, fists raised and ready for a fight.

In romance publishing, series contracts generally leave relatively little room for negotiation; it's simply the way the business works. Mainstream contracts, on the other hand, are far more open to discussion, so your ability to negotiate, along with the attitude you bring to the table, becomes very important in those discussions.

Here are some tips for making sure your contract negotiations are both successful and pleasant, an experience you, with luck, will get to repeat over and over again during your successful career as a romance novelist. As an added bonus, you can apply most of these lessons to any kind of negotiation you find yourself facing:

- ✔ **Remember that you and your editor have the same goal.** Unlike many other sorts of negotiations, where the negotiating parties have very different interests and often need to make major compromises, you and your publisher (represented by your editor) have the identical aim — to publish your book successfully, sell as many copies as possible, and make as much money as possible for both of you.

  Your negotiations probably aren't going to get acrimonious or even cranky, but just in case they do, remember this one fact, because it helps you put everything in perspective.

- ✔ **Don't ask for the moon.** You can negotiate plenty of points, but not all of them, and not forever. Do you want more free author's copies of your book? Your editor can probably do another ten or fifteen, but a hundred is probably pushing it. The same theory holds true for the tougher clauses, too, like the amount of your advance and various royalty rates; if you ask for reasonable increments of change, not huge ones, you're more likely to be successful.

- ✔ **Decide what's most important to you.** For example, is it more important that you get as much money as possible up front, keep your film rights, or negotiate a higher royalty on foreign editions? All or none of those specific things may be on the table, but a variety of things are likely to be under discussion in any negotiation. If the time comes when you have to choose when to push and when to give in, going in knowing what matters most to you helps.

✔ **Don't play drama queen.** Negotiating with someone who cries wolf and threatens to walk over every point, however minuscule, or who takes everything personally, is very frustrating for the editor. Don't pull your overdue mortgage or your kid's orthodontist bills into the negotiation, and don't act as if everything's an insult. Remember, this is business. Your publisher is obviously a business, and now you are, too. So behave professionally.

✔ **Don't drag things out unnecessarily.** You and your editor may naturally play phone tag sometimes, just because you're both busy, but don't let time go by just as a power play.

✔ **Accept that some things aren't going to change.** Every house has clauses that it refuses to alter or delete, whatever the reason. If your editor says something's non-negotiable, don't keep fighting it. Move on, and don't dwell on the points you can't change.

Though it goes against the spirit of win-win, in the interests of facing reality . . . If you have problems with one of these non-negotiable clauses, to the point that it's a deal breaker for you (and I have to assume that neither you nor your editor wants anything to break the deal, and that you wouldn't threaten to walk away frivolously), then say so and get things over with.

None of these strategies are earth shattering, but they're all good to hold on to in the middle of the excitement of making your dreamed-of first sale, and every sale thereafter.

Chapter 18

Tracing the Steps from Page to Press — and Beyond

In This Chapter

▶ Knowing what your editor expects of you at every stage

▶ Understanding the process from manuscript to bound book

▶ Figuring out your role in PR and advertising

*A*fter you've written — and quite possibly rewritten — your romance novel and then sold it, you've done the bulk of the work you'll ever need to do on that manuscript. But you're still not done. You'll likely have additional revisions to make at some point, and plenty of stuff goes on with the manuscript while it's out of your hands.

You need to know what to expect from the publishing process and what others expect of you, starting with the relationship between you and your editor. The way that this working relationship goes — smoothly or not so smoothly — has an effect on your future career, so you want to go into it knowing how to make things go well.

You need to understand the various stages that your manuscript goes through on its way to publication, because you have a role to play in most of them. Every publisher operates slightly differently, but you're likely to see your book at least twice after your editor's done the line edit, and you may have some input on the cover, as well.

Later on — though usually only *later on* in your career — your publisher may advertise your book, or you may decide to advertise it yourself. You need to know about advertising your work, too, so that you can decide what's a sensible use of your money and what isn't. The same holds true for public relations (or PR), where you can do a lot more for less (though sometimes at a high cost of time), if you plan carefully and sensibly. In this chapter, I take you through the entire production cycle of your book and give you tips for helping your book along after it's published, without spending your entire advance and all your writing time doing it.

Every publisher works on its own schedule and has quirks in the process no other house shares, so your first time through is bound to feel a bit like being stuck in a maze. The important thing to know is that everyone wants the same thing: to publish your book as successfully as possible.

Working with Your Editor

The relationship between you and your editor is the most important one of your career. If you have an agent, that relationship probably runs a close second. But the way you and your editor work together affects the progress and success of your book — and all your future books with that house.

Speaking entirely from personal experience, I can tell you that it's a wonderful relationship when it works well — as it usually does. The reason an editor takes on any author in the first place is because she respects that author's talent, enjoys her work, and shares a similar approach to storytelling. It's just — okay, *almost* — as exciting for me to call an author to buy her first book as it is for her to get the call, because I'm eager to publish her and get her work out there in front of thousands of readers. Your editor feels the same way about you and your book. She's as eager to establish a successful, harmonious relationship as you are.

Making the relationship work

The key to making the author/editor relationship work lies in realizing that from the moment she offers you a contract, she's your ally, the person who has chosen to make your book as strong as it can be and shepherd it through the publishing process so that it can be as successful as possible.

If she asks for revisions, as she's quite likely to do, she does it because she thinks those revisions can make the book stronger. When she writes copy or works with the art department on your cover, she's always trying to create a cohesive, persuasive package so that your book sells as many copies as it can.

The fact that you and your editor have the same goal (the successful publication of your book) in mind doesn't mean the two of you agree on everything all the time, so don't worry if you don't always see eye to eye. Mutual honesty and respect can make your relationship a successful one. If you don't agree with a particular revision, for instance, tell your editor so. Just explain your point of view and be polite. I know that should go without saying, but unfortunately, it doesn't. Too often, new writers and even some established authors see their editor as the enemy and the process of working on the book as some kind of power struggle. Get over that now, at least if you want your career to be a long one.

I can't say that every editor out there, or even every romance editor out there, is as open- and fair-minded as an ideal editor should be, but you should operate as if your editor is both of those things, and most of the time you'll be proved right.

What if you and your editor turn out to be a bad match? You can't make an informed decision in this regard until you've worked together for a while, so don't rush to a conclusion while you're doing revisions on your first book or at some equally early stage in the process. Give the relationship time to work. But if you eventually realize that the two of you, despite both of your best efforts, aren't working well together, requesting a change of editor is perfectly fine. You have a few options:

✔ If you have an agent, he or she can handle this request for you.

✔ If you don't have an agent, you have to handle it yourself, even though it's not a lot of fun.

  • If the two of you have good personal rapport, even if you don't see things the same way creatively, talk to your editor directly.

  • If you don't feel comfortable taking the direct approach, talk to your editor's boss, explain the situation, and ask her to handle it.

If you have to initiate that conversation, be polite and matter-of-fact, and don't get emotional or sound like a prima donna. You aren't trying to bad mouth your editor or (inadvertently) make yourself look like someone who's impossible to work with. You just want to create a better working situation for you both, and you can get what you want using a calm approach.

Revising your book one last time

Your first extended chance to get to know and work with your editor probably comes when you're asked to do revisions. (And it usually *is* "when," not "if.") Revisions at this stage are likely to be relatively minor compared to any revisions the editor asked you to do before she offered you a contract (see Chapter 16), because you wouldn't have been offered that contract unless your book was already close to publishable as is. If your editor asked you to do revisions earlier, those revisions were probably big-picture changes. Now you're likely to be dealing with smaller, more specific points.

Most editors prefer to discuss revisions in one of two ways:

✔ By letter (or e-mail, which works out to the same thing)

✔ On the phone

I usually use a letter to outline requested revisions for a new author but tend to switch over to a phone call after a few books. But the key is that you're comfortable with the process. I have authors who prefer a letter because they'd rather have everything neatly typed in full sentences, so that they can consult my notes when they sit down to write. And because that's what they want, that's what I give them. Don't be afraid to ask your editor to follow up a call with a letter, or a letter with an explanatory call, if you need it.

Before you sit down to actually make the revisions, talk to your editor to see how she wants you to do things. She may ask you to print out a clean copy of the manuscript with all the changes made, or she may ask you to give her only the revised pages.

When you become an about-to-be-published author, revisions are a collaborative process in a way they weren't before. Before you're signed, if an editor asks you to revise and resubmit, your only choice is whether to do it or not. Now you get to have an actual conversation. If you have a question about, or a problem with, something your editor has asked you to revise, go ahead and ask her about it, because you can reach an easy compromise most of the time. The two-way communication and honest approach that make the author-editor relationship work also make the revision process go smoothly.

I ask for revisions because I've noticed a point in the manuscript where something isn't working.

- ✔ If I suggest a particular change, 99 percent or more of the time, that change seems most sensible to me but isn't the only possible solution. If my author sees a better solution, or just one she feels more comfortable with, that's fine with me. Her name's going on the cover, not mine, and I want her to feel good about everything on every page.

  Sometimes I'm just not sure what the author's getting at, and she only needs to clarify what she originally meant — something I'd never know if she didn't speak up. After you're under contract, anything and everything can be a conversation.

- ✔ Occasionally, I ask for a change that's non-negotiable — maybe regarding language, or related to plot or characters — but I doubt that happens even 1 percent of the time. And when it does, I'm always happy to explain why.

Line editing set straight

After you've done any last revisions, the line edit is the first time your editor picks up her pencil and starts working on your book. A lot of people don't understand just what a line edit is. Most people think it involves correcting spelling and grammar and nothing else. That description's closer to a description of a copy edit (see the "Diving into details: The copy edit" section later in the chapter), but it's not even complete enough for that.

A *line edit* is a content edit, and a good editor does only as much as necessary to bring all the book's strengths to the fore. She may edit so lightly that the manuscript looks almost untouched, or she can leave a lot of pencil marks on every page. I look for big concerns as I edit — whether every character's behavior is believably motivated, whether the timeline makes sense. I also keep smaller concerns in mind — whether every line of dialogue leads believably into the next, whether each chapter begins and ends effectively. I also correct spelling and grammar when I find mistakes, but some editors leave that for the copy editor to handle.

Ideally, most problems get solved during the revision stage. But some things, even if small ones, always get missed and show up during the line editing process, which by its very nature is a detail-oriented one, as the editor goes through the manuscript with a tight focus on every line.

Every editor handles things a little differently at this stage. I write notes in the margins, some explaining to the author why I made a particular change, others asking for additional revisions (almost always quite small and specific at this point), and still others asking the copy editor to check a fact or the spelling of a particular word. However your editor chooses to handle things, this is the stage when she lets you know what else she needs from you, so just follow her lead. With most publishers, you see these edits and editorial requests at one of two points — either after the line edit or after the copy edit. See the "Diving into details: The copy edit" section later in this chapter, and then check out the "Reviewing the edits" section, also later in the chapter, for more info on the additional work you'll put in.

Often, a book needs a new title because the title you gave it doesn't work for any number of reasons. Your publisher may think that title can't sell, or maybe it's too close to another book they're putting out. Whatever the reason, your editor may ask you to suggest other titles and collaborate with you on choosing one somewhere in the vicinity of this stage, or she may come to you with a suggestion the house likes to see if you like it, too. You may or may not have title approval, but every editor I know works with her authors to be sure everyone's happy with the final choice.

From Manuscript to Bound Book

The real production process — the stages by which a publishing house produces a bound book from your manuscript — begins when the line edit is complete and your novel is handed off to a copy editor. The process truly ends with the printing and binding of your book, but I'm not going to go into the physical end of production, only the editorial parts.

Every house works on its own timetable, but you can forget what you see on TV, where a book's finished on Friday and in the stores a week from Monday. The process of publishing a romance novel usually runs anywhere from six to nine months, but that number isn't inscribed in stone. Your book may take a longer or shorter amount of time. Your editor can tell you how long the process takes with your publisher, and also what your pub (publication) date is, so you can tell everyone when to look for your book on the racks. The specific stages your book passes through, as well as the timing of them and even what they're called, also changes slightly from house to house, so use the following sections as a general guide, not a bible.

Diving into details: The copy edit

After your editor has finished her line edit, the book goes to the copy editor. The copy editor's job is closer to the grammar-and-spelling concept than your editor's, but like the line edit, the copy edit is more than that.

A copy editor looks closely at all the details and all the facts. Does the timeline make sense? Do a character's blue eyes on page 17 turn brown on page 80? When did Montana become a state? Is a brand name being used as a generic? Often, an editor asks the copy editor for additional effort — to flag each mention of a particular name that they may need to change or double-check the use of a foreign language.

A copy editor traditionally notes major or requested changes, or any questions of her own, on perforated pink slips (often called *flags*) attached to the relevant pages of the manuscript. When she's done, the manuscript goes back to the editor, who goes through it and makes any additional changes (or asks the author to make them), and then removes the flags, which leads to the name of that particular stage — the *deflag*.

Reviewing the edits

Depending on the house's or your editor's own methods, you may see a photocopy of your manuscript either after the line edit or after it comes back from the copy editor, but rarely both. At this point, you have a chance to look everything over, make any last-minute corrections to points you catch as you read over the book, and make whatever changes your editor requests of you.

Just as you should feel free to discuss revision suggestions with your editor (see the "Revising your book one last time" section earlier in the chapter), feel free to talk about any questions or problems you have with the line (or copy) edit. At this point, you still have both time and room to make changes that satisfy everyone.

Your editor will explain how she wants you to make those final changes and also how quickly she needs them. At either of these stages, post line edit or post copy edit, time is much tighter than it was earlier when you were revising the book, and you need to meet whatever deadline she gives you or you can hold up the entire production process.

Wholesale rewrites to the manuscript are out of the question as soon as your editor begins the line edit. But during the line- and copy-edit stages, you can still make minor changes if you catch something you're not entirely satisfied with or need to correct an error.

Seeing your book one last time: The galley

After you make changes to the manuscript as requested by your editor (if you're reviewing the manuscript after the line edit), or after the editor deflags the text from the copy editor (if you see the text after the copy edit), the manuscript moves on to the *galley stage.* The galley stage is also sometimes known as the *AA* (or *author alteration*) *stage,* and the *galley* itself is sometimes called the *page proofs.* The galley stage is the point when your manuscript is typeset, sometimes directly from a disk you're asked to provide and other times by a typesetter who inputs the entire book.

You see the book at this stage for only a brief period of time before it goes to press. A proofreader is generally reading through it at the same time, looking for any last glitches that you and the editors missed, and any typos and formatting problems that may have been introduced in typesetting.

You may see a computer printout or a facsimile of exactly what the finished book will look like. Either way, you generally can't make anything but the most minor changes at this point, because major changes would totally throw off the pagination of the finished book.

The galley stage is also the last time you see your book before publication. From this point, the text moves to the printer, where it meets up with your cover (which has been in development simultaneously).

There's sometimes an interim stage between the galley and the bound book, called the ARC. Publishers create an ARC, or *advance reading copy,* almost exclusively for mainstream romances, especially those destined for hardcover publication. Publishers use ARCs so that reviewers and the trade (meaning booksellers) can get an advance look at the book and then create good press and increase pre-publication orders. Some ARCs have fancy covers and others have very plain ones. Publishers set most from *uncorrected page proofs,* which means a galley before it goes through the proofreader. ARCs are costly to produce, and publishers generally reserve them for books that they've decided to support with advertising and PR.

Covering your bases

Only major authors, the kind who've become household names, have guaranteed cover input. And cover approval is even rarer, so don't expect to get either. I strongly recommend against making either a deal breaker when you negotiate your contract. Even so, you should have a basic knowledge of what goes into the process and where you may be able to contribute.

The cover of any book acts as an advertisement; it highlights all the elements that can make a reader pick up the book, check it out, and then plunk down her cash. Often the cover — not the author's name — is the driving force behind the buying decision for the reader, because it's what compels her to pick up the book and check it out in the first place.

Facing front

The front cover is the first thing a reader sees. If it doesn't catch her eye, and if it doesn't intrigue her to want to find out more, it fails in its purpose. Your publisher has too much riding on your book and too much invested in it to slap any old cover on it. A lot of work by a lot of people goes into the design of every cover. You don't see most of that activity, but you can and should rest assured that plenty *is* going on.

Understanding the art and design departments

Every publisher has art and design departments who give you the most appropriate and salable cover possible. They know the market, and they know all the latest bells and whistles in cover decoration. The art and design departments bear ultimate responsibility for creating every cover, but they don't work in isolation. The editorial and often marketing departments also contribute. Your editor probably has input, if only to provide relevant descriptions of characters and setting, as well as a brief synopsis of the book or an idea of its tone — romantic comedy, suspense, paranormal, and so on. She may come to you for additional information, and you can also ask her directly whether she needs anything from you.

If you have ideas for your cover, offer them to your editor. Just be aware that the final cover may look nothing like what you envisioned. If so, be prepared to accept that fact like the professional you now are. But if you see real problems with your cover (if it's inaccurate), you need to bring that to your editor's attention. She may or may not have time to do anything about it, but definitely let her know. Ditto if you just don't like it. Again, you probably can't get anything changed, but it can help your editor next time, when the house designs the cover for your next book.

Maybe as a result of the sheer number of series books that publishers release every month, series authors generally get much more input into their covers than mainstream authors do. Input doesn't mean approval, and as often as not the actual cover turns out differently from the author's vision, but series publishers definitely welcome, even request, ideas.

The art and design departments don't just come up with the cover image, they choose the appropriate type and arrange all the elements of the cover in the most effective way. Category covers have relatively little flexibility in this regard, although mainstream covers can vary hugely. Some readers can be heavily influenced by the type style and its look, while others focus first on the picture. Ultimately, though, a reader looks at both elements, and they both influence her. Both have to be strong, so that both kinds of readers find their eyes drawn to your book amid all the other choices on the racks.

Categorizing covers

In category romance, each series has a basic look that all the books in that series share. Essentially, each series has a branded look, elements that stay the same from book to book and help readers identify the series they're looking for. The cover type and its arrangement are generally equally set. Even the art style is usually similar for all the books in a series — painting versus photography, realism versus a more impressionistic look, close-up versus medium range, and so on. The designer creates the individual cover image for each book to fit that story and those characters, but he or she also creates it to fit into the overall cover format for that line.

In mainstream romances, on the other hand, anything goes. Designers format every cover individually from the ground up. Many people think all romances — especially historical romances — still have the old "bodice-ripper" covers: shirtless manly men bending tousle-haired women with big busts and low-cut necklines backwards and kissing them, or nuzzling their necks like lusty vampires. Those days, I'm happy to say, are gone.

Even when mainstream-romance covers feature the couple, they're posed more realistically and appealingly. Sometimes the cover features only one character or the other; sometimes designers use the look of a still life or a montage; sometimes the cover contains just type and design elements, with no picture at all. Publishers most often save that last possibility for best-selling authors whose names alone can sell books, but it demonstrates the range that mainstream covers can, well, cover.

Big names, fancy foil, and head shots

By the same token, big-name authors are the ones most likely to literally have the biggest names on a book cover. Cover designers usually use a big author's name as the focal point, typewise, of the cover. Because of that, the name often becomes the focal point, period. If you're new, your title is more of a selling point than your name, so you can pretty much expect your title to be in much bigger type or more prominently displayed than your name.

Publishers use fancy treatments (foil, die cuts, embossing, stepbacks, and so on) almost exclusively for mainstream covers, not series. And because they make a cover expensive to produce, they're not used on every book or for every author. Many mainstreams romances have at least one so-called decorative element to make the book stand out. But a cover can be extremely effective with only art, type, and a dramatic design, so don't worry if you don't get any fancy treatment, and don't feel that no one's paying attention to your book or that no one cares whether you succeed or not.

For many authors, getting their pictures on the book marks success, whether on the back cover or inside either the front or back cover. Honestly, whether the publisher includes a picture of the author doesn't indicate much of anything. Some houses never put an author's picture on a book (or, at least, on a paperback), some do it even for new authors, and some do it some of the time and for varying reasons. Yes, it can be a sign that you've "made it" if you get your picture on your book, but sometimes it's just a design element or the publisher can easily include it without incurring an additional cost. If you get your picture on your book, great, but don't take it as some kind of insult or strike against success if you don't.

Facing backwards: Back cover copy

For a best-selling author, the front cover may be the only necessary sales tool. The author's name alone is promise enough that the reader will enjoy the book. But for most other authors — especially first-timers and newer authors — the front cover alone can't seal the deal.

Your front cover isn't going to make every reader pick up your book to find out more about it, but if it does its job well, it attracts all the true potential readers — for example, a clearly historical-romance cover draws historical romance readers but not those readers who only like contemporary romances.

After your cover's done its job and the reader has picked up your book, you're on your way to making a sale. Two elements kick in here to help you close the deal. The first selling point is your writing itself. As I describe in Chapter 12, many readers skim the beginning of a book to get a sense of both the story and the storytelling style. The second key element is the copy, particularly the back-cover copy, which many readers turn to first.

Back-cover copy, as its name implies, runs on the back cover of the book. Back-cover copy tells the reader just enough about the story to hook her into wanting to know more. It introduces her briefly to the characters, the setup, and the source of tension, and then it leaves her hanging. It often ends with a direct question or a cliffhanger:

  ✔ *He's saved her life — but is that life worth living unless he also saves her heart?*

  ✔ *Her first impression was that he was the most irresistible man she'd ever seen. Unfortunately, she might never get the chance to test that theory — because no sooner had he dragged her out of Danko's clutches than the whole world exploded in gunfire.*

In either case, the copy shouldn't reassure the reader that things end well for your characters, much less tell her how, and that's true whether the situation's literally life or death (as in the examples above) or whether emotions, not lives, are on the line. It needs to leave her wondering what happens next and feeling that she has to buy the book and find out.

Some publishing houses have whole departments devoted to writing copy; others use freelancers, ask the editors to write it, or use a combination of the two. Only in extremely rare cases does an author even get input on, much less approval of, the copy. Those rare cases invariably involve brand-name authors who have the leverage to ask for and get privileges that new authors haven't earned.

You generally have to accept the reality that you're not going get input into your copy and most likely won't even get to see it until you see a *cover flat,* a sample cover the way it looks before it's bent and bound around a book. (Cover flats are perfect for framing, by the way, and I know many, many authors with entire walls covered in them.) Even if your editor lets you look at the copy for accuracy and just generally to get your thoughts, she may not have final say, so what ends up on the book may not be what you expect. But that cover copy does represent the best efforts of a lot of people who know what they're doing and want to see your book sell well.

Your lack of copy control is probably a good thing. New authors often write copy on their own and send it in. I've seen a lot of it in my time, and pretty much without exception, it's unusable. Copywriting is a lot harder than it looks, and it takes a long time to figure out that skill. So don't worry that you don't have the knack. You "just" have to write an entire compelling romance, because that's the skill that makes you so valuable to your publisher.

Rather than back-cover copy, hardcovers have *flap copy,* which runs on the inside front flap of the paper jacket and sometimes runs onto the back flap, as well. Flap copy is generally longer than back-cover copy, because the flaps have more available room, and the tone is often different, too. Most romances are published in mass market paperback form, though. So you're probably going to be concerned with normal back-cover copy.

Under the cover: Front sales copy

Most books also have *front sales* (or *page one*) copy, in addition to the back-cover copy. Front sales copy runs on the first actual page of the book, so it's the first thing a reader sees when she flips open the cover. It normally consists of an excerpt taken from the book, often condensed for greatest effect, and it's intended to both give the flavor of the writing and highlight a compelling passage that entices the reader. Occasionally, usually in the case of best-selling authors, the front sales copy consists of reviewers' quotes instead of text from the book, but that's the exception, not the rule.

Asking for quotes: It's all in who you know

Many romances, especially (but not exclusively) mainstreams, have quotes from other authors on the front or back covers, or sometimes along with or instead of front-sales copy. Quotes — especially on the front cover, where space is at a premium — are generally brief and read something like this:

"I couldn't wait to turn the page. Rachel Writer is the best new voice I've seen in ages." — Annie Author, #1 best-selling author of A Great Romance

Finding an author

You've probably come to know at least a few published authors in the course of writing your book, and some of them may have been especially helpful to you, even to the degree that you'd feel comfortable approaching one of them and asking her to give you a quote. If that's the case for you, use your common sense in approaching her. Depending on how well you know her and how often you see her, you can write a letter (or e-mail), call her, or ask her face to face. Be polite and brief, and send her a thank-you note, and even a copy of the published book, afterwards.

Unless the quote comes from someone with an important and recognizable name — a truly recognizable name (to readers everywhere, not just to people in the romance-publishing business) — a quote from her isn't going to help you sell more books. Before you ask her for a favor that may not come to fruition, putting you in an awkward position if you have to tell her your editor decided not to use the quote, think about whether her name really does carry the necessary weight with the reading public. If you're not sure, ask your editor. Giving her the heads-up now rather than later, after you've acquired the quote, is courteous, as well as more practical for you, especially if your editor has to say no.

On the other hand, you may have gotten to know one or more of the really big guns in the industry, because romance authors are some of the most generous people I know. Some of the best-selling authors in the world — and I mean that literally — aren't only romance authors, they're also active members of writers' organizations and willingly share their help with other writers, both published and aspiring.

If you *have* gotten to know an author whose name carries clout, by all means, ask her. Whether you've written a mainstream or a series romance, your editor is likely to cheer at the news that a big-name author has said yes.

Be professional, though. Don't approach an author you don't know or who you've only met in passing. When you ask for a quote, you're asking another writer not only to take valuable time to read your book, so that she can say something about it, but also to put her own reputation on the line by recommending your book to her readers. You shouldn't ask this favor lightly, even when you know someone, so asking someone who's pretty much a stranger is inappropriate.

Even if you don't know another author who can give you a quote, if your publisher thinks a quote may be helpful, the publishing house can handle the request. Your editor or the PR department may go directly to a particular author, or they may talk to her agent and get the book to her that way. Just because they ask doesn't mean they'll get a positive response, but they can make the request more easily than you can. Likewise, if you have an agent, he or she may also be able to help obtain a quote, because agents have a lot of contacts, both directly with authors and with publishers.

Additional sources

After you're published, you may have other options for quotes. Reviewers' quotes on previous books can take the place of author quotes, though you still need the source to carry enough weight. Sometimes your publisher can even get your book reviewed far enough in advance to include a review snippet on the book in question (one of the uses of ARCs, which I discuss in the section "The galley" earlier in this chapter). Additionally, if you place on any notable bestseller lists — and it happens even with first books, though not frequently — your publisher can mention that fact in place of a quote on future books.

Another source, one you're more likely than your publisher or agent to have access to, comes from going to an expert in the field. Your research (or real life) may have introduced you to a "name" who can help you. If your book features anything from stock car racing to rodeo to medical research, you may have gotten to know a pro who'd be happy to give you a quote. Again, check with your editor first, but if the name's big enough, you can gain some real advantages by going outside the romance pool for a quote.

- ✔ Romance readers read a lot, which means they've seen quotes from the same writers and review sources pretty frequently. They probably haven't seen your outside expert before, and novelty is always interesting.

- ✔ An expert's praise may get you readers you wouldn't get otherwise — non-romance readers interested in the subject who recognize the expert's name and decide to give your book a try.

- ✔ A pro's seal of approval may also get you reviewed or mentioned in places (magazines or even newspapers) that wouldn't ordinarily give a romance a second look. This additional attention brings more readers.

Even if you don't know an expert with name recognition, you can be bolder about approaching a stranger who's not in your field. The expert probably doesn't get similar requests all the time, the way best-selling authors do, so he or she will probably be flattered, even if complying is impossible. A quote also gives your expert exposure to your readers, who may take an interest in the pro's work. Ideally, it can be a win-win situation and one that's worth pursuing. As long as you make your request politely, the worst that can happen is that he or she says no.

Including dedications, acknowledgements, and more

At some point during the production process, you have the opportunity to contribute to your book's front matter. *Front matter* includes the front sales copy (which I mention in the "Under the cover: Front sales copy" section earlier in the chapter), the title and copyright pages, and various author-related or author-generated material.

Any front matter you submit, including the following components, is subject to line and copy editing. No one wants to change your voice, but grammar and spelling, as well as appropriateness, are as important in these secondary bits as in the novel itself.

- ✓ **Dedication:** The dedication is your chance to tell the world who you want to thank and why. Many writers like to dedicate their books, and you have complete freedom to dedicate your book to whomever you want: friends, family, people who've helped you along the way, pets, or favorite movie stars. You just need to turn your dedication in to your editor, and she takes care of getting it into the book.

- ✓ **Acknowledgments:** In addition to the dedication, you can add a separate acknowledgment, usually to any helpful experts (or you can include their names in your dedication). Again, your editor takes care of getting your thank yous into the book after you get them to her.

- ✓ **Foreword or afterword:** In some cases, you may include one of these sections, usually written as a letter to the reader or as a first-person address in your own voice, to talk about something relevant to the book — why you wrote it, why this particular story means so much to you, and so on. You may also want to include contact information for a relevant organization or charity. Different publishers have different policies on this practice, so ask your editor.

- ✓ **Biography:** Many romances — especially series — contain a brief writer bio. If your publisher includes biographies, your editor takes care of letting you know what she needs and whether she wants to write the bio based on the information you give her or wants you to write it yourself.

- ✓ **Contact info:** If you want readers to contact you, talk to your editor about your house's policy on including contact info in your bio, whether a snail-mail or an e-mail address. (I strongly caution you to get a P.O. box and never to give out your actual street address.) Save the contact info of anyone who writes to you to create your own mailing list (see the section "Create your own mailing list" later in this chapter), and if you feel comfortable and have time, respond to fan mail to create loyal readers.

Living in a Post-publication World

Life changes dramatically after you sell your first book, and it changes even more after your book's published. Suddenly, not only do you have to focus on writing your next book, but you also need to think about what's happening with the one that's on the stands and about relationships with family, friends, and fellow writers that may change because of your new professional status.

Letting go of your book can be hard, realizing that it's out there in the world, competing with hundreds of other new releases and you can do very little to help it. But, for the most part, you need to do just that. If your publisher gives your book a budget for advertising and PR, great! (And you should know something about the process, in case it does happen.) A first-time author can luck out and get a major push, if her publisher thinks it can drive sales to a highly profitable point by investing in the book's future. But even if that doesn't happen for you now (which is likely), it can happen later. Plus, you can do things to support your book on a smaller scale on your own.

Keeping your expectations realistic

Don't get carried away expecting, or even hoping, to have a ton of money put behind your book. As a first-time author, you probably aren't going to get TV and radio ads, print ads in national magazines and major newspapers, appearances on all the network morning shows and late-night TV shows, interviews in the newsweeklies, awards, or huge sales. Your publisher's also unlikely to send out review copies unless they've created an ARC.

In general, if you expect less, you're more likely to be pleasantly surprised. Always feel free to talk to your editor about the possibilities, though. She's your ally, and she has a lot riding on your book, too. So she's your single best resource at your publisher.

And if your book is a series romance, go ahead and expect even less. Series books don't get advertising and PR support 99.99 percent of the time. Because the publisher is focused on selling and supporting the series, not individual titles, they don't dedicate money to specific books and authors. Publishers are most likely to focus their finances on mainstream romances because, as a rule, mainstreams have the greatest potential for huge sales and bestseller-list appearances.

If your title gets some support, even if not on the best-seller level, here are some of the uses the money may be put toward:

✔ **Back ads:** Your publisher can advertise your book essentially for free inside other books they publish that are aimed at an audience similar to yours, and back ads are quite common. Sometimes they include an excerpt of the advertised book to help hook readers.

✔ **Romance-related magazine ads:** This level of advertising is reasonably priced and well targeted, whereas regional ad campaigns in the mass media are costly, and national coverage costs even more, and neither is as well-targeted at potential readers.

✔ **ARCs:** If your publisher puts out advance reading copies, the cash comes out of your title's advertising budget and often leaves little room for much else. (For more information on ARCs, see the section "Seeing your book one last time: The galley" earlier in this chapter.)

✔ **Public relations:** Labor costs make a full-scale PR campaign for every book prohibitively expensive. Publishers can't afford to dedicate staff time to every book.

Your publisher may have some basic resources to help you — access to advice, inexpensive promo items (pens for book signings, for example), and so on — so ask your editor what's possible and who you should talk to. But help isn't a given, and you may be on your own. Check out the section "Practical strategies for personal PR" for ways to do it yourself.

Advertising and PR: What can happen?

The opportunities for advertising and publicizing your book are endless, and new technology constantly provides new opportunities. Ten years ago, online chats and Web sites were barely a gleam in anyone's eye, and now they're everywhere. Here's just a sampling of the possibilities your publisher may *someday* arrange for you:

✔ **Paid advertising:** Whether it's in print (newspapers and magazines) or in the glamour media (TV and radio), this is the most traditional format for advertising anything. Print ads are much more common in the publishing world than TV or radio ads, which are very rarely used for any book.

✔ **TV and radio guest appearances:** A PR specialist develops contacts so that she can pitch her clients for possible appearances on talk shows. The bigger the show and the market, the harder your PR person has to work to get you on the show. It helps to have a message, so PR reps can present you and your book as being timely or relevant in some way.

Honestly, most romance novels don't meet most big shows' need to be on the cutting edge, but you can sometimes more easily achieve local PR — especially if you live in or near a smaller market — because the angle that you're published and live locally can often be enough.

✔ **Media tours:** A media tour takes time and money. A media tour involves sending you from city to city, where you're already booked on local talk shows, radio stations, and with the local papers, and where you're scheduled to do autographing signings in local stores. Because of the expense, plus the difficulty of creating media interest in authors who aren't well-known, these tours have become relatively uncommon in publishing overall, not just romance publishing.

✔ **Satellite media tours:** These tours are a less expensive variation on the traditional media tour. Instead of traveling from place to place, your PR department makes arrangements, and you go to a studio — usually TV, but you may also find yourself on a satellite radio tour — where you're interviewed by various stations in turn.

✔ **Advertorials:** These print PR devices fall somewhere between advertising (because the space is paid for) and PR (because they look like an article about you and your book, or even an interview, but are written and placed by your publisher). A related form of PR is a press release or review written by or for your publisher. Your publisher pays a specialty firm to place the release in as many places — usually newspapers serving smaller markets — as possible.

✔ **Online opportunities:** Many publishers have areas on their corporate Web sites devoted to publicizing select current releases and profiling authors. In some cases, the sites have room to feature only a few books and authors, although other publishers — and I'm forced to brag about Harlequin here — feature every book and virtually every author. Your publisher's site may also feature online interviews, bulletin boards, and even live author chats.

Practical strategies for personal PR

Whether your publisher has a budget to advertise and publicize your book or not, you can do plenty of things yourself that don't cost you a lot of money and don't take a lot of time away from writing your next book. Bear in mind that you don't need to do anything. It's entirely up to you whether you do something, everything, or nothing. You need to decide for yourself which strategies make sense for you and your book — and your budget.

Attend signings

You've probably already gotten to know your local booksellers, and they may have already talked to you about doing an autographing. Even if you're going in to a bookstore cold, introduce yourself as a local romance author — especially if you know that the store does well with romances — and ask if they'd be interested in having you do a signing. If so, talk to them about what they expect. Some stores make signings real social events, sending out mailings, providing refreshments, maybe even asking you to give a brief talk before you sign. Talk to your publisher, too, because they may have advice or even help in the form of generic posters or giveaway items.

Some autograph signings draw big crowds, and some feel like sitting on the sidelines at the high school dance. Often you don't know which you're in for until the day arrives. Just be prepared for anything to happen and you'll be fine. And it never hurts to personally invite your family and friends, and their friends, and . . .

Offer to sign any unsold books, and come prepared with *Local Author* stickers (or check ahead of time to see if the store has them) to go on the front cover. These strategies make the store more likely to hang on to the extra copies until they sell, rather than return them to your publisher. And bring or buy copies you can sign personally and give to any bookstore employees who've helped set up and execute the event. Even send flowers to the store or stop by with cookies as a thank you. Anything you do to show your appreciation is appreciated right back.

Contact your local media

Depending on where you live, you may want to contact a local paper, or any number of radio and TV stations. In this case, being in a smaller market is actually better for you than living in or around New York City, Los Angeles, or any other big city. Prepare a pitch — your publisher may be able to help you here, so talk to your editor — that talks about you, what makes you PR-worthy, your book, and why it deserves the attention. You can widen your definition of local with radio stations because you can often do these interviews on the phone. For technical reasons, though, a *call-in show* (you talk directly to listeners) may have to be done from the studio.

You may want to briefly touch base with these local media outlets after you know your book's publication date, if only so you know who to talk to when the time comes, but make your real pitch closer to the time your book is published. (When you first make contact, you can even ask when you should get back in touch.) You want any media attention to come right after the book becomes available in stores, so that your sales can benefit from that attention. With any kind of interview, be prepared with some sound bites — including your book's title and the fact that it's available now — that you want to get across.

Also be prepared for trick questions and booby traps. Romances, more than any other kind of book I know, get targeted by the media for everything from good-natured ribbing to nasty cracks, so you need to be ready to deal with anything.

Speak to local clubs and organizations

Often, all kinds of local organizations love to hear a local author speak. You may even belong to some of these organizations. Depending on the organization's focus and the topic of your book, they may be interested in hearing about your novel, your research and how you turned it into fiction, or just your development and career as a writer. Talk to your publisher about arranging to sell books, or your publisher may be willing to donate copies, depending on how many you need. If you can't get either of those options to work, you can sign and give away books at your own expense or direct your audience to the racks. Even if you get only a small attendance, every attendee represents an opportunity to sell additional books through word of mouth, so this kind of local PR can pay off more in the end than you'd expect.

And don't forget your local libraries. Libraries are always looking for ways to draw in more patrons, and with the popularity of the romance genre, a local romance writer can be a good draw, doing both the library and yourself a favor.

Give away bookmarks

For relatively little expense, you can design and print (sometimes on your own, other times through a local copy service) bookmarks with information about your book, and you can distribute them all over the place — at conferences, ahead of and simultaneous with the book's publication date, through your local bookseller (if they're willing, which isn't a definite), and inside every book you autograph.

But I confess to having mixed feelings about bookmarks. Anyone who reads finds bookmarks useful in general, but so many authors use them for PR (especially at conferences) that I'm just not sure how big an impression they make and how good they are at selling books.

Buy print advertising

Though it's probably the most expensive option on this list, print ads still don't have to cost an arm and a leg. Several magazines devoted to the romance industry sell ad space at affordable prices (depending on how much space you buy), especially because you can probably lay out the ad yourself on your computer.

You need to do two things before you buy an ad:

- ✔ **Get the magazine's stats:** Check out the publication's readership, pass-along numbers (how many people they anticipate end up reading each copy), and so on, so that you can determine how many people may see your ad and what you're paying per impression, as marketers say.

 ✔ **Get permission:** Check with your publisher if you're planning to use your book cover or just the cover art in the ad to be sure that your ad is legally acceptable, based on your contract with them and their agreement with the artist.

Create a Web site

Whether you do it yourself or pay someone to do it for you, you may want to take the 21st-century option of creating your own Web site. Check out *Creating Web Pages For Dummies* by Bud E. Smith and Arthur Bebak (Wiley) for how to do it on your own. You can focus your site purely on your book, talk about your life and your interests, or whatever you feel comfortable with.

Do be careful to avoid giving any information that lets people find your street address or phone number. As far as URLs go, your own name or pseudonym probably makes the best domain name, so you may want to reserve that now, if you think you may want to use it later.

Your site should definitely allow readers to e-mail you, though I strongly suggest you create an e-mail address exclusively for reader mail. Answer as much fan mail as you feel you can, given time constraints and your own comfort level, because personal contact builds fans, and fans buy books. Save the addresses of everyone who writes to you, too, and create a mailing list that you can use to alert readers of future books, or autographings and appearances you may be making in their area (see the section "Create your own mailing list" later in this chapter).

As far as letting readers in on your site goes, use every opportunity you can think of. Print the URL on your bookmarks and in any ads you buy, talk it up in interviews, and ask your editor if you can list it somewhere in the book. Your publisher may also be willing to link to your site from theirs.

Look for online PR opportunities

Separate from your own site, you can find all kinds of writers' sites where you can get involved in all sorts of PR opportunities. Depending on the site, it may offer online live chat, as well as bulletin boards. You may also be able to link back to your own site, or post an on-site profile of you or your book. Search around online and talk to other writers to get a sense of what sites are out there and what they offer.

Create your own mailing list

You can create a mailing list of both snail- and e-mail addresses. Start the minute you sell your book. Include booksellers, reviewers, interested local media, and any readers who you already know (including your friends and family). And then add your own readers after your first book is out and fans start writing to you. Alert everyone on your initial list before your first book comes out, and as the list grows, notify the listees of future books, autographings, PR appearances, and so on. Some authors even send out holiday messages. Do whatever you feel comfortable doing as frequently as you feel a need to do it. Personal contact creates a loyal reader base, but don't overload people with information.

Run a contest

You can decide how and where it makes sense for you to publicize what you're doing, but you can run a contest for autographed books, a collectible or unique artifact that's in some way connected to your book (jewelry, a quilt, a hand-knit shawl . . . anything you can think of), a gift certificate, or whatever makes sense to you that may interest readers. You set up the rules, decide on a timeline, choose the winner, and just plain run the show. You also create interest in your book and make it stand out from all the other books being published at the same time.

Speak at writers' conferences

After you're a published author, you have the credibility to speak to aspiring writers, and that helps people get to know you and gets them interested in reading your book. You can spend a lot of time (and money) traveling to conferences to speak, though, so be careful not to take too much time away from your writing.

Write an article

Most writers' organizations have a hard time filling their newsletter or journal pages. When you have a book coming out, offer to do an article. The bio accompanying your article will mention your new book, giving you the opportunity to win new readers.

Dealing with family, friends, and fellow writers

Be prepared for your family to do more than a little bragging about your accomplishments after you become a published author. Your kids may even take you to school for show and tell. If, like many writers, you're relatively introverted, all the attention may embarrass you — but try to bear it. The truth is, you *have* done something extraordinary. Far more people try to publish a book than ever succeed (most of them never even finish writing the manuscript). Let them be proud of you — and be proud of yourself.

Because of the demands writing places on your time, in addition to everything else going on in your life, you may have to make an extra effort to find time for friends and family. A writing career is a wonderful thing, but keep it in perspective and don't forget that people count for the most in the end.

Though these situations occur relatively rarely, and you can expect to find much more genuine enthusiasm and support among your friends and fellow writers than anything else, be prepared for some sour grapes.

- ✔ Whether they're resentful of your success or the increased demands on your time, or they just can't understand why you care so much about things that seem unimportant to them, some of your friends may not stay friends.

- ✔ You may see some of the biggest changes among your fellow writers, especially those who haven't yet published. Most authors are wonderfully generous and are genuinely happy for someone else's success. But sometimes jealousy makes an appearance, and you often can't do anything about it.

In these situations, you can only stay calm, try not to take things personally (which I know can be difficult), be low key around the other person, be reasonable in countering any nastiness that reaches you, and, if necessary, steer clear of the person as much as you can. If you keep a cool head, things may get better over time, and, at the very least, they shouldn't get any worse.

Overall, the time from the sale of your first book until it hits the racks is going to be one of the best of your life. You're busy as you find your way through a whole new world, but it's a good kind of busy, and you find plenty of people who are happy to celebrate with you along the way.

Part VI
The Part of Tens

The 5th Wave   By Rich Tennant

"Why don't you use my computer to write your romance novel? It's got a 64-bit processor — great for crunching data. Think how you could crunch out the romantic prose."

In this part . . .

The famous *For Dummies* Part of Tens — that series of helpful lists that wraps up each and every *For Dummies* book. In this part, I give you tips on avoiding common beginners' mistakes, understanding reasons why publishers reject manuscripts, beating writer's block, and coming up with the perfect title for your romance novel.

Chapter 19

Ten Plots Every Editor Knows — and Why They Still Work

*O*ne of the most common criticisms of romance novels is that they're all the same. As a romance reader and aspiring writer, you know that this criticism isn't true. What *is* true is that certain plot types are so effective that they have names that every editor and most writers know. However, these plot types aren't actual plots, because they don't lay out the middle and end; all they lay out is the beginning. These common "plots" really consist of *setups*, and they're different every time because each writer brings her own spin to them. (Check out Chapter 5 for more on setups and the mechanics of plotting.)

The reason these plots are so effective is that they all contain the seeds of emotional conflict — a must for a well-written romance — which gets your reader invested in your characters' lives and relationship, and it's that invest-ment on the reader's part that keeps her turning the pages. If you begin with a plot that has that emotional component built in from the start, you're already ahead of the game. In this chapter, I lay out some of the best-known setups, and any one of them may give you an idea for your next book.

You bring your own voice, imagination, and characters to any plot — one only *you* can create. Whether you use a setup that's earned a name through frequent use or one that's never been seen before, your job as a writer is to make that plot your own.

Marriage of Convenience

Twenty years ago, a marriage-of-convenience plot was usually financially motivated. For example, the heroine's wealthy grandfather stipulated in his will that she had to marry — sometimes the man of his choice, sometimes the man of her choice — in order to inherit the family wealth. These days, women are more than capable of earning their own livings, and it takes more than a will to make a marriage-of-convenience plot believable.

Today, a marriage of convenience is more likely to be motivated by non-mercenary means. For instance, the hero's chance of maintaining custody of a beloved foster child would be improved if he were married, or the heroine's dying grandmother's final wish is to see her married. The marriage may even be a sham but with genuine emotional consequences; for example, the hero and heroine are undercover cops who have to pose as a married couple in order to bring down a baby-stealing ring.

What makes the plot work is that it involves marriage — the most intimate of human relationships — to someone who's essentially a stranger, which sets up a sense of emotional and sexual tension right from the start.

Stranded with a Stranger

This plot most commonly strands the hero and heroine together via some kind of disaster, like a snowstorm, avalanche, plane crash, or shipwreck. Similar to a marriage of convenience, the plot puts two strangers in a state of forced intimacy, with all the tension that implies. To really up the ante, don't stop at making them strangers; make them strangers who have a good reason — maybe even more than one reason — not to get along. Whether they're just very different types — maybe a corporate CEO who's decided he needs a mountain cabin as a retreat versus a wolf researcher who's totally at home in the wild and has no use for weekend nature boys — or two people with a specific gripe — rival ranchers feuding over the piece of property where they're now stranded — you add a specific source of tension to the obvious discomfort of being locked up with an attractive stranger of the opposite sex, an equation that adds up to more the sum of its parts.

Runaway Bride

The heroine in this story line literally runs away on her wedding day and ends up in the arms of the hero, whether because she hitches a ride in his car, hides in the back of his truck, or runs out of gas in front of his house. A variation of this plot is the kidnapped bride, which involves the hero kidnapping the heroine on her wedding day — for what will turn out to be good and acceptable reasons. Again, the characters are in a forced-intimacy situation, with the two of them getting caught up in each others' lives in emotionally fraught circumstances. The fact that all this happens on her wedding day — often with her still in her wedding dress — adds extra drama, with one dream ending and another, even better one beginning as she meets the hero.

Secret Baby

The secret baby isn't necessarily an infant, although babies or very little kids tend to work better in romances than surly teenagers. The basic setup is that the hero got the heroine pregnant (they may even have been married at the time) but never knew it, and then they were separated. Now he shows up to find she had his child or maybe that she's pregnant with his baby. Whether they want to reunite or not, their lives are now connected, and they have to find a way to deal with the issues that caused their original separation. In real life, babies usually bring a couple together. In a secret-baby romance, at first the baby seems to drive a further wedge between them, because the hero's furious that she never told him about the baby. He may even threaten to sue for custody. But ultimately, the baby is an agent for reconciliation.

Reunion Romance

In this plot, ex-spouses are brought back together and fall in love again or discover that they never stopped loving each other. As with the secret-baby story line, the hero and heroine need to find a way to overcome the issues that drove them apart before. A twist on this plot has them discovering that their divorce was never final. You can even apply the stranded-together setup to ex-spouses (or even ex-lovers) with great effectiveness. The very fact that they were once intimate but have become emotional strangers creates tension any time they meet, and that tension is ratcheted up even higher the longer they're forced to be together.

Back from the Dead

This plot is another type of reunion romance. One of the characters — usually the hero — was declared dead. The heroine has rebuilt her life and is usually on the verge of remarrying when he appears. Suddenly she's torn between two loves and two lives. As an added twist, he may find a child he never knew about, who was born after his "death." In some cases, the new guy turns out to be a creep, so the hero's timely return saves the heroine from genuine unhappiness. In other cases, the new guy is a genuinely good man, adding to the emotional impact of the story (readers often enjoy shedding a tear or two along the way to a happy ending) and possibly providing you with a character worth spinning off into his own story.

Mistaken Identity

This type of plot has several variations. A hero and heroine who have the same last name but are otherwise strangers can be mistakenly assigned to the same cabin on a cruise (which is also a version of stranded with a stranger). Or a heroine with a unisex name can be hired under the assumption that she's a man, finding herself the lone woman on an oil rig, a ranch, or some other bastion of masculinity. Once again, forced intimacy is the name of the game.

Woman in Jeopardy

This plot is an especially good way to showcase an Alpha hero (as described in Chapter 4). Many romantic suspense novels feature this plotline, starring a heroine in danger and the hero whose job is — or who makes it his job — to protect her. She doesn't need to be a wimp, either. She can be strong and capable, but just caught up in a situation where she needs some help — and ends up finding love.

The Dad Next Door

He may not be literally next door, and he may even be the heroine's boss. The basic setup is that he's suddenly a single dad, maybe with a baby he never knew about dumped on his doorstep, or maybe he's inherited a baby (or a bunch of kids), and he needs the heroine's help. This plot works equally well with an Alpha or a Beta hero (see Chapter 4).

Even Sketchier Setups

Other setups are recognizable by name but are even less specific in terms of plot elements. The names of the following setups are pretty self-explanatory, and any one of them can provide an opening for your story:

- Boss/secretary or boss/employee
- Amnesia
- Virgin heroine
- Pregnant heroine
- On the run
- Rancher/cowboy and the city girl

Chapter 20

Ten Tips for Coming Up with a Successful Title

. . . .

. . . .

*Y*our book cover has two main elements — your title and the art. You may not get much, if any, input into the art. But you probably have a lot that you can contribute when it comes to choosing a title. And because your title is such an important factor in getting a reader to pick up your book from the rack, it pays to know everything you can about creating a title that works for you. In this chapter, I talk about how to make sure that your title stands out to a reader in an appealing way, how to find a title that suits your book, how to title connected projects, and the pros and cons of using titling tricks like alliteration, single-word titles, and common expressions.

Speaking the Reader's Language

Accept the fact that no title can appeal to every reader. In fact, you may find that impossibility to be a good thing, because it takes a lot of pressure off you. You want to — and you *can* — create a title that appeals to the bulk of the readers most likely to be interested in your book. The first key to creating the perfect title lies in knowing who your readers are and what they like. If you've written a historical romance, don't worry that readers looking for paranormal romantic suspense may pass your novel by. Focus on getting historical readers to notice you. (I introduce you to romance readers and the various kinds of romances in Chapter 2.)

Use bookstores and the best-seller lists as your resources. Take a look at the names of other books in your segment of the market and think about what those titles have in common, which ones work for you, and which ones are selling best. Many books on best-seller lists are there because of the authors' name, not their titles, but newer authors do sometimes make the lists, too. And, either way, checking out the most successful players never hurts.

The Long and the Short of It

Winning titles can be long or short. (*Long* is a relative term, given the physical limitations created by fitting your title, your name, and the art into the confined space of a book cover.) You can find pros and cons to both:

✔ Longer titles provide real design challenges but often grab the reader, because she hasn't seen anything else out there like them. If you get poetic and let the words flow, you may find that coming up with something unique is easier when you have more words to do it in. A longer title also gives you more space to state your case. You have room to "explain" what your book's all about. But remember that a long title can sound flat and rhythmless, like any old phrase or sentence.

✔ Shorter titles are punchy because they pack a lot into a small space. They can be easier to remember — a plus if a reader wants to ask for your book in the store or tell a friend about it — simply because she has fewer words to remember (and get right). But they can also be so short that they don't say enough to the reader to interest her.

I can't give you any hard-and-fast rules about title length. But longer titles often work best on historical romances or books that focus solely on the relationship. Shorter titles often fit contemporary romances, especially romantic suspense novels, whose fast pacing makes a good match for a shorter, snappier title. Most books fall somewhere in the middle ground, with titles of three or four words.

A Few Words about Single-Word Titles

One-word titles deserve more than a word of their own. They go in and out of favor, and they represent the extremes of the short-title pros and cons (as seen in the preceding section). Finding a word that actually says enough to sum up an entire book is the biggest problem with one-word titles. Plus, the one word you choose has to be memorable and stand out from all the other single-word titles. When a one-word title works, it *works*. It has a real bang to it, and it hits the reader like a wake-up call. But when it fails, it really fails, because it says nothing and doesn't stand out from all the books around it.

Matching Title and Tone Perfectly

You want your title to reflect your book's plot and tone. If you've written a romantic suspense novel, give it a title that reflects the suspenseful, tense, danger-filled tone of the book, not a flowery and generically pretty title. If you've written a historical romance, choose a title that reflects that fact (royal and noble titles always give the reader a good clue), and avoid contemporary phrases that don't fit the period. A paranormal title should sound eerie or a little bit weird, while a romantic comedy should have a light title. When you're titling your book, never pick something so generic that it can fit on any romance. (You know the kind of title I mean — *Love's Perfect Passionate Embrace* and the like.) Instead, think about the specifics of your plot and the tone of your book, and create a title to match.

Hooking Up

A lot of titles, particularly series titles, rely heavily on hooks to indicate the type of story: marriage of convenience, amnesia, pregnant heroine, and so on. A hook-based title does clearly define the story, so any reader looking for that kind of book knows she's found it. It's hard to misunderstand *An Inconvenient Marriage, Missing Memories,* or *Baby on Board.* When you work the hook in cleverly, your title becomes both accurate and memorable. If you don't phrase it cleverly, though, one hook-based title can sound an awful lot like a bunch of others, so a reader may wonder whether she's read this book already. And some titles try to fit in so many hooks that they end up sounding like shopping lists (*The Cowboy's Pregnant Bride,* for instance).

All about Alliteration

An alliterative title fits together well, and it usually has something catchy about it. Alliterative titles also often flow — especially if the initial repeated letter is soft: an *s* or soft *c,* an *f* or an *m.* But alliteration can sound too affected and self-conscious, or more like a tongue twister (Peter Piper picked a passionate pair).

Coining a Cliché

Clichés and other recognizable expressions, as well as common phrases, frequently make for good titles. Readers may like them because the recognition factor makes them feel comfortable, or it may also be because everyone knows what they mean. You can use one exactly as everyone knows it — *Wolf in Sheep's Clothing* (which, depending on the cover art, can come off as suspenseful or humorous) or *Killer Smile* (suspense all the way). Or you can play with the familiar phrase for effect, like *High Crimes and Miss Demeanor* (probably humorous, maybe even historical, depending on when the phrase entered the language).

Naming Names

You can really make your title unique by using one of your characters' names in it, especially if you can work in a full name, since first names alone are less likely to be unique, but a full name will stand out to the reader. That puts a lot of pressure on you to give your characters names worthy of being included in a title (mine, for instance, just doesn't have what it takes — my first name is kind of awkward and my last name is too harsh because of that hard *g*), but this strategy can win you readers if you choose the right name.

Making Connections

If you're writing a *miniseries,* a series of books connected by plot, characters (often family members), or setting, you may want to give each book a title that implies the connection. Whether they all contain the same word (for example, *fire* or *heart*), related words (four connected books may use the four basic elements — earth, air, fire, and water), a family name (if the books all feature related characters), or some other connecting theme, this gimmick can help readers find the books on the shelf and make the connection between them — but only if you make each individual title strong. If I have to make a choice, I'd rather see unrelated but salable titles than related weaker ones.

Following in Others' Footsteps

You can't copyright titles, so don't worry if your title turns out to duplicate someone else's or someone else's title duplicates yours. This situation happens less often than you'd expect, given how many romances publishers put out every year, but it does happen. Just don't choose a well-known title for your book (sorry, but *Gone with the Wind* is unavailable) or knowingly duplicate another title, especially a current or recent bestseller, because you want to avoid confusion when you can and make your book stand out to the reader — not make her stand at the rack wondering whether she's read your book or not, because the title sounds familiar to her.

Chapter 21

Ten Common Writing Mistakes Beginners Make

- -

In This Chapter

▶ Escaping first-timer traps

▶ Keeping your book — and your career — on track

▶ Looking like a pro even when you're not

- -

*E*very writer was a first-timer once, and many still admit to first-timer-style jitters with each new book. But those jitters don't need to hurt you, even when you *are* a first-time writer. When an editor is reading your romance novel, all she cares about is the book. In this chapter, I give you some tips you can use — and some tips for what you should avoid doing — so your book doesn't announce on every page that you're new to the game and are still learning your craft.

Remember the Reader's Expectations

If you remember only one thing, remember this: Give the reader what she wants or find another career. All successful genre publishing is based on knowing what the reader wants and then providing it. And that expectation is never truer than it is in romance. Start thinking about your reader the minute you decide whether to write a contemporary or a historical romance, a series or a mainstream novel, and then make it your goal to satisfy her expectations from page one until the end.

Don't Overwrite

A pro knows exactly what she wants to say and says it. An amateur loads adjectives and adverbs into every sentence, so the simplest idea ends up being as complex (and about as interesting) as a physics textbook. Pare down your prose; make every word count. Too many adjectives say nothing; one carefully chosen adjective says everything. Only describe what's important, because if you lavish equal time on everything, nothing stands out and nothing matters. And don't get cutesy, constantly slipping in puns, inside jokes, and clever turns of phrase. You'll only turn your reader off.

Ya Gotta Love It

If you don't love romance and — especially — love your characters, you're in the wrong business or, at the very least, you're writing the wrong book. In a genre that's all about emotion, don't even think about faking it. If you're not enjoying yourself as you write, if you don't empathize with your characters and care deeply that they get together for that key happily-ever-after moment, you can bet your reader's not going to care, either. You have to believe love is wonderful, possible, and worth working for, or every word you write will be a lie, and any reader (and that includes any editor) will see right through you.

Characters Are Key

And speaking of your characters, make sure that your hero and heroine, in particular, are complex and interesting, and that your reader can identify with your heroine and fall in love with your hero. Introduce your characters — not just to the reader but to each other — early. Get their conflict out on the table, and let them drive the plot, not be driven by it. (For all the ins and outs of creating sympathetic heroines and irresistible heroes, check out Chapter 4.)

Effective Conflict Comes from Within

If a reader wants talking heads debating the issues of the day, she'll turn on a cable news channel. She chooses a romance novel because she wants emotional drama that comes from — and touches — the heart, not the head. Let conflict come from within your characters because of who they are, not what they think. (In Chapter 5, I provide additional insight on including conflict — especially emotional conflict — in your manuscript.)

Make Sure You Have Enough Plot

Whether you're writing a 55,000-word Harlequin Romance novel or a 150,000-word mainstream romantic suspense novel, make sure that you have enough plain old story to support the length of your book. If you're showing every scene from multiple points of view, writing scenes that don't move the plot and romance forward, or digressing into subplots and the details of your secondary characters' lives, you'd better go back and complicate your plot so you can focus on the central love story. If you don't, your book will never see the light of day.

Keep Your Story on Track

The reader doesn't want to hear your every thought or even your characters' every thought. She doesn't care how much research you did or how fascinating you found it. Your job is to focus on the romance, not digress into nonessential information, however interesting it may be. Every scene needs to move the story forward, to take the romance one step beyond where it's been, so don't let your mind or your writing wander. An outline can really help keep your story on track, and I talk about creating one (and using it effectively) in Chapter 7.

The Name of the Game Is Entertainment

Keep your reader interested and having a good time. She may be scared, and you may even make her cry, but never let her get bored. Everything you do should be geared toward entertaining her, because if she loses interest and puts the book down, she may never pick it up again. If you keep your reader happy and entertained, when she reaches the end, she'll be sorry that the book's over and go looking for your next novel.

Don't Forget the Details

Don't move from A to C or D without making it clear what B is. Everything has to add up. Motivations need to be clear, and your plot has to be logical. Your book is fiction, but it has to make just as much sense as if it were real. Make your characters' motivations believable (I talk about creating motivation in Chapter 5), keep your timeline consistent, check your facts (I talk about research in Chapter 13), watch out for contradictions, and don't ever think you can get away with something because "no one will notice." Your readers *will* notice, and they won't like it.

Keep It Moving

Pacing rules. Know where to start, when to stop, how to intercut scenes, and how to create and resolve cliffhangers. Know how to use language to get your reader's heart racing and her hands flipping pages, and then know how to give her a breather before ramping up the tension again. Give her everything she thinks she wants, and then make her want more and keep reading until she gets it. Grab her attention and hold it until she reaches the final page. (I show you how to set the pace in Chapter 10, and how to start, stop, and create cliffhangers in Chapter 12.)

Chapter 22

Ten Reasons Why a Manuscript Gets Rejected

● ●

In This Chapter

▶ Reading between the lines of a rejection letter

▶ Getting inside an editor's mind

▶ Figuring out why your book was rejected when you receive a form reject

● ●

*O*ne of the hardest things you may face as a writer is getting a rejection letter that gives you minimal information or, worse, none at all as to why your manuscript was turned down. In a case like that, all you can do is make your best guess as to why the editor didn't like your book. Often, though, books are rejected for one of several very common reasons, as this chapter demonstrates. If you're willing to be objective about — and tough on — your own work, you're very likely to find your reason for rejection here.

Bad Writing

Lousy writing is, quite honestly, the single most common reason why a book is rejected. Most writing isn't good enough to be published, whether it's ungrammatical, overwritten, juvenile, so stiff you'd swear it was set in plaster, just plain boring, or it contains dialogue even a Shakespearean actor couldn't make work. Every so often a storyteller comes along who just has an indescribable something that overrides the poor quality of her writing, and an editor decides to take on her book anyway. But those types of writers are rare and, frankly, are getting even rarer in this day and age when no one — in any profession — has time to spare. Don't count on being the exception. Learn to write, and write well.

Arrogant Heroes and Unlovable Heroines: Unsympathetic Characters

On the list of reasons why a romance novel gets rejected, right after writing issues, come character flaws. And unsympathetic characters are at the top of the list of character flaws. Maybe as a response to the whole equality-of-the-sexes thing, an awful lot of writers think a strong heroine has to be tough to the point of unsympathetic invulnerability, even bitchiness, but that's just not true. Romance readers don't want to fantasize about being nasty; they want to fantasize about being loved. A too-perfect heroine is equally unsympathetic, but for different reasons.

An unsympathetic — unlovable — hero is often an Alpha male run amok, one who's so nasty, arrogant, dictatorial, even abusive, that no reader wants to wait around for the last chapter, when he suddenly reveals he loves the heroine and finally lets his humanity shine through.

And boring characters — of either sex — are unsympathetic simply because no reader wants to think of herself as dull. (Check out Chapter 4 for more info on character development.)

Cardboard Cutouts: Unrealistic Characters

Unrealistic characters are another losing proposition for a writer. By unrealistic, I don't mean someone who lives a rarified life or has an elite profession. I mean a hero or heroine who doesn't come across as interesting, unique, and driven by a believably drawn personality. Characters whose moods fluctuate with the wind rather than from any coherent inner life are also unrealistic characters, and they're also characters who don't sell.

B-o-r-i-n-g Spells Boring

Simply put, something interesting has to happen in your book. The fate of the world doesn't have to be at risk, no one has to be at death's door, but if your plot can be summed up as "They came, they saw, they dated," you have a problem. A romance novel isn't about two people dealing with the mundane problems of real life. The characters have to be at a crisis in their lives or dealing with something of real importance to them, and the emotional tension in their relationship gives it even more dramatic impact. Stuff happens — interesting stuff — and you build that stuff to a climax. If you have no story, you have no publishable book. Chapter 5 goes over how to create and plot out a riveting story line.

A Tsunami in the Alps and Other Lapses in Logic

Just as bad as characters who don't make sense is a plot that doesn't make sense. Events need to build on each other in a logical sequence, not just come out of nowhere. You have to thread your other characters in believably, not have them descend out of the blue when they're needed to provide information or stir up trouble. An author who has no idea how to develop a story often relies on natural disasters, which are too often arbitrary and are used as a crutch for the author. You wouldn't drive from Boston to Chicago by way of Seattle, but a lot of plots are the written equivalent. Chapter 5 gives you some help in making your plot a lean, mean romance machine.

Outdated Story Line and Characters

Contemporary romance novels are romantic fantasies, but they still bear some relation to the real world. Women in the 21st century aren't limited to the so-called female professions: teaching, nursing, childcare, and secretarial work. They're not spinsters at 22, and they can report abusive bosses. They don't feel obligated to marry just to please Mom and Dad. They can earn a good living and won't be forced to marry to hold on to an inheritance. They don't feel worthless if they can't bear children (even if that fact makes them unhappy) or if they just don't want to have any.

Most men in their 30s don't want to date 18-year-olds, aren't forced to marry to uphold the family name, bear an heir, or inherit the family business, and aren't complete buffoons in the kitchen. As real life goes, so go romance novels. If a manuscript reflects what was popular 20 (or even only 10) years ago, whether in the plot or the characters and their attitudes, back it goes to the author.

Inaccurate (Or No) Research

Particularly in a historical romance novel, where you need to research every detail because you can't just look around you and see how people dress, get around, or use slang, poorly done research can ruin a book's chances for publication. Just one or two obvious errors can destroy an editor's faith in the writer's ability to get the details right. The need for research may be less obvious in a contemporary romance, but it's no less important. Every story almost always has some important aspect that's not common knowledge, and if the writer gets the details wrong — whether she ignores custody law or messes up the stages of a police investigation — she kills her book's ability to sell. Learn how to get your story straight by checking out Chapter 13.

When Your Romance Isn't Really a Romance

Lots of wonderful novels are aimed at a female readership but aren't romance novels. These novels may contain romantic elements, but they're really women's fiction. And if you submit one of them and bill it as a romance — especially if you're targeting series romance — you're going to fail. I talk about the related women's fiction market in Chapter 2.

Wrong Editor/Publishing House

Editors are frequently looking for particular types of romance novels for themselves or for their houses. If you send a Regency romance novel to a house that doesn't publish Regency romances or a paranormal romance novel to an editor who hates paranormal romances, you're not going to make a sale. The book itself may be publishable, but only if you direct it to the proper editor at the proper house. I help you figure out how to target the right publisher and editor in Chapter 15.

Incorrect Formatting

Books that are obviously formatted incorrectly don't even get read. Obvious mistakes include single-spacing your manuscript, improperly paragraphing, making your margins too narrow, having dialogue written in italics instead of quotes, and having your text written in all caps. In Chapter 14, I review exactly what an editor expects from you in the formatting department.

Chapter 23

Ten Ways to Beat Writer's Block

First, a word on what writer's block *isn't*. Writer's block isn't the stage that many writers go through when the book is still forming in their minds — when they may start and stop, rethink, replot, take a break, and then sit down and start writing in earnest, sometimes repeating that sequence several times until they finish the book. If that's your writing process and it works for you, you don't have writer's block, because you don't have a problem. Writer's block isn't the culprit every time you have a break in the writing process — only when that break becomes paralyzing.

I'll be honest and tell you that I'm a big procrastinator, and I think 99 percent of all writer's block is, on some subconscious level, a form of avoidance behavior. I think writer's block grows (quite understandably) from fear — I've experienced writer's block myself for just that reason. I also think the longer you let yourself give in to it, the worse the fear gets, and the harder the writer's block is to overcome.

I don't believe in doing writing exercises to get your creativity flowing or in discovering how to write well by doing practice pieces and then putting the bits together. My suggestions to beating writer's block are pretty practical.

Working Your Way Through It

The best way to beat writer's block is to write your way through it. Sit down at the computer and start typing. At the end of the day, you may decide that 99 percent — or even 100 percent — of what you've written is lousy, and you'll throw it out. But as you keep writing, sooner or later you'll hit on something — even if it's just one thing — that works for you, and now you have something to run with.

Selecting a Different Scene

In general, I think writing a book from Chapter 1 straight through to the end makes sense, because the elements you planned in your outline may change as you write, affecting what happens next (see Chapter 7 for more info). But if you're having trouble with a particular scene, try moving on to the next scene or writing a scene that happens later in the book. A love scene is a particularly good choice, because it's less likely to change radically.

Looking at the Last Scene You Wrote

Sometimes the problem isn't the scene you're trying to write, the problem is the previous scene that sets this one up. The setup scene may be further back — maybe even a few scenes ago, if you took a radical turn. You may need to get a little distance from that earlier scene, and then look at it again, and you'll see what you did wrong. Fix that, and suddenly your characters and story are back on track.

Writing a Scene That You Won't Use

If you feel like you're losing touch with your characters, write an easy scene with them — one that you'll never use but one that will help you get hold of their voices again. Write their honeymoon or the birth of their first child. Write a normal date for them — the kind romance-novel couples never get to have — where they talk all about who they are and discover how much they have in common. Get to know them all over again, and then go back to your story armed with that new knowledge.

Viewing the Scene from a Different Angle

Sometimes just getting another perspective gets your creative juices flowing again. For instance, you can do the scene entirely via description from a third character's point of view. What does the observer see, and what does she think is going on in the characters' minds? You can do the scene entirely in dialogue, so the conversation carries the burden of explanation. Or write the entire scene from your hero or heroine's point of view, as if he or she is remembering what happened and is analyzing what it all meant. Using any one of those treatments as a basis, you can go back and look at the scene with fresh insights as you start writing.

Forgetting about Perfection

Sometimes "good enough" really *is* good enough — for now. You'll have an opportunity later to do a second draft or even a third, so don't expect things to be perfect right away. Get the basics of the scene down on paper (or, technically speaking, on disk), and then move on. Later, you can go back and polish, totally rewrite, or even cut the scene, if you want to. In the meantime, don't let one scene hold you up — keep writing.

Looking Forward — Not Back

Every writer works differently, and as long as what you're doing works for you, keep doing it. There isn't a right or wrong way to work. But if you're not moving forward because you keep polishing or second-guessing the decisions you made in previous chapters, you have to tell yourself no and make yourself move forward.

Analyzing Your Outline

Take another look at what you planned to do and ask yourself whether everything makes sense in terms of plot and character. When you look at your outline again from start to finish, you may see gaps and problems you missed, and those issues may be what's hanging you up now. Fix those issues, and suddenly your writing starts moving again. In Chapter 7, I talk about how to create your outline, and I give you some tips on keeping it a part of the writing process.

Re-energizing Your Creative Instincts

Try thinking about what drew you to this story in the first place. The characters? The chance to try your hand at romantic comedy? The fun of creating a complicated suspense plot? Whatever kind of story you're telling, try taking a break from writing and go watch a movie or read a book that tells a similar story, whether plot- or tone-wise. Lose yourself in that story and just enjoy it. Let yourself remember why you started your own book in the first place, and then go back to writing with that enthusiasm fresh in your mind.

Starting Another Project — If All Else Fails

Sometimes you just need a break from a certain story or character. Maybe you hit a plot snag and need to think about how to solve it before you can move on. Or maybe you've tried everything, nothing has worked, and you just can't get back into the rhythm of the book. In that case, you may have no option but to stop working on it, but don't stop writing altogether. Start working on your next book, whether planning it or actually writing it, but don't let yourself be controlled by writer's block. You need to take charge and control *it,* instead.

Chapter 24

Ten Questions Every Romance Writer Needs to Ask Herself

In This Chapter

▶ Figuring out whether you want to write a romance novel

▶ Handling bumps in the writing process

▶ Deciding whether to get an agent

*B*ecause writing is such a solitary process, you're going to face a lot of times when you have to ask yourself hard questions — and provide your own answers. Even knowing what to ask can be tough, and having some guidance for figuring out the answers can certainly help. So, in this chapter, I provide some questions and considerations that may help you in the writing process.

Should I Write Romance Novels?

You may have a tough time with this question, because everything you're hoping for depends on your answer. But look at the bottom line: If you don't like reading romances, if you don't buy into the fantasy and feel happy every time a hero and heroine get together, or if you're only thinking about writing a romance because you want to make some money, then romance isn't the genre for you. Better to recognize this fact right away and figure out what you *should* be writing.

Why Can't I Get Started?

If you're having problems getting the writing process underway, a number of things could be going on. First, you may not have found the right kind of romance for you yet. Check out Chapter 2 and go through the process of narrowing things down. A change of scene or subgenre may get you on track.

You may also be facing simple fear. Thinking about making your dream come true is scary, and it becomes even scarier when you start working on it, because doubts can creep in: What if I can't pull it off? A lot of times, just recognizing your fear helps you deal with it.

If recognizing why you're afraid isn't enough, you need to just make yourself write without expecting too much. Set a reasonable number of pages as a target and don't judge those pages too harshly after you've written them. Just keep going, and you can probably find your rhythm as your natural bent for storytelling takes over. You can go back later and revise what you've written, but for now, just get the momentum going.

What Can I Do When the Ideas Don't Come?

Sometimes you feel like you've hit a wall. Nothing's coming together, and no idea feels right or interesting enough to get you going. In this situation, you just have to stop pressuring yourself. Get out into the world and do something fun — read a book that you've been looking forward to but haven't had time for, watch TV, rent a movie, go to the beach and daydream . . . anything to relax and open your mind so that you can recognize a good idea when it comes. And a good idea *will* come. You just need to be receptive to it.

How Can I Focus and Stay Positive When Things Go Wrong?

Problems with your writing can often leave you in a slump. But insecurity and depression can strike at any time, often causing your writing train to go off the rails even when your story's not having any obvious problems. When things go wrong and you feel negative (or you feel negative and then things go wrong), remind yourself that every writer goes through phases like this one, so you shouldn't beat yourself up about it. You can give yourself a breather, a day or two to just have fun with life and rejuvenate your mind.

Or you can follow the same advice I suggest in the earlier section about having trouble getting started: Just keep writing, as much as possible without judging, and force yourself through the bad patch. You can go back later and revise — assuming you even need revision. Often, the writing's fine — it's your perceptions that are off.

Finally, reward yourself for your accomplishments, whether that means taking time to cook your favorite meal (or going out to eat), watching your favorite movie from the comfort of your couch, or shopping for a new pair of shoes. Hitting yourself with a stick doesn't help your writing, but holding out a carrot may be just what you need.

When Is It Research and When Is It a Waste of Time?

Get tough on yourself. If you're discovering all kinds of really interesting stuff that you can't honestly say belongs in your book, you're wasting time. Stop it right now and start writing! Procrastination is a cardinal sin. Check out Chapter 13 for more information on drawing the line.

When Should I Send My Manuscript into the Big, Scary World?

Is your manuscript done? Have you polished and rewritten and polished again? Has your critique group told you it's great? Are you just making work for yourself by going over the book again? As terrifying as submitting your book to a publisher can be (and believe me, I know it's scary), you need to do it. Whether you send a query letter or a full or partial manuscript, whether you submit directly or through an agent, the time has come. Be proud of yourself for getting to this point, and then take that crucial next step. You can never sell if you don't submit.

Do I Need an Agent?

If you want to sell a mainstream romance novel, you almost always need an agent. Check out each particular publisher's requirements, but in general, expect to find out that you will need an agent. Series romance is still wide open to authors who want to submit on their own, but a lot of writers choose to work with an agent so that they have an advocate, as well as someone who knows the business side of publishing and can handle all the negotiating. With series submissions, the decision is a personal one, and no answer is wrong. I cover the agent question in more detail in Chapter 15.

How Do I Handle a Friend's Manuscript Selling First?

As the Golden Rule says, "Do unto others . . ." You may be hurting inside, even feeling jealous (a totally human reaction), but practice your acting skills and hide those feelings because, deep down, you know that you *are* happy for your friend. And remember: Publishers always need new authors, so your odds of selling haven't changed and depend entirely on the strength of your book — which you control.

When and How Do I Follow Up on My Book's Status?

As frustrating as it is, be patient. Wait at least three months after you submit a manuscript, and when you do follow up, make a response as easy for the editor as possible. Provide all the relevant information about your book (its title, your pseudonym if you used one, and whether it was a complete or a partial manuscript) and when you submitted it. I prefer getting a letter with an enclosed postcard so that I can quickly fill in the book's status and mail it back. If you call, don't expect an answer immediately. You'll probably need to leave your number so that someone has time to check out what's going on with your book and then call you back.

When Do I Let Go of a Book?

Recognizing that no publisher will accept your book is kind of like accepting the death of a friend. But the sad truth is that most books never sell. If you've submitted to, and been rejected by, every publisher you can think of, if you've revised the book in every way that makes sense to you, if you can't think of anything else to do that doesn't smack of vain hopefulness, you need to let go. Just remember that you learned a lot from this book and that you can take those lessons with you as you write the next book, and the next. And when the day comes that you finally sell, it will be because of every book you've ever written and everything you've learned. So let yourself mourn, but then make yourself look forward to the next book. And never — ever — stop writing. You can take comfort — and find tips for moving forward — in Chapter 16, where I talk about how to handle the difficulties of rejection.

Index

FOR DUMMIES®

A world of resources to help you grow

TRAVEL

Italy FOR DUMMIES
A Travel Guide for the Rest of Us!
0-7645-5453-0

Hawaii FOR DUMMIES
A Travel Guide for the Rest of Us!
0-7645-5438-7

Walt Disney World & Orlando FOR DUMMIES
A Travel Guide for the Rest of Us!
0-7645-5444-1

Also available:

America's National Parks For Dummies
(0-7645-6204-5)

Caribbean For Dummies
(0-7645-5445-X)

Cruise Vacations For Dummies 2003
(0-7645-5459-X)

Europe For Dummies
(0-7645-5456-5)

Ireland For Dummies
(0-7645-6199-5)

France For Dummies
(0-7645-6292-4)

Las Vegas For Dummies
(0-7645-5448-4)

London For Dummies
(0-7645-5416-6)

Mexico's Beach Resorts For Dummies
(0-7645-6262-2)

Paris For Dummies
(0-7645-5494-8)

RV Vacations For Dummie
(0-7645-5443-3)

EDUCATION & TEST PREPARATION

Spanish FOR DUMMIES
A Reference for the Rest of Us!
0-7645-5194-9

Algebra FOR DUMMIES
A Reference for the Rest of Us!
0-7645-5325-9

U.S. History FOR DUMMIES
A Reference for the Rest of Us!
0-7645-5249-X

Also available:

The ACT For Dummies
(0-7645-5210-4)

Chemistry For Dummies
(0-7645-5430-1)

English Grammar For Dummies
(0-7645-5322-4)

French For Dummies
(0-7645-5193-0)

GMAT For Dummies
(0-7645-5251-1)

Inglés Para Dummies
(0-7645-5427-1)

Italian For Dummies
(0-7645-5196-5)

Research Papers For Dum
(0-7645-5426-3)

SAT I For Dummies
(0-7645-5472-7)

U.S. History For Dummies
(0-7645-5249-X)

World History For Dummi
(0-7645-5242-2)

HEALTH, SELF-HELP & SPIRITUALITY

Diabetes FOR DUMMIES
A Reference for the Rest of Us!
0-7645-5154-X

Sex FOR DUMMIES
A Reference for the Rest of Us!
0-7645-5302-X

Parenting FOR DUMMIES
A Reference for the Rest of Us!
0-7645-5418-2

Also available:

The Bible For Dummies
(0-7645-5296-1)

Controlling Cholesterol For Dummies
(0-7645-5440-9)

Dating For Dummies
(0-7645-5072-1)

Dieting For Dummies
(0-7645-5126-4)

High Blood Pressure For Dummies
(0-7645-5424-7)

Judaism For Dummies
(0-7645-5299-6)

Menopause For Dummies
(0-7645-5458-1)

Nutrition For Dummies
(0-7645-5180-9)

Potty Training For Dummi
(0-7645-5417-4)

Pregnancy For Dummies
(0-7645-5074-8)

Rekindling Romance For Dummies
(0-7645-5303-8)

Religion For Dummies
(0-7645-5264-3)

Available wherever books are sold. Go to www.dummies.com or call 1-877-762-2974 to order direct

CPSIA information can be obtained
at www.ICGtesting.com
Printed in the USA
LVOW04s2232040118
561888LV00003B/62/P